Blacks in the New World

August Meier, Series Editor

A list of books in the series appears at the end of this volume.

They Who Would Be Free

They Who Would Be Free

Blacks' Search for Freedom, 1830-1861

Jane H. Pease and
William H. Pease

University of Illinois Press
Urbana and Chicago

Illini Books edition, 1990

©1974, 1990 by Jane H. Pease and William H. Pease
Manufactured in the United States of America
P 5 4 3 2 1

This book is printed on acid-free paper.

Library of Congress Cataloging-in-Publication Data

Pease, Jane H.
They who would be free : Blacks' search for freedom, 1830-61 /
Jane H. Pease and William H. Pease. — Illini books ed.
     p.   cm. — (Blacks in the New World)
Reprint. Originally published: New York : Atheneum,
1974. Originally published in series: Studies in American Negro
life.
     Includes bibliographical references (p.   ).
     ISBN 0-252-06143-8 (alk. paper)
     1. Slavery—United States—Anti-slavery movements.   2. Afro-
Americans—History—To 1863.   I. Pease, William Henry, 1924-
II. Title.   III. Series.
[E449.P38   1990]
973.7′ 114—dc20
                                                    90-34683
                                                        CIP

Preface

WHEN WE were first asked to write this book, we decided against a narrative of black abolitionism in the antebellum North. Instead we determined to analyze the perceptions, attitudes, values, goals, and means of those Northern Negroes who struggled within the abolitionist crusade—and frequently outside of it—to achieve a meaningful freedom for themselves and their brethren in slavery. Because they were black and therefore smarted under restrictions and discriminations which white Americans never experienced, they often found the antislavery crusade, as whites understood it, inadequate. So they worked, wrote, and lectured in separate race organizations and publications as well as in more general reform societies to express their views and achieve their ends.

Perforce we have focused largely upon those who left a record of their plans and perceptions, those who were articulate and active in the press and conventions or those who played significant roles in noteworthy events. Conversely we have largely excluded the self-help activities of non-protest-oriented mutual aid societies and lodges and the otherworldly activity which characterized the central life of most black churches. Concerned with how Northern blacks saw and sought freedom, with their awareness of being powerless and lacking rights, and with their attempts to overcome these deprivations, we have listened most closely to the leaders of and spokesmen for their cause and have probed most acutely those events which best illustrate the evolving patterns which their perceptions created.

To delineate thus the thrust of our inquiry is not to forget that black abolition and protest emerged and evolved in a context of dynamic events whose central theme was the antislavery movement in its broadest dimension. With antecedents in the post-Revolutionary War emancipation enthusiasm and in various attempts to resettle American Negroes outside the United States, that movement's symbolic beginning was marked by the first issue of William Lloyd Garrison's *Liberator* on January 1, 1831. In its first decade, its primary concern was organizing antislavery societies at the local, state, and national levels, principally in New England, New York, Pennsylvania, and Ohio, and spreading the antislavery message through lectures and publications.

By the end of the decade, however, the American Anti-Slavery Society, founded in 1833 to coordinate the work, was badly divided by internal tensions. Long and bitter debates over the issues of antislavery's relation to other reform efforts, its relations with established churches, its initial reliance on moral suasion alone, and its emerging responsiveness to political action marked the progress of dissension. Rejecting the Garrisonian emphasis on universal reformism, anticlericalism, and nonpolitical involvement, the so-called Tappanite wing of the crusade formed the church-oriented American and Foreign Anti-Slavery Society in 1840 and nurtured the emerging Liberty party, led by James G. Birney and Gerrit Smith.

In the decade which followed neither Garrisonian perfectionists nor Tappanite clerics and politicians seemed to make much headway. By the end of the 1840s both national antislavery organizations had markedly declined in importance and in membership, both black and white. Only in 1844 did the Liberty party temporarily slow down that trend. Consequent upon that decline there emerged a more broadly based, and therefore less explicitly antislavery politics aimed chiefly at curtailing Southern slaveholding power in the Union and denying it access to the Western territories. Then, when politics during the last antebellum decade mired because of apparent Southern dominance in the federal government, dedicated abolitionists of both races decided to act outside the political structure as well as within it. They defied federal authority, especially in thwarting the Fugitive Slave Law of 1850, and spoke increasingly of violence and disunion.

Blacks participated in these patterns of change as part of the general antislavery movement, but they also organized and acted on their own. The convention movement (periodic local, state, and national meetings of leaders) was perhaps the principal agency for black activism from the first convention in 1830 right up to the Civil War. It reflected in its interests and concerns many of the ideas, tensions, and directions characteristic of antislavery as a whole. But it also reflected other concerns which explicitly impinged upon and spoke to the distinctive needs and aspirations of the black community. During the 1830s, conventions grappled primarily with questions of economic and social improvement among free blacks, although they maintained simultaneously close contact with the general antislavery movement. Throughout the 1840s, although interest in social and economic improvement persisted, conventions shifted their attention to enfranchisement and political action, acting most often quite apart from abolitionism per se. Finally, in the 1850s, they turned sharply to creating separate black institutions (in addition to the convention movement itself) and to emphasizing emigration outside the United States.

Like the entire antislavery movement, the specific black response was constantly challenged and shaped by the progress of national events. By 1836 the revolution in Texas and her requests for annexation as well as Congressional refusal to receive antislavery petitions had already made slavery a central topic of public debate. During the next decade and a half, as the Mexican War and the question of extending slavery into the newly acquired territory highlighted the new dimensions of the problem, political discourse more and more focused on the slavery issue. In the process, the Liberty party gave way to Free Soil politics.

The 1850s only heightened the increasingly acrimonious dialogue over the peculiar institution. The Compromise of 1850, including the new Fugitive Slave Law so abhorred by abolitionists, was scorned as well by Southern fire-eaters for its failure to guarantee slave state equality in the territories. In 1854 the Kansas-Nebraska Act, which repudiated the very idea of compromise, challenged old-time Unionists and introduced new tension into the already taut situation. Thereafter the major parties broke apart, and the slavery question unequivocally dominated national politics. The predictable sequel was Bleeding Kansas, the rise of the Republican party, the Dred Scott decision, and, in 1861, civil war.

Important as they were for all Americans, these events had particular meaning for Northern freemen. Their freedom, fragile and minimal at best, was constantly threatened. When in 1857 Chief Justice Roger Taney rendered his opinion in the Dred Scott case, he only told black Americans what their own experience had largely taught—that they had no rights which white men were bound to respect.

That reality, which so constricted the lives and hopes of Northern freemen, has shaped our study of their antebellum civil rights and antislavery activity. We believe that freedom, to be meaningful, must involve choices among achievable alternatives and that the nature and number of options available determine the scope of freedom. Realizing that absolute and untrammeled freedom like absolute and unrestricted slavery seldom if ever exists, we believe that the rights which guarantee choice and the power to make choices best define the varying degrees of slavery and freedom. Choice obviously is always circumscribed by the constraints of any society: community mores, legal precepts, religious systems, legislative enactments, economic conditions, and the like. Yet within any given society those who enjoy the most options from which to choose are the freest.

In the twenty years during which we have been studying both the antebellum black experience and the American antislavery movement we have incurred an indebtedness to friends and colleagues too numerous to mention individually here, though they have our continuing appreciation for discussing issues, suggesting obscure sources, and criticizing our techniques and conclusions. There are some, however, whose contribution to this particular study has been so great that we must thank them publicly here. The editor of this series, August Meier, has read and reread our manuscript. While we have not followed all his suggestions, they have enormously improved the structure and emphasis of the book. Both David Katzman and C. Duncan Rice have been extraordinarily generous with their research and reflections on black Detroit and British antislavery, respectively.

In addition the staffs of numerous libraries have aided us in our work. Particularly generous in their permissions and help have been the Boston Public Library, the George Arendts Library of Syracuse University, and the Amistad Research Center in New Orleans. Also providing us with useful manuscript material were the Massachusetts Historical Society, the American Antiquarian Society, the Historical Society of Pennsylvania, Columbia University Library, the Library of Congress and the National Archives, and the Mitchell Library of Glasgow, Scotland. Nor do our debts stop here, for many other libraries provided us with hard-to-find material through the interlibrary loan service. We wish to thank them as well as the Fogler Library of the University of Maine at Orono for facilitating our getting these materials. Finally, we extend our appreciation once again to Betsey Miller Shaffer for preparing the final manuscript with accuracy and imagination.

In order to make for more fluid reading we have made certain modifications in quoted material. Where sense and grammar demanded we have capitalized the initial letter of a sentence without special note, and on occasion reduced upper case to lower. At times we have changed tense and have so noted that by the simple use of brackets. Otherwise the usual conventions have been followed.

Bangor, Maine, February 1974

Contents

PART I

The Setting

THE LAUNCHING of William Lloyd Garrison's *Liberator* in 1831 heralded the revival of post-Revolutionary War emancipation enthusiasm, the decline of antislavery support for African colonization, and the beginning of a search for more effective abolitionist strategies. Among its first supporters were Northern free blacks. Since the American Revolution they had experienced the racist backlash which followed the first emancipation and had created various institutions to serve their race needs. These particular circumstances not only provided them a link with the new abolitionism but gave them a perspective on slavery which separated them from white abolitionists. For the next thirty years these differences generated a relationship of conflict as well as cooperation.

1. TWO ABOLITIONISMS

TO SOME AMERICANS in the decades before the Civil War, the antislavery movement seemed a sinister conspiracy; to others, a consortium of pure idealists; and to still others, a political device to gain power or destroy the Union. Yet, however diverse their responses, observers generally attributed to the antislavery movement a set of common goals and a pattern of unified action. Abolitionists on the other hand had, at least after 1840, no sure belief in their own unity. They fell out not only over methods of action, but also over the very nature of the change they sought. In so doing, they formed many separate and competing organizations, ran a variety of newspapers, and feuded among themselves in public meetings and private letters. Yet neither outsiders, who saw a monolithic movement, nor insiders, who were preoccupied with internal heresy and treason, perceived the nature of the very basic racial split within the movement. It was obvious that there were open controversies among various black and white leaders, but these were most often personal or defined by issues which had already divided the predominately white antislavery crusade. In addition to these frictions, however, a far deeper conceptual chasm separated black from white and generated a distinct black abolitionism.

For each group, slavery and freedom had very different meanings. Whites, especially those reared in the moral environment of New England, understood slavery and freedom as polar absolutes. Individual liberty, enshrined in the Declaration of Independence and fought for in the American Revolution, was their goodly heritage and present reality. At the other extreme stood slavery, an absolute evil, the negation of freedom, the denial of tradition, the antithesis of progress and American ideals.

Blacks, however, defined the terms more complexly. Both experience and history told them that slavery and freedom were not mutually exclusive, separated from each other as righteousness from sin. They were rather terminal points on a continuous spectrum. At one extreme black men had no freedom whatever. Slaves in fact, they could not decide how or where they would live, work, rear their families, order their personal relationships with their fellows, or worship their God. Their condition admitted no options, entertained no choices. It was a world literally bound and fettered. At the opposite extreme was freedom. There, in theory at least, black Americans might enjoy as many options as did fully enfranchised, propertied, middle-class white Americans.

But those were extremes. Between them lay a vast and variegated spectrum. Some slaves hired out their own time and labor, won the confidence of their masters, and traveled widely. Partial though it was, such freedom was real. Frederick Douglass knew it as a caulker in Baltimore, as did Josiah Henson, from traveling throughout the Upper South as his master's agent. Conversely, liberties of free Negroes in the North were sharply curtailed. Frequently excluded from schools, both public and private, as well as from apprenticeships, denied access to ballot box and jury box, they were still partially enslaved. What separated black from white abolitionists were these different perceptions. Whites, conceiving of their own freedom as absolute and never having experienced its opposite extreme, embraced a simple duality. For blacks the alternative was not between slavery or freedom but between more or less freedom and more or less slavery.

different perception of the meaning of slavery & freedom

With such different perceptions of slavery and freedom, white and black abolitionists, though pursuing the common goals of emancipation and civil equality, perceived the relationship between those goals very differently. Whites recognized two distinct problems. First, they must end slavery—immediately and without compensation—for slavery was the root sin. Secondly, they must eliminate discrimination and prejudice. Yet, though they undertook this dual commitment, they often had racial attitudes similar to those of their less committed neighbors. Never fully understanding how a society overtly and covertly racist degraded free Northern blacks as it did the slaves at the South, and therefore, ready to accept political and social restrictions on the newly freed when emancipation should come, these abolitionists remained largely unaware of how much had to be done in their own environment to make black people truly free.[1]

Many indeed simplified the problem and concentrated their efforts exclusively on what to them was the central issue: purging the land of the "sin and guilt of slavery." Yet, in the early days, organized antislavery did act to benefit Northern Negroes. By 1834 the American Anti-Slavery Society had appointed agents to elevate the free people of color by teaching them "Religion, Morals, Domestic Economy, Civil Rights, Education, and the Arts."[2] Similarly, William Lloyd Garrison, leader of New England's

1. In *The Black Image in the White Mind: The Debate on Afro-American Character and Destiny, 1817-1914* (New York: Harper and Row, 1971), 40, George M. Frederickson explores the inability of white abolitionists to recognize that prejudice induced by the racist environment of the North produced the same kind of human degradation which slavery generated. In an earlier study, Leon Litwack explored the inherent contradiction in the abolitionists' demand for immediate emancipation followed by new laws designed to control and restrict the freedom of ex-slaves and to forestall the social disorganization which most abolitionists believed would be the inevitable immediate result of abolition. See his *North of Slavery: The Negro in the Free States, 1790-1860* (Chicago: University of Chicago Press, 1961), 302-303.
2. The Executive Committee of the American Anti-Slavery Society, "In Reference to the Free People of Color," a circular n.d., addressed to the society's agents. Copy bound between 1833 and 1834 volumes of the *Liberator,* American Periodical Series microfilm edition, APS 968, Reel 391.

immediatist abolitionists, encouraged a special educational program, remuneration for involuntary labor, and provision for the employment of freed slaves. Local antislavery societies, too, urged various plans to assist free blacks—apprenticeships, schools, vigilante action against kidnapping, campaigns to abolish restrictions against interracial marriage.[3] If plans for education and moral uplift contained an element of social control, still they reflected an intent to open opportunity and promote greater personal security. Dedication, not hypocrisy, informed the Declaration of Sentiments of the American Anti-Slavery Society in 1833: "We . . . believe and affirm— That all persons of color who possess the qualifications which are demanded of others, ought to be admitted forthwith to the enjoyment of the same privileges, and the exercise of the same prerogatives, as others. . . ."[4]

Antiabolitionist riots and vehement popular denunciation, however, soon provoked a new prudence which made white abolitionists temper their zeal on behalf of Northern Negroes. Their response was, in large part, conditioned by a healthy instinct for self-preservation. Chastened by the mob's depredations in New York City in 1834, the American Anti-Slavery Society's executive committee, including Arthur and Lewis Tappan, both of whose property had been attacked, publicly informed Mayor Cornelius Lawrence that they had no intention of "uniting white and colored people in marriage, . . . encouraging intermarriages, exciting the

3. William Lloyd Garrison, *Thoughts on African Colonization* (orig. publ. 1832. New York: Arno Press, 1969), 85-86. For examples of the concern of various antislavery groups see: for the New England Anti-Slavery Society, Wendell Phillips Garrison and Francis Jackson Garrison, *William Lloyd Garrison, 1805-1889: the Story of His Life as Told by His Children* (4 vols. New York: The Century Co., 1885-1889), 1:282; for the Andover Theological Seminary Anti-Slavery Society, D. T. Kimball and L. F. Laine, to *Genius of Temperance,* August 22, 1833, in *Liberator,* September 28, 1833; and for the New York Anti-Slavery Society, Article 3 of the New York Anti-Slavery Society's constitution in *Liberator,* October 19, 1833.

4. American Anti-Slavery Society, "Declaration [of Sentiments] of the Anti-Slavery Convention . . ." in *Proceedings of the Anti-Slavery Convention, Assembled at Philadelphia, December 4, 5, and 6, 1833* (New York: Printed by Dorr and Butterfield, 1833), as reprinted by the *Abolitionist,* I (December 1833), 179.

people of color to assume airs, &c."[5] This policy encouraged new discretion among agents and lecturers as well. John Thome assured society general agent Theodore Weld two years later, "I was particularly careful to *disclaim* certain things which are confounded with abolitionism; such as social intercourse, amalgamation, etc."[6] And Weld, who had in the past withstood bricks thrown by hostile audiences and who had established black schools while he was working in Cincinnati, had in those same two years begun to draw distinctions between civil rights and social equality.[7]

If prudential considerations made white abolitionists temper their original commitment to full equality, so too did a growing concern for their own civil liberties distract them from it.[8] As black minister and political activist Samuel Ringgold Ward argued, the freedoms of both races should have buttressed each other, for the question was not "whether the black man's slavery shall be perpetuated, but whether the freedom of any Americans can be permanent." [9] Yet as early as 1836, James Forten, Jr., son and namesake of Philadelphia's wealthy sailmaker and early race leader, feared that white abolitionists were already seeking self-protection

5. Arthur Tappan *et al.* to Cornelius W. Lawrence, July 16, 1834, bound between 1833 and 1834 volumes of *Liberator*, American Periodical Series microfilm edition, APS 968, Reel 391.

6. John A. Thome and J. W. Alvord to Theodore Weld, February 9, 1836, in Theodore Dwight Weld, *et al.*, *Letters of Theodore Dwight Weld, Angelina Grimké Weld, and Sarah Grimké, 1822-1844*, edited by Gilbert H. Barnes and Dwight L. Dumond (orig. publ. 1934. Gloucester, Mass.: Peter Smith, 1965), 1:257.

7. Theodore D. Weld to James G. Birney, August 7, 1834, *ibid.*, 1:127-128. See also Birney to Weld, July 26, 1834; Weld to Lewis Tappan, [March 9, 1836]; and [L. Tappan] to Weld, March 15, 1836; all, in order, in *ibid.*, 1:163, 270-274, 276.

8. For a good introduction to the question of white civil liberties and the antislavery issue, see Russel B. Nye, *Fettered Freedom: Civil Liberties and the Slavery Controversy, 1830-1860* (East Lansing: Michigan State College Press, 1949).

9. Samuel Ringgold Ward, *Autobiography of a Fugitive Negro: His Anti-Slavery Labours in the United States, Canada, & England* (London: John Snow, 1855), 77. William Goodell also made the same point when he argued that for the courts to judge on the basis of color was an open invitation to judge on the basis of nationality or even of "freckled-skinned" complexion; in *American Jubilee* for January 1855.

first and reminded them that free blacks and slaves also needed civil rights.[10] Even increasing antislavery activity did not guarantee a commitment to first principles. Presbyterian minister Theodore Wright of New York observed the next year that abolitionists were more interested in "free discussion, petition, anti-Texas [sentiment], and political favor" than in the rights of black men. It was, he said, "an easy thing to talk about the vileness of slavery at the south, but to call the dark man a brother, . . . that is the test."[11] It was clear by 1837 that black civil rights was already subordinate to other interests in the general, white-dominated movement. "It is a strange omission in the Constitution of the American Anti-Slavery Society," James McCune Smith, a New York doctor and druggist, wrote nearly twenty years later, "that no mention is made of Social Equality either of Slaves or Free Blacks, as the aim of that Society."[12]

Strange and unacceptable, for it mirrored the different perceptions of slavery and freedom. For blacks, bondage, prejudice, and discrimination were only varied manifestations of the same problem, so interrelated that to neglect one was to endanger all. The struggles against slavery and racial discrimination could not be separated, for they were reciprocal.[13] Free Negroes argued that they were in psychological bondage as long as their

10. James Forten, Jr., *An Address Delivered Before the Ladies Anti-Slavery Society of Philadelphia . . .14th of April, 1836* (Philadelphia: Merrihew and Gunn, 1836), 4-8.

11. From a speech delivered before the New York State Anti-Slavery Society at Utica, in *Liberator*, October 13, 1837. For additional similar comments see also Samuel E. Cornish's remarks in the *Colored American*, December 16, 1837; and Benjamin F. Roberts to Amos A. Phelps, June 19[?], 1838, Phelps Papers, Antislavery Collection, Boston Public Library (cited hereafter as P-BPL).

12. James McCune Smith to Gerrit Smith, March 31, 1855, Gerrit Smith Miller Papers, Syracuse University (cited hereafter as S-SU).

13. This point has been tacitly assumed in most treatments of black abolitionism; see most recently Benjamin Quarles, *Black Abolitionists* (New York: Oxford University Press, 1969). Charles Wesley, however, is one of the few to develop it explicitly; see his "The Negroes of New York in the Emancipation Movement," *Journal of Negro History*, XXIV (January, 1939), 65-103, particularly on 65.

brothers were physically in chains. Only their emancipation "can set me at liberty," Presbyterian minister Henry Highland Garnet observed in 1840.[14] "Think you ... that I can feel free," James L. Smith asked a year later, "while millions of my countrymen are held in chains and fetters ... [?]"[15] Moreover, teacher William Allen insisted, prejudice, the chain of this psychic bondage, was "in many of its aspects, far more dreadful than that of . . . *bona fide* Southern Slavery...." Its particular destructiveness lay in its effect upon those who had been long free or who had never known slavery because they felt "not at all inferior to the foremost of their oppressors" and were thus ill-prepared to cope with the discrimination they experienced.[16]

Surrounded by prejudice, deprived of civil liberties, barred from economic opportunity, Northern Negroes rejected the notion that they were truly free. "Free indeed!" mocked the New York *Weekly Advocate* in 1837, "when almost every honourable incentive to the pursuit of happiness, so largely and so freely held out to his fairer brother, is withheld from [the black man]."[17] Yet mere elimination of prejudice was not enough, as Boston African Methodist Episcopal clergyman Hosea Easton asserted. Slavery, he wrote in his study of the condition of the American black, destroyed his "moral, intelligent being," and stripped him of "all the innate principles of a freeman." Then, "when the principles of slavery ceases [sic] to act upon him ..., [the former bondsman] is left a mere out-of-use wreck of machinery.... Let the free states," Easton urged, pinpointing white responsibility to take compensatory action, "no longer act the part of them who passed by on the other side, and leaving the colored people half dead,

14. From his speech delivered to the annual meeting of the American Anti-Slavery Society, May 12, 1840; in American Anti-Slavery Society, *Seventh Annual Report* (New York: The Society, 1840), 7.

15. *Liberator*, March 26, 1841.

16. William G. Allen, *The American Prejudice Against Color: An Authentic Narrative, Showing How Easily the Nation Got into an Uproar* (London: W. and F. G. Cash, 1853), 2.

17. *Weekly Advocate*, January 14, 1837.

especially when they were beaten by their own hands, and so call it emancipation—raising a wonderment why the half dead people do not heal themselves. Let them rather act the part of the good Samaritan."[18] The point was never lost; and, on the eve of the Emancipation Proclamation, Frederick Douglass was still contending that "the work does not end with the abolition of slavery but only begins."[19]

One of the most immediate and visible signs of the persistent effects of slavery was poverty. Shunted to the most menial, least attractive, and minimally rewarding jobs and denied access to the education, vocational training, and capital which could extend their options, blacks made considerable efforts to achieve economic parity with whites. Some tried to implant the puritan ethic in the race, others to identify and eliminate the debilitating effects of a culture of poverty. Abolitionists ought to consider, Philadelphia teacher Charles Reason wrote in 1854, that it was "a legitimate part of their great work . . . to abolish not only chattel slavery, but [also] that other kind of slavery, which, for generation after generation, dooms an oppressed people to a condition of dependence and pauperism."[20] Nonetheless whites largely ignored this problem, while much of black antislavery effort was directed to it. Thus different styles as well as different perceptions of principle marked the two abolitionisms.[21]

18. Hosea Easton, *A Treatise on the Intellectual Character, and Civil and Political Conditions of the Colored People of the U. States, and the Prejudice Exercised Toward Them: With a Sermon on the Duty of the Church to Them* (Boston: I. Knapp, 1837, reprint, New York: Arno Press, 1969), 51-52. For similar expressions of the lack of freedom of free blacks see, for example, the speech of Charles Remond delivered in Exeter Hall, London, in 1840, in *Colored American*, August 8, 1840; and the remarks of William J. Watkins at the Cleveland Anti-Slavery Convention, December 4, 1857, *Liberator*, December 25, 1857.

19. *Douglass Monthly*, November, 1862.

20. Charles Reason in Julia Griffiths, ed., *Autographs for Freedom* (Rochester, 1854), 2:12-15, as reproduced in Herbert Aptheker, ed., *A Documentary History of the Negro People in the United States* (orig. publ. 1951. 2 vols. New York: Citadel Press, 1969), 1:363.

21. The attention which black abolitionists paid to the possible ways and means for facilitating economic opportunity is suggested, for example, in Theodore Wright's attack on white prejudice against Negro advancement in an address to the New York Anti-Slavery Society, September 20, 1837, in

Because of these differences, the patterns of black and white antislavery were distinct and sometimes almost mutually exclusive. From 1830 to the Civil War, whites attempted to change public opinion by moral suasion and thus to end slavery immediately in the South. In so doing, they increasingly neglected free blacks in the North. The reliance, especially of Garrisonians, on purging individual consciences of the sin and guilt of slavery shaped their efforts in an ideological and abstract pattern. Consequently they tended to forget "the Negroes as individual human beings."[22] Nor was this attitude unconscious, as Wendell Phillips, second only to Garrison in New England antislavery, proudly admitted. "If we never free a slave, we have at least freed ourselves in the effort to emancipate our brother man."[23] Indeed, both in the battle against slavery and in efforts to overcome prejudice, white abolitionists often put the condition of their own souls first. "There is no way for us to escape from guilt and corruption of heart," urged evangelical cleric Beriah Green, "but by cordially and joyfully yielding to our colored brethren the sympathies of our common humanity."[24] But as Frederick Douglass observed bitterly shortly before the Civil War, the Garrisonian plan to purge the national

---

Carter G. Woodson, *Negro Orators and Their Orations* (Washington: Associated Publishers, 1925), 93; in the demand for careful preparation for emancipation by *Northern Star and Freedmen's Advocate,* March 10, 1842; and in Henry Highland Garnet's linking of land reform and effective abolitionism, in his letter to Sydney H. Gay, September 7, 1848, in *Chronotype,* September 19, 1848.

22. John L. Thomas, *The Liberator. William Lloyd Garrison: A Biography* (Boston: Little, Brown and Company, 1963), 152-153. Others who have observed the abolitionist proclivity to abstraction are Larry Gara, *The Liberty Line: The Legend of the Underground Railroad* (Lexington: University of Kentucky Press, 1961), 4, 76; and Aileen Kraditor, *Means and Ends in American Abolitionism: Garrison and His Critics on Strategy and Tactics. 1834-1850* (New York: Pantheon Books, 1969), *passim.*

23. Garrison and Garrison, *Garrison,* 3:320. For a similar Phillips sentiment see the reference in William L. Garrison to Henry C. Wright, August 26, 1846, Garrison Papers, Antislavery Collection, Boston Public Library (cited hereafter as G-BPL). Similar statements abound for other white abolitionists.

24. *American Anti-Slavery Reporter,* I (June 1834), 88. For Henry B. Stanton's assertion that prejudice is vincible and "that the white man can become a Christian, and the colored man his brother"; see the *Liberator,* May 24, 1834.

conscience by dissolving the Union would do little more than leave "slaves and masters to fight their own battles, in their own way."[25]

Although Garrison's group was only a small part of white abolition, nearly all abolitionists were more concerned with the institution of slavery than with the rights and well-being of Southern slaves or Northern freemen. Thrown largely upon their own resources, therefore, black abolitionists increasingly turned to practical action to achieve equal opportunity and effective civil rights. Very early they had argued that such action was their special function in the broader movement to end slavery. New York editor and Presbyterian cleric Samuel Cornish had suggested in 1829 that whites form abolition societies and blacks concentrate on practical social uplift. Elaborating the same theme, he later contended that white antislavery did best at generating national uneasiness and arousing the national conscience but that black effort was better expended in concrete undertakings for race progress through agriculture, the mechanical trades, education, and a black press.[26]

The meaning of these differing approaches became abundantly clear in 1840. Drawing on experience gained during the early 1830s in several national conventions which they had organized to channel and focus their efforts for improvement and uplift, blacks returned to this mode of action with even greater determination and vigor. While white abolitionists engaged in factional dispute over the relationship of their movement to organized religion and other reform goals, the Negro convention movement launched its campaign for the franchise. Whites, largely ignoring the suffrage issue as such, immediately denounced these conventions as racist separatism within the antislavery movement. Blacks immediately

25. Frederick Douglass, *The Anti-Slavery Movement: A Lecture by Frederick Douglass Before the Rochester Ladies' Anti-Slavery Society* (Rochester: Lee, Mann and Co., 1855), 30-33. Other contemporary critics also condemned the Garrisonian tendency to abstraction; see, among others, James Gordon Bennett, quoted in Garrison and Garrison, *Garrison*, 3:283; and Nathaniel Hall, *The Iniquity: A Sermon Preached in the First Church, Dorchester, on Sunday, Dec. 11, 1859* (Boston: John Wilson & Son, 1859).
26. *Rights of All*, September 18, 1829; *Colored American*, May 3, 1838.

countered that the suffrage was central to American political life, its possession a necessity for those seeking equal civil rights, and its pursuit a vital part of their quest for freedom. To achieve these race goals, political activists argued that they must act in a distinctive fashion in their own conventions. Increasingly, black speakers and writers played upon the theme that they who would be free, themselves must strike the blow.[27]

Cornish, who had long argued for independent black action, saw in it a way to establish the good moral and religious character of blacks in the eyes of whites. Nor was this simply a quest for majority approval, for only such a reputation, he thought, would convince whites that ending slavery was socially safe.[28] Subsequent arguments, less oriented to white sensibilities, continued to tie distinctive black efforts for the elevation of the race to the ultimate ending of slavery. James McCune Smith charged that white antislavery talked of immediate and complete emancipation at the South but practiced only partial emancipation at the North. It was not to be trusted, he continued. "The North cannot collect nor concentrate its moral and intellectual power whilst there is slavery in the North—for semi-emancipation is slavery still. . . ."[29] Nearly twenty years later, in 1855, a short-lived Negro National Council defended its organization and plans in language similar to Smith's. It was impossible, they resolved, to "repose confidence in the genuineness of that Abolitionism which, while it denounces Slavery at the South, scouts as delusive and hurtful all schemes for the moral and social elevation of the free colored people of the North."[30]

That blacks continued to participate in predominantly white

27. For the development of the franchise and separatist strains in the convention movement, see Jane H. Pease and William H. Pease, "Black Power—The Debate in 1840," *Phylon,* XXIX (Spring 1968), 19-26. A writer to the *Weekly Anglo-African,* in the issue for August 13, 1859, insisted on the necessity of black action outside of, as well as within, antislavery ranks, urging efforts to improve the condition and status of Negroes.

28. *Colored American,* March 4, 1837.

29. *Liberator,* June 1, 1838.

30. *Frederick Douglass' Paper,* May 18, 1855. For a similar resolution, adopted by the New York Literary and Productive Union and introduced by James McCune Smith, *ibid.,* February 9, 1855.

antislavery societies up to the Civil War and that white abolitionists actively assisted free Negroes in the North does not contradict the increasingly different approaches which each group evolved. Unfortunately, however, their increasing divergence led to constant misunderstanding. To free blacks, white antislavery became ever more remote and abstract while their needs were immediate, concrete, and personal—not to be satisfied with ideological resolutions. "What the Negro needs," Samuel R. Ward observed in 1855, "is, what belongs to him—what has been ruthlessly torn from him—and what is, by consent of a despotic democracy and a Christless religion, withholden from him, guiltily, perseveringly." All else were "cheap wares" and superfluous.[31]

To whites, black activism based on these premises seemed to manifest self-interest rather than dedication to antislavery principle. Free Negroes' aspirations to material well-being and political power were tawdry goals generating cheap endeavor. The same white abolitionists who preached middle-class virtue, thrift, and hard work, scorned the display and self-seeking which their pursuit involved. Antislavery lecturer Sarah Grimké observed of Samuel Cornish's bourgeois household—she hoped not uncharitably—that it was "like the abode of sanctimonious pride and pharisaical aristocracy."[32] Theodore Weld, who roomed there, found her judgment "lamentably right."[33] From Britain, abolitionist George Thompson commented, in a manner by then common to his American associates when they spoke of their black co-workers, that Charles Remond, lecturer and barber from Salem, Massachusetts, lacked the proper "disinterestedness" and displayed too much "number-one-ishness."[34]

31. Ward, *Autobiography,* 87.
32. Sarah and Angelina Grimké to Theodore Weld, November 30, [18]37, *Weld-Grimké Letters,* 1:487.
33. Theodore Weld to Sarah and Angelina Grimké, December 15, [1837], *ibid.,* 1:496.
34. George Thompson to Richard [Webb], August 12, 1845, Weston Papers, Antislavery Collection, Boston Public Library (cited hereafter as W-BPL). For similar sentiments regarding Douglass, see Maria W. Chapman to Webb, June 29, 1845, Copy, Samuel May, Jr., Papers, Antislavery Collection, Boston Public Library (cited hereafter as M-BPL). On the question of separate standards for blacks, see M. Recard to Mary Estlin, June 29, 1852, G-BPL.

But what did they expect, James McCune Smith wondered. "Recollect," he wrote to Gerrit Smith, philanthropist and political abolitionist from upstate New York, "we are borne along with the tide of wealth-worship, that we are but *men*. . . ."[35] Yet most white abolitionists were no more prepared to understand that than they were to admit the primacy of practical action for race progress in the North. Thus the difference came full circle. Blacks, whose very existence was threatened, found abstraction irrelevant; whites, plagued by guilt and prejudice, failed to comprehend the practical issues. "Consciously or unconsciously," wrote Frederick Douglass in 1860, "almost every white man approaches a colored man with an air of superiority and condescension. The relation subsisting between the races at once shows itself between the individuals, and each prepares, when brought together, to soften the points of antagonism. The white man tries his hand at being negro, and the negro, to make himself agreeable, plays the white man. The end is, each knows the other only superficially."[36]

When mutual understanding failed so completely, agreement was impossible. Neither white nor black quite comprehended the dual nature of the crusade which jointly they sought to wage, for their failure to communicate obscured the difference which tore them asunder. There were in reality two overlapping movements. One was a reform movement seeking to bring practice affecting others into harmony with previously defined ideological commitments; the other was a movement of activists seeking directly to meliorate their own condition and that of their group. For the latter, physical, material, and immediate changes were essential; ideology and theory were useful primarily as they served pragmatic ends.[37]

35. James McCune Smith to Gerrit Smith, December 18, 1846, S-SU.
36. *Douglass Monthly,* October, 1860.
37. This distinction is one which marked a variety of reform-uplift movements of the period. Temperance reformers, who advocated abstinence as a means to improvement and control, operated on very different assumptions and with different goals and programs from Washingtonians, a society of reformed drunkards organized to appeal to and give individual assistance to their fellow alcoholics. Similar differences may also be found in the antebellum Workingmen's movement and the women's rights movement.

Although the two abolitionisms were not movements hermetically sealed off from each other, the basic dualism which characterizes their interrelationship provides the framework for understanding black abolition. It was neither confined by a unified theory of opposition to slavery nor limited to engagement within the framework of antislavery organizations and activities. Compared to its white counterpart, it more emphatically embraced practical efforts to provide economic opportunity and social mobility for Northern blacks, to acquire the franchise and insure civil rights, to establish a sense of black identity and community. This was a far cry from the abolitionism of Wendell Phillips and William Lloyd Garrison, who had not come "into the world to abolish slavery, but to do [their] duty."[38] But it was the only kind with meaning for black America; for it was their search for freedom.

38. Quoted in William L. Garrison to Henry C. Wright, August 26, 1846, G-BPL.

2. COMMUNITY CONSCIOUSNESS BEFORE 1830

WELL BEFORE the antebellum antislavery movement took shape, Northern blacks had evolved a distinctive group consciousness. Their slave heritage left them with experiences and assumptions quite different from those of their white neighbors. The Revolutionary War was not the realization of their freedom, although it did mark a turning point, as sympathetic philanthropists who had previously worked to ameliorate the lot of slaves now sought their emancipation. But even blacks already free were excluded from organized efforts to extend that freedom to all Northern Negroes because early national reform, unlike the Revolution, was largely an upper class affair. Benevolent societies, including emancipation groups, commonly invited to membership only those of established social or political status. Consequently when Northern blacks did achieve general freedom, little sense of personal accomplishment came with it. Moreover it was accompanied neither by equality nor by tolerance, but rather it increased the very racial prejudice which Negroes had long endured as slaves. Particularly hard hit were those who had lived and worked on farms. Although emancipated, many were denied land ownership. Unable therefore to earn a livelihood in the country, they drifted to the cities, where their rural skills were useless.

At the same time, however, the increasing numbers of free Negroes and their concentration in urban areas did provide the necessary precondition for the establishment of black churches and benevolent societies, which first gave the race an organized voice. By 1805 every Northern state had either fully abolished slavery or begun a program of gradual emancipation. In New England and the Middle States, the free black population of 27,000 in 1790 had doubled by 1800 and increased to 75,000 by 1810, to 92,000 ten years later, and had reached nearly 122,500 by 1830. Thus in the forty years since the Revolution a nearly universal emancipation and the concentration of a critical mass provided the basic prerequisite for effective race action.

But they produced increased hostility as well, even from those whites who had backed emancipation. Their sentiment was early expressed in heavily Quaker Burlington, New Jersey, where antislavery whites complained that free Negroes were often "given to Idleness, Frolicking, Drunkenness, and in some few cases . . . Dishonesty."[1] Such views were troublesome enough to abolitionists. But they also increased discrimination and aggravated general race tension; politicians, eager to turn that tension to their own advantage, and laboring whites, fearful of competition, frequently joined forces to enflame prejudice and restrict the scope of black freedom.[2]

In state after state, laws defined different rights and privileges for blacks and whites. Although suffrage was gradually extended to all white males, regardless of their economic standing, most states either retained property qualifications for black voters, or, even worse, totally disfranchised them on grounds of race. Thus in 1807 New Jersey excluded Negroes from the polls and Connecticut did likewise in 1818. Of all Northern states admitted to the Union between 1790 and 1860, only Vermont and Maine never discriminated against blacks in the matter of suffrage. And of the original states, only Massachusetts never compromised color-free voter qualification. Yet in 1820 even Massachusetts considered disfranchising all Negroes. New York, in its constitutional revision

1. Arthur Zilversmit, *The First Emancipation: The Abolition of Slavery in the North* (Chicago: University of Chicago Press, 1967), 223.

2. George M. Frederickson, *The Black Image in the White Mind: The Debate on Afro-American Character and Destiny, 1819-1914* (New York: Harper & Row, 1971), 4-5, follows Zilversmit closely. See also Edgar J. McManus, *A History of Negro Slavery in New York* (Syracuse: Syracuse University Press, 1966), 186-188.

of 1821, not only retained but increased the property qualification for black voters while dropping it for whites. Pennsylvania in 1815 considered controlling the size of its Negro population by curtailing in-migration from other states as Ohio had already done before 1810. And exceeding the Ohio Black Code, which required Negroes to post bonds for good behavior and self-support, Philadelphia city fathers tried but failed in 1813 to require each black in the city to register, pay a special tax, and, if convicted of crime, to undergo special punishment at forced labor.[3] It was little wonder that James Forten, wealthy black sailmaker in the Quaker city, protested "that the advocates of emancipation can enact laws more degrading to the free man, and more injurious to his feelings, than all the tyranny of slavery, or the shackles of infatuated despotism."[4]

As a consequence blacks sought place and identity in organizations of their own in order to sustain their psyches and to promote their physical well-being. Over the years they established lodges, churches, and other similar associations. As early as 1780 Negroes in Providence, Rhode Island, had launched their own benevolent society;[5] and thereafter throughout the North a wide array of mutual aid and fraternal orgainzations grew up to provide both focus and fulcrum for the black community. None, however, was so central to the black experience as the Negro church.

Early developments in Philadelphia set the pattern. There, the Free African Society was founded by Richard Allen and Absalom

3. Emil Olbrich, *The Development of Sentiment on Negro Suffrage to 1860.* Bulletin of the University of Wisconsin, 477, History Series, Vol. 3, no. 1, ([Madison]: University of Wisconsin, 1912), 21-26. Robert A. Warner, *Negroes in New Haven: A Social History* (New Haven: Yale University Press, 1940), 10. McManus, *Slavery in New York,* 185-186. Edward R. Turner, *The Negro in Pennsylvania, 1639-1861* (Washington: American Historical Association, 1912), 152, 151.
4. *Freedom's Journal,* March 14, 1828.
5. Irving H. Bartlett, *From Slave to Citizen: The Story of the Negro in Rhode Island* (Providence: The Urban League of Greater Providence, 1954), 35.

Jones in 1787 as a benevolent society even before white leaders of St. George's Methodist Church had relegated black members to segregated pews. Quickly its initial concern to oversee and guide the moral life and social behavior of its members grew. By 1794 both the African Episcopal Church and the Bethel African Methodist Church had developed from it. Thereafter Bethel Church expanded so widely, with associated branches not only in Pennsylvania but also in New Jersey, Delaware, and Maryland, that in 1816 it became the African Methodist Episcopal denomination. Similarly in New York black Methodists rejected second-class status in the John Street Church, broke away in 1796, and formed the African Methodist Episcopal Zion Church. Like its Philadelphia counterpart it also generated additional congregations and after 1821 assumed denominational status. In Boston, New York, Philadelphia, and other Northern cities Baptists too formed new churches, as did Presbyterians and Episcopalians, though among the latter two no separate denominational structure appeared.[6]

Together with secular benevolent societies these churches, whether within or separate from white denominational structures, provided organizational frameworks through which Northern Negroes could further their physical and spiritual interests. By 1830 Boston, New York, and Philadelphia boasted a diverse array of such groups, while many lesser centers of population offered a choice, though on a restricted scale, among similar institutions.

As useful as separate institutions were, they could not block and counter prejudice, discrimination, and inequality before the law. Thoroughly dismayed and discouraged about their future in America, therefore, some blacks sought total physical separation in Africa. Leader among them was the Massachusetts sea-captain Paul Cuffe, a descendant of Africans and American Indians. Converted

6. Carol V. R. George, *Segregated Sabbaths: Richard Allen and the Emergence of Independent Black Churches, 1760-1840* (New York: Oxford University Press, 1973), 49-115.

to Quakerism and its humanitarian commitments, Cuffe had concluded by 1809 that only the establishment of wholly new African trade patterns would end the persistent Caribbean slave trade. To effect that change, he proposed that black Americans settle on the west African coast and change its economy by introducing new skills.

Pursuing his idea, Cuffe established direct contacts in Sierra Leone, the British colony established for loyalist slaves freed during the American Revolution, and with its sponsoring English organization, the British African Institution. He was delayed for several years by the War of 1812, but in 1816 Cuffe finally settled his first and only group of American emigrants in West Africa: seven families from Northern coastal cities eager to farm in their ancestral homeland. Then, a little over a year later, he died.[7]

The idea of African resettlement did not die with Cuffe. To back his scheme, he had helped establish African Institutions in various Northern cities, led by prestigious free black leaders—in Philadelphia by African Methodist Episcopal bishop Richard Allen, Episcopal minister Absalom Jones, and businessman James Forten.[8] They were quickly overshadowed, however, by the American Colonization Society. Founded in January 1817, the society, including prestigious whites like James Madison, Henry Clay, and Bushrod Washington, pressed for extensive black emigration to Africa. Both groups shared Cuffe's basic premise that many Southern slaveholders, fearful of black revolt, would opt for manumission if free blacks could be removed from the Southern states.[9]

Most Northern blacks, however, feared deportation and responded negatively to the colonization movement. Dubious, on the one hand, that the removal of Southern free blacks would encourage emancipation, they also personally refused to leave their American homeland for an unknown and untried Africa.

7. Sheldon H. Harris, ed., *Paul Cuffe: Black America and the African Return* (New York: Simon and Schuster, 1972), 40-69.
8. *Ibid.*, 229, 235.
9. Paul Cuffe to Samuel J. Mills, August 6, 1816, *ibid.*, 202-203.

Ironically, one of the earliest rejections of colonization occurred at an 1817 meeting called by the Philadelphia African Institution and attended by some three thousand Negroes. Unmoved by the Institution's sympathy for emigration, they dismissed the American Colonization Society's plans out of hand. They denied the society's contention that blacks constitued a "dangerous and useless" class in the United States; and they deplored linking manumission with colonization, which, they claimed, not only would break up slave families but also would fasten slavery ever more securely on those left behind. They intended, they concluded, to remain in Philadelphia where, despite many problems, they had prospered.[10]

The contrary view was not argued. Although Forten favored colonization in principle, sure that Afro-Americans would "never become a people until they came out from amongst the white people," he maintained public silence and, as chairman of the meeting, signed its protest against colonization.[11] Subsequent events, however, suggest that few Northern blacks were so torn. Of the 2886 people whom the American Colonization Society sent to Africa between 1820 and 1833, only 169 of them came from the North.[12] And from the mid-1820s onward, sympathetic whites came to share free blacks' suspicion that the American Colonization Society plan was proslavery. Indeed Garrison family tradition has it that the future *Liberator* editor was induced to oppose colonization in 1827 by William Watkins, a "colored Baltimorean."[13]

The overwhelming rejection of emigration did not, however, indicate that the quality of black life was improving in Northern

10. James Forten to W. S. Porter, June 10, 1835 in *Liberator,* August 1, 1835. Charles H. Wesley, *Richard Allen, Apostle of Freedom* (Washington: Associated Publishers, 1935), 161. William Lloyd Garrison, *Thoughts on African Colonization* (New York: Arno Press, 1969), Part II, 9-10.
11. James Forten to Paul Cuffe, January 25, 1817, in Harris, *Paul Cuffe,* 244.
12. *African Repository,* X (December 1834), 292.
13. Wendell P. Garrison and Francis J. Garrison, *William Lloyd Garrison, 1805-1879; The Story of His Life as Told by His Children* (New York: The Century Co., 1885-1889), I, 145, 148.

cities or that white prejudice was in any respect lessening. When Philadelphia and Boston worried that disproportionately large numbers of blacks were convicted of crime, the Pennsylvania and Massachusetts legislatures sought ways to limit their Negro populations. In 1821 the former passed "An Act to Prevent the Increase of Pauperism," which imposed financial penalties on whites who brought black servants into the state. In the same year, Massachusetts, though it took no consequent action, appointed a legislative committee to explore the possibility of curtailing Negro in-migration. In the West, Cincinnati, immediately across the Ohio River from slaveholding Kentucky and long a haven for manumitted and runaway slaves, experienced a sharp increase in racial tension during the 1820s. Official response through stricter enforcement of the state's black code was insufficient to forestall a race riot in 1829. As a result a large number of black Cincinnatians left the city.[14]

Yet it was not only trauma and despair in the 1820s which stimulated black efforts to end slavery and win civil rights. Like white abolitionists, blacks were encouraged by English antislavery thought, especially by Elizabeth Heyrick's unequivocal publication demanding *Immediate, Not Gradual Emancipation*. They were further heartened by events in Haiti, where by 1822 President Jean Pierre Boyer had ended years of internal strife and opened the way for considerable development of the black republic. Perhaps most encouraging of all was the final ending of slavery in the largest Northern state. On July 4, 1827, New York's process of gradual emancipation was completed and her last slaves were freed. Thus the 18,000 slaves the 1820 census recorded for the Northeast dramatically fell to 3,000 within the decade. New York's action was celebrated as the beginning of a new era.

14. Turner, *Negro in Pennsylvania*, 155-158, 94-95. Frederickson, *Black Image*, 5, Richard C. Wade, "The Negro in Cincinnati, 1800-1830," *Journal of Negro History*, XXXIX (January 1954), 49-51.

Significant of new approaches in the late 1820s was the launching of the first black newspaper in the United States. Early in 1827 *Freedom's Journal* began publication in New York City, jointly edited by John Russwurm, a recent Bowdoin college graduate, and Samuel E. Cornish, a Presbyterian clergyman. Established primarily to serve blacks throughout the North, the paper would also, its editors hoped, change the white image of the Negro, especially among those who were "our friends, to whom we concede all the principles of humanity and religion," but who from misrepresentation had "fallen into the current of popular feeling and [were] imperceptibly floating on the stream—actually living in the practice of prejudice, while they abjure[d] it in theory, and [felt] it not in their hearts." With agents from Washington, D.C., to Yarmouth, Maine, *Freedom's Journal* proposed to elevate and educate the race, to work for black civil rights, to encourage intelligent voting (where the franchise was available), and to promote sympathy for "our brethren who are still in the iron fetters of bondage."[15]

After only six months Cornish resigned his editorship, and the paper, now run by Russwurm alone, slowly declined as it devoted less and less space to black issues, more and more to general items of no particular racial significance. Ironically a major complaint against the paper was that it carried too little about Africa, since Russwurm shortly became one of the small band of Northerners to emigrate. Converted to colonization early in 1829, he gave up his editorship, set off to Liberia, and spent the rest of his life there. Propelled by this emergency, Cornish returned to his editorial post, revived the paper as the *Rights of All* and stressed black Americans' need to communicate among themselves and with whites. Nonetheless the paper failed. Starved for subscriptions despite heroic efforts of stockholders and friends to save it, *Rights of All* ceased publication within the year.[16]

15. *Freedom's Journal*, March 16, 1827; May 18, 1827.
16. Bella Gross, "Freedom's Journal and the Rights of All," *Journal of Negro History*, XVII (July 1932), 241-286. *Rights of All*, May 29, 1829; August [14], 1829.

Short-lived though *Freedom's Journal* and *Rights of All* were, they had both prompted united black action and recorded its results. By advertising private schools in New York City and elsewhere and by promoting interest in the city's African Free Schools, organized in 1787 and run by the New York Manumission Society, they encouraged education for blacks. The papers also led the way in practical action. When the African Free Schools were plagued by declining attendance, editor Cornish became their agent and through newly established visiting committees urged parents to send their children to the schools. At the same time a Dorcas Society was reported to be sewing for children who otherwise would have lacked sufficient clothing to attend classes.[17]

In various articles both papers also participated in the campaign against colonization. They condemned it as a scheme devised by white men fearful of race war to exile free blacks and to perpetuate slavery by removing those who would act against it. Russell Parrott of the old African Institution in Philadelphia wrote in the columns of *Freedom's Journal* that "the free black population have become a source of uneasiness to those who are determined to adhere to a ruinous [slave] system," and Bishop Allen seconded his charges. New York's Thomas Jinnings, in an address to the local mutual relief society, argued that the homeland of Afro-Americans was the New World, not the Old. "Our claims are on America," he said. "It is the land that gave us birth; it is the land of our nativity, we know no other country. . . ."[18]

Yet the inroads of prejudice and discrimination also occasionally led the papers and their correspondents to favor some sort of emigration. For Russwurm, who at one point had toyed with Haiti, Liberia seemed the land of opportunity, promising outlets for his educated talents and the enjoyment of equal rights.[19] Even Cornish, who deplored Russwurm's path, saw in the stringent application of the Ohio Black Code a justification for

17. *Freedom's Journal*, December 21, 1827; January 11, 1828; February 1, 1828.
18. *Ibid.*, July 27, 1827; November 2, 1827; April 4, 1828.
19. *Ibid.*, February 21, 1829; March 7, 1829.

emigration. Though he wished that blacks would stay put and be martyrs for freedom, he conceded that in the face of the Cincinnati riots they might legitimately choose exile. In that event, he urged them to go northward to Canada where they would find a welcome, as well as freedom, equality, and opportunity.[20]

More indicative of changing black temper than the critiques of colonization was the openness with which slavery was attacked in the late 1820s. Cornish occasionally used *Freedom's Journal* for this purpose and, though his remarks were usually veiled, he did assert that Southern self-interest demanded general emancipation rather than individual manumission.[21] Others, like Nathaniel Paul, were more blunt. Addressing an audience celebrating the completion of emancipation in New York, the Albany African Baptist pastor called slavery a "hateful monster, the very demon of avarice and oppression, " a violation of natural and divine law, and a corrupter of republican virtue. Approving England's philanthropic fight against slavery and commending the heroic Haitian struggle of Toussaint L'Ouverture, Paul warned that both slaves and masters were restless in the American South and predicted that the end of slavery was inevitable.[22]

No one else, however, went as far as Boston's David Walker. His *Appeal,* written in 1829 and published the next year, pressed openly for slave revolt. The logical climax of discontent, the *Appeal* was atypical of its time in tone, goal, and focus. Addressing the General Colored Association of Massachusetts, Walker more nearly reflected the temper of the decade. "The primary object of this institution," Walker told the society at its first semi-annual meeting, "is, to unite the colored population, so far, through the United States of America, as may be practicable and expedient; forming societies, opening, extending, and keeping up correspondences, and not withholding any thing which may have the least tendency to meliorate *our* miserable condition—with the

20. *Rights of All,* August 7, 1829.
21. *Ibid.,* August 14, 1829.
22. Nathaniel Paul, "An Address on the Celebration of the Abolition of Slavery in the State of New York, July 5, 1827," in Carter G. Woodson, *Negro Orators and their Orations* (Washington: Associated Publishers, 1925), 65-73.

restrictions, however, of not infringing on the articles of its constitution, or that of the United States of America."[23]

Though Walker of the *Appeal* suggested the direction occasional radical blacks might go after 1830, his 1828 address better summarized the nature of their efforts so far. In the decade of the 1820s Northern free blacks had continued to build race institutions and had initiated the new device of a race newspaper. They had both despaired of their condition in the United States and hoped that changing conditions at home and abroad would bring greater freedom. But how they would act in the future was partly, at least, as it had been in the past, a function of who they were and where they lived.

By 1830 the free Negro population in the North approached 125,000, most of them an unskilled or semiskilled labor force concentrated in and about certain urban areas. In that year more than half of all Northern free blacks lived in the middle states, overwhelmingly in Pennsylvania and New York; of those who lived in the North Central states, somewhat under half were in Ohio; and in New England, their centers of population were Massachusetts and Connecticut. More significantly, with New Jersey, Delaware, and Connecticut as distinct exceptions, they lived disproportionately to whites in a few towns and cities. In 1830 nearly one quarter of all Massachusetts Negroes lived in Boston with a substantial secondary concentration in New Bedford. By 1837, two-thirds of Pennsylvania blacks lived in the city and county of Philadelphia, and at least half of those within the city proper. To the west, Cincinnati's Hamilton county in 1840 accounted for about one-sixth of Ohio's black population. Ten years earlier an estimated one-third of New York State's Negro population lived in New York City. These urban centers of black population in Massachusetts, New York, Pennsylvania, and Ohio were throughout the antebellum period the major centers of black antislavery activism.[24]

23. *Freedom's Journal*, December 19, 1828.
24. *Condition of the American Colored Population, and of the Colony at Liberia* (Boston: Pierce and Parker, 1833), 6. Wilbur Zelinsky, "The Population Geography of the Free Negro in *Ante-Bellum* America,"

Consequently, the problems to which this activism largely addressed itself were imposed by urban setting as well as by minority status. Though some free Negroes like lumber dealer William Whipper and sailmaker James Forten of Pennsylvania had achieved upper-middle-class affluence and others had gained modest economic stability as caterers, barbers, and dealers in second-hand clothing and furniture, the lot of most was that of unskilled or service labor. Nor did the disproportionate number of old people and women among the free population ease the problems of urban poverty—problems which were perpetuated as young people, lacking alternative career models, continued to pursue unskilled labor or service and menial occupations.[25]

It was these constraints and conditions which defined the lot of the free Northern black community. For it the 1820s had been a time of forging and testing. How it could be moved to a politics of social, economic, and legal reform for its own well-being and that of enslaved Southern Negroes was the central task that confronted the spokesmen and leaders of black abolition.

Population Studies, III (1949-1950), 387-388. *African Repository,* XXI (October, 1845), 294. *Liberator,* October 13, 1837. *African Repository,* XXV (November, 1849), 340. Charles T. Hickok, *The Negro in Ohio, 1802-1870* (Cleveland: Press of the Williams Publishing and Electric Co., 1896), 39n. *Freedom's Journal,* June 1, 1827, estimates 15,000 blacks in New York; other estimates run somewhat higher.

25. Statistical evidence on property ownership and annual income is unavailable on any solid basis. But the picture of unskilled and menial labor is clear from contemporary reports devoted to establishing black efforts to gain respectability and from an examinaton of city directories. See, for example, Ohio Anti-Slavery Convention Held at Putnam, on the 22d, 23d, and 24th of April 1835, *Report on the Condition of the People of Color in The State of Ohio* (n.p.: n.p, n.d.); "A Statistical Inquiry into the Condition of the People of Color of the City and Districts of Philadelphia," *North Star,* February 2, 1849; also for Philadelphia, *Douglass Monthly,* October 1860; and for New York, *ibid.,* March 1859. Zelinsky, "Population Geography," 388. Robert Ernst, "The Economic Status of New York City Negroes, 1850-1863," *Negro History Bulletin,* XII (March 1949), 131-143.

PART II

Cooperation and Conflict Within the Antislavery Movement

BLACKS WERE early financial backers of the antislavery press, popular lecturers on prejudice, and effective limners of the evils of slavery; yet they were prominent neither as officers nor as decision-makers in antislavery societies. The paradox begot praise and tension both. Blacks never wholly forsook predominantly white abolition societies; yet black abolition was never exclusively expressed through them. Over the years Negroes performed important functions in these societies; but as time went on they increasingly criticized their limitations and prejudices. Some rejected white abolitionism altogether; some merely shifted from one faction to another; still others continued loyally within the original societies. Few, however, remained wholly satisfied with the movement.

3. AGENTS AND AGITATORS
AT HOME

WHEN WILLIAM Lloyd Garrison launched the *Liberator* on January 1, 1831, he sounded the militant note for which Northern blacks had been waiting and hoping. Even before the first issue appeared, they began to work for it. Spurred by James Forten, Philadelphia Negroes voted it support and provided charter subscribers. Soon after, groups in Boston, New York, and Middletown, Connecticut, followed suit. Within a year there were over a dozen black *Liberator* agents in such widely separated places as Cincinnati, Baltimore, New York, New Haven, and Boston. Because of their efforts, nearly three-fourths of *Liberator* subscribers in the early years were Negroes.[1]

The *Liberator* heralded the birth of a new antislavery movement in which blacks joined whites to form both local and national societies. When Garrison and a dozen white Yankees initiated in 1832 a New England Anti-Slavery Society, blacks contributed a fourth of the signatures on the new society's constitution.[2] The next year Samuel Cornish participated in the early meetings called to launch a New York City antislavery society. And in Philadelphia, where the American Anti-Slavery Society was founded in December 1833, three of the delegates were Negroes.

1. James Forten to [William L. Garrison], December 31, 1830; and Forten to Garrison, February 2, 1831, both in G-BPL. *Liberator,* February 12, March 12, 19, July 23, August 6 and 20, 1831, and January 21, 1832. Benjamin Quarles, *Black Abolitionists* (New York: Oxford University Press, 1969), 20.
2. Wendell P. Garrison and Francis J. Garrison, *William Lloyd Garrison, 1805-1879: The Story of his Life as told by his Children* (4 vols. New York: The Century Co., 1885-1889), 1:280, 282.

James McCrummell, Garrison's host in Philadelphia, James Barbadoes, a Boston barber, and Robert Purvis, son and heir of a Charleston, South Carolina, merchant and now a Philadelphia resident, all signed the society's Declaration of Sentiments.[3]

The black role in this new abolition was not limited to getting subscriptions and signing documents, though the mere fact that they joined societies was a major departure from earlier antislavery organizations whose membership was confined to whites.[4] In New York, David Ruggles, activist grocer, responded to American Colonization Society attacks on the new movement with a denunciatory pamphlet, *The Extinguisher Extinguished*. Tendentious and ad hominem though much of his argument was, Ruggles drove home his charge that prior to 1832 no genuine Northern exertions had been made to free Southern slaves.[5] Theodore Wright made a similarly energetic defense of the new abolitionism as the sole vehicle for antislavery progress. Without it, Southern slaves, both powerless and without rights, had no hope for freedom. Garrison was, Wright concluded more than "the friend of the colored man," he was a virtual Messiah.[6]

The overwhelmingly positive nature of this early enthusiasm came, in time, to haunt some of its spokesmen. Recalling in the 1850s the zeal with which they had joined the new crusade,

3. Bertram Wyatt-Brown, "Partners in Piety: Lewis and Arthur Tappan, Evangelical Abolitionists, 1828-1841" (Ph.D. The John Hopkins University, 1963), 125. *Liberator*, December 14 and 21, 1833.

4. One of the most significant changes in Jacksonian reform movements from late 18th- and early 19th-century reform societies was the change from a restricted and elite invited membership to an open and voluntary one. Had this structural change not occurred, it is hard to see how blacks could have played any more significant organizational role from 1830-1863 than they did in the period of Northern emancipation activity (ca. 1775-1805), from which, with few exceptions, they were excluded. The shift from closed to open membership was occurring in the 1820s, but there is little record among the few really active Northern antislavery societies, most notably the Philadelphia-based American Convention for Promoting the Abolition of Slavery, that blacks played any significant role then either.

5. David Ruggles, *The "Extinguisher" Extinguished! or David M. Reese. M.D., "Used Up."* . . . (New York: David Ruggles, 1834, reprint, Philadelphia: Rhistoric, n.d.), 8.

6. *Liberator*, June 25, 1836.

Presbyterian minister James W. C. Pennington regretted that their absolute trust in it had made his colleagues give up their independent efforts and rely on white abolitionists who had "taken up the labouring oar."[7]

Antislavery efforts in the early 1830s depended heavily on writing, publishing, and distributing pamphlets, tracts, and newspapers. As time went on, however, lecturers and agents came to be the principal proselytizers for the abolitionist message. Here free blacks were especially useful. By 1840 several of them had become regular speakers on the antislavery lecture circuit. Rev. John W. Lewis worked in New Hamsphire; Jehiel C. Beman, pastor of the African Baptist Church in Middletown, Connecticut, was active there and in Massachusetts; and Charles Remond frequently left his Salem barber shop to lecture throughout New England. In this work, blacks had a real advantage over their more numerous white comrades, for their color gave their message an immediacy to which white audiences particularly responded.[8]

In 1841 abolitionists also discovered that if black lecturers could be more convincing than white, so a slave could be more effective than a freeman. At a local antislavery convention on Nantucket Island, Frederick Douglass, recently escaped from Maryland slavery, gave his first antislavery talk. His success was immediate. He was a living demonstration of what other lecturers, whites and free blacks alike, could only talk about. Almost at once

7. James W. C. Pennington, *The Fugitive Blacksmith; or, Events in the History of James W. C. Pennington, Pastor of a Presbyterian Church in New York, Formerly a Slave in the State of Maryland, United States* (3rd ed. 1850. Westport, Conn.: Negro Universities Press, 1971), 55.

8. For Lewis, see *Liberator*, October 18, 1839; for Beman, Quarles, *Black Abolitionists*, 26; *Colored American*, November 16, 1839; *Massachusetts Abolitionist*, September 12, 1839; for Remond, *Liberator*, July 20, 1838, and 1840-44 *passim*.

antislavery leaders hired him as an agent for the Massachusetts Anti-Slavery Society.[9]

In his first lectures in this new capacity, Douglass drew almost exclusively on his personal history. He talked in the first person of his slave experience, of his escape, and of his life as fugitive in New York and New Bedford. It was the drama of his position which moved his listeners; the content of the message was subordinate to the persona. As he became a more polished lecturer, therefore, his white sponsors began to worry. "Better have a little of the plantation speech," John Collins, general agent of the Massachusetts society, warned him. "It is not best that you seem too learned." And Stephen Foster, a dynamic radical and visceral lecturer, advised him not to become too good at speechmaking. "People won't believe that you were ever a slave, Frederick," he cautioned.[10]

Yet there was little reason to worry. Wherever they went, black speakers, fugitive or free, were at a premium on the lecture platform. What they said, how they looked, the ease with which they discoursed, and the dynamics with which they portrayed slavery won attention. The better they spoke, the better their message came across. At first, indeed, Douglass could not match the practiced oratory of Boston Brahmin Wendell Phillips or the fiery denunciations of Quaker Abby Kelley. Yet within five months of his Nantucket debut he was making a "very good impression" on skeptical auditors, and within the year he had converted at least one self-confessed non-abolitionist, who had attended a single lecture and was completely won over by this fugitive slave who was "chaste in language, brilliant in thought, and truly eloquent in delivery."[11] By 1845 Douglass' platform command was unchallenged. As Wendell Phillips reported to

9. Philip Foner, ed., *The Life and Writings of Frederick Douglass* (4 vols. New York: International Publishers, 1950-55), 1:27. Garrison and Garrison, *Garrison*, 3:20.

10. Foner, *Douglass*, 1:59.

11. E. D. Moore to Amos A. Phelps, January 10, 1842, Phelps Papers, Antislavery Collection, Boston Public Library (cited hereafter as P-BPL). "Othello" to the *Nantucket Islander* Editor, n.d., in *Liberator*, July 8, 1842.

English friends, he combined the best of black and white and was "the most remarkable & by far the ablest colored man we have ever had here."[12]

His talent and his condition made him overshadow other Negro speakers. It was true that other fugitive slaves had lectured before Douglass, but men like Henry Highland Garnet and Samuel Ringgold Ward had kept their slave backgrounds quiet for reasons of personal security. Therefore when Douglass became an antislavery agent, he created, in effect, a new type: the slave lecturer whose closeness to the peculiar institution quite captured public imagination. It was not long before others followed his example and capitalized upon the appeal he had demonstrated.[13]

From Kentucky came Henry Bibb, who began to lecture in 1843 in Michigan, only a couple of years after he had escaped to Detroit.[14] Another Kentuckian, William Wells Brown, was among the most successful of slave lecturers. Although he had settled in upstate New York shortly after his 1834 escape, it was only in 1843 that he began to lecture for the Western New York Anti-Slavery Society. Subsequently, also like Douglass, he campaigned extensively in England. Then, in 1855, after a five year stay abroad, he returned to the United States to become an agent for the American and Massachusetts antislavery societies. In this capacity he undertook a new role, giving public readings of his semi-autobiographical drama, "The Doughface Baked," written to counter the popular pro-Southern portrayal of slavery recently published by a Boston clergyman, Nehemiah Adams.[15]

12. Wendell Phillips to [?], February 24, 1845, G-BPL.
13. Larry Gara, "The Professional Fugitive in the Abolition Movement," *Wisconsin Magazine of History*, XLVIII (Spring, 1965), 204; also his *Liberty Line:The Legend of the Underground Railroad* (Lexington: University of Kentucky Press, 1961), 122. Foner, *Douglass*, 1:46.
14. Henry Bibb, *Narrative of the Life and Adventures of Henry Bibb, An American Slave* (orig. publ., 1849. Miami: Mnemosyne, 1969), 175-187.
15. William E. Farrison, "William Wells Brown in Buffalo," *Journal of Negro History*, XXXIX (October, 1954), 298-314. *Liberator*, December 28, 1855, May 23, 1856, August 1, 1856. For further evidence about Brown's lecture tours, *ibid.*, September 3, 1847, February 23, 1855, and October 16, 1857.

Henry "Box" Brown, whose fame began when he escaped slavery by being crated and shipped to Philadelphia, also showed a considerable theatrical flair. In 1850 he toured with Bostonian Benjamin Roberts, displaying a diorama which depicted Brown's experiences. Roberts would describe the scenes for the audience and lecture on the "Condition of the Colored Population in the United States," for which Brown was a living exhibit, telling stories of his slavery days and singing spirituals.[16] Similarly Anthony Burns, a fugitive recaptured in Boston and then bought free, joined promoter H. C. Garcelon and toured the country in the late 1850s. In the evenings they showed a panorama called "The Moving Mirror of Slavery" and in the daytime peddled copies of the *Life of Anthony Burns.*[17]

Few of those who lectured or performed for antislavery audiences, however, lasted as long as did Douglass, Remond, and William Wells Brown, each of whom appeared quite regularly for at least twenty years. Collectively however, all of them demonstrated that black lecturers interested and convinced a public which had "itching ears to hear a colored man speak, and particularly *a slave.*"[18] Yet to suppose that their appeal was derived simply from their dramatic status as fugitive slaves or the happy circumstance of their plantation patois is to assign them an easy but false vaudevillian role. Undeniably their mere presence as lecturers was used to demonstrate to the doubtful the essential humanity and talent of a race largely consigned to slavery. It is equally true, however, that to the thoughtful and perceptive they brought a variegated message.

First and foremost they emphasized the brutalizing conditions and consequences of the slavery which many of them had experienced at first hand. The humblest speakers confined themselves to describing the long and unrewarded hours of toil; the whip, ever present to prod or punish; the physical violence to enforce discipline or satisfy sadistic appetites of vicious overseers

16. *Liberator,* May 31, 1850.
17. *Ibid.,* September 3, 1858.
18. John A. Collins, in Foner, *Douglass,* 1:46.

and tyrannical masters; the destruction of family life by sale, concubinage, and even escape. More sophisticated lecturers discussed the complex restrictions on personal freedom: the systems of passess and papers, the denial of religious worship, the proscriptions against learning to read and write. A few, like William Wells Brown, conceptualized still more broadly from the specific illustration to the generic condition. A slave, he explained to the Female Anti-Slavery Society of Salem, "is a thing. He is a piece of property in the hands of a master, as much as is the horse that belongs to the individual that may ride him through your streets to-morrow. Where we find one man holding an unlimited power over another . . . what can we expect to find of his condition?"[19]

It was a cruelly direct question from which there was no escape. Black lecturers quickly disabused those whites who consoled themselves with Panglossian reassurance that some masters were kind and some slaves fortunate. The kind masters might, ex-slaves argued, be less brutal or provide religious training or even connive to circumvent the laws against literacy—but by so doing they only made their slaves more restless, more eager to break their bonds and run for freedom. In thus asserting their full manhood and demanding recognition of it, these lecturers left no leeway for those who would content themselves with ameliorating conditions as part of gradual emancipation.

So Douglass wrote in his *Narrative*, published in 1845, that having lived in the city and having had a lenient master were the two crucial factors which nourished his sense of self and propelled him to flight. The independence that the urban environment provided him and the kindness that his master bestowed upon him only increased his distain for the system which denied him freedom. J. W. C. Pennington made the same point more explicitly in his *Fugitive Blacksmith* when he argued that "the mildest form of slavery . . . is comparatively the worst form . . . ." Aware of the

---

19. William Wells Brown, "A Lecture Delivered Before the Female Anti-Slavery Society of Salem at Lyceum Hall, Nov. 14, 1847," in *The Narrative of William W. Brown, A Fugitive Slave* (1848 edition. Reading, Mass.: Addison-Wesley, 1969), 82.

psychological anxiety it created, he probed the reasons for it. "It not only keeps the slave in the most unpleasant apprehension . . . but it actually . . . trains him under the most favorable circumstances the system admits of, and then plunges him into the worst of which it is capable."[20] "Tell me not of kind masters under slavery's hateful rule!" apostrophized Henry "Box" Brown, turning the tables in a bitter denunciation of the system. "There is no such thing as a person of that description. . . ."[21]

Both white and black lecturers buttressed their analysis of slavery with shocking atrocity stories to rouse their audiences' emotions. For most whites these stories came secondhand from compilations like Theodore Weld's *Slavery As It Is* or the writings of the Rev. George Bourne, whose sadistic tales bordered on pornography. But most black lecturers could rely on firsthand experience—albeit often supplemented by stock tales. And Douglass, who dealt little with specific atrocity themes, derived verification from his own *Narrative* for his insistence that terror, however exerted, was basic to slavery. Without the constant threat of violence, he contended, no slave would work.[22]

Those who dealt more specifically with the subject relied most heavily on shocking tales of the sexual use and abuse of female slaves. Sarah Remond, who later became a physician, generalized on their implication. There were 800,000 mulattoes in the South, she informed her audiences. They were "the fruits of licentiousness—bringing nothing but desolation in the hearts of the mother who bore them, and it ought to have brought shame to the father, but there was no respect for morality while the ministers of the gospel and statesmen of the south did not act an example which even their slaves could follow."[23] Remond's light color

20. Pennington, *Fugitive Blacksmith*, v.

21. Henry Box Brown, *Narrative of Henry Box Brown, Who Escaped from Slavery Enclosed in a Box 3 Feet Long and 2 Wide. Written From a Statement of Facts Made by Himself. With Remarks Upon the Remedy for Slavery. By Charles Stearns* (orig. edition 1849. Philadelphia: Rhistoric Publications, n.d.), 13.

22. In this connection see also Douglass' "Appeal to the British People," 1846, in Foner, *Douglass*, 1:158.

23. *Warrington* [England] *Times*, n.d., quoted in *Liberator*, March 11, 1859. For a more general use of the shock technique, by William Wells

must have reinforced audience imagination of the dilemmas of the women she discussed, "unprotected," as Garnet had once put it, "from the lusts of tyrants."[24]

Much more than did white abolitionists, black lecturers explored the economic debt that white America owed slave labor. Whites did, it is true, discuss the alleged unprofitability of slavery and the debilitating laziness and extravagance it presumably bred in whites. Some few also proposed that antislavery folk refuse to buy the produce of slave labor. But by and large they ignored the benefits which black labor had brought the national economy. By contrast, Henry Highland Garnet based his claims for full citizenship not only on Negroes' participation in the American Revolution and War of 1812 but also on their heavy economic contribution to national growth.[25] As he told the 1840 American Anti-Slavery Society convention, "In the Middle States . . . we have contributed our proportionate share in tilling the soil," while in the South, "from the Chesapeake Bay to the Sabine River, there is not a foot of cultivated ground that has not smiled beneath the hard hand of the dark American."[26]

Others, like Sojourner Truth, as well known on the lecture circuit as on fugitive escape routes, thought that white people throughout America "owed the colored race a big debt, and if they paid it all back, they wouldn't have any thing left for seed."[27] Equally directly William Wells Brown, addressing a New York audience in 1862, summarized thirty years of black frustration. "The nation," he charged, "owes the colored people a great debt. You, the people of New York, owe us a great debt. You have kept us down, helped to degrade us by your odious laws . . . you have loved to keep us in chains, while the slaveholders have deprived us

Brown, see *Manchester* [England] *Evening Examiner and Times,* August 5, 1854, cited in *Liberator,* September 1, 1854.

24. Henry Highland Garnet, *The Past and Present Condition, and Destiny of the Colored Race* . . . (Troy: J. C. Kneeland and Co., 1848, reprint, Miami: Mnemosyne, 1969), 14-15.

25. Speech to American Anti-Slavery Society Annual Meeting, in *Liberator,* May 22, 1840.

26. *National Anti-Slavery Standard,* June 11, 1840.

27. *Liberator,* July 14, 1854.

of our liberty and everything; and now the time has come for you to do your duty in this matter."[28]

Useful as the speaking tour was for exposing black anguish and shaping white antislavery opinion, it was not the sole means for so doing. One of the most popular and effective alternatives was the slave narrative. Frequently ghost-written or heavily edited by whites, sometimes fictional in style, these narratives nonetheless impressed white readers with the immediacy of slavery. More than fifty of them were published in the half century before Emancipation, and at least one authority has argued that they did more than any other form of presentation to illuminate for Northerners the wrongs of slavery.[29] Even when they came to rely only minimally on books and pamphlets to spread their message, white abolitionists continued to back the publication of slave narratives. Exaggerated though his claims for them may have been, Elizur Wright, Boston abolitionist editor, expressed the prevailing opinion when he said the narratives were an "easy and infallible means of abolitionizing the free states" because they went "right to the hearts of men."[30]

Because they thought them so important, white abolitionists took great care to insure their credibility. Consequently the American Anti-Slavery Society withdrew James Williams' *Narrative of an Escape from an Alabama Plantation* from circulation when it discovered discrepancies in family and place names that opened Williams' central contentions to challenge.[31] In so doing they highlighted a real problem, for fugitives were leery of being too explicit and accurate lest they subject themselves to recapture by their former masters. Nonetheless when Henry Bibb was chastised by Liberty party leader James G. Birney for the imprecise names

28. *Ibid.*, May 16, 1862.
29. Charles H. Nichols, *Many Thousands Gone: The Ex-Slaves' Account of their Bondage and Freedom* (Bloomington: Indiana University Press, 1963, 1969), 180-181.
30. Quoted in Nichols, *Many Thousands Gone*, 178.
31. *Liberator*, November 2, 1838. The full title of the book was *Narrative of James Williams, An American Slave Who Was for Several Years a Driver on a Cotton Plantation in Alabama* (New York: American Anti-Slavery Society, 1838).

and dates which marred his narrative, whose publication had been subsidized by the American and Foreign Anti-Slavery Society, Bibb promised to gather the data necessary to verify his story.[32]

Of the many slave memoirs, none surpassed Douglass' *Narrative* in style, popularity, or accuracy.[33] Highly literate and aggressively independent, Douglass had written his story without assistance. Welcomed joyously by the antislavery press upon its publication in 1845, it was puffed in New York by the *National Anti-Slavery Standard*, official organ of the American Anti-Slavery Society. In Boston the *Liberator* was joined by the non-abolitionist *Transcript and Courier* in praising its interest and credibility.[34] So vivid was his story and so precise his descriptions that Douglass received letters from the South which, in denying some of its more gruesome details, implicitly vouched for its general accuracy. Indeed fear of being seized and returned to slavery shortly drove Douglass out of the country.[35] In 1846 and 1847, supported in part by proceeds from the sale of his book, he traveled throughout Great Britain, selling the *Narrative* and giving antislavery lectures. Yet even in England the explicitness of Douglass' descriptions, especially of slave breeders, created problems. The second British edition of the *Narrative*, printed in Dublin by antislavery Quaker Richard Webb, was bowdlerized to eliminate those "disgusting details" which made it unfit reading for proper young Victorians.[36] But whatever the form, it was immensely popular, selling over 30,000 copies by 1850.[37]

32. Henry Bibb to James G. Birney, February 25, 1845, in Dwight L. Dumond, ed., *Letters of James Gillespie Birney, 1831-1857* (2 vols. New York: D. Appleton Co., 1938), 938. Henry Bibb to Executive Committee, American and Foreign Anti-Slavery Society, March 6, 1850, in American Missionary Association Papers, Amistad Collection (cited hereafter as AMA-ARC).

33. Frederick Douglass, *Narrative of the Life of Frederick Douglass, An American Slave, Written by Himself* (Boston: Anti-Slavery Office, 1845, reprint, New York: Dolphin Books, 1963).

34. *Liberator*, June 6, 1845.

35. *Ibid.*, February 27, 1846. Frederick Douglass to Editor of the [Belfast, Ireland] *Protestant Journal,* July 23, 1846, *ibid.,* August 28, 1846.

36. Frederick Douglass to Richard D. Webb, January 30, 1846, in G-BPL. The quotation is in John B. Estlin to Samuel May, Jr., November 10, 1845, M-BPL.

37. Quarles, *Black Abolitionists,* 64-65.

Two years after Douglass' book appeared, William Wells
Brown's autobiography similarly entranced antislavery people.
Brown had taken his manuscript to Edmund Quincy, aristocratic
Boston abolitionist, for revision. But Quincy, impressed by its
force, refused to make any significant changes in it. It was, just as
it stood, "a terrible picture of slavery, told with great simplicity,"
even more striking than Douglass' narrative, Quincy thought,
because Brown drew on a more varied experience of slavery.
Completely taken with the author, Quincy could scarcely contain
his delight. He had never, he said, "cottoned to" any man as he did
to Brown. "I do not know that his intellectual power is equal to
that of Douglass," Quincy wrote fellow Bostonian Caroline
Weston, "but he is of a much higher cast of character."[38] The
press echoed Quincy's praise. The *Liberator* found his *Narrative*
"very creditable" to its author; spokesmen for organized religion in
the *Christian World* and the *Christian Citizen* were impressed with it;
and the Herkimer, New York, *Freeman* found it exciting and
convincing.[39]

By the 1850s empathetic portrayals of slave life boomed, in part
because of the popularity of Harriet Beecher Stowe's *Uncle Tom's
Cabin*. Whether authentic autobiography, semifictional recollections, or novels, like William Wells Brown's *Clotelle* of 1853,[40]
they addressed themselves to by-now-familiar themes. Descriptions
of violence, especially of whipping, were commonplace and
frequently linked to the corollary themes of resisting force with
force or of running away to avoid being slashed. The narratives also
explored the means by which slaves improved their physical
condition. They became skilled laborers, or they hunted, fished,
and made various commodities for sale or trade. Often, if they
were accomplished craftsmen or even petty entrepreneurs, they
hired their time, acquired a competency, and became virtually

38. Edmund Quincy to Caroline Weston, July 2, 1847, W-BPL.
   39. *Liberator,* July 30, 1847. Other press comments, *ibid.,* October 1,
1847. Also *ibid.,* November 26, 1847.
   40. Originally published as *Clotelle, or, The President's Daughter: A
Narrative of Slave Life in the United States,* and issued in a second edition
(1864) as *Clotelle: A Tale of the Southern States,* the book was the first
novel written by a black in America.

and were
taught by
women
like
our
Grimké

independent. More clandestinely, they learned to read and write, studied the Bible, and conducted religious services for fellow slaves. Similarly, inventiveness and diligence held slave families together under almost impossible circumstances. The importance of the family was constantly borne out by the narratives, and reluctance to break family ties was often cited as a major obstacle in the way of escape to the North. These tales, in short, played heavily upon the humanity, intelligence, and perseverance of slaves and thereby challenged contemporary American race theory in a way not easily ignored.[41]

The eagerness with which white abolitionists utilized the special talents of blacks did not mask a wide variation in their responses to them. Superficially, at least, they delighted in interracial effort and celebrated the color and caliber of their coworkers. There were already, Nathaniel P. Rogers' New Hampshire *Herald of Freedom* announced happily in 1840, enough black men "in action . . .to maintain the anti-slavery enterprise, and to win their liberty, and that of their enslaved brethren,—if every white abolitionist were drawn from the field."[42] Moreover Rogers took particular pleasure in the accomplishments of very dark Negroes because, he said, they best demonstrated the humanity of the race. So when he reported a Fourth of July address given by young Garnet in 1835, while he was a student at the Noyes Academy in Canaan, New Hampshire, Rogers not only praised the speech's "great simplicity, pathos and beauty" but the speaker's "full, unmitigated, unalleviated and unpardonable blackness."[43] Even the New York *Tribune*, far less extreme in its antislavery stance, waxed enthusiastic over Samuel

41. Among the many slave stories the following are representative of the genre: Douglass' *Narrative* (1845); William Hayden, *Narrative of William Hayden* (1846); William Wells Brown, *Narrative of William W. Brown* (1848); Henry Bibb's *Narrative* (1849); Josiah Henson, *Life of Josiah Henson, formerly a Slave* (1847); Pennington's *Fugitive Blacksmith* (3rd ed., 1850); Henry Box Brown's *Narrative* (1849); and Mattie Griffiths, *Autobiography of a Female Slave* (1857).

42. Quoted in Monroe N. Work, "The Life of Charles B. Ray," *Journal of Negro History*, IV (October 1919), 364.

43. *Liberator*, July 25, 1835.

R. Ward, who was a living refutation of the belief that talented
Negroes drew on their partial white ancestry for the abilities they
displayed. About Ward there could be no doubt, the paper
explained in a favorable report, for he was a "genuine Nigerian,
black as the ace of spades in a deep cellar on a rainy midnight."[44]

Abolitionist response to Ellen Craft, who thoroughly charmed
them, demonstrated a quite contrary vein. Craft was so
light-skinned that she and her husband had masqueraded their way
out of slavery with Ellen playing the role of master and William her
manservant. "To think of such a woman being held as a piece of
property," commented Massachusetts Anti-Slavery Society general
agent Samuel May, Jr., "subject to be traded off to the highest
bidder (while it is in reality no worse or wickeder than when done
to the blackest woman that ever was) does yet stir a community
brought up in prejudice against color a thousand times more deeply
than could be effected in similar circumstances."[45]

The initial enthusiasm which whites showed for blacks,
whatever their hue, often sank under reservations and skepticism as
the novelty wore off. Charles Remond, whose extensive antislavery
activity made him a frequent colleague of Garrisonian leaders in
Boston, was early a favorite. Maria Weston Chapman, their chief
money-raiser, had praised Remond's "prudence & tact" when she
first heard him speak.[46] Yet before long she and her sisters Anne,
Emma, Deborah, and Caroline Weston all had their misgivings.
Remond could not, Anne reported to Deborah in 1842, "speak at
all. At least," she added, "he has nothing to say, for his manner
merely is good & gentlemanly."[47] And Deborah shortly thereafter
confided to Emma that, when Remond objected to sharing his

44. New York *Tribune*, May 8, [1850], quoted in *Liberator*, May 17,
1850. The American and Foreign Anti-Slavery Society, *Annual Report*
(1849) also specifically noted Ward's very dark complexion.

45. Samuel May, Jr., to Joseph Estlin, February 2, 1849, quoted in Gara,
"Professional Fugitive," 199. See also reports in the *Liberator*, March 2 and
May 11, 1849.

46. Maria W. Chapman to Deborah Weston, January 19, [1840?], in
W-BPL.

47. [Anne Weston] to Deborah Weston, February 4, 1842, fragment in
W-BPL.

lecture time with a fund-raising collection, the complaint deserved no more notice than "an ass' kick."[48]

The causes of such disaffection were varied. There was, most simply, concern that antislavery spokesmen, black or white, slave or free, might behave poorly or accomplish little. But more particular were the pointed fears among many white abolitionists that black coworkers might become too independent, as Douglass eventually did, or that they might very likely turn the cause to their own profit, because, as Quincy noted specifically of Remond, they felt the bitterness of their position and would soothe their feelings as opportunity offered.[49] In turn, some blacks were made uneasy by what they considered their spokesmen's servility to white abolitionists. In 1840 Charles Remond went to London as a delegate to the World Anti-Slavery Convention. There, in company with Garrison and Nathaniel Rogers, he refused to take part in the proceedings because the women delegates from America were denied the right to participate. The *Colored American* objected to Remond's action. "Although he went not as a delegate from the colored people, he was nevertheless a colored man. . . .And he ought therefore to have taken his seat, and seized the first opportunity, to lay before the Convention as the only one there immediately concerned, all the disabilities of the nominally free people of his own country, to be made the especial business of the Convention. . . ."[50] Remond defended his action on grounds of moral obligation. His expenses had been borne, in large part, by

48. Deborah Weston to Emma Weston, March 16, 1842, in W-BPL. Deborah also complained that Remond was "rather sulky at times"; see her letter to Lucia Weston, June 15, 1847, in W-BPL.

49. Edmund Quincy to Richard D. Webb, May 26, 1843, in Edmund Quincy Papers, Massachusetts Historical Society (cited hereafter as Q-MHS). There were those also who feared that Remond would use antislavery as a way to accumulate wealth and physical comfort; see Wendell Phillips to Elizabeth Pease, August 29, 1847, in G-BPL. Among white abolitionists Remond was also frequently compared to Douglass, to the general disadvantage of the former; see Abby Kelley to Stephen S. Foster, January 21, 1845, in Foster Papers, American Antiquarian Society (cited hereafter as F-AAS); and Wendell Phillips to Richard D. Webb, May 30-July 27, 1845, in G-BPL.

50. *Colored American,* August 8, 1840.

various ladies' antislavery societies in Maine and Rhode Island and, as a result, he had felt duty bound not to participate in a convention which excluded women.[51] Nonetheless, he later told a Boston supporter that, while he "should have been [happy] to see the ladies seated as delegates," he had "not lost a night's sleep in consequence of their rejection."[52] There was something to the suspicion at home that Remond had acted less out of principle than out of a desire to continue in the aura of Garrison's fame and approval.

Even more divisive were the questions raised when Negroes appeared before segregated audiences. The issue had been widely discussed because the popular singer, Elizabeth Greenfield, the "Black Swan," made such appearances. Militants had condemned the practice roundly. When, therefore, in 1850 Samuel Ward accepted an invitation to address a meeting in the Second Presbyterian Church on St. Mary Street in Philadelphia at which blacks were to be relegated to the balcony, he was subjected to heated criticism. In the regular issues of the *North Star* and in a special extra, which he published in Philadelphia, Douglass called Ward an apostate. "Where was his sense of justice?" the Rochester editor asked bitterly. "Where was his manly indignation? Why did he not denounce the whole transaction at once, and declare either that he would not speak under such a call," or else make the circular which announced the segregated meeting "the basis of his discourse, and show the impropriety of sending forth such a handbill?" That he made no such declaration, Douglass continued, was an "insult offered to colored citizens," made still worse by the fact that Ward had "made an eloquent speech," amused his auditors, and "never raised a whisper against the infamous handbill."[53] Remond, too, joined in the attack. Participation in a meeting which sanctioned "the cruel and depressing customs and

51. Charles L. Remond to Charles B. Ray, June 30, 1840, in *Liberator,* October 16, 1840.
52. Charles L. Remond to Thomas Coles, October 2, 1840, *ibid.,* October 30, 1840.
53. *North Star,* May 30, 1850. The *North Star Extra,* n.d., published in Philadelphia, has a copy of the handbill.

laws" that had harassed Negroes "for a long series of years," was a "gratuitous, palpable . . . humiliat[ion] ."[54] Nor were his critics moved by Ward's defense that had he not given the lecture under segregated conditions, he could not have reached that particular audience at all. To Douglass it was still sycophancy. "You are seen, Samuel Ringgold Ward," he intoned.[55] No more need be said.

In the face of numerous hazards and despite persistent criticism, black agents, writers, and lecturers, both free and fugitive, made a distinct and positive contribution to the American crusade against slavery. To their work they brought an experience as Negroes and as slaves which gave them insights and weapons unique among antislavery workers. It was not surprising, then, that British abolitionists welcomed them when they chose to travel abroad or that their lecture tours made an equally distinctive contribution in England, Scotland, and Ireland.

54. *North Star*, May 30, 1850.
55. *Ibid.*, June 13, 1850.

4. AGENTS AND
AGITATORS
ABROAD

JUST AS organized antislavery in the United States was emerging in the 1830s, the British antislavery movement reached its climax. Begun in the late eighteenth century by Thomas Clarkson and William Wilberforce, nourished by the evangelical movement, pressed by Elizabeth Heyrick from gradualism to full and immediate emancipation in the 1820s, British abolitionism triumphed in 1833 when Parliament acted to end slavery in the British empire. But the mechanics of emancipation, complicated by paying compensation and establishing systems of apprenticeship, took time. It was therefore not until 1840 that slavery came completely to an end in the West Indies and not until 1843 in India. Nonetheless British enthusiasts had, by then, already turned their zeal toward the United States, where Americans who were building their own crusade welcomed their experience, their assistance, and the model for action which they had set.

In order to promote cooperation between the two national movements, a pattern of American abolitionist visits to England was rapidly established. Virtually from the beginning, Negroes participated in this exchange and rapidly became in England, as they were at home, popular and effective symbols both of the despair of slavery and the hope of emancipation. "Frederick Douglass has been working wonders," wrote an English correspondent to Maria Chapman in the mid-1840s. "He is a living example of the capabilities of the slave, & . . . he proves that *they are not* what they have been misrepresented [to be]—mere chattels—with bodies formed for Herculean labour, but without minds—without souls."[1]

Black spokesmen also, consciously or unconsciously, served other British purposes. At times they were convenient vehicles for British scorn of American life and values. When, for instance, Robert Purvis, who was touring England in 1834, was introduced to Daniel O'Connell, the great Irish leader refused to shake hands with him as an "American Gentleman," but happily extended the hand of friendship to an abolitionist and a black.[2] So too in a way ironically similar to the American pattern, blacks were frequently used as pawns in the infighting among competing groups of British abolitionists.[3] Although it was, therefore, from a mixture of motives that British supporters welcomed them, that did not deter them, for black abolitionists were equally willing to use and manipulate their British sympathizers when their cause demanded it.

A significant number of American Negroes who made the Atlantic crossing had gone with quite other purposes than engaging in the antislavery crusade. James McCune Smith, for instance, attended college and medical school in Glasgow in the 1830s. Alexander Crummell, Episcopal clergyman, studied at Cambridge and took a degree there in 1853. Robert Purvis was simply on the grand tour, traditional for young men of means, in 1834. Others, like Nathaniel Paul, who in 1831 was raising money for the

1. S. Hildreth to Maria W. Chapman, October 31, 1846, in W-BPL. In addition their lecturing was useful to stir up interest and reinvigorate antislavery work in England. C. Duncan Rice, "The Scottish Factor in the Fight Against American Slavery, 1830-1870" (Ph.D. University of Edinburgh, 1969), 103, dates the beginning of this stimulation as early as 1833 when Nathaniel Paul was visiting Great Britain.
2. *Liberator*, August 23, 1834.
3. Rice, "Scottish Factor," 4.

Canadian Wilberforce settlement, were agents of special groups in North America. Josiah Henson, alleged prototype for Uncle Tom, spent 1849-1850 in England soliciting contributions for the British-American Institute, a projected manual labor school at Dawn, Upper Canada. And Samuel Ward toured the British Isles in 1852 on a general fund-raising mission for destitute refugees who had fled to Canada in the wake of the 1850 Fugitive Slave Act. Some went simply because they themselves were fugitives. Douglass had feared reenslavement after his *Narrative* was published, so fled to England and stayed there until his freedom was bought. William and Ellen Craft sailed from Boston late in 1850 with the slavecatchers quite literally at their heels. And in 1853, William G. Allen, recently a professor at Central College in McGrawville, New York, chose exile in England to escape the personal abuse and violence heaped upon him for having married one of his white students.[4]

Regardless of the reasons for which they came, once they were in England nearly all turned to antislavery work. For most, their very presence was testimony to the evils of slavery and prejudice. Their problem lay in finding ways to convert general sympathy into specific support for the antislavery work in America. William Wells Brown, highly conscious of means and technique, agreed that British hatred of oppression was genuine enough and easily roused. Yet it was difficult for those so far removed from the fact to understand the "real condition of the slaves in the United States." Even the visual presence of a bona fide slave, though it added immediacy, was not enough. In Britain as in the American North, potential sympathizers had to be jolted from their apathy by detailed descriptions of the conditions of bondage presented by those who had suffered under them.[5] For five years, therefore, Brown lectured to British audiences on the antislavery circuit, verbally and visually indoctrinating them with the horrors of the

4. For a more extended list of blacks who visited Europe in the antebellum period see Benjamin Quarles, *Black Abolitionists*. (New York: Oxford University Press, 1969), 130-140.

5. William Wells Brown, *The American Fugitive in Europe: Sketches of Places and People Abroad* (Boston: John P. Jewett, 1855), 297-298.

peculiar institution.[6] Ex-slaves Douglass, Pennington, and Henson varied the specifics, but all operated on Brown's assumptions. And those who, like Charles and Sarah Remond and William Allen, had never known slavery, were most telling in their presentation of prejudice and discrimination. Thus, free or fugitive, they served the same cause with messages shaped by personal experience.

Much of the substance of their British appearances was identical to the fare they presented in America. They told of the horrors of slavery and of exhilarating and dangerous modes of escape. The Crafts and Henry "Box" Brown were platform exhibits whose very existence thrilled audiences. Both Browns presented large panoramas picturing their experiences in slavery and their escapes.[7] The demand that the lecturers be specimens on exhibit was not always pleasant, as Douglass' experience in northern Ireland demonstrated. Arriving in Belfast after his initial speaking tour in the South he found he was to be quartered in a centrally located hotel so that he would be "accessible to every one that wish[ed] to see [him]." Deprived of all privacy, Douglass found his stay thoroughly disagreeable.[8]

To be fully effective in Britain lecturers had to vary the American pattern and develop arguments which appealed directly to local concerns and interests. To do so demanded some variations on contemporary American patriotism. Early in the antislavery crusade, blacks no less than whites had expressed pride in America's revolutionary heritage. Reflecting Jeffersonian assumptions enshrined in the Declaration of Independence, they had blamed the British for slavery's existence in the United States. Lecturing in New York city in 1827, Nathaniel Paul had argued that it was the strength of the imperial system, of which the United States had been a part, which had forced slavery on a people who would otherwise have been "led by the spirit of pure repub-

6. *Liberator*, September 28, 1849.
7. *Liberator*, January 24, 1851. William E. Farrison, *William Wells Brown: Author and Reformer* (Chicago: University of Chicago Press, 1969), 175-176. Richard D. Webb to Maria W. Chapman, November 12, 1850, W-BPL.
8. Frederick Douglass to Richard D. Webb, December 6, 1845, G-BPL.

licanism" and would have "guarded against its intrusion," thus sparing the country "so great a curse." [9]

Emancipation in the Empire, however, forced white and black antislavery spokesmen to curb their chauvinism and praise the imperial approach. Yet even then some of them had reservations. Fully exposed to the British antislavery program during his student days in Scotland, where he was a member of the Glasgow Emancipation Society, James McCune Smith warned American abolitionists in 1838 of its loopholes. The apprenticeship system instituted as a transition from slavery in Jamaica and elsewhere was ominously like emancipation in the Northern states for it produced only a very partial and unsatisfactory freedom. [10]

Once British emancipation was complete in the West Indies such reservations gave way to unstinted praise for the British example, and British audiences responded accordingly. Glaswegians were delighted with Remond, and several other Americans, who on August 7, 1840, suggested to a local group that Britain's action should be a model for the United States. [11] Five years later Douglass, who at home contended that lack of economic opportunity was a restriction on the freedom which Northern blacks allegedly enjoyed, denied that the poverty-stricken Irish peasants were slaves. It was impossible, he contended, because under British law everyone was free. Not surprisingly, his characteristically middle- to upper-class Belfast audience cheered him enthusiastically. [12] At least among American antislavery lecturers in Great Britain, England had been wholly exonerated from responsibility for American slavery. Few worried, as did missionary-oriented James Pennington, that Britain and France were

9. Nathaniel Paul, *An Address, Delivered on the Celebration of the Abolition of Slavery in the State of New York, July 5, 1827*...(Albany: Printed by John Van Steenbergh, 1827, reprint, Dorothy Porter, ed., *Negro Protest Pamphlets,* New York: Arno Press, 1969), 12.

10. *Liberator,* June 1, 1838.

11. Glasgow Emancipation Society, Minute Books, Collections of Mitchell Library, Glasgow, Scotland. Minutes for August 7, 1840, whole number page 175.

12. Belfast *Banner of Ulster,* December 9, 1845, reported in *Liberator,* February 6, 1846.

both currently engrossing Africa with little care for the evangelization and conversion of the natives.[13] Rather, with William
Wells Brown, they lauded English virtue. If, indeed, Great Britain
was responsible for introducing slavery into colonial America, why
could it not be argued that, as she "abolished slavery in the West
Indies, she would have done the same for the American States if
she had had the power to do it"? That query led Brown to wonder
whether America's revolutionary independence was not "(to say
the least) a great misfortune to one sixth of the population of that
land." Only swift action in the United States to end slavery could
put the question to rest.[14]

Not only were Englishmen absolved of responsibility for
American slavery, they were also praised for their freedom from
the race prejudice in which Americans wallowed. By ringing the
changes on this theme, black lecturers won sympathy for their
plight at home and simultaneously fed Britons' belief in their own
superiority. Remond was a master of the argument. He was, as
William Wells Brown said, "sensitive to a fault about prejudice,"
and much of his American speech-making revolved about the
endemic racism which he accused his audiences of sharing.[15] In
England he reversed his technique to commend his listeners for
their lack of prejudice. Among them he found no Jim Crow cars or
other forms of discrimination which made liberty in his own
country only "the grossest licentiousness."[16]

13. James W. C. Pennington to Editor, *American Missionary*, n.d., and
Pennington to George Whipple, February 20, 1850, both in AMA-ARC.
14. Brown, *American Fugitive in Europe*, 219. At a meeting in
Edinburgh in December 1850, Brown urged the Ladies Emancipation
Society to show their preference for the British model of emancipation by
supporting the free produce movement and boycotting American slave-
produced goods. Remond also followed the same pattern when, in a speech in
Massachusetts in 1859, he argued that British emancipation had brought
more real and meaningful freedom to blacks than had the American
Revolution; see *Liberator*, January 24, 1851, and August 5, 1859,
respectively.
15. William Wells Brown, *The Black Man, His Antecedents, His Genius,
and His Achievements* (4th ed., 1865. Miami: Mnemosyne, 1969), 247.
16. *Liberator*, August 28, October 2, and October 16, 1840, the
quotation in the final issue, in Charles L. Remond to Charles B. Ray, June
30, 1840.

Remond's praise for their color-blind culture, whether deserved or not, provoked from Englishmen a most favorable response which extended to others who contrasted it with American practice. William Wells Brown, Garnet, Allen, and Sarah Remond were all well received when they handled the subject in a similar way.[17] In its extreme, the self-satisfaction thus inspired was reflected in an otherwise trivial episode that occurred when Brown and the Crafts visited the Crystal Palace Exhibition with English friends. Conspicuously the three blacks promenaded about with thirteen Englishmen grouped so that a young white girl was always juxtaposed to a black man and Ellen Craft was paired with one of the English hosts. The display, one English participant later wrote Garrison, thoroughly annoyed other Americans at the exhibition. "Unostentatiously, without the least parade," he wrote in adverbs not wholly convincing, "we gave the Americans a practical demonstration of the anti-slavery feelings of Englishmen. We asserted the principle, recognized by the whole civilized world— from which America must be practically excluded, so long as she holds slaves—of the perfect equality, in civil and social standing, of the black and white."[18]

Their perception of an England free not only of slavery but also of prejudice led black visitors to identify with Great Britain and feel increasingly alienated from their homeland. This response too became a frequent component of their lectures and, of course, won sympathy from their flattered listeners. Remond broached the alienation theme as early as 1840. In a lecture before the British and Foreign Anti-Slavery Society in London, he insisted that slaves had more grievances by far than American revolutionaries had had in 1776. How could it be otherwise when the simple act of stepping on British soil made a free man of the slave who, had he stayed at home, would still be in bondage. Though Remond insisted that he "entertained not the slightest wish to . . . traduce his country," which he then accused of "legalised murder," his in-

17. See, for example, *Liberator,* October 19, 1849, July 22, 1853, May 5, 1854, and April 8, 1859; also *Impartial Citizen,* May 17, 1851.
18. *Liberator,* July 18, 1851.

tent seemed quite otherwise. Nonetheless he concluded on the bland note of hoping that "the voice of every friend of this country would go forth for the abolition of that most iniquitous system."[19]

Douglass was yet more open in his criticism. "I have," he wrote Garrison in a letter subsequently published in the *Liberator*, ". . .no government to defend; and as to nation, I belong to none. . . .I am an outcast from the society of my childhood, and an outlaw in the land of my birth."[20] Nor was his appeal for British action as timorous as Remond's. He told a packed meeting in Cork in November 1845, two months before he had written Garrison, that he wanted "Americans to know that in the good city of Cork" he had "ridiculed their nation" and that he hoped "to excite the utter contempt of the people . . . upon them."[21]

Neither Douglass nor Remond was interested simply in catharsis. Their goal was to arouse British opinion and bring its pressure to bear on the United States to end slavery.[22] And sometimes, at least so their American critics thought, they were aiming for more than moral pressure from foreign public opinion. Just before he left England to return to America, Douglass urged his well-wishers to agitate the antislavery question. "I am met," he noted, "with the objection, that to do so in this country, is to excite, irritate, and disturb the slaveholder." Precisely so. "I wish the slaveholder to be irritated. I want him jealous; I desire to see him alarmed and disturbed."[23] Was he appealing only to conscience or did he, as some Americans believed, hope for a more menacing display of British power, perhaps finally even war between the United States and England?[24]

19. *Ibid.*, July 31, 1840.

20. *Ibid.*, January 30, 1846.

21. *Cork Examiner*, n.d., quoted in *Liberator*, December 12, 1845.

22. *Liberator*, June 26, 1846. Philip Foner, *The Life and Writings of Frederick Douglass* (4 vols. New York: International Publishers, 1950-1955), 1:156.

23. "Farewell Speech to The British People," in Foner, *Douglass*, 1:227.

24. For American press notices of Douglass' English tour see *Liberator*, February 13, 1846.

Though neither Remond nor Douglass ever completely re-
nounced America, others came close to it. Both William Wells
Brown and Ward eventually identified themselves more closely
with England than with the United States. Ward, who settled
abroad, consistently referred in his 1855 autobiography to Englishmen as "we" and Americans as "they."[25] And Brown, before he
returned to the United States after his five year sojourn in England,
commented, "I had become so well acquainted with the British
people and their history, that I had begun to fancy myself an
Englishman by habit, if not by birth."[26]

The close identification which many lecturers made with
English life not only aroused the enthusiasm of their hosts, but also
facilitated their ability to exploit other issues which would
reinforce their antislavery message. One such issue was the
persistence until 1843 of slavery in India. During his tour from
1840 to 1842, Remond seized upon this situation to rouse British
awareness of their responsibility to end slavery everywhere. By
lecturing on Indian slavery and then turning to American bondage,
he made each cause subserve the other. Well aware of the British
textile industry's reliance on American-grown cotton, Remond
urged the English to complete emancipation in India and then turn
its free labor to the cultivation of cotton in such a way as to bring
economic pressure to bear on American exporters of slave-
produced cotton. Thus would Britain serve not only the cause of
freedom on two continents, but her own imperial interests as
well.[27]

Another issue which, with effort, could be used to antislavery
purpose was temperance. While in Cork in 1845 Douglass met
Father Edward Mathew, the internationally-known temperance

25. Samuel Ringgold Ward, *Autobiography of a Fugitive Negro. His
Anti-Slavery Labours in the United States, Canada, and England* (London: J.
Snow, 1855), particularly 290-300.
26. Brown, *American Fugitive in Europe*, 303.
27. Rice, "Scottish Factor," 195. Glasgow Emancipation Society,
Minute Books. Minutes for September 14, 1840, whole number page 178.

avoided broader social issues & reform

advocate, and was lavishly entertained by him. Douglass in turn enthusiastically took up Mathew's cause and lectured in both Ireland and England on the evils of alcohol. As in America, so in Great Britain it was possible not only to link the two crusades but to lead sympathetic audiences from one topic to the other and thus increase the support for each. How one reform might be used to supplement the other Douglass illustrated in 1846 when he urged Englishmen to boycott the World's Temperance Convention if slaveholders were admitted as delegates. At least one temperance enthusiast threatened to withhold his £50 donation if Douglass' advice were not heeded.[28]

If there were social issues, like alcoholism, which could be taken up to combine English and American reform interests, so too there were issues which abolitionists, both black and white, better avoided if they were to win upper and upper middle-class British sympathy. Foremost among these were the conditions of factory labor and urban slums. Almost without fail, antislavery lecturers either ignored or condemned the Chartist movement, at its height in the 1840s, much as at home they refused to relate the problems of impoverished urban immigrant labor in the North to those of Negro slaves in the South. So, in the first year of the Irish famine, Douglass blamed the profusion of beggars in Irish towns on intemperance.[29] Likewise William Wells Brown insisted that the more he saw and learned "of the condition of the working-classes of England, the more [he became] satisfied of the utter fallacy of the statements often made that their condition approximate[d] to that of the slaves in America."[30] Such statements eased the way for the English, as for Yankees, to condemn social injustice without endangering their own institutions.

Only once, when Douglass battled with the Free Presbyterian Church of Scotland, did a black lecturer venture on a social issue

28. *Liberator,* November 28, 1845, and March 27, 1846. *Ibid.,* June 26, 1846. Samuel Ward also lectured extensively on temperance; see his *Autobiography,* 330-398.
29. *Liberator,* March 27, 1846.
30. Brown, *American Fugitive in Europe,* 140.

which threatened directly the British status quo. Like many white abolitionists, Douglass refused to associate with any church which extended membership to slaveholders or fellowshipped with other churches admitting slaveowners. When he lectured in Great Britain he tried to extend this cordon sanitaire designed to place the American South outside Christendom. In Dublin, he had bitterly recalled his master's good standing in the Methodist Church and excoriated the sect. His remarks were ill-received by Irish Methodists, who had made special efforts to open their chapels to his antislavery lectures and who feared that in so doing they had only facilitated "infidelity."[31]

Neither perturbed nor dissuaded by this Irish experience. Douglass in the spring of 1846 went on to Scotland where he found a local crisis cut absolutely to his tactics. The Free Presbyterian Church of Scotland had recently conducted an extensive fund-raising drive in the American South and had received contributions from slaveholders. The opportunity this situation offered for driving home the message of church complicity in slavery was too good to be ignored. Speaking in the Abbey Church at Arbroath, Douglass lashed out at the greed which had led the Free Church to give moral support to slavery. Reaching the climax of his address, he exhorted them to "send back that money." The effect was electric as the audience picked up the line and began to chant it on the spot.[32]

Douglass could scarcely have been happier. Within weeks the slogan had engulfed the country. "SEND BACK THE MONEY" appeared as graffiti on fences, buildings, and pavements. On the walls of the Free Church at Arbroath "THE SLAVE'S BLOOD" was printed in large letters.[33] Amazingly Douglass gained pop-

31. Cork *Examiner,* October 20, [1845], reported in *Liberator,* November 28, 1845. For another Douglass contretemps with the Methodists, see Durham County *Herald,* September 25, 1846, reported in *Liberator,* November 13, 1846. John B. Estlin to Samuel May, Jr., November 10, 1845, M-BPL.

32. Arbroath *Guide,* February 14, 1846, reported in *Liberator,* April 3, 1846.

33. James N. Buffum to William L. Garrison, April 14, 1846, *Liberator,* May 15, 1846.

ularity by his role in the matter. He had not only struck a responsive chord among abolitionists but had become somewhat of a folk hero. He played his role so well that what might have seemed an outsider's interference in local matters became a welcome commentary on the sin and guilt of slavery. Avoiding involvement in more wide-ranging criticism of the Free Church, he consistently confined himself to its links with the slavery question.[34] "My work is to make slavery disreputable," Douglass wrote John Scoble of the British and Foreign Anti-Slavery Society, "and I cannot do this while Christian churches in [Great Britain] are extending the hand of Christian fellowship to the slaveholders and endorsing their character as slaveholders."[35]

In so doing Douglass came close to involvement in forbidden class issues. The popularity of his Free Church stand led him to make street corner addresses to working-class audiences which won their sympathy and support. "How forcibly he preached his people's wrong!" wrote one humble Scot, greatly impressed by Douglass. "*Strong* language indeed. O let us be up to send back not only the money but the people—Why are they treated by whites as fishes of the sea. O raise up your voice, ye shall yet be heard Africa!"[36]

For some, the tactics seemed dangerous and the message insurrectionary. Fearful of mob violence and revolutionary upheaval, conservative church members were frightened off by Douglass' vigorous attacks. But in the long run his radical Scottish presentations caused him little trouble, for at the same time he was appealing successfully to ministers of other sects, who were soon praying publicly for emancipation, giving antislavery sermons, and proclaiming the exclusion of proslavery preachers from their pulpits.[37] Even John B. Estlin, a socially conservative abolitionist

34. Rice, "Scottish Factor," 291. Glasgow *Argus*, April 27, 1846, reported in *Liberator*, May 29, 1846.

35. Quoted in Rice, "Scottish Factor," 33-34.

36. Quoted in George Shepperson, "Frederick Douglass and Scotland," *Journal of Negro History*, XXXVIII (July 1953), 313-314. Also Rice, "Scottish Factor," 332.

37. Shepperson, "Douglass and Scotland," 308-309, 313. *Liberator*, June 19, 1846.

from Bristol, who had feared that Douglass would turn the clergy from antislavery, was reassured. He had turned back from the brink, regained clerical support, and enlarged British antislavery audiences. Within six months after he had launched his Free Church attack, Douglass lectured in Bristol to Estlin's complete satisfaction. "His speech was marked by pathos, humour, sarcasm, seriousness, & unanswerable argument."[38]

Douglass was, as Estlin realized, a superb tactician. "My mission to this land," he had written Webb in Dublin, "is purely an Anti-slavery one, and although there are other good causes which need to be advocated,—I think that my duty calls me strictly to the question of Slavery." Ever seeking the proper issue for the proper moment, adapting parochial interests to larger antislavery ends with an unmatched timing and agility, Douglass never forgot that he was "a man of one idea."[39]

Although no subsequent black lecturers offered the novelty of Remond or engendered the widespread enthusiasm which greeted Douglass, they did pursue similar goals with similar tactics. Garnet, for example, pressed British Presbyterians and Congregationalists to refuse fellowship to their American brethren who accepted slaveholders as church members; and Ward urged British abolitionists to develop the economy of the West Indies, so that its free produce would compete with slave-grown American merchandise. They also sought official British action to cut off the illicit slave trade which filtered slaves into the United States through Cuba and to stand firm against the imprisonment of black British sailors in American ports.[40] In all these ways they essayed to turn British domestic and diplomatic issues to the purposes of their antislavery crusade.

The zeal of black lecturers in rousing antislavery enthusiasm made them successful in raising money as well. Paul, on his

38. John B. Estlin to Samuel May, Jr., September 3, 1846, M-BPL.
39. Frederick Douglass to Richard D. Webb, November 10, 1845, G-BPL.
40. "Extracts from the Minutes of the Belfast Anti-Slavery Society," *Impartial Citizen*, May 17, 1851. Rice, "Scottish Factor," 368. *Frederick Douglass' Paper*, June 23, 1854.

fund-raising tour in 1831, gathered some $8,000. Henson, during his 1849-1850 tour, raised equally significant sums of money for the British-American Institute.[41] And when Ward came seeking aid for fugitives in Canada, he received at least £1,200.[42] Similarly Garrisonians lecturing in England garnered funds for the American Anti-Slavery Society and solicited articles from women's groups which might be sold at Boston's annual antislavery bazaar. Both Remond and Douglass engaged long-range support in this way.[43]

Sometimes lecturers inspired generosity to themselves directly in a way which annoyed British antislavery purists. From Dublin, Richard Webb, who was unusually eager to criticize black foibles, wrote Chapman that Remond had left Ireland during his 1842 tour with more money for himself than the white agent John Collins had been able to raise for the American Anti-Slavery Society. As Webb recalled it, some three years later, "He begged too much and too undisguisedly. . . ."[44] George Thompson concurred in the assessment. In 1846 Webb also fretted over Douglass' success in making money "hand over hand" from the sale of his *Narrative*.[45] Yet such carping was minimal and did not deter Douglass, William Wells Brown, and Pennington from receiving the generous gifts

41. William H. Pease and Jane H. Pease, *Black Utopia: Negro Communal Experiments in America* (Madison: State Historical Society of Wisconsin, 1963, 1972), 60, 73-74. Dawn's finances were too tangled to be able to set any exact sum. Of the $8,000 Paul collected nearly all of it went to meet his expenses while he was in England. The rest he lent Garrison for fare home from England. Garrison then refused to repay it.

42. British *Banner*, n.d., reported in *Frederick Douglass' Paper*, April 21, 1854. *Provincial Freeman*, April 15, 1854.

43. "An Appeal to the Abolitionists of Great Britain for the American Anti-Slavery Society," a broadside dated November 12, 1840, G-BPL. Mary Mannix and Isabel Jennings to Maria W. Chapman, November 15, 1841, Chapman Papers, Antislavery Collection, Boston Public Library (cited hereafter as Ch-BPL). *Liberator*, November 28, 1845. Mary Ireland to Maria W. Chapman, January 24, 1846, W-BPL. Jane J. D. Carr to Maria W. Chapman, November 4, 1846, Ch-BPL. Jane Jennings to Maria W. Chapman, November 26, [1846], W-BPL. Lucy Browne to Maria W. Chapman, October 15, 1846, Ch-BPL, and April 14, 1847, W-BPL.

44. Richard D. Webb to Maria W. Chapman, February 22, 1842, G-BPL. Webb to Chapman, n.d., W-BPL.

45. George Thompson to Richard [Webb], August 12, 1845, W-BPL. Richard Webb to Maria W. Chapman, February 26, 1846, W-BPL.

which made it possible for each of them to buy his freedom. And Douglass received in addition a purse of $2,000, originally presented to provide him a steady income but eventually used with the donors' approval to establish the *North Star*.[46]

Not only did Britishers give money to blacks, they lionized them as well. Their color was a novelty which intrigued curiosity and interest. Even Garrison suffered by comparison. The story went that when the British antislavery leader Thomas Folwell Buxton first met the Bostonian he was deeply disappointed that the editor was not a Negro. Although his predecessors had been well received, it was probably Remond, made highly visible by his association with Garrison at the 1840 World's Antislavery Convention, who precipitated the lionizing of black abolitionists which continued for the next twenty years. "Our colored friend Remond," Garrison wrote his wife, Helen, "invariably accompanies us, and is a great favorite in every circle. . . ."[47] And the circle was as heady for the Boston printer turned editor as for the Salem barber, for they were entertained by the Duchess of Sutherland and Lady Byron as well as by merchants, industrialists, and professionals.[48]

Unquestionably the lionizing was partly an inverse snobbery, a self-satisfying display of English superiority over American racism, and an illustration of lords and ladies bountiful willing to mix with the worthy poor. The role of those thus received was necessarily ritualized. One was expected not only to be humble but to accept the values of one's benefactors. Remond had the particular knack for conveying exactly the right image. London Quaker Ester Sturge thought he was "modest & unassuming," and gave everyone a very good impression of the "coloured Race." Elizabeth Pease of Midlands railroad wealth praised him for his "gentle and Christian

---

46. Foner, *Douglass,* 1:72, 82. William E. Farrison, *William Wells Brown* : *Author and Reformer* (Chicago: University of Chicago Press, 1969), 238-241. *Liberator,* June 20, [30?], 1851.
47. William L. Garrison to Helen Garrison, July 3, 1840, G-BPL.
48. *Liberator,* August 28, 1840. Rice, "Scottish Factor," 166.

forbearance, his candor and honesty—and his ability in serving the great cause."[49]

Douglass too was constantly solicited and puffed. Although he was considerably more conscious than Remond of the implications of the process, he also had the wit to make the very most of it. Sensitive to his admirers' wishes that he be a "full blood black,"[50] he strove to fit their preconceptions. "I find I am hardly black enough for british taste," he wrote, "but by keeping my hair as woolly as possible—I make out to pass for at least half a negro at any rate."[51] His poise combined with his slave status more than made up for his half-white ancestry. "He is," Isabel Jennings wrote from Ireland with delighted approval, "the first intelligent *slave* who has ever visited Cork and it is only natural that he should excite more sympathy than any of the others."[52] The local press in Cork thought him "aimiable [sic] and interesting" as a private man and "original and eloquent" as a lecturer.[53] He was, wrote another Anglo-Irish supporter, "an honor to America."[54] A decade later New Hampshire antislavery radical Parker Pillsbury, by then a committed enemy of Douglass, warned his American colleagues not to attack Douglass in Great Britain because he was still the single most popular American abolitionist.[55]

The impact of the many blacks who went to Great Britain in the thirty years before the Civil War was both intensive and extensive. Their very success, however, generated excessive British expectations which in turn led to hostility when their accomplishments

49. Ester Sturge to Maria W. Chapman, March 2, 1844, W-BPL. *Liberator*, May 21, 1841. One thing that undoubtedly helped, as Rice notes, "Scottish Factor," 202, was that Remond "was prepared to come to terms with British abolitionists at their own relatively conservative level."

50. Catherine Clarkson to Maria W. Chapman, August 2, 1846, W-BPL.

51. Frederick Douglass to Francis Jackson, January 29, 1846, G-BPL.

52. Isabel Jennings to Maria W. Chapman, [1846?], W-BPL.

53. Cork *Examiner*, October 27, 1845, quoted in *Liberator*, November 28, 1845.

54. George C. Pim to Maria W. Chapman, October 31, 1846, Ch-BPL.

55. Parker Pillsbury made this point in several letters which he wrote to Samuel May, Jr. during 1855; see M-BPL, 1855, *passim*.

failed to conform to them. The reception of both Remond and
Douglass, the two best received, is an instructive case in point.
Their most ardent supporters were women, who wrote the
preponderance of the many letters which brought testimony to
American friends of the two men's success and personal charm.[56]
One might attribute their disproportionate numbers to the vagaries
of chance or the likelihood that women had more time than men
for letter-writing, were it not for the British men's hostile
commentary on the attention women gave Douglass. "You can
hardly imagine how he is noticed," wrote John Estlin to Samuel
May, Jr., with clear pique, "*better*, I may say, by *ladies*: Some of
them really a little exceed the bounds of propriety, or delicacy, as
far as *appearances* are concerned. Yet," Estlin grudgingly admitted,
"F.D.'s conduct is most guardedly correct, judicious and de-
corous." Then, still obviously uneasy, he added, "I doubt if he
forms intimacies much with gentlemen."[57]

Estlin was not alone. Webb, remembering Douglass' mid-1840s
tour some years later, reflected on the fact that it was young,
impressionable women whom the black man swept off their feet.
That Webb had clashed with Douglass as his Irish publisher and as a
participant in antislavery infighting scarcely invalidates the observation, for it was precisely Douglass' prickly independence which
rankled his white male associates in Great Britain as in the United
States. Webb could not think of a single man who supported
Douglass.[58] "I should think him of a suspicious turn of mind,"
Estlin had written in an 1847 letter to May and it was "not very
easy to advise, or serve him, as he manifest[ed] suspicion, &

56. See, for example, [Seven Members of the Cork Ladies Anti-Slavery
Society] to Maria W. Chapman, December 1, 1841, W-BPL. Isabel Jennings
to Maria W. Chapman, April 12, 1843, W-BPL. Mary Howill to Sister,
[1847], quoted in Eva Beatrice Dykes, *The Negro in English Romantic
Thought; or a Study of Sympathy for the Oppressed* (Washington:
Associated Publishers, 1942), 148. Mary Brady to Maria W. Chapman, n.d.,
Ch-BPL. Copy of an extract of a letter from Miss S. Carpenter in Maria W.
Chapman to [?], April 1846, W-BPL.
57. John B. Estlin to Samuel May, Jr., January 12, 1847, M-BPL.
58. Richard D. Webb to Maria W. Chapman, January 22, 1854, W-BPL.

jealousy, towards those whose disinterested kindness for him was not to be doubted."[59]

In England as in America those who were accustomed to set policy and make decisions were troubled by the independence of one whose revolt against slavery made him unwilling and perhaps unable to accept their directions unquestioningly. Those Negroes who took the advice of their British hosts and conformed to their wishes had a much easier time. The accommodating William Wells Brown won praise for being more open and confiding than Douglass, less "haughty and impatient."[60] But even Brown was put on the defensive when his British hosts discovered that he was separated from his wife. Similarly Henry Bibb was warned not even to come to England because he had married a free woman after having left a wife who was unwilling to escape with him from slavery.[61]

Lack of decorum was almost as much an issue in public performances as in private life. Proper Victorians were made uneasy by the show which Brown and the Crafts first put on when they arrived in England. "We have been endeavoring to improve the tone of Brown and Crafts *Exhibition*," Estlin wrote to fellow abolitionist Eliza Wigham, "[by] altering their too showman like hand bills, and securing a higher position for Ellen."[62] When lecturers were suitably refined, however, there was no trouble. Sarah Remond was just fine as even Webb conceded in his backhanded way. She "goes on firmly," he wrote May, and "is not unworthy to be present at a concert or an opera when [the] way opens."[63]

59. John B. Estlin to Samuel May, Jr., January 12, 1847 and July 16, 1846, both in M-BPL. Estlin had earlier had reservations about entertaining Douglass in his own home; see Estlin to Richard D. Webb, November 13, 1845, W-BPL.

60. Richard D. Webb to [Maria W. Chapman], August 3, 1849, W-BPL. Mary Estlin also found Brown more personally acceptable than Douglass; see Mary Estlin to Maria W. Chapman, April 25, 1850, quoted in Farrison, *Brown,* 167. Nine years later she was still fearful of Douglass' potential treachery; see Mary Estlin to Maria W. Chapman, October 20, 1859, W-BPL.

61. *Liberator,* July 12, 1850. William Smeal to Maria W. Chapman, March 21, 1848, W-BPL.

62. John B. Estlin to [Eliza] Wigham, May 3, 1851, Copy, W-BPL.

63. Richard D. Webb to Samuel May, Jr., March 29, 1859, M-BPL.

This mixed reception was not really surprising. Victorian standards of behavior set guidelines which, under the best of circumstances, were difficult to meet. Beyond this, nineteenth-century mores only exaggerated the latent sexual fears, so obvious in some of the criticism, which haunted Anglo-Saxons when they encountered other races. Yet at no time did these obstacles significantly impede the work of the talented black agents who lectured and labored in Great Britain from Remond and Douglass in the 1840s to William Wells Brown, Ward, Pennington, and Garnet in the 1850s. The key factor was less one of private personality than of public appeal—and all of these men did win the attention and support of large numbers. By contrast there were those lacking personal resources and public personae who made little impression. The Crafts, who, when they arrived, were widely welcomed and personally popular, won little attention after their novelty wore off, and they soon dropped out of sight as students in an English school.[64] Neither they nor Henry "Box" Brown were able to sustain themselves by lecturing. Similarly the highly-educated William Allen lacked platform appeal and could do little more than patch together a tenuous living by giving private elocution lessons.[65]

What these experiences taught, William Wells Brown tried to pass on to his fellows. England, he told them, was no place for a fugitive who lacked some special talent. In 1851 unemployment was high among Negroes living there, many subsisted on public charity, and all of them faced the competition of skilled refugees from the continental revolutions of 1848. By 1853, the British *Anti-Slavery Advocate* warned that blacks in Great Britain were increasingly becoming beggars and tramps.[66]

Few who sought public attention actually gained it. Those without special talents and sound credentials from white-

64. *Liberator*, January 2, and October 22, 1852. *Anti-Slavery Advocate*, No. 3 (December 1852), 22.
65. *Anti-Slavery Advocate*, No. 10 (July 1853), 76; and No. 12, Vol. II (December 1857), 90-91.
66. *Liberator*, July 23, 1851. *Anti-Slavery Advocate*, No. 11 (August 1853), 85.

dominated American antislavery or missionary societies were largely ignored. But those who gained the necessary initial entree into British benevolent circles and exploited it with competence accomplished much in the British Isles. It was they who largely shaped Britishers' sympathetic vision of American slavery and in turn molded the nature of their antislavery response to it.

5. FACTIONALISM, POWERLESSNESS, AND PREJUDICE

AT THE heart of white antislavery thought was the premise of equality, the assumptions that blacks were not inherently inferior to whites, that they were equally entitled to the natural rights of man. Yet the attitudes and actions of individual abolitionists often belied the assumptions of their ideology. Subject to the pressure of their neighbors' contrary beliefs and heirs to social usage grounded in racial distinctions, they hesitated to fly full face against the customs of their time. So it was that in the 1830s they hesitated even to admit blacks to their antislavery societies. The immediate obstacles were twofold. In the first place tradition in America as in England had, before the 1830s, limited the membership of benevolent societies to a social elite specifically invited to serve in them. The newer practice of opening participation in such groups to all interested had just begun. Secondly, many among those Americans who were committed to equality still believed that separation of the races was normal, desirable, and, perhaps, inevitable. To institute interracial associations, therefore, violated well-established customs and seemed to presage more harm than good for their cause.

Not all white abolitionists shared these reservations. Garrison pleaded with Unitarian minister William Ellery Channing to stop preaching that antislavery societies "ought never to have permitted our colored brethren to unite with us in our associations."[1] Blacks, so the popular author Lydia Maria Child argued in 1836, had given

1. Leon F. Litwack, *North of Slavery, The Negro in the Free States, 1790-1860* (Chicago: University of Chicago Press, 1961), 304.

68

substantial support to the new and struggling American Anti-Slavery Society in its first few years. "It is true," she conceded, "that a very small number of intelligent colored people do belong to our societies. The very circumstance of their feeling an interest in their degraded brethren is an indication of moral worth. When such men and women ask to give a portion of their hard earnings to a righteous cause, who could justify us in refusing their offer?"[2]

But Child's rather patronizing tolerance betrayed the very attitudes which made many Negroes prefer to establish their own segregated auxiliary antislavery associations.[3] Others, however, simply fretted about the unwillingness of Afro-Americans to participate actively in any antislavery society. "We need more radicalism among us, before we can speak as becomes a suffering, oppressed and persecuted people," Remond wrote Garrison in 1841 surveying the race apathy he thought had marked the past decade. "We have been altogether too fearful of martyrdom . . .too slow in our movements."[4]

Without doubt both white prejudice and black hesitance to become involved in white-dominated groups limited the role that Negroes played in antislavery societies throughout the antebellum decades. Conspicuous as they were as agents and lecturers, there are real questions about the degree to which they shaped or directed society policies and actions.

There is no question that blacks did participate during the 1830s in the formation and the work of national, regional, and state societies. Following the lead of James McCrummell, Robert Purvis, and James Barbadoes, who had attended the founding convention of the American Anti-Slavery Society, Negro participants at subsequent meetings of the national society presented resolutions, served on committees, and offered prayers for benedic-

2. *Liberator,* April 3, 1836.
3. Charles H. Wesley, "The Negro in the Organization of Abolition," *Phylon,* II (Third Quarter, 1941), 223-235. Benjamin Quarles, *Black Abolitionists* (New York: Oxford University Press, 1969), 29-30.
4. *Liberator,* May 21, 1841.

tion upon their labors.[5] In 1837 the Rev. Charles Gardiner, a Presbyterian pastor from Philadelphia, was probably the first Negro to address a national convention and thus began a practice which made the black presence considerably more evident.[6] In state and local societies their participation was still more active and their numbers more telling.[7] Beginning with its first meeting in 1834, a sizeable Massachusetts delegation regularly attended the sessions of the New England Anti-Slavery Convention and were joined on the first occasion by New Yorkers Theodore Wright and Charles B. Ray. Likewise, blacks participated in the conventions of the New York and Pennsylvania Anti-Slavery Societies, both of which they had helped found. And, in each of the three conventions of antislavery women from 1837 to 1839, black delegates were unusually active as speakers and officers, reflecting the greater opportunities available when all participants represented groups customarily excluded from such roles and could share their inexperience equally.

Despite this widespread engagement in major and minor antislavery meetings and, in the early years, monetary contributions which supplied as much as one-seventh of the national society's total annual budget, blacks played, in fact, a limited role in making the societies' decisions. In state and regional organizations the officers were overwhelmingly white, with only an occasional token black among them. During its second year, the Rev. Samuel Snowden of Boston was chosen to be one of nine

5. See, for example, *Colored American,* May 20, 1837 and June 2, 1838; *National Enquirer,* April 29, 1837 and June 3, 1837; and *Liberator,* May 18, 1838.
6. *Liberator,* May 19, 1837.
7. The material which follows in this and the following paragraph is compiled from reports of various antislavery groups and reported in *Liberator, passim,* throughout the 1830s. See also the various annual reports of the American Anti-Slavery Society. Secondary sources dealing with the question of black participation include Quarles, *Black Abolitionists,* 25, 27-28; Wesley, "The Negro in the Organization of Abolition"; and Gerda Lerner, "The Grimké Sisters and the Struggle Against Race Prejudice," *Journal of Negro History,* XLVIII (October 1963), which quotes a letter of Angelina Grimké to Jane Smith, April 17, 1837, discussing the formation of a black women's antislavery society, 285.

counselors of the New England Anti-Slavery Society. Throughout the rest of the 1830s one or two Negroes usually occupied similar posts in that society or in its successor, the Massachusetts Anti-Slavery Society. At the national level, five Negroes were elected to the seventy-four-member Board of Managers of the American Anti-Slavery Society when it was founded; and for the rest of the decade between five and ten served with the constantly expanding, though largely honorific, group. More indicative of decision-making power was the presence, throughout the 1830s, of Cornish and Wright on the ten to twelve member executive committee of the American Anti-Slavery Society, which allocated funds, planned campaigns, and actually administered the society's business.

It was not only the prejudice of abolitionists which dictated the paucity of blacks in organized antislavery work. Peter Williams, pastor of New York's St. Philip's Episcopal Church, was chosen a member of the first excutive committee of the American Anti-Slavery Society. A sound choice, he had been active in the affairs of the African Free School. Like Wright and Cornish, he was a New Yorker and could easily attend the regular meetings of the committee, which were customarily held in the city. Within a year of his appointment and after an anti-abolitionist riot had vandalized St. Philip's, Bishop Benjamin Onderdonk, Williams' superior, demanded that the priest give up his antislavery work and confine himself to his ecclesiastical duties.

Williams, minister first and race spokesman second, agreed. The extended apologia which he subsequently published disclosed his predicament. In an effort to maintain his following, he pointed out that he had resigned only from the executive committee, not from the society. At the same time he tried to appease the bishop by denying that he had ever been active in the society.[8] A thoroughly

8. *African Repository*, X (August 1834), 185-188. Peter Williams to Gerrit Smith, July 26, and September 4, 1834, S-SU. Carter G. Woodson, ed., *The Mind of the Negro as Reflected in Letters Written During the Crisis, 1800-1860* (orig. publ. 1926. New York: Negro Universities Press, 1969), 633-634. Bishop Onderdonk also prohibited blacks from attending General Theological Seminary and refused Alexander Crummell a place as minister in his diocese without embarrassing and unusual restrictions on his activities.

unsatisfactory resolution, it nonetheless spoke eloquently to the perennial problem of competing loyalties.

Williams' case highlighted the tensions of individuals who were torn between antislavery imperatives on the one hand and economic and professional survival on the other. Despite them, however, active and articulate free Negroes did support the new antislavery societies throughout the 1830s. They applauded abolitionist condemnation of colonization.[9] They welcomed the American Anti-Slavery Society's famous "Seventy," the itinerant agents who, beginning in 1837, preached the abolitionist message from Maine to Ohio. Especially did they commend men like Augustus Wattles in Ohio and Hiram Wilson in Canada, who were assigned to "labor for the improvement of the free colored people."[10] When Elijah Lovejoy, an antislavery editor in Alton, Illinois, was killed by an anti-abolitionist mob, Negroes in Boston and New York held memorial meetings eulogizing him. Similarly, blacks praised James G. Birney, Henry B. Stanton, and Wendell Phillips when they testified before a Massachusetts legislative committee against slavery in the District of Columbia.[11] In Philadelphia, the American Moral Reform Society, an offshoot of the black convention movement in the 1830s, lauded Garrison for having "pointed out to us the hope of immediate and unconditional liberty."[12] Thus, Cornish spoke clearly for his fellows when he addressed delegates at the 1838 meeting of the American Anti-Slavery Society as "wise men of the nation . . .great and good men . . .the salt of the earth, the leaven which preserves our nation, morally and politically, and which will wipe off American reproach, and eventually be America's glory."[13]

    9. *Colored American,* March 4, 1837.
    10. Circular Letter from ministers of Negro churches in New York to the Free Colored People of the United States, *Weekly Advocate,* February 18, 1837. *National Enquirer,* March 4, 1837.
    11. *Liberator,* December 29, 1837, and March 23, 1838.
    12. *Ibid.,* November 3, 1837.
    13. *Ibid.,* June 8, 1838.

Yet all this did not prevent white abolitionists from trying to marshal black support for their own purposes when, in the late 1830s, the antislavery movement was rent by internal feuding. The controversy began in earnest in 1837 and continued for the next three years, until the American Anti-Slavery Society split in two, spawning the rival American and Foreign Anti-Slavery Society. At issue was the nature of reform and specifically the means which should be used to end slavery. The radicals, led by Garrison, sought far-reaching and fundamental changes in society and government which went well beyond the eradication of slavery. They broke with organized religion, disdained political action within the prevailing system, and would rely solely on moral suasion in pursuit of a variety of interrelated reform movements. The conservatives, who centered around the Tappan brothers and a number of New York and Massachusetts clerics, rejected Garrisonian multi-reformism, sought to work through established denominations, and utilized the political system. Their view of reform potential and the nature of the change to be effected was far more limited. As the two groups squabbled ever more viciously, blacks felt tossed about on waves of a debate often irrelevant to their interests. The longer the controversy raged, the more convinced they became that the infighting was only weakening and disrupting the movement on which they had pinned their hopes.

The struggle had begun when several Massachusetts clerics denounced Garrison's personal attacks on specific ministers and church members who had links with slavery or fellowshipped with slaveholders. In Boston, where Negro ministers played a minor role in antislavery, the black community came quickly and persistently to Garrison's defense. For the next three years they met repeatedly, adopted numerous resolutions which praised him, branded his opponents "foe[s] to liberty," and anathematized the clerically dominated Massachusetts Abolition Society.[14] In New York, seat of the Tappans' strength, the black response was muted.

14. *Ibid.*, September 22 and November 24, 1837, October 25 and November 1, 1839, and *Colored American*, April 11, 1840. The quotation is from *Liberator*, June 7, 1840.

Cornish, a cleric and long-time associate of Lewis Tappan, was then editing the *Colored American*, and in it he tried to play down the issue. The response from Boston was instantaneous and well aired in the *Liberator*. Cornish had failed in his pledge to serve American Negroes because he refused to give all sides of the dispute. In response, Cornish said that, because the paper served all colored Americans, he would refuse to publish the recriminatory documents which Boston blacks were sending on to him.[15]

Attacked on one flank by Garrisonians, the *Colored American* was soon under the guns of New York abolitionists, who would have had it support plans for an antislavery third party. When Wright moved in 1839 that the New York State Anti-Slavery Society endorse the paper, the society's president, Gerrit Smith, countered that unless it "changed its course on politics" it should not be supported. Cornish, in an effort to sting the consciences of his white critics, replied that of all persons "abolitionists should be the last to infringe upon the right of opinion and free discussion."[16] His defense only made matters worse. Both Smith and upstate editor William Goodell became as incensed as the Garrisonians had been. Smith, denying that he had tried to pressure Cornish, then accused him of supporting proslavery candidates and thereby upholding sin and crime. Goodell, for his part, charged Cornish with an unthinking partisanship that made him reject an antislavery party in favor of openly anti-Negro Whig candidates for office.[17] At this point it was obvious that antislavery feuding was not only destroying what had been a unified movement, it was subverting black effort as well. The only cure, "Sinceritas" of New Haven contended in the *Colored American*, was to jettison white supporters and act independently. "Rally around our press, and save it and our cause from destruction," he urged his comrades in an appeal which became ever more common as factional disputes within the antislavery movement multiplied.[18]

15. *Liberator*, October 6, 1837. *Colored American*, October 14, 1837.
16. *Colored American*, October 5, 1839.
17. *Ibid.*, October 19, 1839.
18. *Ibid.*, November 2, 1839.

Exhortation, however, was easier than achievement. No more than whites could black abolitionists avoid the discussion of conflicting techniques and philosophies once the issues had been raised. Could antislavery people continue to work within churches linked, however remotely, to slavery? Must they form a third party to make political action a viable tool of antislavery? Was nonresistance or the total renunciation of force the necessary preliminary to ending slavery? Was women's rights a relevant part of the antislavery crusade? Would the abolition of slavery be meaningful if real property were still privately owned and subject to speculation and monopoly control? These questions and dozens more crowded in upon them. Although blacks variously joined each of the conflicting factions, they shared common ground in preferring to confine their attention to slavery and the rights of free Negroes and to regard other questions as delusory. The *Colored American* put it bluntly. Arguing that nonresistance, women's rights, and sabbatarianism were "*neither parts nor parcels of that great and holy cause,*" it objected to their being "intruded into its measures."[19] New Bedford blacks, critical of the unthinking factional loyalty of their Boston colleagues, denounced them for "introducing into anti-slavery meetings, subjects foreign to the cause of the slave," which had a "direct tendency to cripple the efforts of a large portion of the true friends of the slave, and clog the wheels of the abolition car."[20]

A more serious and decidedly indicative contretemps occurred somewhat later, in 1843. Frederick Douglass and Charles Remond, both thoroughly identified with the multi-reformist Garrisonian Massachusetts Anti-Slavery Society, clashed publicly with the society's white general agent, John Collins. When, late in the summer, the three men were lecturing together in upstate New York, Collins, an ardent utopian socialist, cut one of their meetings short in order to hold an antiproperty meeting in the same hall. Remond, denied his lecture time, angrily charged Collins with using antislavery as a stepping stone to communitarianism. Collins,

19. *Ibid.*, May 11, 1839.
20. *Liberator*, October 18, 1839.

characteristically connecting the two reforms, cut down Remond's short-sightedness. "To recognize property in soil is worse than to enslave men. . . .The universal reform movement will do more for the slave than the antislavery movement." Thoroughly upset, Douglass threatened to resign his antislavery agency if the Massachusetts board sustained Collins. The ensuing exchange elaborated persisting race differences even within the same antislavery faction. Collins put down black criticism to intellectual insensitivity and social disadvantage. Douglass as a fugitive slave and Remond as a victim of color prejudice were simply unable to cope with "higher claims than antislavery."[21] At society headquarters Maria Chapman made a similar response. In attacking Collins, "Remond & [D]ouglas[s] have made a mistake in conduct, but they [k]now they may rely on their friends in Boston to put the most friendly construction on hasty acts, & to forget & forgive them as . . . 'Divine Justice' (I speak transcendentally not Calvinistically) will permit."[22] Here converged a series of fundamental problems. For white Garrisonians, an elaborate reform theory became more pressing than the specific action which blacks put first.

Underlying this conflict ran the whites' assumption that their experience better fitted Negroes for carrying out policy than making it, and they acted accordingly. There was, therefore, little room for independent black spokesmen among the more highly ideological Garrisonians. Consequently, blacks previously active in antislavery organizations either opted out or turned them, as best they could, to their own ends. One of the first open clashes occurred over a decision to correct what many blacks thought was a lacuna in American Anti-Slavery Society concerns—their economic advancement. In 1840, the Rev. Jehiel C. Beman, then living in Boston, opened an employment agency for free Negroes under the auspices of the Massachusetts Abolition Society. For his temerity he was charged with venality in selling out to new organization, as the Garrisonians called their opponents. He had,

21. Frederick Douglass to Maria W. Chapman, September 10, 1843, W-BPL. John A. Collins to Chapman, August 23, 1843, W-BPL.
22. Maria W. Chapman to Sydney H. Gay, August 22, 1843, G-CU.

said Garrison, lent "his influence to subvert the old society, and destroy the Liberator."[23] Beman offered a twofold pragmatic retort. First of all, Boston blacks needed such an agency, and the Garrisonian Massachusetts Anti-Slavery Society had refused to back one. And secondarily, Beman himself needed employment, which he sought from the Abolition Society only when the old Anti-Slavery Society told him "they had nothing for him to do."[24]

For weeks the issue was not only hotly debated in the white antislavery press of Boston but was also aired at black meetings in the city. One writer, probably Beman himself, used the new organization press to blister the Garrisonians for talking about equality and opportunity for free Negroes but doing nothing to effect it.[25] In response a meeting of black Bostonians, three of whom had earlier exonerated Beman because of the extenuating circumstances of personal need which had led him to work for the Abolition Society, came to the old organization's defense. Neither Garrison nor the Anti-Slavery Society was "recreant to the first principles of abolition," and the attack which had so branded them was the "most unkind and ungrateful expression that could ever escape the lips of any colored man." Pushed from all sides, Beman, who had earlier considered himself a Garrisonian, was driven completely into the opposition. Shortly thereafter he became the publisher of the new organization's *Massachusetts Abolitionist*.[26]

The bitterness of Beman's experience in trying to revise and enlarge abolitionist policy explains why others simply dropped out of formal antislavery activity. In New Hampshire John Lewis was similarly pressed from old organization ranks. He had, when the factional feuding became intense in 1839, vigorously supported the

23. *Liberator,* February 28, 1840.
24. Certified statement signed by John T. Hilton, John Levy, and John B. Butler, March 17, 1840; J. V. Himes to William L. Garrison, March 17, 1840; and John E. Scarlett's certified statement, March 17, 1840, which contains the quotation, all in *Liberator,* March 20, 1840.
25. "A Colored Man" [probably Beman] to Editor, March, 1840, from a typed copy headed "For the Abolitionist ANTI-SLAVERY IN 1840" in Elizur Wright Papers, Library of Congress (cited hereafter as W-LC).
26. *Colored American,* April 11, 1840; *Massachusetts Abolitionist,* April 2, 1840. *Liberator,* March 20 and April 3, 1840, which contains the quotations. *Massachusetts Abolitionist,* September 3, 1840.

Boston position. One more year of exhausting discussions of universal reform, however, thoroughly disillusioned him. "As a colored man, and a representative of my people," Lewis wrote the executive committee of the Garrisonian New Hampshire Anti-Slavery Society in 1840, "I feel it a duty to make the advocacy of the [antislavery] cause the paramount question."[27] Although he said he would continue to give antislavery lectures, he did not wish to waste his effort on debilitating and pointless infighting. The *Herald of Freedom*, organ of the New Hampshire society, responded vituperatively. Lewis too much enjoyed the flattery of "great congregations at sectarian meetings" and the fun of being a black man ogled at by curious white audiences to be a good agent. Because he lacked the stamina to labor in difficult vineyards, the *Herald* concluded, he was no great loss.[28]

The difficulties which Lewis and Beman faced were not exclusive to the American scene. Many of the British antislavery disputes in the 1840s and 1850s in which black agents were involved were but mirror images of them. Much of the hostility between Douglass and Richard Webb in Dublin stemmed from the fear of Boston leaders that Douglass would defect to the British and Foreign Anti-Slavery Society, which was closely associated with the Tappan group.[29] In 1850, when Pennington helped establish a new and anti-Garrisonian female antislavery society in Glasgow, Boston's response to it was familiar. As Wendell Phillips had earlier warned Elizabeth Pease in Darlington, "Pennington is with you just what he was here, self-seeking, trimming & utterly unreliable. . . ."[30]

British abolitionists, in short, responded to black lecturers according to their American factional alliance. Garrisonian John

27. John W. Lewis to William L. Garrison, November 20, 1839, *Liberator,* December 6, 1839. The quotation in *Liberator,* January 15, 1841.

28. *Herald of Freedom,* n.d., in *Liberator,* January 15, 1841.

29. Maria W. Chapman to Richard D. Webb, June 29, 1845, January 23 and February 24, 1846, Extracts, M-BPL.

30. Andrew Paton to Anne Weston, November 10, 1850, W-BPL. William Smeal to William W. Brown, December 12, 1850, Extract, W-BPL. Rice, "Scottish Factor," 383. Quotation in Wendell Phillips to Elizabeth Pease, February 19, 1850, G-BPL.

Estlin and his daughter Mary constantly wailed and warned against the duplicity of "colored ministers" like Pennington, Henson, Ward, and Garnet, whom the British and Foreign Anti-Slavery Society sponsored on their lecture rounds.[31] They even, when the occasion offered, staged platform confrontations between old and new organization black lecturers in an effort to put down the latter.

Unwilling to be used as counters in a white antislavery movement at home or abroad, black abolitionists evolved new views of their place within it. When members of the American Anti-Slavery Society had left its annual meeting in 1840 to found the competing American and Foreign Anti-Slavery Society, they found that the black clergymen in attendance were with them. Methodists Jehiel Beman, his son Amos Gerry Beman, and Christopher Rush, second bishop of the Zion Methodist Connexion, joined Presbyterians Samuel Cornish and Theodore Wright, both former members of the executive committee of the American Society; the somewhat less-activist Philadelphians Andrew Harris and Stephen Gloucester; and the young Troy minister, Henry Garnet, who had already made his mark in the old society and in independent race organizations.[32]

Some regulars remained in the Garrisonian ranks—among them Purvis and Remond—and the two most talented fugitive slave speakers, Douglass and William Wells Brown, were soon recruited to it. But the simple fact remains that the old organization for the next twenty years failed to attract and use black talent as it might have and paid dearly for not doing so. Almost never after 1840 did blacks serve on the decision-making executive committee of the American society. It is true that Thomas Van Rensselaer was appointed to the group in 1840, but he served no longer than three

31. John B. Estlin to Eliza Wigham, May 3, 1851, W-BPL. Mary Estlin to [Anne?] Weston, May 28, 1851, W-BPL. Mary Estlin to Caroline Weston, May 16, 1857, W-BPL.

32. Quarles, *Black Abolitionists*, 46.

years, a tenure scarcely matching the service that Cornish and Wright had given the Society before the split. Nor was the problem a geographical one after the society's headquarters moved to Boston in 1843, for Remond always lived in Salem, Douglass' home in the 1840s was in New Bedford and Lynn, and Brown spent several years in Boston in the 1850s. None of them was called to serve on this tight-knit committee.

Nevertheless black Garrisonians did participate in local, state, and regional conventions and societies. Throughout the late 1840s and during most of the 1850s, for example, Remond was president of the Essex County (Massachusetts) Anti-Slavery Society. In Philadelphia Purvis held the same position in the Pennsylvania Anti-Slavery Society. And just prior to his break with the Garrisonians, Douglass was president of the New England Anti-Slavery Convention. Even more extensive was their speech-making at conventions, their appointment or election to lesser societal offices, their membership on various convention committees, and their ubiquitous presence on the long lists of vice-presidents which antislavery conventions chose.[33] There is little question that Negro participation was made as visible as possible. Yet this visibility seldom carried with it the leverage with which to mold the antislavery movement, at least on the national level.

At first sight the role which Negroes played in the American and Foreign Anti-Slavery Society seems considerably more important. Conspicuous among its founders, they usually held at least two seats on its executive committee. Cornish, Wright, A. N. Freeman, Ray, Pennington, and Smith were regulars at its deliberations. Yet even in the new organization blacks were excluded from top national offices, which led Brooklynite William Wilson to speculate sarcastically whether "the hungry white crowd [was] so large that the black specks pass[ed] unobserved by the chiefs in command."[34]

33. The preceding evidence is drawn largely from various reports in *Liberator, National Anti-Slavery Standard,* and *Anti-Slavery Bugle.*
34. The preceding evidence is drawn largely from *American and Foreign Anti-Slavery Reporter* and American and Foreign Anti-Slavery Society annual reports. The quotation is in *Frederick Douglass' Paper,* April 15, 1853.

In short, neither old nor new organization allowed blacks to play a key role at the national level. At the same time, it is true that after the 1840 split, the American Society never regained its strength and the American and Foreign soon became the shadow organization it remained for most of its presumptive existence. Especially among antislavery conservatives therefore church-sponsored antislavery organizations became more functional and viable outlets for antislavery zeal.

In one of these groups, the Union Missionary Society, black clerics played important roles. The Union Society was organized in 1841 to carry on antislavery missionary work at home and overseas. Although Lewis Tappan controlled most of its operating funds and it was not an exclusively black group, its officers and members were predominantly Negro, including such new organization stalwarts as Cornish, Garnet, Ward, Ray, and Alexander Crummell, then of Providence. Its first president was J. W. C. Pennington; Amos Beman, its corresponding secretary; and Theodore Wright, its treasurer.[35] Moderately successful, the Union Missionary Society was absorbed in 1845 by the American Missionary Association, a larger, newly-created group which coordinated the wide variety of antislavery missionary groups that had developed over the years. Among its many activities in the 1850s it supported, as home missionaries, Amos Beman, who had given up his New Haven parish to become an itinerant preacher; Jarmain W. Loguen, who combined home parish work in Syracuse with preaching to small black settlements throughout upstate New York; and Garnet, who was a city missionary as well as pastor of New York's Shiloh Church in the late 1850s. Like the American and Foreign Anti-Slavery Society, the American Missionary Association had Negroes on its executive committee and, less frequently, on its lists of officers.[36] In this respect at least

35. Lewis Tappan to Amos A. Phelps, January 16, 1844, P-BPL. *American and Foreign Anti-Slavery Reporter*, II (June 1842), 54, and II (November 1842), 98.

36. Union Missionary Society and American Missionary Association records, AMA-ARC, *passim*; Richard B. Drake, "The American Missionary Association and the Southern Negro, 1861-1888" (Ph.D. Emory University,

clerically oriented branches of antislavery were more concerned
with the black voice than were the more radical organizations.
Although, like the more radical groups, they experienced internal
racial tensions, these were more readily bridged by shared ties,
which were conspicuously lacking or at least more tenuous
between black and white Garrisonians: affiliation with the same
basic church structure, more nearly similar professional preoccupations, and a shared preference for pragmatic action. It is also
significant that nearly all black officers in non-Garrisonian organizations were ministers and that none of them came from
exclusively black denominations. Thus church ties proved critical.

If the preoccupation with ideological struggles made blacks
restive, particularly within Garrisonian organizations, so too did
their growing awareness of anti-black prejudice among their white
confreres. Early in the 1830s, black abolitionists had thought—or
hoped—that it would be otherwise. In his address to the Convention of the Free People of Color in 1834, New Yorker William
Hamilton announced sanguinely, "That hitherto strong-footed, but
sore-eyed vixen, Prejudice, is limping off, seeking the shade. The
Anti-Slavery Society and the friends of immediate abolition, are
taking a noble, bold, and manly stand, in the cause of universal
liberty."[37] Elsewhere, when Theodore Wright castigated northern
whites for neither employing free Negroes nor giving them equal
education, nor admitting them to apprenticeships, he expressly
excepted abolitionists.[38] Similarly Cornish commended the various
antislavery societies for having "created A CONSCIENCE on the
subject of Slavery, and prejudice against color, throughout the
length and breadth of our land."[39] Even Smith, looking back long
after he had lost his early enthusiasm, recalled that antislavery in

---

1957. Third Draft, on deposit, Berea College Library), Appendix A; Quarles,
Black Abolitionists, 79-80.
    37. *Liberator,* June 14, 1834.
    38. *Ibid.,* November 5, 1836.
    39. *Colored American,* May 6, 1837.

the 1830s had seemed to him an interracial "honeymoon" when "all went merrily as a marriage bell."[40]

These ecstatic endorsements were very soon modified. In 1837 Cornish warned that the American Union for the Improvement of the People of Color was too full of prejudice to be serviceable. They would hinder more than they would help "until they have buried their prejudice of heart, and learned to view [blacks] , as brethren of the same family and the same blood, with themselves."[41] In the same year, Wright urged antislavery societies to exclude prejudiced whites from membership. Many societies' constitutions, he observed ruefully, failed to mention "the giant sin of prejudice," and many individual abolitionists had not yet "annihilate[d] , in their own bosoms, the cord of caste."[42]

Understandable as such prejudice was in terms of prevailing mores and understandable also as white abolitionists' caution about challenging deep-seated racial fears was at a time of mob violence against them, still these attitudes created problems within the movement. Only a few, like Angelina Grimké, Charleston-born Quaker lecturer, faced the problem bluntly, entreating blacks to help whites overcome their prejudice. "You must be willing to mingle with us whilst we have the prejudice," she pled, "because it is only by associating with you that we shall be able to overcome it."[43] But even those numerically few white abolitionists who mingled frequently with black colleagues did not overcome it—as Sarah Forten told Grimké frankly. Daughter of James Forten, she frequently met white antislavery crusaders in her father's house, and she knew at first hand that prejudice "obscure[d] their many virtues and chok[ed] up the avenues to higher and nobler sentiments."[44] "There are, I am sorry to say, two kinds of

40. *Frederick Douglass' Paper,* January 26, 1855.
41. *Colored American,* March 25, 1837.
42. *Liberator,* October 13, 1837.
43. Quoted in Lerner, "The Grimké Sisters," 286.
44. Sarah Forten to Angelina Grimké, April 15, 1837, in Gilbert H. Barnes and Dwight L. Dumond, eds., *Letters of Theodore Dwight Weld, Angelina Grimké Weld, and Sarah Grimké, 1822-1844* (2 vols. New York: D. Appleton-Century Co., 1934), 1:380.

abolitionists," Nathaniel Paul observed somewhat later; those who
hate slavery and prejudice equally and those "who hate slavery,
especially that which is 1000 or 1500 miles off," but who, "as bad
as they hate slavery . . . hate a man who wears a colored skin
worse."[45]

Although throughout the 1830s black abolitionists bore with
their white associates, they became less and less sanguine of their
contributions toward the goals of full equality. Measured by the
assistance they gave free Negroes seeking economic improvement,
whites fell far short of their professed ideals. As early as 1838
Cornish condemned the American Anti-Slavery Society for dropping those agents assigned to educate and elevate free Negroes. If
white men would give their advice and influence and lend their
money to stimulate "husbandry, manufactures and mechanism by
colored men, the result would be most salutary," he thought.[46]
But they did not do so. Stephen Myers, editor of the Albany, New
York, *Northern Star and Freeman's Advocate*, argued that white
abolitionists lectured at length on egalitarian principles but then
failed to practice them. Blacks had no desire, Myers assured them,
to seek "their daughters in marriage" or "to ride in their carriages."
What they wanted was the economic opportunity which equal
access to jobs would provide. "We do not ask for money," he
noted sharply, "neither do we wish [abolitionists] to educate our
children; these we will endeavor to provide for by the sweat of our
brow, but we *do* ask that their workshops may be opened to our
youth, and that those of us who are already in business may be
patronized."[47] Considered objectively, Myers concluded somewhat

45. Speech to the Albany Anti-Slavery Convention, March 1, 1838, in
Friend of Man, March 14, 1838. For the general problem of prejudice among
abolitionists, see William H. Pease and Jane H. Pease, "Antislavery
Ambivalence: Immediatism, Expediency, Race," *American Quarterly*, XVII
(Winter 1965), 682-695; Leon F. Litwack, "The Abolitionist Dilemma: The
Antislavery Movement and the Northern Negro," *New England Quarterly*,
XXXIV (March 1961), 50-73; his *North of Slavery*, particularly 304-316;
and Louis Filler, *The Crusade Against Slavery, 1830-1860* (New York:
Harper and Brothers, 1960), 143.

46. *Colored American*, October 27, 1838.

47. *Northern Star and Freeman's Advocate*, March 3, 1842. The article is
signed "M." and was doubtlessly written by Myers.

later, abolitionists had done nothing for Negroes, North or South.[48]

What was said in the early 1840s had not changed a decade later. Sharply and pungently William Wilson told his white antislavery colleagues that they must "toe the mark" and do more than lecture "colored people to merely be good and honest and not to think too highly of themselves, and hence get out of their place." Thousands for sympathy but "not one dollar to make a practical example of the capacity of a single colored man" was the appropriate description of their efforts to date. No abolitionist had or would "admit him, nor his son, nor his son's son to [his] counting-room, nor [his] work-bench nor to any other respectable station in [his] gift."[49] The reality and immediacy of Wilson's dismay was born out at the annual meeting of the American and Foreign Anti-Slavery Society in 1852. On the floor of the convention Edward V. Clark, a jeweler, accused Lewis Tappan of refusing to employ a black clerk. James McCune Smith harangued Tappan for refusing to hire a black sea captain, and merchant John Rankin for refusing a $500 loan to help a young Negro druggist get established in business.[50] Seven years later Garnet repeated the litany to a Boston convention, tightening the screw even more. "I think I find, most generally, that the men who take our sons and daughters into their stores and work-shops, are not Abolitionists. Abolitionists say it is not part of their work to do this."[51]

Even the employment patterns within antislavery societies fed the bitterness. Here, as in the commercial and business world, blacks were hired only in certain race-cast roles. Their color gave them a positive advantage as agents which whites simply could not match, and so they were hired to lecture and collect funds. With the exception of William Still, who served for fourteen years as general clerk of the Pennsylvania Anti-Slavery Society in Philadel-

48. *Ibid.*, March 17, 1842. In 1855 Myers repeated essentially the same charge, see *Frederick Douglass' Paper*, May 18, 1855.
49. *Frederick Douglass' Paper*, April 22, 1852.
50. *Ibid.*, May 27, 1852.
51. *Weekly Anglo-African*, September 17, 1859.

phia,[52] Negroes were generally taken on only in subservient positions in antislavery offices. William Nell, for instance, was hired as an office helper by the Massachusetts Anti-Slavery Society in 1840 and three years later dismissed when the society ran short of funds. One could argue the logic of dispensing with the helper rather than the manager of the office, but that was just the point. Negroes were almost never in charge. This point Maria Chapman overlooked when she wrote in despair about the aftereffects of firing Nell. "The col'd people," she told *National Anti-Slavery Standard* editor David Child, "were ready to [desert to] N[ew] Organiz[ation] about it. . . ."[53]

With tenacious persistence blacks protested against their exclusion from significant policy-making, administrative, and editorial positions. Van Rensselaer, editor of the *Ram's Horn*, asserted that Negroes were never offered the really good antislavery posts. "Why is not some colored man receiving a salary of a thousand dollars a year from some of these [antislavery political] parties?" he asked bitterly early in 1848. "Why are not colored men employed as editors of anti-slavery papers?"[54] To other Negroes the answer was obvious. Quakers and Garrisonians, Ward observed, cared not a whit about blacks as people. "Whatever [the former] do for us," he charged, "savors of pity, and is done at arm's length, on a sort of *noli me tangere* principle." The Garrisonians lacked even the veneer of pity in their refusal to encourage a black man "as clerk in an anti-slavery office, or editor, or lecturer to the same extent as . . . [they did] white men of the same calibre."[55]

Other occasions apparently reflecting white abolitionist equivocation aroused still more strident attacks in the 1850s. In Philadelphia Charles Reason publicly condemned antislavery

52. William Still to Executive Committee, May 29, 1861, Copy, in Pennsylvania Anti-Slavery Society, Minutes of the Executive Committee, M. J. Burleigh Collection, Historical Society of Pennsylvania.
53. Maria W. Chapman to David L. Child, [1843?], Child Papers, Antislavery Collection, Boston Public Library (cited hereafter as C-BPL).
54. *North Star*, February 25, 1848.
55. *Frederick Douglass' Paper*, April 13, 1855.

feminist Lucy Stone for having addressed a segregated audience.[56] Douglass rejected her disclaimers that she had been unaware of the ban on Negroes until it was too late to withdraw. She had already shown her hand by lecturing throughout the South on women's rights without ever mentioning slavery, a phenomenon which was, he thought, something like preaching "about the exceeding sinfulness of sin, without defining what sin is."[57] In Washington, Myrtilla Miner, who had opened a school for Negro girls, was chastised by George T. Downing, Newport, Rhode Island, hotel owner, for displaying underlying hostility to the race. Allegedly she preferred light-colored students because she thought their white ancestry made them more educable than darker girls.[58] Along these same lines Downing charged Elizabeth Cady Stanton with having said that the *few drops of Saxon blood flowing in Frederick Douglass' veins [gave] him his clear perception of Humanity, of his inalienable rights."*[59] White abolitionists as a group, Ward and Douglass had both concluded by the mid-1850s, wished to keep blacks in "the short frocks of childhood."[60] They have fallen "away from their first love, touching the recognition of the entire manhood and social equality of the colored people," said Douglass.[61] "They assume the right to dictate to us about all matters," Ward told an English audience; "they dislike to see us assume or maintain manly and independent positions; they prefer that we should be a second-rate set of folks, in intellectual matters." "There are many *professed* abolitionists, on both sides of the Atlantic," Ward concluded in his 1855 autobiography, "who have no idea that a black man should feel towards and speak of his tormenters as a white man would concerning his."[62]

56. *Ibid.*, February 10, 1854.
57. *Ibid.*, February 17, 1854.
58. George T. Downing to Frederick Douglass, December 6, 1854, *Frederick Douglass' Paper*, December 22, 1854.
59. George T. Downing to Samuel Rhoades, January 13, 1855, *Frederick Douglass' Paper*, January 19, 1856.
60. *Provincial Freeman*, June 10, 1854.
61. Frederick Douglass to Charles Sumner, April 24, 1855, in Foner, *Douglass*, 2:362.
62. *Provincial Freeman*, June 10, 1854. Ward, *Autobiography*, 13.

This growing disaffection was vividly dramatized in the late 1840s and 1850s by several causes célèbres. The fracas over Douglass' break with the Boston Garrisonians was the most prolonged and complex. Well known on both sides of the Atlantic, Douglass had the ability and backing, as well as the will, to insist on his independence and still survive as the leading black abolitionist. The Garrisonians, who had already worried about his overly-smooth lecture style and his rebellion against mixing utopian socialism with antislavery, feared that when he was in England he might go yet further astray and be lured by self-interest into conservative British and Foreign Anti-Slavery Society circles. Therefore Chapman had written Webb to keep Douglass under careful surveillance. When Douglass learned of this surreptitious maneuvering, he was incensed. "If you wish to drive me from the Antislavery Society—" he wrote Chapman, "put me under overseership and the work is done."[63]

That, however, was only the beginning. After he returned from England in 1847, Douglass established the *North Star* against the advice of Boston antislavery headquarters from whom, as Ward observed, he received "about as much *dis*couragement as *en*couragement."[64] Then in 1851 he broke with the Garrisonian doctrine that the federal constitution was a proslavery document. This was the final severing of Douglass' earliest antislavery ties and marked the completion of his swing to a politically oriented abolition. It also exposed him to a series of withering attacks from his erstwhile associates which lasted until the Civil War. Their immediate response in 1852 was to charge him, at the American Anti-Slavery Society annual meeting, with nine points of treason to the antislavery cause.[65] But they failed to isolate him from rank and file white abolitionists who, hearing his vigorous defense, elected him, with but one dissenting vote, to a position on the powerless but presumably prestigious board of managers.

63. Frederick Douglass to Maria W. Chapman, March 29, 1846, W-BPL.
64. *Impartial Citizen,* May 31, 1851.
65. Frederick Douglass to Gerrit Smith, May 15, 1852, in Foner, *Douglass,* 2:180-181. For the tenor of the attack on Douglass, see *Frederick Douglass' Paper,* May 20, 1852.

Throughout the next year the Garrisonian antislavery press charged Douglass with dishonesty, marital infidelity, self-serving ambition, and desertion from the cause. The *National Anti-Slavery Standard*, the *Liberator*, the *Pennsylvania Freeman*, and the *Anti-Slavery Bugle* in Ohio all questioned his moral fitness to lead American blacks, alleging that he was a traitor, an ingrate, and the willing tool of that English Jezebel, Julia Griffiths, who had come to America to assist him with the *North Star* and was now sowing dissention within Douglass' own family.[66] As Collins had privately charged in 1843, Garrison now publicly charged that Douglass, as a black, could not fully understand the depth and breadth of abolitionism. "The Anti-Slavery cause," he wrote in December, 1853, "both religiously and politically, has transcended the ability of the sufferers from American slavery and prejudice, *as a class*, to keep pace with it, or to perceive what are its demands, or to understand the philosophy of its operations."[67] Douglass was driven to utter fury as ideological dispute descended to prejudice and character assassination. "Who will doubt, hereafter," he asked in despair, "the natural inferiority of the *negro*, when the great champion of the negroes' rights, thus broadly concedes all that is claimed respecting the negroe's [*sic*] inferiority by the bitterest despisers of the negro race."[68]

Not surprisingly, Negroes fought back on their own behalf and on Douglass'. Across the North from Providence to Albany to Chicago they gathered in angry meetings to give him support. Characteristically beginning with an acknowledgment of abolitionists' past assistance, they went on to laud Douglass' "unswerving fidelity" to antislavery and his readiness "to 'crucify all personal considerations' to the cause of his people."[69] But most of all they

66. Particularly bitter was the attack of Wendell Phillips in August 1853, which Douglass reports in *Frederick Douglass' Paper*, August 19, 1853. For Julia Griffiths see the *Liberator* attack, November 18, 1853, and her refutation, December 2, 1853, *ibid.*, December 2, 1853.

67. *Liberator*, December 16, 1853.

68. *Frederick Douglass' Paper*, December 9, 1853.

69. *Ibid.*, November, December 1853, January 1854, *passim*. The quotations are from sentiments adopted by a Providence, Rhode Island, meeting in December, 1853, *ibid.*, December 30, 1853.

denied their inability to understand a movement they well understood as one to gain full freedom for their race. Nonetheless the feud raged on, too well advanced for either party to pull back. In 1857 Garrison refused to speak to Douglass; and by 1860 he declined even to sit on the same platform with this "thoroughly base and selfish" man who was "more and more . . . destitute of every principle of honor, ungrateful to the last degree, and malevolent in spirit." He was, Garrison concluded, "not worthy of respect, confidence, or countenance."[70]

Although similar incidents pale by comparison with the Douglass imbroglio, they define a pattern of white antislavery attitudes discouraging in the extreme to black leaders. Even so faithful a Garrisonian as Robert Purvis was not immune. Scheduled to speak at the twentieth anniversary celebration of the American Anti-Slavery Society in 1854, he was introduced by Garrison to a Philadelphia audience which, in the large, was familiar with him. Nonetheless Garrison told the delegates proudly that Purvis was "one of that proscribed class" of whom many were "held as chattels personal" and others "treated as lepers." With the fatal wit of the humorless, Garrison referred to Purvis' light skin. "If he be a colored man, ay, a black man, who of us is white?"[71] Purvis, understandably galled, responded that "it was no great compliment to him to say that he was honest enough to acknowledge his blood." Then the Rev. Dr. William Furness, Philadelphia's leading Unitarian and a prominent abolitionist, congratulated Purvis for not taking advantage of his wealth and light skin to marry a white woman. Cruelly cut but still cool, Purvis again asserted his pride in "his blood" and "hoped that nothing of the sort would be said again."[72]

Still another round of white insensitivity and outright rancor grew out of James McCune Smith's charges that black speakers had been deliberately excluded from an 1854 lecture series sponsored

70. William L. Garrison to Helen B. Garrison, February 17, 1857, G-BPL. Garrison to Samuel J. May, September 28, 1860, G-BPL.

71. *Liberator*, May 19, 1854.

72. *Ibid.*, May 26, 1854.

by Garrisonians in New York and Boston. For him it was one more indication that abolitionists would not employ blacks in capacities that paid well. Developing this larger point he charged that the American Anti-Slavery Society paid Sydney Gay, white editor of the *National Anti-Slavery Standard*, a $1,200 salary. This drew from the *Standard* a sharp response as much off the subject at hand as Smith's reference to Gay had been. Smith, the *Standard* asserted, was in collusion with the apostate Douglass, in whose paper the charges appeared and who had not been invited to give one of the lectures under discussion. But this did not represent exclusion of Negroes, for William Wells Brown was one of the lecturers. It must then be, the *Standard* concluded, that Smith thought no man was "really 'coloured' who [had] not by faithlessness to old friends proved his heart to be as black as his skin."[73] The real reason for the paucity of Negroes in the lecture series, it concluded, lay in the same apathy which accounted for their limited membership in the American Anti-Slavery Society.

Smith, who was himself dismayed by the small number of black activists, retorted that, even so, it was only the existence of the race which gave the white antislavery movement purpose. Hinting, as whites in reverse so often did about black abolitionists, that their pursuit of the cause was self-serving, he went on to elaborate, "My dark face is one of the *grievances* on which all the pennies are collected: so you *are* my debtor, after all—no blacks, no coppers. . . ."[74] Flailing about in his "Communipaw" column in *Frederick Douglass' Paper*, Smith carried on the dispute for nearly a year. Garrisonians were, he contended, racist, impractical, fickle, and ineffectual. In sum, they were willing to leave blacks "poor, and blind, and bleeding, whilst . . . they . . . followed, first the $100,000 fever, then anti-Sabbath, then something else, and lastly, the Phantom of Disunion."[75]

73. *National Anti-Slavery Standard*, December 23, 1854. The same material is also copied into *Frederick Douglass' Paper*, January 19, 1855.

74. *Frederick Douglass' Paper*, January 19, 1855.

75. *Ibid.*, October 5, 1855.

These incidents and the underlying strains which they illustrated made Negroes, especially in the 1850s, demand either separate race action or new power to make decisions within the antislavery movement. Martin Delany, Pittsburgh physician and editor, who was well on the way to black nationalism in 1853, contended that the only white abolitionist leaders who had ever bothered to consult blacks at all were Gerrit Smith, Garrison, and Hester Moore of Philadelphia. He doubted that things would change for the better.[76] We must not be "mere objects of sympathy," William Watkins, Douglass' assistant editor, concluded in 1855. "We must try the management of the concern awhile [ourselves] , and if after '*twenty-five years*,' . . .we are then no nearer the port of our destination than today, we will relinquish to those, who by virtue of their superior endowments, are more competent than we. . . ."[77]

Still more insistent was James McCune Smith. The "battle against caste and Slavery . . . ,' he said in 1855, "is emphatically our battle; no one else can fight it for us, and with God's help we must fight it ourselves."[78] Even Remond, whom Smith had earlier lumped with Purvis and William Wells Brown as "*yellow* men"[79] because of their loyalty to the Garrisonian faction, admitted that the white abolitionists did not fully understand the problem. "There were certain questions," the *Liberator* quoted him as saying, "upon which the judgment of the colored man was the best, because the peculiarity of his position better fitted him to understand them."[80]

That was the point which white abolitionists either could not or would not grasp. And because they did not grasp it, they never permitted their black fellow workers to shape the crusade to peculiar race needs. Consequently those fellow workers had little choice but to fashion their own antislavery movement. By the

76. *Ibid.*, May 6, 1853.
77. *Ibid.*, February 9, 1855.
78. *Ibid.*, May 18, 1855.
79. *Ibid.*, January 19, 1855.
80. *Liberator*, December 28, 1855.

1850s their disillusionment was overt. But it had been building slowly over the years. As early as the 1830s and more positively in the 1840s, many Negro spokesmen began to pursue goals through separate and independent action. In their own conventions, through their own press, in race-oriented societies they pressed, even while they cooperated with their white brethren, for that full manhood of which the abolition of slavery was but the first step.

PART III

The Means to Advance the Race

NOT ONLY did free Negroes support the new antislavery movement, they also organized separate black institutions to unify the race, fight prejudice, and improve their economic position. In conventions, as well as in newspapers and other publications, they attacked racial segregation and the denial of civil rights and economic opportunity, which white abolitionists so often ignored or considered only of secondary importance. Thus they developed alternative ways to extend black freedom, both in the North and the South.

6. ESTABLISHING THE ARGUMENTS AND INSTITUTIONS

CLEARLY NOT all black goals could have been achieved by working within the general antislavery movement, even if relationships between black and white participants had been more smooth. Thus as race-based churches and mutual-aid societies had emerged very early to counteract prejudice and provide economic and social security for free Negroes, so in the thirty years before the Civil War, other separate institutions developed with similar goals. Their racially exclusive nature, as well as their being the means by which their members and supporters sought to change the conditions of their own group rather than shape the conditions of another, necessarily set them apart from those predominately Northern and white reform societies whose major efforts were directed at blacks in the South. Furthermore, black speakers, writers, and editors not only encouraged separate race action but sought also to build pride, dignity, and a sense of worth among their audience. But, because whites were the numerical majority and exercised economic and political power, blacks also had to speak to them, to challenge their prejudices and persuade them to open those opportunities which free blacks needed to achieve the goals of their group.

These self-conscious but diverse race goals implied some internal conflicts. On the one hand Negroes had to learn to respect themselves and their race, to act independently to improve their lot, and to shape their own institutions—press, schools, churches, businesses, and even antislavery societies. On the other hand, they had to demonstrate their similarity to whites, physiologically as well as mentally and morally. Contradictory as these positions might seem, they proved reciprocal more often than not. Pride in race was seen not as a way to separate blacks from whites but rather to bring them together in equality. Much black press coverage sought to mold white attitudes. And reform conventions of whatever sort tried always, as one of their goals, to change whites' opinion of blacks and thereby induce them to open to blacks the full possibilities of American life, which whites largely controlled. Thus much of distinctive black abolition and civil rights activity not only complemented white antislavery, it also offered a vehicle by which the Negroes hoped to achieve the full promise of American life.

To these ends blacks published speeches, pamphlets, and newspapers. First among the tasks of such publications was shattering race stereotypes which fed white prejudice and, by their prevalence, subverted black self-respect. Frederick Douglass well illustrated the problem in an analogy with portraiture. Customarily, he noted, white artists portrayed blacks first as Negroes and only secondarily as individuals because they "have adopted a theory respecting the distinctive features of negro physiognomy. . . .The temptation to make the likeness of the negro, rather than of the man, is very strong. . . ."[1]

White theories not only about the Negro's appearance but about his morality, physical structure, and intellectual capacity shaped the racism which marked the dominant culture. Political egalitarianism was confined to whites only. Departures from economic equality were most spectacularly masked by Jacksonian attacks on monopoly but were also more subtly veiled in racist illusions that guaranteed even the poorest white some sense of his own superiority.[2] This very appeal, of course, fed white, and especially

1. *Liberator,* April 20, 1849.
2. George M. Frederickson, *The Black Image in the White Mind: The Debate on Afro-American Character and Destiny, 1817-1914* (New York: Harper & Row, 1971), 90-91, 94-95. Leonard L. Richards, *"Gentlemen of Property and Standing," Anti-Abolition Mobs in Jacksonian America* (New York: Oxford University Press, 1970), 85, 129, 151, 154. Richard Bardolph, "Social Origins of Distinguished Negroes, 1770-1865," *Journal of Negro History,* XL (July 1955), 230.

immigrant, antipathy for economic competition with blacks. During the 1840s and 1850s immigrants threatened the jobs of blacks working as artisans, mechanics, and even barbers. Caught in the pressures of population growth, immigrant competition, and the tensions of urban life, all groups within the black community increasingly found themselves economically squeezed out, constantly pushed lower on the socioeconomic ladder.[3]   Nor, as studies of antiabolition and race riots make clear, was racial tension confined to the poor and middling classes. "Gentlemen of Property and Standing," fearful of the political unrest and economic dislocation which radical antislavery portended, either joined or led antiabolitionist mobs whose venom spilled over in attacks on the persons, homes, and churches of urban black people.[4]

Concomitant with white racial unity at a time when growing economic differences among classes conflicted with egalitarian rhetoric was the evolution of a racist ideology. Both North and South produced writers who publicized a new ethnology designed to explain the physiological, mental, and spiritual inferiority of blacks. Racial differences in cranial structure and facial angles were exploited to link Negroes more closely to apes than to Caucasians. Other theories asserted that Africans had never developed a high civilization but had languished in savagery, paganism, licentiousness, and cannibalism.[5]

Related to these ethnological and biological theories were charges of specific patterns of Afro-American behavior which presumably proved them in practice. None more consistently sparked vigorous black refutation than evidence offered to prove

3. Herman D. Bloch, *The Circle of Discrimination: An Economic and Social Study of the Black Man in New York* (New York: New York University Press, 1969), 26-34; Theodore Hershberg, "Free Blacks in Antebellum Philadelphia: A Study of Ex-Slaves, Freeborn, and Socioeconomic Decline," *Journal of Social History,* V (Winter, 1971-1972), 183-209.
4. Richards, *Gentlemen of Property and Standing,* 85, 129, 151, 154.
5. Frederickson, *Black Image,* particularly pages 49-50, 71, 74-75. William Stanton, *The Leopard's Spots: Scientific Attitudes Toward Race in America, 1815-1859* (Chicago: University of Chicago Press, 1960) covers the subject in detail.

that American Negroes were morally deficient and more criminally inclined than whites. Prison statistics did seem to lend credence to the belief. The 1827 Prison Discipline Society's report, for instance, showed that, although blacks in the Northern states constituted between one seventy-fourth of the total population in Massachusetts and one thirteenth in New Jersey, they constituted between one sixth and one third of the entire prison population. In Massachusetts, Connecticut, New York, and Pennsylvania, according to the figures, blacks were more than ten times as likely to be convicted for crime and imprisoned as their total proportion of the state population would indicate.[6]

Blacks refuted the conclusions drawn from these figures. While some challenged the statistics, others accepted them and addressed themselves to their explanation. One of the latter, Russell Parrott, found the origins of that "looseness of morals" in the state of slavery from which these criminals had come and in the temptations of the environment in which they were forced to live. Crime and vice were the inevitable consequences of urban slums.[7] A *Freedom's Journal* editorial developed the point, attributing the high crime rate to antisocial behavior engendered by poverty and prejudice. By contrast white crimes were "most generally . . . premeditated and vicious," the result of personal evil rather than environmental pressures. Therefore, the *Journal* concluded, the higher prison rate for Negroes did "not prove them more subject to crime, or their characters more debased."[8]

Some years later, in 1836, Thomas Van Rensselaer took up the same theme. In answer to the charge of New York's City recorder, Richard Riker, that blacks contributed disproportionately to the city's crime rate, he rehearsed the usual arguments about slums and poverty. But he also added that blacks had been deprived of the education necessary for them to earn decent livings and to understand the laws. Consequently, when they were brought into

6. *Condition of the American Colored Population, and of the Colony at Liberia* (Boston: Pierce & Parker, 1833), 10-11.

7. *Freedom's Journal*, July 27, 1827.

8. *Ibid.*, March 30, 1827.

court they seldom had defense counsel to lead them successfully through the intricacies of courtroom procedure. Little wonder, then, that so many ran afoul of the law and were convicted for offenses customarily forgiven others.[9]

Samuel Cornish went still further, probing the motives behind white exposes of black crime. The practice of "searching out instances of degradation and crime among our people, and publishing them in contrast with our white population generally," he wrote, had falsified the record by singling out Negroes for special publicity. "If we must be brought into comparison," he suggested, "let it be with those in the same walks of society—any other method is ungenerous and calculated to do harm." Not only did it feed white stereotypes but it ate away at the self-assurance of introspective blacks who blamed their "more than ordinary degradation" on race.[10]

Virtually all black commentators agreed that it was not race but the conditions of slavery, prejudice, urban slums, and poverty which made Negroes appear more inherently criminal and brutal than whites. And for those conditions, as David Ruggles asserted, whites were directly responsible. That Negroes were a "degraded and ignorant" people, Ruggles readily admitted; but the fault was not their own. Whites had created the environment of degradation, ignorance, and crime which made them so. There was no evidence, he flatly asserted, "anatomical or physical," "to warrant the *charge*, that [blacks were] but little above brutes."[11]

Despite such vigorous refutation, the stereotypes were embodied in the very names which identified the race, and for a while blacks attempted to escape the attributions by changing the names. "Why do our friends, as well as our enemies," one writer asked in 1831, "call us 'negroes'? We feel it to be a term of reproach, and could wish our friends would call us by some other name."[12]

9. *Liberator,* November 12, 1836.
10. *Colored American,* March 25, 1837. During its early years the *Liberator* had made a practice of reporting crimes committed by blacks but not of giving any general crime statistics or averages for comparison.
11. David Ruggles, *Extinguisher Extinguished* (New York: David Ruggles, 1834), 41.
12. *Liberator,* June 4, 1831.

Agreement upon an appropriate nomenclature, however, defied attainment. Throughout the 1830s and even after the debate raged. Should they call themselves colored people or Negroes, blacks or Africans? Or should they avoid all race designations?[13] When Garrisonians Whipper and Purvis pressed the Fifth Annual Convention for the Improvement of the Free People of Color to adopt a resolution to give up "as far as possible" the use of the word colored, the convention chose to organize a society with absolutely no race designation, calling it only the American Moral Reform Society.[14]

That action was, however, atypical. As race consciousness and activism grew, the major question became one of how best to use specific nomenclature to stimulate race pride and identity. Charles Ray, for example, suggested that when a Negro did something praiseworthy he should be identified as "colored" but when the reference was derogatory, no race designation should be given. But such tergiversations went nowhere; and in 1848 Garnet, by then well known as a militant, urged blacks to stop debating terminology and get on with substantive antislavery work.[15]

Nonetheless the implications of the long debate bore fruit in the 1850s when black speakers increasingly took pride in their color and in other distinctive physical characteristics. Mulatto Henry Bibb wrote in his autobiography that whites had not only robbed him of his "labor and liberty," but had very nearly stripped him of his "dark complexion."[16] Ward took such open and great delight in his own rich blackness that Douglass thought he almost exceeded the bounds of "good taste."[17] Late in the 1850s, Boston lawyer and dentist John S. Rock anticipated the twentieth-century

13. See, for example, *Liberator*, July 16, 1831; and *Colored American*, March 4, 1837.

14. *Liberator*, August 1, 1835. Convention for the Improvement of the Free People of Colour, *Minutes of the Fifth Annual Convention...1835* (orig. publ. 1835. New York: Arno Press, 1969), 15.

15. *Colored American*, November 3, 1838. H. H. Garnet, *Past and Present Condition, and Destiny of the Coloured Race,. . .* (Troy: J. C. Kneeland, 1848), 19-20.

16. H. Bibb, *Narrative of the Life and Adventures of Henry Bibb. . .* (New York: The Author, 1849), 49.

17. *Frederick Douglass' Paper*, June 3, 1853.

slogan that black is beautiful. In public lectures he contrasted the "fine tough muscular system, the beautiful, rich color, the full broad features, and the gracefully frizzled hair of the negro, with the delicate physical organization, wan color, sharp features and lank hair" of the white man, and concluded that "when the white man was created, nature was pretty well exhausted."[18]

Although positive emphasis upon color helped generate race pride, it did lamentably little to counteract the denigration implicit and explicit in the white man's perception and use of color terms. To get at the assumptions and conclusions which tradition and contemporary ethnology propagated, blacks presented a variety of arguments. One of the most persistent was the attribution of color and other distinctive physiological characteristics to environmental origins. As early as the late 1820s, John Russwurm espoused the theory linking skin color and hair texture directly to climate.[19] Subsequently physician James McCune Smith elaborated a much more complex version of Russwurm's theory. Locating the key to stages of civilization in the way in which men of various cultures utilized food and air, he explained character attributes by a much greater variety of environmental forces.[20]

Both Smith's and Russwurm's arguments were in harmony with theories well known to white Americans of the period, and they were widely propagated by Pennington, Allen, and others.[21] Yet, although they emphasized the equal excellence if not the actual identity of the races, they failed adequately to account for the inferior position of blacks in nineteenth-century America. For many, the problem was self-evident: Slavery, both immediately and in its long-range effects, was the factor which set American Negroes apart and degraded them.

18. *Liberator*, March 12, 1858. Some, however, like William Allen, showed a clear preference for white attributes. See his *The American Prejudice Against Color* . . . (London: W. & F. G. Cash, 1853), 72.

19. *Freedom's Journal*, May 9, 1828.

20. *Anglo-African Magazine*, January, 1859, 5-9.

21. See, for example, James W. C. Pennington, *A Textbook of the Origin and History &c. of Colored People* (Hartford: L. Skinner, Printer, 1841), 91-96; and report of a lecture by Allen, *Liberator*, August 30, 1850.

Cornish and Wright explored the most evident links between slavery and prejudice in their detailed analysis of emancipation in the British West Indies. Writing rather prematurely in 1840, they concluded that as soon as slavery had ended there, prejudice was "on the wane" and "men began to be respected according to their worth."[22] The experience of free Negroes in the North, however, belied this easy formula, as William Wells Brown pointed out in 1847. Neither prejudice nor slavery balked at having Negro waiters in close proximity to whites; but let those same blacks sit down at table with whites and the cry at once went up, "Odor! niggers! nastiness!"[23] The heritage of slavery had left the black man a menial. In that role he was acceptable; in others which implied equality he was not. Caste, so Smith asserted in his ethnological study, was the fruit of slavery, which excluded even free blacks from all opportunities for advancement. "The inferiority . . . is not by color," Douglass mused ironically, "but by condition. With a hundred thousand dollars . . . I could make a very black man white."[24]

Fundamental for most antebellum black spokesmen was the belief that there were no essential differences among the races of mankind. If this was so, it followed that miscegenation was both natural and logical. Yet to accept nature and logic was dangerous on two counts. Amalgamation, as it was called, threatened whites at their most emotionally vulnerable spot. Their "hideous fear of amalgamation" aside, however, miscegenation still contradicted the imperatives of race pride. What that pride demanded for separate identity, the struggle for equality and acceptance in general American society undercut. The issue generated neither any commonly accepted solutions nor even very much clear-cut debate.

22. Samuel E. Cornish and Theodore S. Wright, *The Colonization Scheme Considered, in Its Rejection by the Colored People—in Its Tendency to Uphold Caste—in Its Unfitness for Christianizing and Civilizing the Aborigines of Africa, and for Putting a Stop to the African Slave Trade . . .* (Newark: Printed by Aaron Guest, 1840), 9.

23. *Liberator*, July 30, 1847.

24. *Frederick Douglass' Paper*, July 22, 1853. For similar observations see William Wells Brown to William L. Garrison, October 12, 1849, *Liberator*, November 2, 1849; and James McCune Smith in *Anglo-African Magazine*, January, 1859, 16-17.

Cornish, a light man with one son able to pass as white, stood half-heartedly against amalgamation, opposing it if it weakened race pride. At the same time he frequently spoke with approval of the advantages which accrued to light-skinned Negroes. Even militants sidestepped the issue. Ruggles said that personally he hoped intermarriage would never come, though in principle he saw nothing inherently wrong with it. It worked well in South America and, save for public opinion, it would work in the United States. The exception was, of course, the substance of the problem, but Ruggles preferred to shift the argument to equality in other areas and ignore the question of miscegenation.[25] Similarly Garnet refused to discuss it, calling it a dead issue. "It is too late to make a successful attempt to separate the black and white people in the New World," he wrote in 1848. *"This western world is destined to be filled with a mixed race."*[26] For him this irreversible fact signified no diminution of black pride, since the process depended upon Negroes' having become fully rooted in America. Paola Brown, on the other hand, treated the issue as a matter of individual domesticity by agreeing with David Walker that the black who marries a white woman will be twice a slave for she will treat him like a "NIGER."[27] That Brown also urged the repeal of antimiscegenation laws only confirms the one persistent point of agreement which ran through the discussion—that no legal obstacle should block interracial marriages.

These discussions, while they touched on the raw edge of white racial and sexual fears, did not come to grips with the underlying nature of racism. By contrast, blacks grappled rigorously with the

---

25. *Colored American,* July 29, 1837. Ruggles, *Extinguisher Extinguished,* 10-17. In 1852 Cornish still preferred light skin, for it meant that the process of assimilation was advancing; see *Frederick Douglass' Paper,* February 5, 1852.

26. Garnet, *Past and Present Condition,* 25.

27. Paola Brown, *Address Intended to be Delivered in the City Hall, Hamilton, February 7, 1851, on the Subject of Slavery* (Hamilton: Printed for the Author, 1851), 8-9. David Walker, *Walker's Appeal in four Articles; Together with a Preamble, to the Coloured Citizens of the World, but in Particular, and very Expressly, to Those of the United States of America* . . . (3rd ed. Boston: David Walker, 1830. Reprint, New York: Arno Press, 1969), 19.

explicitly intellectual arguments used to justify white America's endemic hostility to darker races. In so doing they had to attack popular religious beliefs of the day which justified slavery from biblical text, contending particularly that Africans, as the descendants of Ham, were destined by God to be the hewers of wood and the drawers of water for other races; or that Africans were heirs to the curse which God had placed on Canaan, the son of Ham.

Pennington, in his *Origin and History of the Colored People*, proposed that American race prejudice glorified neither God nor man but was rather, in generating hypocrisy, "blindness of mind," "insubordination, bloodshed, and murder," fundamentally un-Christian. More specifically he argued that Negroes were not "the seed of Cain as the stupid say," for all Cain's descendants perished in the flood. In sum, he concluded, an honest and honorable reading of the Bible provided no endorsement either of enslavement or of discrimination against Negroes.[28]

Pennington's fellow cleric Garnet elaborated the theme still more, saying that African descent from Ham only proved the common origins of all mankind, since Asians and Europeans were the descendants of Noah's other sons. Thus he pursued the biblical route to demonstrate identical roots for all humankind and to answer charges that Negroes were a separate biological order.[29] Others, making the same point, pitted the Bible against science. Russwurm thought that the creation of Adam was the origin of all mankind and rejected evolutionary arguments of Linnaeus, Buffon, and Helvetius, who taught that "our primogenitor is the Monkey"

28. Pennington, *Origin and History of the Colored People*, 77, 7-18.
29. [Wilson Armistead], *Calumny Refuted, by Facts from Liberia; with Extracts from the Inaugural Address of the Coloured President Roberts . . . and Extracts from a Discourse by H. H. Garnett . . .*(New York: W. Harned, 1848), 39. Outside of clerical ranks probably the most convincing argument was that which stressed that Christianity condemned all forms of oppression. It was from this point, in fact, that Pennington had started. See, for example, *Northern Star and Freeman's Advocate*, January 2, 1843; and Samuel R. Ward to the Christian Anti-Slavery Convention, [April 1850] in its Minutes, 66-68, reproduced in *Journal of Negro History*, X (October 1925), 755.

as he did Erasmus Darwin, who said that "the Oyster is the favoured animal."[30]

James McCune Smith preferred using reason and his medical training to attack prevailing scientific theories which identified different races as different species. Disputing the selection of evidence and measuring techniques used in experiments reported in an appendix to Lyell's popular *Lectures on Geology*, Smith challenged the relevance of comparative craniology, denying that skull measurements were the sole criteria by which to determine race characteristics or that they even indicated mental capacity.[31]

A much better way to explore the intellectual and creative abilities of Negroes was to turn to the history of the race and develop from its high points an awareness of the accomplishments of the past. Important as this was in answering white aspersions, it was equally important for developing self-respect. Black writers and speakers determined to restore the roots torn up in the forced migration from Africa and to recall the experiences forgotten in prevailing American histories. That there was a conscious effort to develop black history was born out in the persistent complaints against John Russwurm who, as editor of *Freedom's Journal*, failed to write about ancient Africa. If "we have produced some worthy sons of such [slave] sires [as our fathers], ought we not to have the benefit of these creditable facts?" Samuel Ward was still asking thirty years later. "If we do not vindicate ourselves, who will do it for us?"[32]

One of the functions of black history, whether ancient or modern, African or American, was to furnish models to inspire future action. Lecturers and writers therefore delved into the past for heroes and heroines of varying sorts. Garnet, Ward, Thomas Jinnings, and William Allen, among others, all explored the ancient prestige of Africa from the Queen of Sheba to Hannibal to

30. *Freedom's Journal*, April 18, 1828.
31. *Anglo-African Magazine*, August, 1859, 225ff.
32. *Freedom's Journal*, December 5, 1828, Samuel Ringgold Ward, *Autobiography of a Fugitive Negro* ... (London: J. Snow, 1855), 270.

Cleopatra to the early church fathers Cyprian and Augustine. Similarly writers and orators expounded on the exploits of Toussaint L'Ouverture in the Haitian revolution and on black participation in the American Revolution and the War of 1812.[33]

All these were efforts to counteract the facelessness of black America which William Wilson described in an "Ethiop" column in the *Frederick Douglass' Paper* in 1853. "At present, what we find around us, either in art or literature, is made so to press upon us, that we depreciate, we despise, we almost hate ourselves, and all that favors us. Well may we scoff at black skins and woolly heads, since every model set before us for admiration, has pallid face and flaxen head, or emanations thereof."[34] Only with a history of their own would scoffing turn to pride.

Not only did race spokesmen seek to change attitudes, they also sought vehicles for common action. They therefore sought ways to link Northern free Negroes who, although concentrated in urban centers, were widely separated in various states and often isolated in their separate enclaves. If more than local concerns were to unite them, they needed efficient printed communication. *Freedom's Journal* and the *Rights of All* early tried to meet that need, but they failed to attract the subscribers necessary to sustain them. As a result, during the first years of black activism, occasional pamphlets were the mainstay of their efforts. The minutes and proceedings of the various Negro conventions provided, during the 1830s, the staple of that literature. Overshadowing them all in drama and importance was David Walker's *Appeal*, written in 1829 and published in Boston in 1830.

Walker, born a freeman in North Carolina in 1785, had moved to Boston as a young man and become a clothes dealer. Although he was active during the 1820s in the Methodist Church and in the

33. See, for example, Garnet, *Past and Present Condition*, 11-12; Ward, *Autobiography*, 87; *Freedom's Journal*, April 4, 1828; *North Star*, June 16, 1848; *Liberator*, October 29, 1852; *Freedom's Journal*, April 6, 1827; *Liberator*, August 9, 1839; and American and Foreign Anti-Slavery Society, *Annual Report . . . 1850*, 22-23.
34. *Frederick Douglass' Paper*, March 11, 1853.

Massachusetts General Colored Association, nothing from this period suggests the vigor of his *Appeal,* published shortly before the first issue of the *Liberator* appeared.[35]

In spite of his minimal education and a dense and rambling writing style, Walker developed an argument which both frightened whites who read it and pressed its black readers to change their bearings. He described American Negroes as "the *most wretched, degraded* and abject set of beings that ever *lived* since the world began," enslaved as they were by white men and treated like *"Monkeys* or *Orang-Outangs."*[36] The cause of this treatment, he continued, was greed, which drove whites to exploit blacks either as slaves or as free labor, employing them in menial jobs like barbering, shoeshining, and domestic service, which could never bring them happiness or security. Economically trapped and socially ill-treated, blacks were also absolutely deprived of political power and prestige.[37] "Can our condition be any worse? Can it be more mean and abject?" he asked his fellows. Caught at the very bottom, they were in a position where defiance could cost them nothing and might possibly prove beneficial. So he counseled resistance. "If there are any changes, will they not be for the better, though they may appear for the worse at first? Can [the whites] get us any lower?"[38]

The beginning of freedom, Walker explained, was the fight against slavery. Free Negroes in the North must assist their brothers in bonds, teach them the meaning of freedom, and refute white charges that black men were inferior. So far, however, action had

35. Donald M. Jacobs, "David Walker: Boston Race Leader, 1825-1830," *Essex Institute Historical Collections,* CVII (January, 1971), 94-107. "Leo," a black correspondent from Philadelphia, doubted that Walker could have written so sophisticated a work and implied in his letter to the editor that Bishop Richard Allen had written it; see *Liberator,* January 29, 1831. The Boston *Daily Courier* also challenged Walker's authorship and charged that he was covering for a New Yorker; see Jacobs, "David Walker," 106.

36. David Walker, *Walker's Appeal in Four Articles,* 17, 20.

37. *Ibid.,* 24, 41, 18.

38. *Ibid.,* 12. In 1828 Walker was tried and acquitted for receiving stolen goods and was thereby convinced of the inutility of white legal systems for blacks; see Jacobs, "David Walker," 101.

been blocked by apathy. When blacks had organized, it had been in benevolent societies and fraternal organizations, in Masonic lodges, temperance societies, and Sabbath associations, which did nothing to end slavery. Not only did they dissipate their energy on trivia, but they curried favor with their *"natural enemies"* and in failing to stand united against whites actually strengthened slavery's hold.[39] They could, Walker predicted optimistically, produce their own Hannibal; but he also cautioned that the first Hannibal had suffered defeat because Carthage did not unite behind him. Divided, apathetic, and passive. American blacks confirmed the popular image that they were "ignorant, abject, servile, and mean." White men know, Walker charged with blistering directness, that "we are too servile to assert our rights as men—or they would not fool with us as they do." Even slaves, he taunted, "are too servile, they love to have Masters too well!!!!!!"[40]

There was but one way out in Walker's view: militant action. "The man who will stand still and let another murder him, is worse than an infidel, and if he has common sense, ought not to be pitied."[41] There was no reason why black resistance, once it occurred, should fail, for millions would then prefer death to slavery. Indeed, he predicted that Negroes could achieve self-government within the present United States. "Our sufferings will come to an *end*, in spite of all the Americans this side of *eternity*," he prophesied. " 'Every dog must have its day,' the American's is coming to an end."[42] Though he concluded his *Appeal* by calling for white action to end slavery and open the way for future amity between the races,[43] Walker never really contradicted his premise that whites were brutal, murderous, and perfidious. There was, consequently, no mistaking his message. They "know well if we are *men*—and there is a secret monitor in their hearts which tells them we are—they know, I say, if we *are* men, and see them treating us

39. *Ibid.,* 40, 52-53, quotation 21.
40. *Ibid.,* 30, quotations 74-75.
41. *Ibid.,* 37; see also 23.
42. *Ibid.,* 40, quotations 26.
43. *Ibid.,* 80, 86.

in the manner they do, that there can be nothing in our hearts but death alone, for them; notwithstanding we may appear cheerful, when we see them murdering our dear mothers and wives, because we cannot help ourselves."[44]

When he began the *Liberator*, Garrison proclaimed that he would be heard and proceeded to shock the sensibilities of white America. Yet the bravado of Walker's *Appeal* shocked even Garrison. The *Appeal*, he cautioned, was too violent and irreverent in its "spirit and tendency" and sought vengeance, which was the prerogative of the Lord.[45] With such a response from the most sympathetic of whites, the black response to Walker's subsequent sudden disappearance was not surprising. There were rumors of foul play, perhaps precipitated by a Southern price on his head.[46] No one really knows what happened to Walker, but of his *Appeal* there can be no doubt. It was a clarion call at the time and became a legacy of central importance to Afro-Americans.

In stark contrast to the *Appeal* was a pamphlet published eight years later and marked by its tone of utter despair and alienation. Hosea Easton's *Treatise on the Intellectual Character, and Civil and Political Conditions of the Colored People of the U. States,* though less widely discussed, was equally provocative in its argument. Challenging one of the oldest justifications for slavery—that bringing Africans into contact with Europeans had civilized and elevated them—Easton denied that Africa was an uncivilized territory and its inhabitants barbarians. He argued that its civilization had been, before Europeans destroyed it, vastly superior to that of the destroyers. It was their forced exile in America which had debased Africans' character, intellect, and physique. Their reduction to slavery as well as their remoteness from their native environment had cost them their inherent superiority. Americanized Negroes were, he argued, inferior not only to their free ancestors in Africa but to newly imported slaves as well.[47]

44. *Ibid.,* 72.
45. *Liberator,* January 8, 1831.
46. *Ibid.,* January 22, 1831.
47. Hosea Easton, *A Treatise on the Intellectual Character, and Civil and Political Conditions of the Colored People of the U. States* (Boston: I.

The tragedy which this loss implied was still more acute because Americanization offered them no compensations. It was purely a negative process, Easton thought, which stripped the Negro of his African identity but provided him no substitute. Alienated from both cultures, American slaves had been reified into objects of avarice and foci of exploitation. Furthermore prejudice and discrimination by white Americans successfully blocked every channel whereby, whether free or slave, they might seek justice and decency.[48] Neither constitution nor statute law protected them; legal guarantees, like the rest of America, were for whites only. "There can be," Easton concluded, "no appeals made in the name of the laws of the country, of philanthropy, or humanity, or religion, that is *[sic]* capable of drawing forth any thing but the retort—*you are a negro!*"[49]

Even suppose, Easton hypothesized, that a free black managed, by dint of hard work and good fortune, to achieve economic independence and prove himself a man of rectitude and piety. It would avail him nothing. Prejudice would deny him effective freedom of thought, speech, and movement; and in death as in life it would grant him no greater recognition. "Let them seek a decent burial for their departed friend in the church yard—and they are immediately made to feel that they are as a carcass destined to be preyed upon by the eagles of persecution. Thus are they followed from life's dawn to death's doom."[50] Even the promises of the Christian afterlife eluded Negroes, for as a people they were excluded, almost universally, from adequate religious training. Thus they were totally isolated. "They belong to no people, race, or nation; subjects of no government—citizens of no country— scattered surplus remnants of two races, and of different nations— severed into individuality—rendered a mass of broken fragments, thrown to and fro, by the boisterous passions of this and other

---

Knapp, 1837), in Dorothy B. Porter, ed. *Negro Protest Pamphlets* ... (New York: Arno Press, 1969), 18-19, 21, 25.
48. *Ibid.*, 42, 38.
49. *Ibid.*, 32-33.
50. *Ibid.*, 40.

ungodly nations."[51] From this alienation Easton saw no escape. The only action he proposed was a powerless appeal to whites to give up their murderous ways.[52] Thus he was both more and less desperate than David Walker.

As provocative as the *Appeal* and *Treatise* were, single pamphlets of this sort did not provide the continuity either to unify free Northern blacks or provoke them to action. Only a regularly issued and widely read press could meet those needs. At first the *Liberator* served this function. Staunchly supported by James Forten in Philadelphia, John B. Vashon and George Cary in Pittsburgh, and Theodore Wright in New York, as well as by the Massachusetts black community, it drew most of its subscribers and most of its agents from the ranks of free Northern Negroes.[53]

But the *Liberator* was not a race paper. Its major energies were devoted to expounding the theory and tactics of Garrisonianism; and in time it had little room for items of specific interest to blacks. Still, it was not until 1837 that a paper emerged with the mission, stability, and popularity of the earlier *Freedom's Journal*. In January of that year the *Weekly Advocate* appeared; by March it had become the *Colored American*, owned by Philip Bell and edited by Samuel Cornish. Subsidized at first by Arthur Tappan, it nevertheless was specifically dedicated to serving the interests of Northern blacks and establishing effective communication among them. In the spirit of the times, the *Colored American* devoted most of its space to "the moral improvement and melioration" of blacks, to creating race pride and a sense of identity, and to refuting white misconceptions and prejudices about Negroes.[54]

51. *Ibid.*, 36-37.
52. *Ibid.*, 49.
53. Donald M. Jacobs, "William Lloyd Garrison's *Liberator* and Boston's Blacks, 1830-1865," *New England Quarterly*, XLIV (June, 1971), 259-277. James Forten to William L. Garrison, May 21, 1831, G-BPL. George Cary to [Garrison], June 6, 1831, G-BPL. *Liberator*, March 31, 1832 and May 28, 1836. Convention for the Improvement of the Free People of Color, *Minutes of the Fifth Annual ...1835* (orig. publ. 1835. New York: Arno Press, 1969), 13.
54. Lewis Tappan, *Life of Arthur Tappan* (New York: Hurd & Houghton, 1870), 185. *Colored American*, March 4, 1837. Quotation from *Weekly Advocate*, January 7, 1837.

Editor Cornish urged his readers to support the paper so "that by it our people may be reached, their minds cultivated, their habits changed, and their moral and religious character raised and made uniform."[55] High hopes and exhortation were unfortunately not enough for a paper launched in the year of a major panic and depression. For the four years it survived, its financing was always precarious. In June 1837 it had only nine hundred subscribers; Cornish went unpaid, and Bell's books were in the red. In November, after a reorganization, a committee of "colored gentlemen" came to Bell's assistance and undertook to raise funds to guarantee the paper's stability. Five months later subscriptions had not increased, and in June 1838 a second reorganization occurred. At the end of that year Cornish was still unpaid and eager to transfer much of the editorial burden to James McCune Smith. The following June they both resigned. Amazingly the paper survived for two more years under the editorship of Charles Ray, and died finally only in 1841.[56]

Fundamentally the *Colored American* failed to generate, in the community it served, the enthusiasm necessary to maintain it. The fault was not wholly the editors' and publishers', however, for every other black newspaper of the period suffered the same fate. Perhaps it was the poverty of potential subscribers, who could not afford to buy nonessentials. Perhaps illiteracy reduced the possible readership below the level necessary to sustain a press. Perhaps the tendency to launch papers without a backlog of resources augured sure failure. Certainly these were among the reasons for the minimal success of the black press during the antebellum period.

Their lack of success betokened no absence of will, as was attested by the numbers of papers planned and even issued in the following years. In 1838 in Philadelphia the American Moral Reform Society undertook to publish the *National Reformer*. In New York City, at the same time, the equally ephemeral *Champion*

55. *Colored American,* March 18, 1837. The paper clearly addressed itself to free blacks and paid very little direct attention to the issue of antislavery.

56. *Ibid., passim.* See, particularly, issues for November 11, 1837, June 2, 1838, and June 22, 1839.

of Equal Rights was proposed. And in Boston, Benjamin Roberts attempted to issue an antislavery paper "edited & published entirely by colored men."[57]

With somewhat more success David Ruggles launched the *Mirror of Liberty* in 1838. Utilizing his reputation as leader of the New York Vigilance Committee and the author of various pamphlets, he set out to publish an independent quarterly. The *Mirror*, according to its prospectus, was "consecrated to the genius of liberty," would be "trammelled by no sect, association or company of men," and would expose those evils which blocked the progress of "a scattered, peeled and downtrodden people."[58] Although it promised to avoid "long and theoretical disquisitions on abstract questions" in favor of disclosing the "errors which have evidently proved snares" to black advancement in America,[59] the *Mirror of Liberty* was almost as ephemeral as its fellows. After four issues in two years it died, largely the victim of Ruggles' making it an organ for his personal feuds.

The failures of the 1830s did not dampen the desire to establish a strong press. Various groups, among them the national conventions held in Buffalo in 1843 and in Troy in 1847, devoted considerable effort and debate to the question of establishing newspapers. "Circumstances make it absolutely necessary, that we should have a press of our own," the Pennsylvania state convention of 1841 announced, expressing the general sentiment.[60] If, as the delegates at Troy thought, education was the central vehicle for advancement, then "a press [was] needed to keep this very fact before the whole people, in order that all [might] constantly and unitedly labor in . . . the right direction." If there were better ways to improve the race, they only made a press "more necessary,

57. Benjamin F. Roberts to Amos A. Phelps, June 19, 1838, P-BPL. See also *Colored American,* September 22 and November 10, 1838 for the other two attempts. Roberts, in his venture, hoped to set up a printshop where he would not only issue a newspaper but employ black apprentices.

58. *Liberator,* July 27, 1838.

59. *Mirror of Liberty,* July, 1838.

60. State Convention of the Colored Freemen of Pennsylvania, *Proceedings of . . . Held in Pittsburgh, on the 23rd, 24th and 25th of August, 1841* . . . (Pittsburgh: Matthew M. Grant, 1841), 13.

inasmuch as it [would] afford a field in which the relative importance of the various means [might] be discussed and settled in the hearing of the whole people, and to the profit of all."[61]

The convention talk and planning came to little. The newspapers established in the 1840s were the results of individual efforts and as ephemeral as most of those similarly produced had been in the previous decade. In 1842, for example, Allen and Garnet published, for a short while, the *National Watchman* in Troy. The next year Garnet undertook the *United States Clarion*, a paper primarily aimed at the moral and religious uplift of his Troy congregation. Across the Hudson River in Albany Stephen Myers launched his temperance and race paper, the *Northern Star and Freeman's Advocate*, which had a somewhat longer if sporadic career. In 1842 the *Herald of Justice* was published in New Haven; the *People's Press*, in New York City; and the Methodist-sponsored *Zion's Wesleyan*, in Boston. Three years later Ward began the politically oriented *True American* in Cortland, New York, which in 1850 he melded with Myers' *Northern Star* to form the *Impartial Citizen*, published first in Syracuse and then in Boston. More Liberty party than race papers, Ward's ventures were comparatively more enduring and successful than either Martin Delany's *Mystery*, published in Pittsburgh; the *Colored Citizen*, sponsored by a group in Cincinnati; or Thomas Van Rensselaer's *Ram's Horn* of New York.[62]

Not until Douglass established the *North Star* in December 1847, was there much real hope for a vital national press. Douglass had substantial financial backing from English supporters, a wide and distinguished reputation among abolitionists of both races, and recognized literary talent. He also drew upon the editorial talents

61. Report of the Committee on a National Press and Printing Establishment for the People of Color, *North Star*, January 14, 1848. See also State Convention of the Colored Freemen of Pennsylvania, *Proceedings . . . 1841*, 13; National Convention of Colored Citizens, *Minutes of. . . . Held in Buffalo, On the 15th, 16th, 17th, 18th, and 19th of August, 1843* (New York: Piercy & Reed, 1843), 27-30.

62. Irving Garland Penn, *The Afro-American Press and its Editors* (Springfield, Mass.: Willey and Co., 1891, reprint, New York: Arno Press, 1969), 52; *American and Foreign Anti-Slavery Reporter*, II (June, 1842), 60; *Northern Star and Freeman's Advocate*, February 3, 1842; Cortland, New

of Delany, who was initially his associate editor, and of Ward, who late in 1851 acted as his New England agent. But even Douglass found the going difficult. Caught in antislavery infighting, he also suffered from the internal bickering among blacks over the nature and location of a race press. The Troy convention of 1847, which endorsed the speedy establishment of a black press, spurned the projected *North Star*, because, based in Rochester, it would not be a national paper.[63] Simultaneously Garrison and his white Boston associates, fearing competition from a new antislavery paper and irked by declining Negro support for the *Liberator*, tried vigorously to dissuade Douglass from his new undertaking. When they failed to do so, they took pleasure in the obstacles he encountered. Samuel May, Jr., in 1848, placed the blame for the difficulties Douglass was already experiencing at the doorstep of all blacks. "*We* KNOW that people will *not* do, dare not do, what they ought to do, to sustain the anti-slavery cause."[64] May's assessment contained a kernel of truth, for Douglass admitted early in the year that 80% of *North Star* subscribers were white. In fact, it never became independent of white support, as increasingly during the 1850s Douglass relied upon Gerrit Smith for subsidies in one form or another.[65]

York, *Democrat*, February 19, 1845; *North Star*, February 2, 1849; *American and Foreign Anti-Slavery Reporter*, III [IV] (May, 1846), 7; Penn, *Afro-American Press*, 62-63. These papers were all troubled by limited subscriptions, unstable financing, and were, as a result, relatively short-lived. They suffered frequently as well from editorial problems and were the subject of criticism from the white antislavery press for such things as amateurism and poor grammar; see, for example, *Northern Star and Freeman's Advocate*, December 8, 1842, and *Liberator*, July 23, 1847.

63. *North Star*, January 14, 1848.

64. Samuel May, Jr., to John B. Estlin, October 31, 1848, M-BPL. See also May to Estlin, May 29 and September 30, 1847, both in M-BPL; *Liberator*, June 25 and July 23, 1847; and Abby Kelley Foster to Maria W. Chapman, October 5, 1847, W-BPL. Garrisonian whites feared the potential competition of a black press with the established antislavery press. Garrison, already bitter about declining black support for the *Liberator*, carried very little race news during the 1840s. The tenor of feeling was well put by Foster, who told Chapman that she had little confidence in Douglass: "*Confidential[ly] I have always feared him.*"

65. *North Star*, February 11, 1848. Douglass to Julia Griffiths, April 28, 1848, in Foner, *Douglass*, 1:306. Samuel May, Jr., to John B. Estlin,

In a *North Star* editorial early in 1849, Delany claimed that an independent, self-sustaining black press was simply impossible. By a long chain of somewhat dubious reasoning he concluded that 2500 subscribers were the maximum possible for an undertaking which required at least 3500 to survive. The weakness of Delany's arithmetic and logic notwithstanding, his message was convincing. There were apparently too few Negroes who both could and would support their own press.[66]

In this situation, competition among several papers was folly. Nevertheless, during the 1850s still more papers struggled briefly for existence and then died. In 1851 Henry Bibb started the *Voice of the Fugitive* in Windsor, Canada West. It drew its support, as did the subsequent Canadian-based *Provincial Freeman*, largely from fugitives in Canada and their friends and relatives in the United States. Other new journals were launched closer to home shortly after the *North Star* began publication. The *Hyperion* made its brief appearance in New York as did the temperance paper the *Delevan Union*. Ohio state conventions persistently urged the establishment of a western newspaper and in 1853 William Day of Cleveland decided to publish his *Aliened American*.[67] Douglass now feared the new competition as Garrison had earlier feared the *North Star*. Obviously piqued, he reprinted a New York *Tribune* editorial comment that with the *Aliened American* Day was fishing

---

October 31, 1848, M-BPL. Douglass to Gerrit Smith, May 1, 1851, S-SU. Douglass to Smith, July 14, 1852, S-SU.

66. *North Star,* April 13, 1849. Delany's argument went as follows: There are 500,000 free blacks in the United States. Of these only 62,489 are males residing in the North. Of them only one-third are literate, which drops the total pool to 20,849. But three-fourths of that group are indifferent to a race press. Thus there are left but 5,207 potential subscribers and of them one-half are too poor to subscribe. Hence there is a real subscribing audience of only about 2,500 persons.

67. State Convention of the Colored Citizens of Ohio, *Minutes of the State Convention...Convened at Columbus, January 9th, 10th, 11th, and 12th, 1850* (Columbus: Printed at the Ohio Standard Office, by Gale & Cleveland, 1850), 7-8; and *Minutes of the State Convention...Convened at Columbus. Jan. 15th. 16th, 17th, and 18th, 1851* ([Columbus?]: E. Glover, Printer, 1851), 14-15. Convention of the Colored Freemen of Ohio, *Proceedings of the Convention...Held in Cincinnati, January 14, 15, 16, 17, and 19*

"with a naked hook—or rather, with the frying-pan—and so [was] quite unlikely to catch any but the slowest chubs."[68]

Finally, in July 1859, after Douglass had converted the *North Star* into the *Frederick Douglass' Paper* and then, despairing of sustaining a weekly, had undertaken the *Douglass Monthly*, James McCune Smith started the *Weekly Anglo-African* in New York, the outgrowth of a monthly already published in the city. "We need a Press—a press of our own," he wrote. "We need to know something else of ourselves through the press than the every-day statements made up to suit the feelings of the base or the interests of our opponents. . . . Our *cause* (for in this country we have a cause) demands our own advocacy."[69] The *Anglo-African* excelled in printing stories of black activity in a number of eastern cities and drew upon the talents of diverse contributors. In its pages appeared material by Pennington, Garnet, Amos Beman, Ray, Mary Shadd Cary, formerly of the *Provincial Freeman*, Delany, Reason, Douglass, and young Ohio lawyer John Mercer Langston. Its scope and effort made it more truly than its predecessors a national race paper serving the Northeast and Midwest, if not the South. Even so it did not survive the exigencies of the Civil War.

For more than thirty years free blacks in the antebellum North tried to create a viable press as a vehicle for achieving advancement and respect. Although their successes were few, both the periodical and occasional publications they did issue provided, however sporadically and unevenly, new channels through which blacks spoke to blacks and incidentally to whites. Still, the printed word was not action. Other means were needed to educate and elevate black Americans to the point where they could effect change in the laws and institutions among which they seemed destined to live.

The national convention movement embodied much of the planning which blacks undertook to elevate the race. The first

---

(Cincinnati: Printed by Dumas & Lawyer, 1852), 10. *Aliened American*, April 9, 1853.

68. *Frederick Douglass' Paper*, May 13, 1853. Douglass' fears went back as far as 1849, see *North Star*, June 29 and August 3, 1849.

69. *Weekly Anglo-African*, July 23, 1859.

convention met in Philadelphia in 1830. Originally proposed by Hezekiah Grice, a Baltimore ice dealer and butcher, to discuss emigration to Canada, it was expanded in scope even before it assembled. His enthusiasm had been shaped by Quaker Benjamin Lundy's plans to settle free blacks in North America outside the United States and whetted by the 1829 emigration of Ohioans who, driven from their state by the newly enforced black code, had started their own settlement in Wilberforce, Canada.

The suggestion Grice made in April 1830 for a meeting of Northern race leaders soon bore fruit. In August Bishop Richard Allen of the African Methodist Episcopal Church, eager to control such a venture and aware that New Yorkers were ready to take it up, urged Grice to join him in arranging the convention, which met a month later in Philadelphia. The group that gathered on September 15 was small. At first only five Pennsylvanians were on hand, but they were soon joined by seven more delegates from Philadelphia and by fourteen others representing New York, Connecticut, Rhode Island, Maryland, and Virginia.[70]

Despite its small size, the gathering proposed forming an American Society of the Free People of Color to encourage Canadian Emigration. More importantly, it discussed the desirability of holding national race conventions. The idea caught fire. For the next five years conventions met annually and thereafter somewhat less regularly. Of the one hundred and five different delegates who attended during the first half-dozen years, many attended two or more conventions, and several participated in all five of the meetings.[71] From the outset these conventions explored the problem of national organization, convinced that it alone could provide proper communication and stimulate effective action among the "people of color." "Under present circumstances," admonished William Hamilton in his 1834 presidential address to the convention, "it is highly necessary [that] the free people of color should combine, and closely attend to their own particular interest. All kinds of jealousy should be swept away from among them, and their whole eye fixed, intently fixed on their own peculiar welfare."[72]

70. *Anglo-African Magazine,* I (October, 1859), 306-308.
71. Howard H. Bell, *A Survey of the Negro Convention Movement,*

For the first year or two, emigration was the major project of the meetings. But the persistent mismanagement of the Wilberforce community soon made it little more than a barely preferable alternative to the detested Liberian program of the American Colonization Society. Subsequently the interest of the conventions lay elsewhere. Regularly they encouraged the formation of temperance societies, mental improvement societies, benevolent associations, and educational institutions. So strongly influenced were they by white abolitionists, some of whom regularly attended the conventions, that in 1835 they voted to establish the American Moral Reform Society, whose purview would embrace the full sweep of Garrisonian multi-reformism. Even so the interests of previous conventions shaped the specific platform of the society so that education, temperance, universal liberty, and economic opportunity led the list of concerns.[73]

Despite the enthusiasm of its founding, the American Moral Reform Society never flourished. The absence of a race designation in its sweeping title suggested its major flaw—that its program was so all-embracing that it deflected the group from the convention movement's main purpose, the fostering of race pride and cohesion. Indeed the society never really got under way. It was approved in principle at the 1834 convention; the next year its Declaration of Sentiments and constitution were adopted. But not until 1837 was the first annual meeting held. And the vigorous plans projected at that meeting soon came to naught. The society's decision to send out agents and to raise $1,000 with which to pay them was effectively cancelled by the panic of 1837, which doomed fund raising of any sort.[74] Moreover, by adopting a Garrisonian resolution that "those *women* who are

1830-1861 (Ph.D. Northwestern University, 1953. Reprint, New York: Arno Press, 1969), 19.

72. William Hamilton, *Address to the Fourth Annual Convention of the Free People of Color of the United States* . .(New York: S. W. Benedict, 1834. Reprint, in Dorothy Porter, ed., *Negro Protest Pamphlets* [New York: Arno Press, 1969]), 4.

73. Convention for the Improvement of the Free People of Colour, *Minutes of the Fifth Annual . . .1835,* 25-31.

74. American Moral Reform Society, *The Minutes and Proceedings of the First Annual Meeting . . .Held at Philadelphia . . .the 14th to the 19th of August, 1837* (Philadelphia: Printed by Merrihew and Gunn, 1837. Reprint, Philadelphia: Rhistoric Publications, n.d.), 25-26.

now pleading the cause of humanity., and devoting their time, talents, and industry, to the cause of Universal Freedom, deserve the blessings of Heaven, and the gratitude of posterity,"[75] it ventured into the morass of controversy in which the national antislavery movement was to founder for three years and thus further diverted its attention from specific race needs. The extreme to which this sweeping program led was that the only plank the society adopted that might conceivably be labeled a peculiarly Negro issue was opposition to American annexation of the newly independent and slavery-supporting Texas. And that position was scarcely unique to blacks.

Caught up in the vagaries of universal reform, both the Moral Reform Society and the 1830s convention movement as a whole lost focus. They embraced a variety of piecemeal reforms but lacked a system of priorities; they talked ideals and theory but devised few programs of practical action. They blossomed, then withered and died. The Moral Reform Society, Cornish complained bitterly, was neither a "great BATTERING RAM" nor a "MIGHTY ENGINE" of the black community, but rather a weak reed, "scattering its feeble efforts to the winds," lacking both *"definite* objects of benevolence, and *definite* measures of action."[76] By 1840 the early convention movement had, in large part, become dysfunctional.

Yet the movement did not die. The bridge leading from the early national conventions to those of the 1840s was the state convention, primarily concerned with gaining suffrage and participating in political action. Petition campaigns and lecture tours promoting manhood suffrage unrestricted by race were undertaken by both blacks and whites throughout the North; but in the states with sizeable black populations and restricted suffrage, race conventions ensured a concentration of effort precisely where, in their supporters' eyes, it would most likely succeed. And, on the heels of these conventions in the early 1840s, national meetings, while they still worked for social and economic gains, gave special attention to political goals.

Revitalized, the convention movement expanded markedly as local and regional, in addition to state and national assemblies,

75. *Ibid.,* 24.
76. *Colored American,* August 26, 1837. Bell, *Negro Convention Movement,* 37, makes essentially the same point about the entire convention movement.

became increasingly common. Their growth provided an opportunity for new spokesmen and leaders to emerge. James McCune Smith and Ulysses Vidal of New York, Martin Delany and John B. Vashon of Pittsburgh, J. W. C. Pennington and Amos Beman of Hartford, and Uriah Boston of Poughkeepsie, all of whom played active roles in subsequent national conventions, first assumed leadership in the smaller and more restricted groups. In addition, these groups also sought to translate into reality the schools, libraries, and debating societies which national conventions proposed.

The proliferation of these smaller conventions breathed new life into the national movement. Both the Buffalo convention of 1843 and the Troy assemblage of 1847 drew participants in significantly greater numbers than had the Philadelphia and New York meetings of the 1830s; and in 1848 at Cleveland a plateau of cooperation and harmony prevailed which made Frederick Douglass believe that the time had finally come when national conventions should be supplemented by a permanent national organization with regular council meetings. Within five years the dream was realized at the Rochester convention of 1853.

Two years later the national council collapsed. Yet that it disintegrated so soon is less significant than that it was established in the first place, for its demise reflected not dissatisfaction with national organization but competing forms of nationalism jockeying for support in the 1850s. Douglass and the Rochester convention had urged the development and extension of separate race institutions within the United States. But Martin Delany and the 1854 Cleveland convention pressed for emigration outside the country. Thus quickly did national unity shatter, and after the ill-starred Philadelphia meeting of 1855, national conventions seemed futile. For the rest of the antebellum decade state and local meetings carried the burden of organized action.

Despite the discontinuities of form, leadership, and primary programs, however, the convention movement provided for black reformers an arena in which to exchange ideas, formulate programs, and discover a group identity. Much if not all self-consciously black antislavery and civil rights activity either shaped or was shaped by this central institution.

7. SEEKING ECONOMIC ADVANCEMENT

IN EFFORTS to break the hold which ignorance, poverty, and humble station had on their race, black abolitionists quested after that equality and unlimited opportunity which Middle Period rhetoric promised all Americans. Unlike so many white reformers who tried to transcend the materialism of their times, blacks, virtually without exception, sought a worldly prosperity scorned by transcendentalists and Utopian socialists. Moral reform, like education, both major considerations of the convention movement throughout its thirty-year existence, was largely conceived of as a means toward economic and social well-being.

Temperance, for example, was but one of those reform movements popular in antebellum America which Northern free black leaders turned to the purposes of achieving for themselves and their community dignity and recognition and ultimately freedom in its fullest sense. Thus they espoused temperance not because alcoholism or drunkenness was a race preoccupation, but because abstinence so well represented the moral uplift and social control which lay at the heart of much antebellum reform. Temperance societies abound throughout the Jacksonian period. Varyingly devoted to reforming drunkards, practicing total abstinence as preventive public medicine, and Americanizing immigrants, their supporters were propelled by sundry motives. Blacks likewise turned their temperance organizations to meet special group needs. "Circumstanced as we, the people of colour, are in this country," one proponent of social respectability noted in 1827, "intemperance is more hurtful to us than others."[1] Living

1. *Freedom's Journal*, June 1, 1827.

already on the outer fringes of American society and prosperity, Negroes could afford neither the economic drain of intemperance nor the social image of tippling. To succumb to liquor was to close still more tightly the chains which held them in poverty and slavery.

In Ohio antislavery and temperance were particularly interrelated. Cincinnati's dynamic early abolitionist Theodore Weld and his fellow students at Lane Seminary had worked vigorously for both causes. By 1840 at least one-quarter of the black population in the city belonged to one or another temperance society.[2] Throughout the 1830s, national conventions urged local groups to form temperance associations. As early as 1833 Negroes in Washington, Philadelphia, Carlisle, New Haven, Hartford, Middletown, Boston, Princeton, Albany, Schenectady, Utica, Syracuse, Catskill, Poughkeepsie, Newburg, Newtown, Troy, Brooklyn, and New York City had acted to establish societies. Later in the 1830s and 1840s, statewide societies emerged which, at least in Connecticut and New York, held extended annual meetings. In New England a regional society met for several years during the late 1830s and subsequently in 1842 a tristate (New York, Connecticut, and Massachusetts) Delevan Union Temperance Society of Colored People was established.[3]

Although, as one critic has noted, these societies were "stronger on planning than on performance,"[4] they offered a useful mechanism for improving the race image through individual action. Especially did the New England Temperance Society focus its attention on the social disorganization which drunkenness produced. Contending that, in spite of their poverty and other

2. Benjamin Quarles, *Black Abolitionists* (New York: Oxford University Press, 1969), 96-97.

3. *Ibid.*, 93. Convention for the Improvement of the Free People of Colour, *Minutes and Proceedings of the Third Annual Convention . . . Held . . . in the City of Philadelphia, From the 3rd to the 13th of June inclusive, 1833* (New York: Published by Order of the Convention, 1833: Reprint. New York: Arno Press, 1969) 15-16. *Liberator,* May 7 and 14, August 27, 1836. Robert A. Warner, *New Haven Negroes: A Social History* (New Haven: Yale University Press, 1940), 90-91.

4. Quarles, *Black Abolitionists,* 97.

deprivations, blacks were proportionately less given to drunkenness than whites, it warned Negroes of the impending disaster which lay in a descent to the level of Caucasian intemperance.[5] The Rev. John Lewis of the society linked temperance both to economic survival and moral salvation, for the "grog-shop" was associated with those other scenes of iniquity, "the gaming table, the brothel and the theatre," where blacks wasted both their money and their souls.[6]

As Lewis' concern suggested, temperance comprised but one part of a larger campaign both to shelter black effort and funds from dissipation and to channel them to economically productive undertakings. The press constantly linked sober morality with shrewd thriftiness in exhortations drawn from the spirit of Benjamin Franklin's Poor Richard. Avoid display and waste. Buy only necessities. Save against hard times. Invest surplus income carefully. *Freedom's Journal* warned its readers not to squander their substance on the "superfluities of life" lest they fall into beggary and crime.[7] A "Colored Baltimorean" pressed the same point unmercifully. "Instead of profiting by the many lessons we have had, on frugality and economy, and diligently pursuing that which contributes to the moral, intellectual, and political elevation of any people, too many of us are grasping at unsubstantial forms; lavishing our hard earnings upon those glittering bubbles which characterise the giddy and the gay in the higher walks of fashionable life."[8] The *Colored American* damned playing the numbers as the most empty of these bubbles. Lotteries, editor Cornish explained, were both illegal and poor investments, almost always rigged to favor the dealers. And even if one held a winning policy ticket, he warned, one was unlikely to be paid off, so dishonest were the operators.[9]

The moralists were not simply negative. For every vice spurned they proposed a positive substitute. Cornish advised that the time

5. *Liberator,* October 29, 1836.
6. *Ibid.,* September 14, 1836.
7. *Freedom's Journal,* May 30, 1828. Also *ibid.,* March 21, 1829.
8. *Liberator,* February 19, 1831.
9. *Colored American,* February 23, 1839.

saved from gambling and drinking be invested in hearing lectures, reading, and generally improving the mind.[10] William Nell, as Douglass' assistant on the *North Star*, urged young men to follow the course which had led him to his respectable position. Work hard, excel, waste no time. Even social events could be put to educational purposes if young men would turn soirées into serious discussion groups to improve their own minds and those of their young ladies. Trotting out familiar aphorisms, Nell assured his readers that "one blow of the chisel does not make a statue," and that "a pigmy is a pigmy still, though he sat [sic] bestride the Alps; [while] a giant *is* a giant, though always in the valley."[11]

That young men responded to these Alger-like encomiums, the Moral Lever Association of Allegheny City, Pennsylvania, attested. Its fulcrum was acquiring real estate and its members were "fast accumulating property and must eventually hold a large amount."[12] By contrast, those who smoked Havana cigars, dressed in flashy clothes, sassed their superiors, and showed "careless indifference" to their work were held up as negative models. William Wilson, Brooklyn correspondent for *Frederick Douglass' Paper*, described one black clerk thus disporting himself and concluded that such playboys were doomed to "situation to-day, and evacuation to-morrow."[13]

Again and again black writers and speakers praised honesty, punctuality, restraint, modesty, enterprise, skill, thriftiness, and diligence. By 1860 the *Weekly Anglo-African* was advising a concentration on economic competence so single that it urged abstinence from feeble churches and "deceptive" politics in favor of "quiet, steady, earnest progress in the paths of industry, frugality, competency, intelligence, and virtue."[14] Garnet sounded the same theme in the call for the national convention of 1864. "Sound morality must be encouraged; education must be pro-

10. *Ibid.*, March 18, 1837.
11. *North Star*, May 4, 1849.
12. *Ibid.*, July 6, 1849.
13. *Frederick Douglass' Paper*, March 11, 1853.
14. *Weekly Anglo-African*, February 25, 1860.

moted; temperance and frugality must be exemplified, and industry, and thrift, and everything that pertains to well-ordered and dignified life, must be exhibited to the nation and the world."[15] Early and late, race leaders demanded group endorsement and individual exertion of the Puritan ethic. High thinking, plain living, and hard work would surely profit the individual and dignify the community.

Sounding their paeans to abstinence, and reifying their zeal in a variety of reform structures, black leaders also struggled to open new occupations and professions to young people in order to break the well-based stereotype of Negro as domestic or manual laborer. Inasmuch as white youth learned skilled trades as apprentices, so young blacks needed access to the skills and experience of master craftsmen. James Forten, whose business success stemmed from his own apprenticeship to a sailmaker, early encouraged the extension of this kind of training to the race. He fretted when a Mrs. Stansbury of Trenton, New Jersey, donated $1,000 to the American Colonization Society to aid free Negroes when that money could have been used to pay master mechanics who would apprentice young blacks.[16]

In the long run, so small a sum would have been meaningless, for Northern blacks were almost universally blocked from learning the secrets of skilled labor. "Poor Layman" reported to the *Liberator* that there were, so far as he knew, "only two colored mechanics" in all of Boston in the middle 1830s; and that, with the exception of two or three apprentice printers, no young Negro was then learning any needle or mechanical trade. Only slightly less devastating was the report of the white Rev. R. Spaulding to the Boston auxiliary of the American Union for the Relief and Improvement of the Colored Race, which listed no more than a dozen and a half black Bostonians who were skilled workers in 1834.[17] Surveys of labor in other Northern cities repeated this

15. *Liberator*, September 9, 1864.
16. James Forten to William L. Garrison, February 23, 1831, G-BPL.
17. *Liberator*, November 22, 1834. *African Repository*, XIII (March, 1837), 188-190.

pattern and even suggested that as time went on the situation further deteriorated. Douglass reported in 1853 that New York whites were pushing blacks out of the service jobs they had traditionally held and thereby plunging them still further down the economic scale.[18]

Not surprisingly, efforts to gain access to skilled trades, business, and the professions were backed by denunciation of those menial tasks which society had traditionally assigned blacks. Critics found domestic service particularly degrading. Here, Negroes were not only confined to unskilled labor and poor pay, but they were demeaned by serving as lackeys to whites. "O, horrible idea, indeed!" admonished Maria Stewart, the first woman, black or white, to lecture publicly against slavery. Young women hired out for "mean, servile labor" because they could get no other jobs. By this means ambition was stifled, ignorance deepened, and shiftlessness encouraged. There were none, she thought, who had "enriched themselves by spending their lives as house-domestics, washing windows, shaking carpets, brushing boots, or tending upon gentlemen's tables."[19]

The argument was not that menial labor was, in itself, denigrating, for no "needful labor" was dishonorable; nor did any insist that blacks should never perform any kind of necessary and useful work. But, as the address of the Cleveland National Convention of 1848 made clear, "such employments have been so long and universally filled by colored men, as to become a badge of degradation, in that it has established the conviction that colored

18. *Frederick Douglass' Paper*, March 4, 1853. As Douglass suggested, so did others, urging as did the National Council in 1855, that where the opportunity to learn trades in schools did not exist blacks turned to other methods, such as opening up apprentice shops, to train their young men; see *Provincial Freeman*, May 26, 1855.

19. *Liberator*, November 17, 1832. The *Northern Star and Freemen's Advocate*, February 10, 1842, further explored the damage done by excluding Negroes from the trades. The children of slaves grew up in households whose masters trained them only to be "living stock." Denied education, except to suit the convenience of masters, they established homes which did little to educate children beyond the same level. "It was formerly thought by their masters that any thing was good enough for slaves, and now any thing is good enough for the blacks."

men are only fit for such employments."[20] Wherever the issue was discussed, the response was much the same. The colored citizens of Gallia County, Ohio, resolved in 1851 that young people should be urged to undertake "mechanical, agricultural and professional pursuits" to avoid the stigma of unskilled work.[21] Thomas Duff advised his fellow Californians to "abandon such positions as bootblacks, waiters, servants, and carriers, and other servile employment," for only thus could they improve their standing. "If they cannot engage in trading, mechanical pursuits or farming," he counseled, "let them pitch into mining from which they have not yet been debarred. . . ." There, diligent application and thrift would provide almost anyone the capital needed to buy land and start a farm.[22]

No one explored the issue of menial labor more thoroughly than Martin Delany. In his own newspaper, the *Mystery*, in the columns of the *North Star*, and in his book, *The Condition, Elevation, Emigration and Destiny of the Colored People of the United States*, he probed the dilemmas and delusions which it generated. First of all, he emphasized, blacks must not content themselves simply with making a steady income or they would never understand how badly off they were, and all efforts to elevate them would fall as "pearl cast among swine" or be useful only in the hereafter.[23] Indeed, in *Condition, Elevation, Emigration, and Destiny*, he chastised blacks for their preoccupation with religion, which led them to wait for God to rescue them from worldly tribulations while they sat with hands idly folded in prayer. "Their hope is largely developed, and consequently," he scoffed, "they usually stand still—hope in God, and really expect Him to do that for them, which it is necessary they should do themselves." And when they were not depending on God, they depended on whites. "White men are producers—we are consumers," he wrote in acid comparison. "They build houses, and we rent them. They raise

20. *North Star*, September 22, 1848.
21. *Frederick Douglass' Paper*, January 1, 1852.
22. *Mirror of the Times* (San Francisco), December 12, 1857.
23. *North Star*, February 18, 1848. The quotation from the *Mystery*, December 16, 1846.

produce, and we consume it. They manufacture clothes and wares, and we garnish ourselves with them. They build coaches, vessels, cars, hotels, saloons, and other vehicles and places of accommodation, and we deliberately wait until they have got them in readiness, then walk in, and contend with as much assurance for a 'right,' as though the whole thing was bought by, paid for, and belonged to us."[24]

The cure for their ills, Delany admonished, was neither sorrow nor prayer nor shame, but work. "Our elevation must be the result of *self-efforts*, and work of our *own hands*."[25] His conclusion differed from that of other thoughtful observers not in its emphasis on work or even on the kind of work that was most desirable but in his blunt advice to refuse most of the jobs then available to Negroes. They must be producers. They must do labor which instilled pride and self-sufficiency. Neither men nor women should perform domestic labor for whites. Especially should Negro wives stay home, bring up their own children, and nourish their own hearth in good middle-class fashion.[26] It is the "duty of the Free, to elevate themselves in the most speedy and effective manner possible," Delany concluded, making his advice a race obligation, for "the redemption of the bondman depends entirely upon the elevation of the freeman."[27]

Given the quest for economic well-being and social status, it is not surprising that both national and state conventions and local groups adopted another of the major antebellum reform preoccupations to their needs—education. If black youth could gain access to schools, and particularly schools which offered training for particular trades and skills, they could free themselves from menial labor and, in so doing, share the choices available to middle-class Americans. With such opportunity in mind Peter Williams

24. Martin R. Delany, *The Condition, Elevation, Emigration, and Destiny of the Colored People of the United States Politically Considered* (Philadelphia: The Author, 1852. Reprint, New York: Arno Press, 1969), 37-38, 44-45.
25. *Ibid.*, 45.
26. *Ibid.*, 193-195.
27. *Ibid.*, 205.

praised Gerrit Smith's Peterboro school for furthering the goal of Negroes' "equality with [their] white fellow citizens."[28] David Ruggles asserted that without education blacks would remain *"depressed & degraded,"* while with further schooling they could prove to whites that black minds were as capable of "indefinite Expansion" as their own.[29] If blacks failed to take education seriously, James Forten, Jr., warned, they courted disaster. "Are we content," he asked delegates to the moral reform convention in 1837, "to wrap the mantle of ignorance, around us, and cry out 'a little more sleep, a little more slumber, a little more folding together of the arms?' Shall we, when told that we aspire to no other stations than hewers of wood and drawers of water, respond Amen, even be it so?" No, Forten replied. Let us "give the lie direct to these foul accusations, by examples of talent, genius, honesty, and sobriety,—by rearing in our midst the broad standard of education[.]"[30] When they had the same opportunity to get an education that whites enjoyed, Garnet predicted that blacks would show themselves fully their equals.[31]

A good education, however, was the key not only to public image but to economic opportunity and improved status as well. "Philanthropus" anonymously pointed out in 1827 that the depressing pattern of black employment at menial labor was clear testimony to inadequate schooling.[32] Viewing the same phenomenon, Samuel Ward argued that it fed white convictions that the Negro was "naturally, morally, intellectually, or socially inferior to the white."[33] Similarly, Lewis Woodson, Pittsburgh barber and preacher, assured readers of the *Colored American* that white

28. Peter Williams to Gerrit Smith, August 19, 1834, S-SU.

29. David Ruggles to Gerrit Smith, April 22, 1836, S-SU.

30. American Moral Reform Society, *The Minutes and Proceedings of the First Annual Meeting,* 36-37.

31. Baldwinsville, New York, *Republican,* November 20, 1845. On the eve of the Civil War, Douglass was still sanguine enough to predict that if blacks had equal educational opportunities, equal suffrage would follow as a matter of course; see *Douglass Monthly,* March, 1859.

32. *Freedom's Journal,* March 30, 1827.

33. Samuel Ringgold Ward, *Autobiography of a Fugitive Negro...* (London: J. Snow, 1855), 88.

prejudice existed because blacks, lacking skill and training, were poor workers.[34]

Just as education would widen horizons and expand opportunities, so also its proponents hoped it would function as a means of social control, defining the community's expectations and inculcating its mores. "Philanthropus" urged blacks to avoid "balls, theatrical and numerous other trivial amusements" so that they could afford better education.[35] Only thus could a vicious circle be broken in which poor education contributed to delinquency, which, in turn, diverted young people's attention from education. Sound schooling, he continued, would eradicate antisocial behavior. "The evils accruing to our whole community from the loose and depraved habits of many of the rising generation," he warned, "are incalculable."[36] Community leaders agreed. Austin Steward, grocer of Rochester, thought schools should teach children temperance principles and an abhorrence of nighttime carousing. Cornish, echoing Steward's viewpoint, planned a public reading room as a substitute for the porter house.[37] The proliferation of schools, reading rooms, literary societies, and libraries in the 1830s was universally viewed by their sponsors as the vanquisher of grog shops, gambling dens, and bawdy houses.[38]

"Be righteous, be honest, be just, be economical, be prudent, offend not the laws of your country," the national convention admonished in 1832. "In a word live in that purity of life, by both precept and example—live in the constant pursuit of that moral and intellectual strength, which will invigorate your understandings, and render you illustrious in the eyes of civilized nations. ..."[39] Or, as Samuel Cornish put it, blacks' failure not only to prosper

34. "Augustine" in *Colored American*, February 16, 1839.

35. *Freedom's Journal*, March 30, 1827.

36. *Ibid.*, April 6, 1827.

37. *Ibid.*, July 27, 1827. *Rights of All*, May 29, 1829.

38. See, for example, *Liberator*, May 11, 1833; *Colored American*, June 24, 1837 and November 10, 1838.

39. Convention for the Improvement of the Free People of . . .Color, *Minutes and Proceedings of the Second Annual . . . Held . . . in . . . Philadelphia, From the 4th to the 13th of June inclusive, 1832* (Philadelphia: Published by Order of the Convention, 1832. Reprint, New York: Arno Press, 1969), 35.

economically but also to acquire the necessary skills to do so lay in
a tendency to "grasp after flowers, and neglect solid and
whol[e]some fruits!!!"[40] Thrift and enterprise must precede as
well as flow from education. William Nell, in 1847 assisting
Douglass with the *North Star*, commented that "any person, of
ordinary calibre, must know that to become elevated, they must
cultivate and practice the same traits which are elevating others
around them...."[41] Not so very different was the viewpoint of
the 1854 Emigration Convention which urged the formation of a
Negro nation. Arguing that in "the present social system of
civilized society, the equality of persons is only recognized by their
equality of attainments," it urged blacks to learn the vocations
"pertaining to the Industrial and Wealth accumulating occupations" as a way out of their subserviency.[42]

Practically, the way out had to be marked with schools or other
organizations which would teach the knowledge and skills needed
for success. In this respect the early national conventions looked to
state and local groups, some of which dated from the 1820s, to
activate social and intellectual improvement among blacks. On the
whole they did generate considerable enthusiasm. "I care not how
many societies, whose objects are moral or mental improvement,
are raised up," an anonymous writer to the *Colored American*
asserted fervently. "They will do good among us. They will tend to
clear us from the charge of indolence, or indifference, to our own
welfare, which has been heaped upon us; and also, from that foul
aspersion, as to the inferiority of our intellectual capacities, with
which many has [*sic*] been pleased to brand us."[43]

40. *Rights of All*, September 18, 1829.
41. *North Star*, December 3, 1847.
42. *Proceedings of the National Emigration Convention of Colored People; held at Cleveland, Ohio . . .24-26 August, 1854* (Pittsburgh, 1854), quoted in Aptheker, *Documentary History,* 1:366. Beginning with the same premises about education, M. H. Freeman argued some years later that parental and economic class influences were also important parts of education. In white children these influences are felt and were "the means that first develop . . . that due self-respect and self-reliance which must lie at the foundation of any just and harmonious development of mind." *Anglo-African Magazine,* I (April 1859), 116.
43. *Colored American*, March 11, 1837.

Among the societies so founded, New York City's Phoenix Society was outstanding. Originally organized in 1833 by white abolitionist Arthur Tappan and subsidized by both Tappan brothers until 1837, the society was composed principally of "colored young men" and dedicated to the "improvement of the colored people in morals, literature, and the mechanic arts."[44] It boasted a meeting hall and a library, ran a high school for Negro youth and an evening school for adults, and organized a visitation scheme to encourage parents to send their children to school. For those who were utterly destitute, the Phoenixians encouraged the formation of Dorcas Societies, whose women would "help clothe poor children of color, if they will attend school."[45]

The Phoenix Society was only one among many similar groups throughout the North. New York also had a Garrison Literary and Benevolent Association for boys from four to twenty. Across the river in Jamaica there was another benevolent society, and upstate in Geneva a Mental and Moral Improvement Society. Boston boasted its Philomatheon Society of young persons who wished to promote the interests of liberty and literature. New Bedford had a Colored Association, which served as an auxiliary group to the national conventions. In Pennsylvania the Philadelphia Library of Colored People and an Agricultural and Mechanic Association catered to the needs of their members; while in Pittsburgh the Young Men's Literary and Moral Reform Society was an arm of the American Moral Reform Society. These, and scores of other societies like them, provided "literary, moral and intellectual improvement of the young and rising generation" wherewith to "baffle" their foes, "taught the useful trades [and] the arts together with the rudiments of a common education," and "in every other way ... endeavor[ed] to promote the happiness of the people of color by encouraging them to improve their minds and to abstain from every vicious and demoralizing practice."[46]

44. *Liberator,* June 29, 1833.
45. *Ibid.,* June 29, 1833. Also Lewis Tappan, *Life of Arthur Tappan* (New York: Hurd and Houghton, 1870), 158.
46. Young Men's Literary and Moral Reform Society of the City of Pittsburgh, Constitution, Article II, in *Colored American,* September 2,

Despite the plethora of local schools and societies the national conventions also attempted to develop model schools for both higher education and vocational training. The earliest of them was for a manual labor college in New Haven. The original proposal came not from blacks but from Arthur Tappan and Simeon S. Jocelyn, an antislavery pastor to a black congregation in New Haven, who had conceived the plan in 1828 or 1829. In 1831, together with Garrison, Benjamin Lundy, and Philadelphia philanthropists Thomas Shipley and Charles Pierce, they presented it to the convention of the free people of color. The response was immediate and enthusiastic endorsement, with one significant amendment. To make sure that blacks would control its destiny, they insisted that a majority of the trustees be Negroes. Once this was done, the convention appointed committees of community leaders in Boston, New York, Philadelphia, Baltimore, New Haven, Brooklyn, and other major eastern cities to raise an initial fund of $20,000. At the same time they appointed Cornish to coordinate these local groups.[47]

The New Haven Manual Labor College, which was to provide, "in connexion with a scientific education, . . . a useful Mechanical or Agricultural profession,"[48] never materialized. No sooner were the plans publicized than New Haven officials condemned them, and a town meeting backed their resolution to prohibit the school. Thus citizens who feared an influx of blacks into their small city determined to block the enterprise.[49]

They were successful. Yet, though the New Haven venture failed, other attempts were made to establish such a school. In fact,

1837. Preamble to the constitution of a literary society of young Negroes in Philadelphia, in *Colored American,* February 2, 1839. Agricultural and Mechanic Association [of Philadelphia], Preamble to the constitution, Ms, Leon Gardner Collection, Historical Society of Pennsylvania. *Liberator,* June 29, 1833, reporting on the purposes of the Phoenix Society.

47. Gilbert Barnes, *The Antislavery Impulse, 1830-1844* (orig. publ. 1933. Gloucester, Mass.: Peter Smith, 1967), 25-27. New Haven *Advertiser,* n.d., in *Liberator,* November 12, 1831. Minutes and Proceedings of the First Annual Convention of the People of Color, in *Liberator,* October 22, 1831.

48. Minutes and Proceedings of the First Annual Convention of the People of Color, in *Liberator,* October 22, 1831.

49. *Liberator,* October 29, 1831.

the action of the New Haven town fathers did not stop local blacks and others in Boston and Providence from continuing to endorse the project and to raise money for it.[50] The following year the national convention pressed hard for no more than a shift of location in the original plan. After branding New Haven's action "a disgrace to themselves" and "a stigma on the reputed fame of New England and the country," the 1832 convention "determined to present to another portion of the country not far distant, and at no very remote period, the opportunity of gaining for them[selves] the character of a truly philanthropic spirit, and of retrieving the character of the country...."[51] It was not, however, a race convention but rather the New England Anti-Slavery Society which organized a second campaign and sent Garrison to England to gather funds. Assisted by James Forten in Philadelphia, John B. Vashon in Pittsburgh, Peter Williams in New York City, and Charles L. Remond in Salem, and endorsed by public meetings in Boston, Philadelphia, New York, and Newark, the New England society planned to raise $50,000 in the United States and England to launch a new school.[52]

The flurry of Negro meetings and letters was all somewhat delusive. Both the New Haven venture and the New England Anti-Slavery Society project were engineered and dominated by whites. Furthermore Garrison's English tour competed directly with Nathaniel Paul's efforts to raise funds for a seminary at the Canadian Wilberforce Settlement. Beset by a profusion of plans— for other schools were planned in New York and Pennsylvania[53]—and by their competition for limited funds, the national convention of 1833 seriously wondered "whether there [was] any prospect that a Manual Labour School for the instruction of coloured youth [would] shortly be established, and if so *where*, and what progress

50. *Ibid.,* November 5 and 12, 1831.
51. Convention for the Improvement of the Free People of Color, *Minutes and Proceedings of the Second Annual...1832,* 34.
52. *Liberator,* September 29, 1832, March 9 and 23, April 13, and May 11, 1833.
53. Convention for the Improvement of the Free People of Colour, *Minutes and Proceedings of the Third Annual,* 14.

[had] been made towards it[s] completion."[54] Ironically, excepting the short-lived and mismanaged Wilberforce institution, the only other advanced school established for black students in the 1830s was Gerrit Smith's equally short-lived school at Peterboro, in whose planning and direction blacks played a distinctly peripheral role.[55]

After the early failures to launch manual labor schools a decade and a half passed before the idea was again seriously broached. Then, in 1847 and again in 1853, national conventions drew up new plans. At the 1847 Troy convention, the New York City delegation, headed by professionals Alexander Crummell and James McCune Smith, proposed establishing a highly academically oriented college. The suggestion triggered a long and hot debate. Its supporters argued that a black college would stimulate the race to self-improvement by creating a reservoir of teachers, providing employment for Negro professors, and shielding students from the prejudice they would otherwise experience in predominantly white schools. Opponents, led by Douglass, Garnet, Van Rensselaer, and Amos Beman, questioned the need for separate colleges because the number of good white schools which would admit Negroes was growing. Given this development, why try again what had so miserably failed in the 1830s?[56]

Nonetheless the delegates voted 26-17 to establish a college strong in classical and scientific studies. Defending its decision, the convention argued that the poor quality of their secondary education left blacks unprepared to compete successfully in white schools. Moreover the high cost of attending white schools, most of which lacked the work-study plan of the manual labor school,

54. *Ibid.*, 7.
55. The black role in the school was apparently confined to Smith's request that New York ministers Samuel Cornish, Peter Williams, and Theodore Wright screen applicants and recommend candidates for admission. Williams, Wright, and Cornish to Gerrit Smith, May 3, 1835, S-SU. See also Williams to Smith, April 22, 1834, and Cornish to Smith, March 24, 1834, both in S-SU.
56. *North Star*, December 3, 1847. The opponents also questioned whether black students were all that discomfited in white schools.

excluded many of their promising young men.[57] As important as either of these factors to the convention's decision was its concern that black students, thrust into white colleges, would be "separated from their people, inasmuch as there is no point of interest, or of contact, between the colleges of our country and the colored people of the Union."[58] A separate college would benefit many others than the students who attended it.

Although the Troy project never went beyond the planning stage,[59] its failure did not preclude discussion of a race college at the 1853 Rochester convention. The emphasis here, however, was more heavily vocational, with pursuit of traditional classical and scientific studies less important than training in agricultural and mechanical skills. In the process, the manual labor plan was to be exploited financially as well as educationally. The prospectus for such a school, as Douglass sketched it for the delegates, had roots at least as far back as the 1835 convention, which had endorsed schools designed to teach trades and prepare students for good jobs in a manner similar to the apprenticeship system.[60]

Well before the Rochester meeting, Douglass had speculated editorially about the best method of job training, even toying with the idea of endowed workshops where white craftsmen would train black apprentices.[61] By the time the convention assembled, however, he had shifted his sights to a single school capable of

57. National Convention of Colored People, *Proceedings of the National Convention. . . Held in Troy, N. Y. on the 6th, 7th, 8th and 9th, October, 1847* (Troy: J. C. Kneeland and Co., 1847. Reprint, New York: Arno Press, 1969), 33-37.

58. *North Star*, January 21, 1848.

59. There was a Manual Labor Institute in Woodstock, Michigan, founded about 1847 and another, The British-American Institute, in Dawn, Canada, founded in 1842. Neither was at the collegiate level. The Woodstock Institute was brought to our attention by David Katzman, who kindly made his notes of the Detroit area available to us. See also William H. Pease and Jane H. Pease, *Black Utopia: Negro Communal Experiments in America* (Madison: State Historical Society of Wisconsin, 1963, 1972), 64-67. It is interesting to note that in all of these plans for educational institutions, local and state groups worked at the secondary level; national organizations always planned for collegiate level institutions.

60. Convention for the Improvement of the Free People of Colour, *Minutes of the Fifth Annual . . .1835*, 16.

61. *Frederick Douglass' Paper*, March 11, 1853.

offering a varied program. It was substantially his plan which the convention adopted. In the projected institution, literary training would be secondary to the vocational programs. The agricultural courses would be supplemented by a working farm; the mechanical arts program, with various workshops. So extensive a program required a sizeable faculty and plant, and the delegates anticipated that a minimum endowment of $50,000 was needed before the school could open. Once running, its substantial budget would be partially sustained by the sale of products made in the various workshops. Thus it could hope to become self-supporting and to reduce student fees as well. "In such wise" the Rochester meeting hoped to make the school a stepping-stone for race progress, giving its youth the "means of success, adapted to their struggling condition, and ere long, following the enterprise of the age, we may hope to see them filling everywhere positions of responsibility and trust, and gliding on the triple tide of wealth, intelligence and virtue, reach eventually, to a sure resting place of distinction and happiness."[62]

Probably the best conceived of all the educational efforts proposed by national conventions, the Rochester plan soon ran afoul the major obstacle which had foiled all its predecessors—inability to raise funds. Initially the convention undertook to collect $50,000 of operating capital by selling $10 shares. In addition, they hoped to raise $100,000 through contributions from benefactors and well-wishers. Within the year the planning committee realized its goal was too high and the national council, a permanent working group established by the convention, lowered its sights from $50,000 to $30,000 in shares and to $10,000 in outright gifts.[63] This decision was as much a recognition of defeat as it was a concession to reality. Few blacks had capital to invest in so untried a venture, and hoped-for white support failed to materialize.

62. Colored National Convention, *Proceedings of . . . Held in Rochester, July 6th, 7th, and 8th, 1853* (Rochester: Frederick Douglass' Paper, 1853. Reprint, New York: Arno Press, 1969), 18, 31-32, quotation on 33.
63. *Frederick Douglass' Paper,* August 5, 1853 and March 24, 1854.

Douglass and others had expected that Harriet Beecher Stowe would give the school at least $1,500 from funds she had collected in England. Admittedly she had made no firm commitment, but her decision not to contribute led to complaints and further wrangling between white and black abolitionists.[64] The latter were especially bitter with the Garrisonians, whose open hostility to the Rochester project and influence on Stowe had probably discouraged her gift. James McCune Smith observed caustically that the same Garrison who twenty years earlier had gone to England expressly to raise funds for a Negro manual labor college, now accused blacks of being in a *"morbid state of mind"* for trying to establish their own school.[65] Maria Chapman, whose control of American Anti-Slavery Society funds lay in her money-raising skill, publicly condemned *"exclusive* instruction, teaching for *blacks,* a school founded on color" as simply being a way to herd Negroes "ignominiously apart from the refining influence of association with the more highly educated and accomplished." A separate school, she concluded, was "a direct way of fitting white men for tyrants, and black men for slaves";[66] it would assuredly receive no funds through her hands.

Nor was dissension limited to white hostility. In 1855 the national council, on the verge of collapse only two years after its founding, refused further endorsement for a separate school. The council was already shattered by many issues, not least of which was the debate over support for separate or integrated schools. Long troublesome as a theoretical issue, it had by 1855 created a national and well-publicized crisis in the black community which played itself out in the heated Philadelphia meeting of the national

64. *Frederick Douglass' Paper,* January 20, 1854. Charles H. Nichols, *Many Thousands Gone: The Ex-Slaves' Account of their Bondage and Freedom* (Bloomington: Indiana University Press, 1963), 170, claims that when Mrs. Stowe returned from Europe and did not give any money to the black venture, she also did not account for what she did do with the money. See, for example, *Frederick Douglass' Paper,* January 13, 1854.

65. *Frederick Douglass' Paper,* February 16, 1855.

66. Maria W. Chapman, *How Can I Help to Abolish Slavery? or, Counsels to the Newly Converted.* Anti-slavery Tract No. 14 (New York: American Anti-Slavery Society, [1855]), 4-5.

council in July of that year. Victim of the larger debate, the Rochester plan for a manual labor school was lost by a single vote. Arguments about its organization and financing and even about its practicality and necessity gave way to the broader and decisive question, should education at any level be integrated or segregated.[67] In sum, despite at least three major convention efforts no national model of a manual labor school for blacks ever emerged.

Moreover, as time went on, various spokesmen began to question whether education of whatever kind and however achieved would really fulfill the hopes that had been vested in it. If, as Lewis Woodson put it, the goal of education was to acquire the means by which one might "decently maintain himself in society,"[68] subsequent employment patterns had to be the test of educational efficacy. And as things stood, whites had to be willing to hire blacks, and they were not. Even abolitionists, who established schools to educate and train Negroes, failed to employ their graduates. If, the *Northern Star and Freeman's Advocate* observed caustically, anyone thought "that colored people believe that opening seminaries form[s] the most effectual means for bettering their condition, we can assure him that he is very much mistaken." Directly challenging the abolitionists, the *Star* demanded that they "inform us how many colored young men from the multitude of seminaries which . . . have been opened 'through abolition influence' are employed by abolition merchants and lawyers as clerks, and . . . what is the objection to employing colored persons who are sufficiently qualified for such purposes."[69] John Rock, who first practiced dentistry and then law, was particularly sensitive to the dilemma faced by highly trained persons. No matter how skilled they were, they would have little scope for their talents. Drawing on the bitterness of his own experience, Rock explored the irony of the situation in which "education aggravates . . . suffering. The more highly educated the colored man is,"

67. *Liberator*, July 27, 1855. See also *Frederick Douglass' Paper*, January 18, 1856.

68. State Convention of the Colored Freeman of Pennsylvania, *Proceedings . . . 1841*, 13.

69. *Northern Star and Freeman's Advocate*, March 17, 1842.

he observed, "the more keenly he suffers." Even in Massachusetts, where blacks triumphed over school segregation in 1855 and were permitted to attend "the free schools and colleges," they were still victims of economic discrimination. So in 1862 Rock questioned whether that victory had not been counterproductive. "The more ignorant the colored man, the more happy he must be. If we are never to derive the benefits of education, it would be a misfortune for us to see inside of a school-house."[70]

The dismay and despair which Rock voiced were hardly to be gainsaid, for the experience of more than thirty years' quest for reasonable—let alone equal—economic opportunity had taught black Americans the tremendous opposition and difficulty they faced. They had, like their white antislavery counterparts, sought advance through multiple reforms; they had, like Americans generally, accepted the premise that education was a nearly infallible talisman. Seeking at first for an equal place in America, they were thwarted in that most basic of arenas—economic advancement. Increasingly, therefore, they attacked segregation, both formal and informal, where it blocked their access to the opportunities they sought.

70. *Liberator,* August 15, 1862.

8. ATTACKING SEGREGATION AND EXCLUSION

A MAJOR block to race advancement was Negroes' exclusion from public and private institutions. Churches, schools, militia units, railroads, steamboats, courts, theatres, and restaurants were often either completely closed to them or open only on demeaning terms. Exclusion from basic institutions and public facilities, therefore, was a constant preoccupation in the antebellum years. Where efforts to gain access to existing institutions promised success, blacks sought merely to end segregation. Where structural change was impossible, as in the courts, they insisted on equal rights. But where no accommodation seemed likely, they turned their efforts to establishing separate institutions in order to promote the advancement of their race.

Often, however, the choice was not clear-cut. General principle and immediate practicality both clouded the issue. Indeed, the debate over integration and segregation reflected the most fundamental dilemma which black activists faced. Should they strive for acceptance in white America or struggle to achieve a distinctive and separate culture? Should segregated facilities be viewed as an end in themselves or as a transition device and so be shaped to bridge white and black communities? How these questions were answered defined the nature of the struggle.

Efforts to achieve desegregation were undertaken in churches, transportation, and a variety of public facilities; but nowhere was the effort more important than in schools. Here the debate was shaped by whether or not public or charitable schools were available to blacks in a given city or state. Where they were completely excluded from the educational system, they most frequently focused their energies on obtaining special schools. But where their children attended segregated classes over a period of time, they more likely strove for integrated education. Furthermore, since no two states had identical requirements and since local practice was often more important than statute law, the school issue took a variety of shapes and inspired little race cohesion. In New York, for example, an 1845 law permitted local option on separate schools and granted the towns which established them the same state subsidies allowed for other schools. Ohio had no provision for the education of black children until a law adopted in 1847 allowed the use of state funds for separate schools, and a second law passed in 1852 made separate facilities mandatory under certain conditions. Massachusetts practiced de facto local option in regard to separate schools until 1855, when it prohibited segregated education. In Pennsylvania there was no official provision for segregated facilities until 1854, although state instructional funds after 1820 could be used for privately operated black schools.[1]

Frequently, and especially in the early years, the only schools for Negroes were sustained by white philanthropy. In New York City the African free schools of the 1820s and 1830s were administered and subsidized by local benefactors. But New York was a special case, for until 1842 all the city's free schools were controlled by private societies with state subvention. Boston's separate schools were funded and partially sustained by an endowment left by Abdiel Smith early in the century after blacks had petitioned that such schools be established. In Ohio by the middle 1830s scattered separate schools were supported by white benefactors, special subscriptions, and similar means. But even these private and tenuous beginnings were sometimes frustrated by white opposition. Prudence Crandall's school for girls in Canter-

---

1. Franklin Johnson, *The Development of State Legislation Concerning the Free Negro* (New York: Arbor Press, 1918), 52-53; and Edward R. Turner, *The Negro in Pennsylvania, 1639-1861* (Washington: American Historical Association, 1912), 131-132.

bury, Connecticut, was forced to close in 1834 because of local hostility and a resultant state law prohibiting the establishment of schools for out-of-state Negroes. Shortly thereafter the integrated Noyes Academy in New Hampshire was shut down by mob action.

Consequently, for most Negroes, the basic concern was simply getting some kind of school for their children, without regard to their theoretical preferences for integration or segregation. "We will never cease to urge our claims either for admission on terms of equality into the Public Schools, or for the establishment of separate Schools for our children until our object is attained," Jamaica, Long Island, blacks maintained with an eye to the possible.[2] And their resolution captured the thrust of much black thought. In the late 1820s and early 1830s Negroes began to found private schools for their children. In Philadelphia a group of "respectable people of colour" planned such a school in 1827. The Phoenix Society was only one of several groups in New York City to establish schools during the period. In Cleveland canal boat captain John Malvin solicited funds for a school, and in Pittsburgh the African Education Society was similarly engaged. Many schools thus begun were short-lived, and most separate schools were not black-sponsored. In 1837, for instance, of the twenty schools in Ohio which admitted blacks, only four were controlled by Negroes.[3]

Exciting as race efforts to found schools were individually, they were collectively inadequate to meet the minimal needs of the community. Consequently, black Americans, like white, turned to local and state government for educational assistance. Those of Philadelphia petitioned the state legislature in 1832 to admit their children to the public schools on the grounds that they, like whites, paid taxes to support public education.[4] Their request failed and twenty

2. *Voice of the Fugitive,* July 16, 1851.

3. *Freedom's Journal,* May 11, 1827. Charles T. Hickok, *Negro in Ohio, 1802-1870* (Cleveland: Press of Williams Publishing and Electric Company, 1896), 88. Benjamin Quarles, *Black Abolitionists* (New York: Oxford University Press, 1969), 108-109. *Colored American,* October 14, 1837.

4. *Hazard's Register,* IX (June 1832), 361-362. The contention was also made that blacks constituted a proportionately smaller part of the pauper population than whites and were therefore less of a financial burden on the community.

years later, in a rather more dramatic fashion, wealthy suburban landowner Robert Purvis of Byberry refused to pay taxes for schools from which his children were excluded. The suggestion of local officials that he send them to the nearby Mechanicsville school brought only denunciation from Purvis, who called the segregated school a "flimsy and ridiculous sham." A man of property and a substantial tax payer, Purvis won his contest.[5] For most, however, such assaults upon the citadels of power were scarcely possible.

On the West Coast the problem was no different. The Sacramento Common Council in 1855 appropriated money to educate Negro children. The mayor, contending that their action might alienate local citizens of Southern background, vetoed it and won. Joining with several aldermen, he argued that the state constitution limited citizenship to whites and forbade tax appropriations for noncitizens.[6]

Wholly excluded from Ohio's common schools during the 1830s, blacks there relied completely on the inadequate facilities provided by private schools, many of them run by abolitionists. It was not until they established the School Fund Institution in 1838 that there was any statewide coordination in providing schools. Within the year this privately funded agency opened nine schools for Negroes. Although the available facilities were still insufficient, a state convention in 1839 failed to devise a better system.[7] Constantly thereafter Ohio meetings sought ways to educate black children. The state conventions of 1851, 1852, and 1857 all debated the question at length, acting on Ohio laws passed in 1848 and 1849 which provided that in towns where their children were excluded from the public schools the taxes blacks paid might be used to fund schools built, directed, and managed by officials chosen by Negroes.[8] On the whole, these laws met the minimal

5. *Liberator*, December 16, 1853. Also *ibid.*, September 21, 1860.
6. *Ibid.*, December 14, 1855.
7. *Ibid.*, October 18, 1839. *Colored American*, October 19, 1839.
8. State Convention of the Colored Citizens of Ohio, *Minutes . . . 1851* ([Columbus]: E. Glover, [1851]). 12. Convention of the Colored Freemen *of Ohio*, Proceedings . . . [1852] (Cincinnati: Dumas & Lawyer, 1852), 8.

goals set by early conventions in the state, yet soon the apparent success began to fade. Legislation passed in 1853 put black schools under the supervision of the white district in which they fell. Only sharp protest from Cincinnati, where the black population was most dense, gained an exception for that city's schools. There, after 1856, black schools were returned to the control of boards elected by Negroes.[9]

Despite all the energy consumed in extracting any schools at all from a reluctant society, blacks, especially in the East, vigorously debated the relative merits of segregation and integration. As early as 1827 *Freedom's Journal* condemned the common assumption that in Negro schools the standards for teachers and pupils should be significantly lower than those in white schools. "A little smattering, and a few words recommendatory from his teacher, are all [school examiners] look for from a boy of colour. The very idea of his colour, is enough to elicit praise . . . when the same exercise performed as well by another boy, would pass unnoticed, and be considered as a thing of course."[10] In consequence children in segregated schools inevitably received an inferior education and their talents went largely undeveloped. "The fatal practice," Cornish noted a decade later, "of HALF qualifying, and then HALF paying a colored brother for his services, has long discouraged and well nigh ruined our very best men."[11]

Charles Reason, a professor at the biracial Central College in McGrawville, New York, argued a somewhat different point. Separate schools, he told a Boston Equal School Rights meeting in 1849, existed only where one race felt superior to the other. The mere fact of separation made Negro children believe they were inferior and thus dashed their hopes and crushed their ambitions.[12] And the previous year, Garnet, invigorated by

---

State Convention of the Colored Men of the State of Ohio, *Proceedings of . . . Held in the City of Columbus, January 21st, 22nd, and 23rd, 1857* (Columbus: John Geary & Son, 1857), 7. Hickok, *Negro in Ohio, 90-91.*

9. Hickok, *Negro in Ohio,* 101-102.
10. *Freedom's Journal,* June 1, 1827.
11. *Colored American,* August 12, 1837.
12. *Liberator,* February 6, 1850.

Europe's turmoil in 1848, predicted radical change in America as "revolution after revolution" occurred "until all men [would be] placed upon equality." Integrated education was, he thought, a necessary step in that revolution.[13]

For others, the case against separate schools was neither clear nor convincing. Lewis Woodson envisaged quality black schools as a prod to race pride. He would not tell those who wished to establish separate churches and schools that they were wrong, for to do so "would destroy all confidence in themselves; paralise [sic] their energies; and prevent them from doing by half what they might do. I would tell them," he continued, emphasizing their separateness, "to 'go ahead,' and build themselves up in every thing, to a perfect level with their white brethren; and then the passage from one side to the other would be easy, because the way would in fact be smooth and *level*."[14]

Others argued that young Negroes needed models whom they could emulate. A Poughkeepsie man, writing to the *Colored American* in 1840, insisted that black youth needed black teachers if they were themselves to aspire to that profession. Pennington went further when he endorsed separate normal schools to train and supply black teachers to race schools.[15] Conversely, the *Impartial Citizen* pointed out, only black schools could forestall the "crippling and discouraging of competent teachers" in the black community because white schools would not hire them.[16]

The issue was not exclusively providing a circular supply of more black teachers. Preachers and teachers constituted the core of community leadership. To be independent and effective in stimulating race pride, they must serve black institutions and black institutions must be served by them. Thus on the eve of the Civil War, a correspondent of the *Weekly Anglo-African* deplored black churches' seeking white pastors, who had no roots in the community they would serve.[17] The 1865 Pennsylvania State

13. *North Star,* May 19, 1848.
14. *Colored American,* November 10, 1838.
15. *Ibid.,* May 23, 1840. *North Star,* May 19, 1848.
16. *Impartial Citizen,* June 28, 1851.
17. *Weekly Anglo-African,* January 7, 1860.

Equal Rights Convention attested that the point was valid for teachers as for the clergy when it resolved that black teachers should be given preference in black schools because they were "better qualified by conventional circumstances outside of the schoolhouse."[18]

The arguments pitting the merits of segregation against those of integration clashed head-on at the Rochester convention of 1853. Integrationists were convinced that "precisely the same species of learning imparted to white youth [would] best serve for colored youth." Moreover, since white academies and colleges were clearly superior to the few Negro schools then in existence, blacks should attend them. Separatists questioned these assumptions. They doubted that Negro youths, already far behind their white counterparts, could profit from the higher education which white colleges offered without the special assistance and encouragement that only a segregated education could provide. "Neither schools nor educators for the whites, at present," they argued, "are in full sympathy" with the black student. Furthermore they doubted the merits of a white education for a potential race leader. "He must either abandon his own state of things which he finds around him, and which he is pledged to change and better, or cease to receive culture from such sources, since their whole tendency is to change him, not his condition—to educate him out of his sympathies, not to quicken and warm his sympathies, for all that is of worth to him is his elevation, and the elevation of his people."[19]

Both points of view shaped a series of school battles which individual communities fought out. One of the earliest erupted in New York City late in the 1830s. Attendance at the African free schools had been falling off badly when the trustees moved in 1839 either to curtail or abandon their operation altogether. In immediate response to this threat to the community's already meagre educational facilities, a group of race leaders, primarily

18. State Equal Rights' Convention, *Proceedings of the . . . Convention . . . Held in the City of Harrisburg, February 8th, 9th, and 10th, 1865 . . .* (Philadelphia: Printed For and By the Order of the Convention, 1865. Reprint, Philadelphia: Rhistoric Publications, n.d.), 19.

19. *Frederick Douglass' Paper*, July 29, 1853.

preachers and teachers, rallied to defend their segregated school system. They formed a committee which developed a program to "secure a full attendance at all the schools, and carry the benefits of our school system to all the families of our colored population."[20] The committee hoped thus to close the gap between parents and schools and, in so doing, it did forestall the projected closings. Yet more than community apathy and disunity were involved in the crisis, for criticism of the schools' deficiencies, characteristic of publicly supported separate schools, was a constant theme in local discussions. Both Ruggles and Cornish, in their respective journals, condemned the poorly trained teachers, the inadequate funding, and the deficient buildings.[21] Some gave up altogether on the free schools to back quality private schools, especially the New York Select Academy, which in 1840 was run completely by Negroes. Thomas S. Sidney, one of the most promising young blacks in the city, was then its principal with the talented Alexander Crummell his assistant.[22] Hopes for the academy, however, were soon dashed by Sidney's death and Crummell's decision to pursue the Episcopal ministry.

The entire question of the role of the African free schools was thrown into further confusion by state legislation passed in 1841 to end the New York City system in which private societies controlled publicly supported schools. Although the struggle for a genuine public school system was primarily an issue between Protestant and Catholic forces, the administration of black schools was affected by it. And, much as control of the city schools remained in Protestant hands despite the new law, so it was whites who decided to continue separate race schools. Some progress was made in the late 1840s and early 1850s when a special Negro board was appointed to supervise these schools.[23] Nevertheless the black schools remained the stepchildren of the city system. A study made in 1857 by the New York Society for the Promotion of

20. *Colored American,* January 26, 1839.
21. *Mirror of Liberty,* January, 1839. *Colored American,* October 19, 1839.
22. *Colored American,* May 18 and October 19, 1839.
23. *Voice of the Fugitive,* June 4, 1851.

Education among Colored Children again condemned the neglected state of the buildings and the overcrowding which resulted from placing all the city's Negro children in eight small schools. The solution they proposed was to abandon school segregation. But cognizant of white hostility, they also suggested as a second choice that, if separate schools were continued, a minimum of two new buildings should be erected to replace and consolidate the eight outdated schools then in operation. The city failed to take even that step, although it did demolish and rebuild the most dilapidated school, the one on Mulberry Street. The Laurens Street school, located in the worst section of the city where parents feared to send their children, was neither closed nor rebuilt but only remodeled. All others remained untouched.[24]

Upstate in Rochester, on the other hand, developments were somewhat more satisfactory. There, a publicly financed separate school had been established in 1832 at the request of black residents whose children had been largely excluded from the town schools. As in New York, however, the school was always inadequately financed both before and after the 1841 law which required its incorporation in the city school system and participation in public funding. Subsequent state legislation designed to force towns to provide adequate schools for Negro children left the situation equally untouched until in 1847 Frederick Douglass moved to Rochester and led an attack on the whole segregated system. Publicized in the columns of the *North Star* and well-received among white abolitionists in this upstate antislavery stronghold, Douglass' critique concentrated upon the city's renting the cold and clammy basement of the Zion Methodist Church for the school—an approach which exposed both governmental unconcern and black collusion in the unsatisfactory conditions.[25]

24. *Anglo-African Magazine,* I (July, 1859), 222-224.
25. Judith P. Ruchin, "The Abolition of Colored Schools in Rochester, New York: 1832-1856," *New York History,* LI (July 1970), 376-382. Douglass' first school conflict in Rochester was with the private Seward Academy to which he had sent his daughter. She was soon excluded because of the objections of white parents. See his protest in *North Star,* September 22, 1848.

When this first effort failed to achieve integration, Rochester blacks mounted a second attack in 1854 to improve the quality of the segregated school. They castigated the school board for hiring a prejudiced white teacher rather than the Negro teacher whom they had recommended. Yet it was neither black attacks on segregation nor demands for community control which ended separate education in Rochester in 1856. Practical action both by blacks and by whites rather than theoretical considerations doomed it. First, the Zion Church trustees no longer wished to rent their basement and no alternative location was available. Secondly, whites realized that the per pupil cost of segregated education was exorbitantly high.[26] Thus Rochester residents quietly ended segregation on the purely pragmatic grounds of economic utility.

Of all the antebellum school segregation fights, Boston's is best known. Public drama peaked there in 1849 when, in the Roberts case, Charles Sumner eloquently, though unsuccessfully, argued the case for integrated schooling. But this court encounter was only one act in the larger, black-dominated drama staged to end segregation. Central to it was the labor of William Nell. Childless himself, Nell was driven by his own searing experience in the city's separate school in the 1820s. An excellent student, he had been denied the customary prize for academic merit solely because he was a Negro. Smarting from that scar and encouraged by white Garrisonians, Nell in 1844 undertook an attack on the heart of segregation in Boston. With the aid of his fellow townsmen, he led an extended war which finally, in 1855, achieved the integration which the schools of Salem, New Bedford, Nantucket, Worcester, and Lowell had already achieved, also with broad white support.[27]

---

26. *Frederick Douglass' Paper*, September 1, 1854. Ruchin, "Abolition of Colored Schools in Rochester," 392. Douglass' campaign against segregated education throughout New York state failed, however, as the state passed legislation in 1864 permitting separate schools; see *Douglass Monthly*, March, 1859, and Johnson, *Development of State Legislation*, 52.

27. *Liberator*, December 28, 1855. Carleton Mabee, "A Negro Boycott to Integrate Boston Schools," *New England Quarterly*, XLI (September, 1968), 341-361. Leon F. Litwack, *North of Slavery. The Negro in the Free States, 1790-1860* (Chicago: University of Chicago Press, 1961), 143.

The first round of the Boston drama concentrated on the harsh discipline and lackadaisical teaching of Abner Forbes, the white master of the Smith School. He feruled the boys on the soles of their bare feet and the girls on the backs of their hands. He used abusive and obscene language to students and parents. He neglected his classroom duties, sometimes reading newspapers during class time, sometimes failing to appear at all. Worse yet, he acted so as to make his pupils feel inferior. In publicizing these charges, a special committee, sparked by Nell and chaired by John Hilton, not only requested the city school committee to replace Forbes but to abolish the Smith School. The school committee made no response to either request. Forbes was retained and the school in Belknap street remained open.[28]

Although in the following year the school committee again refused petitions urging integration,[29] in 1846 it did undertake a thorough study of the entire issue. Its two antislavery members presented a minority report urging an end to segregation. Because republican government conferred "civil equality and legal rights upon every citizen," the minority contended that it could not create any "difference between rich and poor, learned and ignorant, white and black." The majority rejected their argument and voted to retain segregation as a necessary barrier against amalgamation and racial tension. Denying, in any case, that the separate schools were inferior, they openly doubted that the minority position represented the views of most Boston Negroes.[30]

The doubt was, in fact, quite justified, for the argument over the relative merits of segregation and integration split Boston's black community as it divided opinion elsewhere. Over the next few years the integrationists continued their petition campaigns to end segregated schooling. They also backed Benjamin Roberts' 1849 recourse to the courts, where he challenged the legality of excluding his daughter Sarah from the schools in her immediate neighborhood and forcing her to walk to a distant segregated

28. *Liberator*, June 28 and August 2, 1844.
29. *Ibid.*, June 27, 1845.
30. *Ibid.*, August 21, 1846.

school. It was on her behalf that Charles Sumner, not yet a United States Senator, argued that separate facilities were inherently unequal and thus inconsistent with the Massachusetts constitution.

Equally insistent, however, was pressure from those who would use segregation to build strong black institutions. Led by Thomas Paul Smith, they successfully pressured the school committee to appoint Thomas Paul, a black Dartmouth graduate, principal of the Smith School.[31] If temporarily this group seemed to have the upper hand, it was not for long. In September 1849, as soon as Paul was appointed, the newly formed Committee of Supervision of the School Rights Question began a boycott of the Smith School which lasted somewhat longer than a year. Those participating sent their children to a temporary school taught by a local minister where efforts were made to prevent further damage to their educational experience. Concomitant with the boycott were a series of weekly meetings held to keep the community informed, to support the boycotters, and to spur on the fight against segregation. Although their efforts flagged for a while when the Roberts case was decided against them, they effectively refocused their campaign on petitioning the state legislature to end school segregation throughout the commonwealth.[32]

Finally, in 1855, the legislature acted to ban separate schools within Massachusetts, and in September Boston integrated its schools. Nell, who had organized the petition campaigns and the boycott, and Roberts, who had joined these efforts when his court case failed, received the thanks of their community at a victory celebration, where the "valiant" children and "vigilant" mothers who bore the brunt of the boycott were also lauded.[33] As Charles Remond observed, they had collectively forced both city and state to end school segregation and, in so doing, had demonstrated "that the colored people were beginning to understand the necessity of

31. Thomas P. Smith to James McCune Smith, August 2, 1849, *Liberator,* January 4, 1850.

32. *Ibid.,* September 7, 14, and 21, October 5, November 9, 1849, and April 26, 1850.

33. *Ibid.,* November 10, 1854.

adhesiveness and consistency."[34]

Unhappily the Boston experience was exceptional, as the case of Rhode Island soon demonstrated. Moved by the Massachusetts example, Providence blacks in 1857 petitioned their state legislature to end segregation. Pointing to the inadequate faculty and facilities which characterized the segregated schools of Newport and Bristol as well as of Providence, they argued that separate schools necessarily instilled a sense of inferiority in the students they served. Yet this contention, which had borne fruit in Massachusetts, failed to convince the legislators of its southern neighbor. The 1857 petition not only failed to produce change but presented an occasion for a legislative committee report in 1858 excoriating desegregation in any form.[35] There the matter stood until after the Civil War.

If separate schools offered a possible alternative, separate courts did not. Consequently efforts to gain full legal rights as witnesses, jurors, and defendants were aimed largely at changing state laws governing the trial process. In many states, including Ohio, Indiana, Illinois, Iowa, and California, blacks could not testify against whites. A whole series of Ohio conventions, which regularly opposed the state's black code, challenged blacks' exclusion from the witness box. Indiana Negroes devoted a major part of their conventions of 1851 and 1857 to being able to testify in court without racial restrictions. In 1848 and 1852 conventions in Illinois firmly protested against Negroes' exclusion from the witness box. And on the West Coast, the California black community was vocal and vociferous in demanding that their testimony be admitted equally in the courts. Whether their particular zeal derived from a higher degree of property holding or from the ethos of a new frontier is not clear, but between 1851

34. *Ibid.*, December 28, 1855.
35. Colored People of Providence, *Will the General Assembly Put Down Caste Schools?* ([Providence]: n.p., December, 1857), *passim.*

and 1855 San Francisco Negroes annually petitioned for the right to testify in court. In 1852 California blacks organized a statewide Franchise League, whose prime concern was less the vote than the right to testify against whites. And state conventions held in 1855, 1856, and 1857 all placed the witness issue at the head of their grievances.[36]

Equally as important as the right to be witnesses was the right to serve on juries, from which Negroes were almost universally barred. This issue was particularly acute in the 1850s as cases deriving from the stringent Fugitive Slave Law of 1850 came to court. Even in Massachusetts, where the law made no racial distinctions in legal rights, practice excluded Negroes from juries. It was only constant agitation which forced a change in 1859 when the Commonwealth's first Negro jurors were impaneled in Worcester.[37] In Ohio, where they were specifically excluded by law, the debate was more dramatic. Long an issue, it came to a head late in the decade when Charles H. Langston, schoolteacher and activist, was arrested for his role in the Oberlin-Wellington fugitive rescue case of 1859. Found guilty of violating the 1850 law, Langston, in his plea to the court, contested the court's right to try him. In so doing, he based his argument on the injustice done any black defendant judged by an all-white jury.

Central to Langston's contention was the explicit assumption that all whites were prejudiced against all blacks. Why that was so was not his mission to explain. It was simply a fact amply borne out in his own trial, where the "jurors are well known to have shared largely in these prejudices." Consequently, he said, "they were

36. Litwack, *North of Slavery,* 93. Emma Lou Thornbrough, *The Negro in Indiana: A Study of a Minority* (Indiana Historical Collections, XXXVII. Indianapolis: Indiana Historical Bureau, 1957), 146, 164. *North Star,* September 29, 1848. *Frederick Douglass' Paper,* January 14, 1853. James A. Fisher, "The Struggle for Negro Testimony in California, 1851-1863," *Southern California Quarterly,* LI (December, 1969), 314-320. Rudolph M. Lapp, "The Negro in Gold Rush California," *Journal of Negro History,* XLIX (April, 1964), 95-98. Colored Citizens of California, *Proceedings of the First State Convention ... [1855],* 3. *Liberator,* January 11, 1856, as taken from the Sacramento *Tribune,* November 21, 1855. *Liberator,* July 3, 1857.

37. *Liberator,* December 28, 1855. Litwack, *North of Slavery,* 94.

neither impartial, nor were they a jury of my peers. . . . I was tried by a jury who were prejudiced; before a Court that was prejudiced; prosecuted by an officer who was prejudiced, and defended, though ably, by counsel who were prejudiced. . . . I have not been tried," he concluded, urging the injustice of his conviction, "either by a jury of my peers, according to the principles of the common law, or by an impartial jury according to the Constitution of the United States." Whether as a result of his plea or of the rather tenuous evidence presented against him, the presiding judge sentenced Langston to a much shorter prison term and a much lighter fine than that imposed on the only other defendant who was found guilty, Simeon Bushnell, a white man.[38] Significantly, however, Langston was sentenced and Ohio law continued until after the Civil War to exclude Negroes from the jury box.

In contrast to the quest for jury duty, efforts to attain access to the militia embraced both the formation of separate units and attempts to alter the laws excluding blacks from militia duty. In the antebellum North, membership in certain militia companies gave social prestige. Consequently German and Irish immigrants, often denied admission to the most desirable units, gained permission, in various states, to organize their own militia groups. Blacks, excluded by law from militia duty in all states, also sought redress in the same way; but more often they pressed for broader legal changes.

The idea surfaced first in 1845 at the New York State Convention in Syracuse. There Garnet and Thomas Van Rensselaer clashed over Negro exemption from military duty. The latter argued against demands that blacks be admitted to a militia which upheld proslavery government. Garnet, however, insisted that

38. Charles H. Langston, *Should a Colored Man be Subject to the Pains and Penalties of the Fugitive Slave Law? Speech . . .Before the U.S. District Court for the Northern District of Ohio, May 12, 1859* (Cleveland: Ohio Anti-Slavery Society, 1859), 11-12, for the quotations. Jacob R. Shipherd, comp., *History of the Oberlin-Wellington Rescue* (Boston: J. P. Jewett & Co., 1859), 169, 170, 178.

training in arms was the right and duty of all citizens, like the franchise and jury duty. As long as he lived under the aegis of a government, he said, he would demand all those rights.[39]

Garnet's position, with slight qualification, won almost unanimous approval at Syracuse, strong support at Troy in 1847, and similar support at Cleveland the following year. At both of the latter conventions the militia question extended into a debate over the requirements of self-defense. Since Negroes in America must provide their own armed protection, the delegates argued, they especially needed militia training. At Troy they commended "the propriety of instructing their sons in the art of war,"[40] though at Cleveland, they failed to adopt a resolution urging blacks to study the art of military science "so as to enable them to measure arms with assailants without and invaders within."[41]

During the decade preceding the Civil War, the militia question took on even more urgency. Negroes sought duty in regular militia units. They organized extralegal units of their own. They debated the occasions when they might properly fight for their country. At least twice during the decade Massachusetts blacks pressed the state legislature for access to the state militia. In 1853 Bostonians formed a Garrison Association to agitate for a black militia unit. Both William Watkins and Robert Morris testified before a legislative committee for a "colored Military Company."[42] Noting that an Irish company had recently been approved by the legislature, Morris sought the same privilege for blacks. "We do not want . . . a step-mother in the case," he said, "who will butter the bread for one, and sand it for another."[43] It was important, Watkins added, that blacks have "an unrestricted right to the enjoyment of full civil privileges." To exempt them from militia

39. *National Anti-Slavery Standard,* September 11, 1845.
40. National Convention of Colored People, *Proceedings . . .1847,* 17.
41. *North Star,* September 29, 1848.
42. *Liberator,* March 11, 1853.
43. William C. Nell, *The Colored Patriots of the American Revolution with Sketches of Several Distinguished Colored Persons: to which is added a Brief Survey of the Conditions and Prospects of Colored Americans* (Boston: Robert F. Wallcut, 1855. Reprint, New York: Arno Press, 1968), 102.

duty effectually classed them with idiots, lunatics, drunkards, vagabonds, paupers, and criminals.[44]

Defeated when both the legislature and a constitutional convention refused to entertain their request,[45] blacks tried again in 1860. This time they drafted a petition to strike the word "white" from the state's militia law. John Rock addressed the Committee on Federal Relations of the Massachusetts House of Representatives in its support, delivering to them large parts of the speech he had first given at the 1858 Boston Massacre celebration, refuting charges of Negro cowardice. Unmoved, the legislature failed to act. Fifteen months later, with civil war already begun, it defeated still another measure to remove the restrictions on black service in the militia.[46]

When the state government most sympathetic to their rights refused blacks militia service, little could be expected elsewhere. Nonetheless unauthorized private militia companies sprang up throughout the North. In Cincinnati, in 1857, the Attucks Blues was organized to study military tactics and to "become more proficient in the use of arms." The unit pledged itself to serve "our State, our people and country."[47] In Reading, Pennsylvania, the Douglass Guards was established with somewhat less dynamism, and soon its members evinced only "luke-warmness in regard[to] their company."[48] More successful, Harrisburg's Henry Highland Garnet Guards attracted members with smart uniforms and "new muskets."[49] The military company in Paterson, New Jersey, stressed both physical training and race consciousness and won praise from a correspondent to the *Weekly Anglo-African* for

44. William J. Watkins, *Our Rights as Men. An Address Delivered in Boston, Before the Legislative Committee on the Militia, February 24, 1853* . . . (Boston: Benjamin F. Roberts, [1853]. Reprint, in Dorothy Porter, ed., *Negro Protest Pamphlets*, New York: Arno Press, 1969), 18, quotation on 7.
45. *Liberator*, May 13 and July 1, 1853.
46. *Ibid.*, March 2, 1860, May 24, 1861.
47. State Convention of the Colored Men of the State of Ohio, *Proceedings . . . 1857*, 6.
48. *Weekly Anglo-African*, September 24, 1859; quotations, *ibid.*, October 29, 1859.
49. *Ibid.*, August 6, 1859.

making guns as well as letters, "aids to elevation, and assistants to the work of reformation."[50] But despite their efforts, Northern blacks had to wait well into the Civil War before their military services were wanted or utilized by the states whose militias had continued, until then, to deny them entry.

The issue of segregation and discrimination in predominately white churches proved a more complex issue both because the matter was not governed by law and because separate black churches offered clear advantages. They played a central role in providing leaders and in uniting their members in a variety of self-help activities. Contrary to conditions pertaining in almost all separate schools, separate church policies and practices were usually shaped and governed by their members and ministers. In most Northern cities, furthermore, if a Negro attended church at all it was more likely to be a black than a predominately white one. But not even the pride and loyalty which black churches generated lessened resentment of Jim Crow treatment in other Christian churches, where "Negro pews" effectively separated blacks from whites.

None were more vocal in protesting such discrimination than those clergy who, in denominational matters, suffered professionally the same ostracism that laymen met in the pews. Samuel Cornish, always a loyal Presbyterian, persistently attacked such practices, especially in his own sect. One of his most vigorous denunciations arose from parental indignation as well as clerical status. In the columns of the *Colored American*, he described how his children had, on one occasion when he could not take them to his own black congregation, attended a white church in their neighborhood and been relegated to the Negro pew. They returned home to ask their father in perplexed wonderment, "Why do white people hate us so?" Cornish could do no more than take their question straight to his fellow clergymen. Charging them to look

50. *Ibid.,* October 8, 1859.

into their own hearts, he beseeched them to alter their church practices. To fail to do so was to fail in the Christian ministry. "You are verily guilty—you are *Slaves* to a wicked public sentiment—you dare not warn the people—God will hold you responsible. . . ."[51]

Cornish also exposed the injustice of never calling black ministers to serve white churches, although white clerics frequently served black congregations. The offense was double since it encouraged white prejudice and, at the same time, deprived Negro churches of ministers expertly qualified by experience and training to meet their needs.[52] And from this premise it followed logically that black laymen should attend their own churches. But if they did belong to a white parish, they should refuse absolutely to sit in Negro pews and "sanction their own degradation." If there was no alternative, they should stand in the aisle.[53]

Among other churchmen, the response was much the same. Baltimore Methodists in 1840 protested the action of the General Conference of the Methodist Episcopal Church which forbade blacks to give testimony "against the white members of the church" in states where Negro testimony was barred in civil and criminal proceedings. The fact that their petition against "this soul-sickening resolution" was not even presented to the Conference delegates suggests the attitudes of white churchmen generally.[54] Three years later New York Negroes objected when Episcopal Bishop Henry Onderdonk refused to allow Alexander Crummell to hold a parish in his diocese unless Crummell guaranteed not to send a delegate from his church to any diocesan convention.[55] The decision, consonant with an earlier one denying Crummell admission to the Episcopal Theological Seminary in New York, rankled so much that Crummell went to England to take a divinity degree and then settled in Liberia

51. *Colored American,* March 11 and 18, 1837, quotations in the latter.
52. *Ibid.,* April 1 and August 12, 1837.
53. *Ibid.,* August 19, 1837.
54. *Ibid.,* July 4, 1840.
55. *Liberator,* July 21, 1843.

Frederick Douglass went well beyond protesting Jim Crowism in white churches and denounced separate black churches themselves as a form of segregation. Exclusively black institutions of any kind, he argued in 1848, merely encouraged discrimination and prejudice. "Negro pews in the church; negro boxes in the theatre; negro cars on the railroad; negro berths in the steamboat; negro churches and negro schools in the community, are all the pernicious fruit of a wicked, unnatural, and blasphemous prejudice against our God-given complexion; and as such stand directly in the way of our progress and equality."[56] On the matter of churches, Douglass went unheard, for the separate church constituted a uniquely black-controlled institution and was thus a major vehicle for expressing race solidarity and fostering leadership. Yet the rest of his argument reflected the general antebellum protest against segregation.

On facilities other than church and school there was virtually no defense of segregation. Yet some discriminatory patterns drew less attention than others. A case in point was the fight to repeal the Massachusetts antimiscegenation law. Launched by Garrison in the second issue of the *Liberator*, it was pressed by Massachusetts abolitionists for the next twelve years.[57] Boston Negroes, however, remained largely silent on the subject until, early in 1843, rumor whispered that they did not care about repeal. Unwilling to let the aspersion stand, they held a public meeting in the Belknap Street church on February 1 and dismissed "with indignation, the attempt which designing individuals have made to persuade the public that the colored people, as a body, do not approve and support the efforts . . . to efface from the statute book of Massachusetts the law, and destroy the customs, which make a distinction in regard to the rights of citizens on account of color."[58]

Clear-cut as their resolution was, it is significant that it failed to mention the nature of the statute under attack and focused rather

56. *North Star*, March 10, 1848.
57. Louis Ruchames, "Race, Marriage and Abolition in Massachusetts," *Journal of Negro History*, XL (July, 1955), 250-273.
58. *Liberator*, February 10, 1843.

on all discrimination based on color. Indeed the other business of the meeting indicated that Massachusetts Negroes were far more concerned about segregated transportation and found "the illegal and oppressive customs of some of the rail-road corporations of the State" a "more immediate and trying grievance than any other."[59] Except for schools, Jim Crow cars and forward-deck boat accommodations spurred, throughout the North, more protest than any other form of discrimination. Nearly a decade before the Belknap Street meeting, the national convention of 1834 had recommended that blacks "patronize those conveyances and establishments only, in which are granted us equal privileges for our money."[60] Since segregation in public conveyances and places of amusement was largely a matter of practice and custom rather than of law, selective economic pressure offered a sound strategy for effective action. Here blacks could do considerably more than pass resolutions and petition the legislature. Where social custom and corporate usage alone stood in their way, they could and did respond with immediate and personal resistance in an attempt to force decisive change.

David Ruggles exemplified the pattern of resistance. Partially blind, he tried in 1841 to buy a first-class ticket on the Nantucket and New Bedford steamer. For his initial impertinence he was physically attacked by the captain. When he protested that action in a letter to a New Bedford newspaper, his private papers were seized. Incensed New Bedford blacks held a mass meeting, presided over by the then obscure Frederick Douglass, to protest Ruggles' treatment. Its inefficacy was demonstrated when Ruggles, now widely identified as a trouble-maker, bought a first-class ticket on the New Bedford and Taunton Railroad and insisted on keeping the seat in the all-white car to which his ticket entitled him. Not to be outdone by the steamboat officials, the conductor tried to oust him, and when Ruggles refused to budge, the superintendent and

59. *Ibid.*, February 10, 1843.

60. Convention for the Improvement of the Free People of Colour, *Minutes of the Fourth Annual Convention . . . Held . . . in . . . New York, from the 2d to the 12th of June inclusive, 1834* (New York: Published by Order of the Convention, 1834. Reprint, New York: Arno Press, 1969), 15.

several supporters beat him, tore his clothes, threw him bodily from the train, and refused to get his trunk from the baggage car.[61]

Ruggles, not to be thwarted, promptly took the matter to court, charged the "minions" of the railroad with assault, and tried to force them "to explain, under oath, the object of their pretended rule and their fraudulent practices upon the public." Pressing his luck, he planned to use the evidence thus obtained to challenge the railroad in civil court. The court, however, refused to cooperate. Judge Henry Crapo, a stockholder in the railroad, heard the assault case and decided that since Ruggles had refused to sit where he was told, attempts to remove him did not constitute assault.[62]

For a while, the railroad was smug in its victory; but Ruggles' challenge had set a new tone locally. Determined to end discrimination on a line which served one of the largest concentrations of blacks in the state, Negroes continued to bring pressure on it. Twice in 1842, for example, the opponents clashed. Once Shadrack Howard, incensed because he was denied a place on the cars, fought it out with fisticuffs—and lost. Another time Richard Johnson and his daughter were denied the places they had purchased. When remonstrance failed to alter official policy, Johnson hired a private conveyance to take them to Boston and then publicized the incident. Although individually such challenges seldom won their immediate points, their collective impact was sufficient to end Jim Crow facilities on Massachusetts railroads. In spite of the fact that the 1842 legislative hearings on the question of railroad discrimination brought no change in Massachusetts law, the practice was soon ended by voluntary action.[63]

Like Ruggles, Henry Highland Garnet battled persistently against Jim Crow transportation. He well remembered how, as a "cripple[d], weak, sickly, feeble" lad, he had had to ride atop a railroad car to get to the Noyes Academy in Canaan, New Hampshire, because on that line Negroes were not allowed to ride

61. *Liberator,* July 9 and 23, 1841.
62. *Ibid.,* August 6, 1841.
63. *Ibid.,* February 18 and October 7, 1842.

inside.[64] As an adult therefore he fought the system, even though by then he had already undergone the amputation of one leg. When, early in the 1840s, he had refused to move from the first-class car, reserved for whites, to the second-class car, where blacks were permitted, he had forced the Utica and Schenectady Railroad to change its policy. Then, in 1848, he happened to be in Providence when a protest meeting assembled to condemn the Stonington Railroad for having forced Jeremiah Myers to ride Jim Crow up to Worcester. Garnet urged an all-out attack. Calling the "aristocratic, purse-proud" railroad "the meanest and the most iniquitous" on American soil, he advised his audience to resist its conductors when they tried to enforce segregated seating. "He would not pretend to say how they should resist, *but they should resist*," one auditor reported. "For his part, he generally hugged the seats, and sometimes they would go with him as a whole or in part."[65]

The hazards of Garnet's course were demonstrated when, two months later, he set out for Canada. As he boarded the cars at Buffalo for Niagara Falls the conductor ordered him to move to the car directly behind the engine. "Not being accustomed to yield up my rights without making at least a semblance of lawful resistance," Garnet wrote, he refused to move, and was thrown from the train, severely beaten, and forced to seek medical attention.[66]

Despite the examples of Ruggles, Garnet, and Howard, other challengers sought test cases rather than physical violence. This was especially true of efforts to end discrimination on city street car lines where, in cities big enough to make commuting to work a necessity, transportation was critical to economic survival.[67]

64. Alexander Crummell, *Africa and America: Address and Discourses* (Springfield: Willey and Co., 1891), 279.
65. *North Star*, April 14, 1848.
66. *Ibid.*, June 23, 1848. Quotation in *Anti-Slavery Bugle*, July 7, 1848.
67. In a letter to the editor of the *New York Evangelist* (ca. 1853), J. W. C. Pennington emphasizes this point of economic necessity and public transportation: see Carter G. Woodson, *Mind of the Negro as Reflected in Letters Written During the Crisis, 1800-1860* (Washington: Association for the Study of Negro Life and History, 1926), 650.

Elizabeth Jennings, a young organist in New York, used the Third Avenue line regularly to get to the Congregational Church where she played. One Sunday in 1854 when she was traveling to her job, she was denied a seat on the first car and was referred to the second, already crowded, as "reserved for her people." She refused to move, and the conductor told her that she might remain in the first car if no one objected. When she rejected those demeaning terms, she was summarily ordered from the car for her boldness. Refusing to leave, she was thrown out by the driver and the conductor. Undaunted, she boarded again and this time a policeman threw her off. Thoroughly enraged, Jennings sued the car line for damages. Her case eventually reached the State Supreme Court, and there her lawyer, a young man named Chester A. Arthur, won her a judgment of $225.[68]

Victory though it was, it did not convince the black community that their rights were permanently secure. Thus Elizabeth Jennings' father, Thomas, a dentist, and clergymen James Pennington and M. H. Freeman led in organizing the New York Legal Rights Association to press the campaign against "the rules of the various public conveyances" which deprived them of the "use of common carrier conveyances."[69] To test the "legal rights in travel, &c. &c., in the Courts of Law"[70] Pennington sued, unsuccessfully, the Sixth Avenue Railroad Company in a case similar to that which Jennings had won.[71] Nonetheless this group, in which women with the spirit of Elizabeth Jennings were active from its beginnings in 1855, achieved within four years considerable equality of treatment in the city's transportation system.[72]

In Philadelphia, where technically all the city's "public conveyances [were] forbidden to the black man," efforts to gain equal access to city and suburban transportation were less successful.[73]

68. Leo H. Hirsch, "New York and the Negro, from 1783 to 1865," *Journal of Negro History*, XVI (October, 1931), 425-426.
69. *Frederick Douglass' Paper*, September 7, 1855.
70. James McCune Smith to Gerrit Smith, March 31, 1855, S-SU.
71. *Frederick Douglass' Paper*, September 7, 1855.
72. *Ibid.*, March 18, 1859.
73. *Douglass Monthly*, October 1860.

The first well-publicized challenge there came from George W. Goines, a bookseller, who was "forcibly ejected" from the Spruce and Pine Street line in 1859 and then sued the company.[74] His fight was a catalyst for the formation in 1860 of the Social, Civil, and Statistical Association. Originally a small group of only seventeen men, its strong leadership, including William Still and lumberman Stephen Smith, attracted members, and the society soon grew to more than eighty people. It collected information about discrimination in the state and investigated specific cases, especially those involving street car transportation and the Pennsylvania Railroad.[75] Its efforts to change what it found, however, were still blocked by the courts, for in 1861 the district court ruled that in denying blacks the franchise, the state constitution of 1838 had validated a broader pattern of differential treatment for the races. There was, therefore, nothing illegal or unconstitutional in segregating Negroes in transportation facilities or in excluding them altogether. Not until 1867 did Pennsylvania finally abolish legal discrimination in public transportation.[76]

Of all the antebellum fights against transportation discrimination, none attracted more attention nationally than that waged against the Cunard Steamship Company. Serving as a major link between the United States and Great Britain, its packets carried passengers and mail from all parts of the country. Consequently challenges to the British company were highly visible and distinctly dramatic. Here, as in few other cases, Northern black civil rights action could touch slaveholders directly. When, for example, Douglass purchased passage to England on the *Cambria* in 1845, he was obliged to travel steerage. But company policy was countered by the decision of the captain, who was so impressed by Douglass that he permitted him not only to mingle on deck with the first-class passengers but, on the last night out, to give them an antislavery lecture. Some Southern passengers were so infuriated

74. *Weekly Anglo-African,* July 23 and October 8, 1859.
75. Social, Civil and Statistical Association of Colored People of Philadelphia. Executive Committee, "Minute Book, 1860-1867," MS, Historical Society of Pennsylvania, 1860, *passim.*
76. Turner, *Negro in Pennsylvania,* 198.

that they tried to attack Douglass and desisted only when the captain threatened to put them in irons. As the English cheered the event, Southerners denounced the captain and the line.[77]

Two years later, when Douglass prepared to return home, Cunard officials once again refused to sell him a first-class ticket. Once again English opinion responded, this time in fuming fury. So fierce were the press attacks that a leading Cunard official publicly apologized and announced a new company policy for the future.[78] Still problems persisted, Six years later Samuel Ward, although allowed to occupy a state room on a Cunard packet, was directed to take his meals there alone. Mightily peeved, Ward did some investigating and found that all the second-class passengers were Englishmen who, with one exception, had no objection to eating with him. So he defied the line and its white American passengers by taking his meals pleasantly with Her Majesty's subjects.[79] It was another instance of what the Richmond, Virginia, *Whig* had complained about some years earlier when it warned Southerners to avoid traveling on the same ship as Henry Bibb. "Credulous John Bull [is] fleeced by our cunning Cuffees."[80]

On street cars and railroad trains, aboard ferries and ships, and even occasionally in theaters and restaurants, blacks kept up a prolonged campaign, variously pleading for or insisting on equal accommodations. Some, when pressed, stood firm; others resorted to violence; many appealed to public opinion or took their challenges to the courts. When Julian McCrae and John Stephenson bought tickets to the Howard Atheneum in Boston, they managed to combine a variety of these responses. Asked to leave the theater, they refused and after a great ruckus, had to be put out by the police. They then took their case to the press and to the courts "to test the question of color in its relation to places of public

77. Philip Foner, ed., *The Life and Writings of Frederick Douglass* (4 vols. New York: International Publishers, 1950-1955), 1:62.

78. *Ibid.*, 1:74.

79. Samuel Ringgold Ward, *Autobiography of a Fugitive Negro* .... (London: J. Snow, 1855), 227-231.

80. *Liberator,* June 18, 1847.

amusement."[81] Though their victory was only partial, it symbol-
ized the testing of their fellows.

For more than thirty years, blacks wrestled with the problems
of segregation. Experiencing modest success in achieving adequate
separate schools, they almost universally failed in efforts for
integration. In churches, the Negro pew remained commonplace,
though because of the large group served by black churches the
issue of segregation was of more theoretical than practical concern.
And in the broad sweep of other segregated public facilities, the
gains made in integrating transportation, though significant, were
of limited scope. Seldom did theoretical argument, political action,
or economic expediency change the prevailing patterns of prejudice
which, because whites constituted an overwhelming majority and
held the reins of power, blocked change. And failure generated
despair which tempted all but the most persistent to surrender.
Indicative of the hopelessness which powerlessness bred was
George Downing's decision in 1861 to give up his successful
Newport hotel as well as his leadership of the Rhode Island
integration campaign to move to Boston. Only thus could his
children enjoy the benefits of "equal school rights."[82] But many
who pleaded and protested for integration were at the same time
fighting for the political rights which they hoped would give them
the ability to institute social change. They did not dare give up.

81. *Ibid.*, December 26, 1856. George W. Forbes relates a similar story
about William Nell and the Remond sisters which occurred in the spring of
1853. He claims that they won damages in a civil suit; see "William Cooper
Nell," Typescript in "Biographical Sketches of Eminent Negroes, Correspondence, etc., Boston etc., 1906-1936," Antislavery Collection, Boston Public
Library.
82. *Liberator,* June 7, 1861.

PART IV

A New Amalgam of Civil Rights and Abolition

LIKE THE entire antislavery movement, black abolitionism, particularly after 1840, was challenged and shaped by national events as well as by internal dynamics. Many abolitionists responded politically to the annexation of Texas, the Mexican War, and the extension of slavery into new territory. Even so, the political response of blacks had a special dimension, for they were also struggling simply to gain access to the political process. Similarly, the concerns they shared with white abolitionists in the 1850s—the new fugitive slave law, the crisis in Kansas, and the Dred Scott decision—not only encouraged cooperation with the broader movement but also generated ever more insistent demands for race action—for violent resistance, institutional separatism, or emigration from the United States.

9. SUFFRAGE AND POLITICS—THE THRUST OF THE 1840s

IN AUGUST 1840, the New York State Convention of Colored Men, meeting in Albany, resolved "That in proportion as we are treated with disrespect, contumely, and neglect, in our political, literary, and ecclesiastical relations, from the want of the elective franchise—so would we command respect and influence in these different relations by the possession of it."[1] It was not the first time that Negroes publicly demanded the vote, for it was only in Massachusetts and northern New England that they long possessed full suffrage. Elsewhere just a select few had ever voted, or the many had cast their ballots for limited periods of time. Thus in Providence, Rhode Island, blacks petitioned the state legislature in 1831 for full suffrage or exemption from taxation. Less militantly, Connecticut blacks at the 1836 state temperance society meeting considered their need for the franchise. And the 1834 national convention proposed a committee to investigate voting rights and practices in the various states.[2] The new emphasis on political action in 1840 was, therefore, less a radical departure than a revived and intensified interest in achieving and exerting effective political power.

1. *Colored American,* January 9, 1841.
2. *Liberator,* March 19, 1831. Howard H. Bell, *A Survey of the Negro Convention Movement, 1830-1861* (New York: Arno Press, 1969), 56-68. Convention for the Improvement of the Free People of Colour, *Minutes . . . 1834,* 18.

173

In all probability the Pennsylvania crisis of 1837 triggered the heightened interest in political action. Ever since the adoption of the state constitution of 1790, which neither authorized nor denied Negroes the franchise, blacks had voted regularly in many parts of Pennsylvania, though not in Philadelphia where the force of public opinion and the threat of violence usually kept them from the polls. But even there, by the 1830s, individual blacks had begun to press for the vote. "Now is their time," wrote "C.D.P." to the *Liberator* in 1831, drawing a lesson for Philadelphians from the recent Rhode Island petitions. "Let them hold themselves in readiness for the ensuing election. . . ."[3]

The actual test did not come until four years later. Then, in 1835, a black man named Fogg, qualified to vote by residence and payment of taxes, challenged his exclusion from the polls in Philadelphia's county court. Although he won his case, his victory was short-lived, for two years later, a state constitutional convention undertook to settle, one way or the other, the question of Negro suffrage. Their deliberations were shaped by the fall elections of 1837, which fell between the convention's two sessions, and in which Bucks County Democrats were defeated, so they claimed, by black votes. As a result of that defeat, the Democrats appealed the question of black suffrage to the county court, which ruled that blacks were not "freemen" as defined in the 1790 constitution and could not, therefore, vote. The second session of the constitutional convention then decided to follow the latter ruling, not so much for legal consistency as to avoid attracting more Negroes into the state.[4] Their decision was, in short, a realization of the wishes of their white constituents, who thought blacks were inferior and undesirable as fellow citizens.

During the convention's debates, blacks had optimistically mounted a statewide petition campaign on behalf of full suffrage.

3. *Liberator,* March 19 [26], 1831. See also Emil Olbrich, *The Development of Sentiment on Negro Suffrage to 1860* (Madison: University of Wisconsin, 1912), 51-69.
4. Edward R. Turner, *Negro in Pennsylvania, 1639-1861* (Washington: American Historical Association, 1912), 188, 169-177, 190.

After the convention denied them the vote entirely, they sought to defeat the new constitution's ratification through an "Appeal of Forty Thousand Citizens Threatened with Disfranchisement, to the People of Pennsylvania."[5] All their efforts, however, came to naught. In October 1838, white voters upheld the convention's decision. Blacks remained disfranchised in the state until shortly after the Civil War.

The events in Pennsylvania undoubtedly alarmed New York State blacks, who responded by organizing a strong enfranchisement movement. In August 1837, even before the Pennsylvania constitutional convention had acted, a group of impatient young New Yorkers met to challenge both the suffrage provision in their state constitution and the conservatism of older race spokesmen who had failed to attack it. Among these rebels were Henry Highland Garnet, still a student at the Oneida Institute; Charles Reason, later a distinguished teacher but then only in his teens; and George Downing, a son of restaurateur Thomas Downing, who was also under twenty. They and several others organized a Young Men's Convention to launch a petition campaign throughout the state demanding constitutional revision to extend Negro suffrage.[6]

Although their youth and radicalism alarmed some, their earnestness captured reluctant support from many of their elders. Older leaders with little previous enthusiasm for political action followed the young Turks and joined their campaign to repeal the 1821 constitutional provision which required a $250 property qualification for black voters—and only black voters. Early in the year Samuel Cornish had organized a petition campaign, which the convention carried on. Philip Bell, publisher of the *Colored American*, and Charles Ray, already a well-established clergyman at thirty, circulated petitions upstate while Cornish, then forty-two, served as campaign coordinator from his New York City base.[7]

5. *Colored American*, July 1, 1837, March 15, 1838. *Liberator*, April 13, 1838.

6. *Colored American*, September 2, 1837.

7. Olbrich, *Development of Sentiment on Negro Suffrage*, 35-36. *Colored American*, March 11 and August 19, 1837.

No sooner was their petition campaign under way than city blacks, in 1838, organized the Association for the Political Elevation and Improvement of the People of Color "to make exertions and sacrifices to obtain for themselves, and ensure for their posterity, the enjoyment and exercise of the right of suffrage."[8] Similarly the pages of the *Colored American* were filled with editorials urging New Yorkers to press the franchise issue. The foundation was laid for the surge of political action which dominated New York civil rights activity in 1840 and the years thereafter. The stage had been set for a series of state conventions whose goal was gaining and using political power.

How to get political power admitted of no easy answer; and the debate over means provoked major disputes. Part of the wider debates sundering the antislavery movement at the time, the issue of political power and political action was inextricably intertwined with others like the question of multi-reformism and abolition's proper relationship with churches. This general political debate was directly relevant to issues which puzzled blacks in 1840, for central to both groups were questions about the potential use and value of the franchise. Should abolitionists, as Gerrit Smith and his followers contended, organize an antislavery party and press their cause through politics as well as through moral suasion? Should they, as the Garrisonians argued, shun political involvement in an immoral government; or, if they must use political action, confine themselves to supporting antislavery candidates within the old parties?

Although such questions focused on problems generic to abolitionist theory and practice, they nevertheless spoke indirectly to that which concerned blacks specifically. Not surprisingly, therefore, many Negroes who thought that the suffrage question was critical gravitated to the political action group within the antislavery movement. Yet they did not automatically line up with one side or the other in the antislavery debates over politics. On

8. *Colored American,* June 16, 1838. See also Daniel Perlman, "Organizations of the Free Negro in New York City, 1800-1860," *Journal of Negro History,* LVI (July 1971), 189-190.

the whole, the *Colored American's* condemnation of internal antislavery differences reflected the majority hope on political no less than on other issues. "We are not pleased with seeing Anti-Slavery men quarrel."[9] It was partly to escape the wheel-spinning these quarrels involved that black abolitionists undertook separate race action to gain the franchise.

Predictably, however, blacks no more than whites avoided factionalism over political action, albeit their splits followed lines quite different from those dividing whites. At the very outset supporters of political action clashed over using exclusive race conventions to forge a black politics appropriate to conditions in individual states. The *Colored American*, edited by Charles Ray from 1839 to 1841, enthusiastically endorsed the state suffrage convention idea. "While we believe that, being of the *American nation*, we ought to identify ourselves with the American people, and with American interests," Ray wrote in the spring of 1840, "yet there are and will be, special interests for us to attend to, so long as American caste. exists, and we have not equal rights, in common with the American people."[10] Although former editor Cornish was doubtful about this separatism, Ray simply said the older man was out of date. Cornish, he wrote, "stands by the old paths, but does not enquire for the new. . . . He is inclined to call every thing 'enthusiasm and visionary or human measures' which devides [*sic*] in the least from old tradition. . . ."[11]

If it was easy to dispatch Cornish as old guard, it was not possible to dismiss the young activist James McCune Smith so cavalierly. Smith, an ardent supporter of the franchise, nevertheless disagreed with the convention enthusiasts. Although he was elected a delegate to the state convention in Albany in the fall of 1840, he had reservations about the separatism on which it was based and attended only reluctantly. Convinced that a similar meeting in Pennsylvania in 1837 had spurred disfranchisement there, Smith worried that all separate conventions might prove counterpro-

9. *Colored American,* May 2, 1840.
10. *Ibid.,* May 2, 1840.
11. *Ibid.,* November 9, 1839.

ductive. He was convinced that "separate action, distinguished by the complexion of the skin," had within it "a virtual acknowledgment that there are rights peculiar to the color of a man's skin." "A movement based on the complexion of the skin," he warned, "will end in riveting still more firmly the chains which bind us." At the same time Smith feared sabotaging the drive for suffrage; and so, "for the common good" of his fellows, he decided to "attend the Convention, and labor to promote its objects."[12]

Support for separate conventions was unintentionally boosted by the inept opposition to them of the American Anti-Slavery Society's *National Anti-Slavery Standard*. In patronizing tones it warned blacks against responding viscerally to white prejudice. They should be patient and leave the matter to white abolitionists. "The fetter galls and cuts deeply," the paper observed, "but we cannot unlock it instantly. In your desire to become freemen . . . be careful that you do not tear down what you build up. You cannot be free until [the] community shall see and feel that you are men."[13]

The response was as vigorous as it was prompt. Thomas Van Rensselaer, otherwise a good Garrisonian, sharply challenged the *Standard*. It was blacks, not whites, he pointed out, who suffered discrimination. Therefore it was they who had the right and duty to call conventions to redress their grievances.[14] Samuel Ward also jibed at the *Standard*. "There are too many Abolitionists in *profession*," he said, "who have yet to learn what it is to crucify prejudice against color within their own bosoms."[15] Even more pointed was the analysis of the *Colored American's* acting editor. "As long as we attend the Conventions called by our white friends we will be looked upon as playing second fiddle to them. They will always form the majority of such Conventions, and the sentiments and opinions thus promulgated will go forth as the sentiments and opinions of white men, but when *we act* then they will see that the

12. *Ibid.*, August 15, 1840.
13. *National Anti-Slavery Standard*, June 18, 1840.
14. *Colored American*, July 4, 1840.
15. *National Anti-Slavery Standard*, July 2, 1840.

worm is turning."[16] It was another instance in which those who would be free had themselves to strike the blow.

That the debate broke the ranks of black Garrisonians is borne out by more than Van Renesselaer's comments. The loyal American Moral Reform Society, it is true, resisted race separatism in its sparsely attended last annual meeting in 1840. At that time the delegates voted that they regarded "the custom of associating Conventions for philanthropic purposes, under the badge of complexional distinctions, as contrary to the principles of our Society, and the genius of republicanism."[17] In so doing, they were rejecting their fellow Garrisonian David Ruggles' request that the society send delegates to a national convention of "disfranchised and enslaved people." Ruggles nonetheless continued to argue that a convention based on "complexional distinctions" was imperative. "It is no where to be found in history containing the rise and progress of nations from the earliest ages of the world down to the present period of time . . . that a people who have felt 'the *scorpions lash,* and *vipers sting,*' ever extricated themselves from the tyrant's yoke, without considering their own exclusive, their every condition and employing individual, collective, unanimous and energetic action in the cause of reform and equal rights." Complexion, Ruggles insisted, was a "badge to our condition as *disfranchised and enslaved* Americans." Therefore, "until equal liberty comes to crown us all with emancipation and the franchise," black attempts to join together with enfranchised Americans "as free men and women" would be mere sham.

There was no alternative, Ruggles continued, to complexional conventions if able young Negroes were to be allowed to exert their talents. Those who had acted within the general antislavery movement were there considered "*exceptions*" and cut off from their fellow sufferers. Only in a separate movement could they work effectively for the race. "IMMEDIATE EMANCIPATION" was meaningless without "full ENFRANCHISEMENT"; without

16. *Colored American,* June 27, 1840.
17. *Liberator,* October 9, 1840.

civil rights blacks could neither be nor act as the equals of whites. To gain the vote and other civil rights, to become the equals of other citizens, they must act on their own.[18]

This was Ruggles' message to the Moral Reform Society. Its leaders, however, feared that separate action conveyed the impression that equal suffrage was a race issue and thus ran the danger of backfiring. If the Negro's color justified separate action, William Whipper observed, then "the white man will be equally able to establish the dignity of his Anglo-Saxon blood, and the *virtue* of his complexion."[19]

Whipper's contention was difficult to counter. Yet a pseudonymous writer to the *Colored American* undertook to demolish it. "We maintain," wrote "Sidney, "that what is morally right for one man to do, may be morally wrong for another; and thus of entire classes of a whole people. Duties arise from relations. Our responsibilities and obligations receive their hue and coloring from the situation we may maintain, and the connections we may have. . . .We sustain relations to our own people, so peculiar that white men cannot assume them; and according to these relations are our attending duties."[20] Whether it was the logic of situational ethics or a pragmatism generated by finding no functional alternative which won general support for race conventions is moot. The fact is the debate was over by 1842, and exclusive conventions were commonplace for the next twenty years.

Easier of compromise because it involved primarily practical and procedural issues was the question whether state or national conventions provided the better base from which blacks could organize their forces and press for political as well as other goals. Nonetheless it too was hotly fought out in 1840. If, as a Hartford group insisted, slavery was the central issue, then only national conventions and societies were appropriate. Early in the debate they had contended that "no measure [was] better adapted to meet the necessities of our critical case, than the concentration of

18. *National Anti-Slavery Standard,* October 1, 1840.
19. *Colored American,* February 6 and 20, 1841, quotation in latter.
20. *Ibid.,* March 13, 1841.

our *energies, intelligence*, and *sympathies*" in national conventions which could aid and nourish a national organization and, in turn, propagate black views and civil rights activity year-round.[21] Essentially they sought to carry on the convention patterns of the preceding decade and to replace the Moral Reform Society with a similar but more effective and race-conscious organization.

The response from Wilmington, Delaware, to Worcester, Massachusetts, and from New York to Pittsburgh supported this familiar device as public meetings called for yet another national convention in 1840.[22] Thus encouraged, David Ruggles launched a call for a "National Reform Convention of the Colored Inhabitants of the United States of America." Scheduled to meet in New Haven, the convention was summoned to give special attention to the franchise question.[23] Yet no sooner had this call, with ninety-seven signatures appended, gone out, than presumed signers began to protest. Several claimed they had not authorized the use of their names at all; others complained that they had assented neither to the timing nor the place, both of which were ill-chosen.[24] But despite these protests the convention met. Apparently the disaffected were right. When the opening gavel fell, five delegates and twenty onlookers embarrassedly faced each other. Nonetheless the five worked hard and founded the American Reform Board of Disfranchised Commissioners, charged with achieving "equal human rights" and the "immediate relief and enfranchisement" of Northern blacks. So ambitious a program with so small a base, however, was doomed to fail, and, although the board met once the following year, it never again reassembled.[25]

Those who supported state conventions were able to build more solidly. It was easier for substantial numbers to get to a central meeting place. With greater participation, state conventions both

21. *Ibid.*, June 13, 1840.

22. Both *Colored American* and *Liberator* carried numerous notices of support during the spring and summer of 1840.

23. *Colored American*, July 25, 1840.

24. *Ibid.*, August 8 and 15, 1840.

25. *Liberator*, July 30, 1841, which contains the quotations, and August 13 and October 22, 1841. *Colored American*, September 19, 1840.

promised continuity and offered an opportunity to base national meetings on local units. Furthermore, with the franchise their substantive focus, they could more readily address themselves to the various state laws and constitutions which determined the electorate. Finally, special conditions prevailing in New York State constituted a particular impetus to suffrage conventions there. In that state were both a group of Negro voters who met the special property and residence requirements and a much larger group waiting to be enfranchised. Unlike Pennsylvania, where none could vote, or Massachusetts, where all could, there was both a political base and a compelling incentive for change. Perhaps equally important, New York was the heart of political abolitionism and the home of the Liberty party. Thus a particularly favorable environment encouraged a black suffrage campaign in the Empire State which simply did not exist in states like Connecticut and Ohio. The particular virtues which state conventions seemed to have over national conventions in 1840 and the particular political conditions prevailing in New York made it no accident, therefore, that a vigorous state convention movement emerged there or that its principal concerns were nearly always political.

The first New York state convention met in August 1840. Proposed in independent meetings in Jamaica, Long Island, and in upstate Troy, the convention, which was proudly heralded and fiercely opposed in preliminary meetings from Buffalo and Rochester to Albany, Poughkeepsie, and New York City, finally assembled in Albany.[26] There, some 130 delegates gathered "to shake off the putrid garments of . . . degradation, and move for a giant effort for . . . natural and imprescriptable rights."[27] There were present some older leaders like Austin Steward, who had attended the first national convention in 1830 and who now

26. In almost every issue from the beginning of June until mid-August 1840 the *Colored American* contained arguments for and against a national convention. For the two proposals, *ibid.*, May 9 and June 6, 1840.

27. The language is that of a resolution adopted by blacks of Oswego, New York, *Colored American*, August 1, 1840.

presided at the Albany meeting. Younger men, however, dominated the sessions. Outstanding among them was Garnet, already known as a political activist, who increased his stature by preparing the convention's major documents, writing its address, acting as one of its secretaries, and serving on the permanent central committee which it established.

Shaped by Garnet's preliminary activity, the convention explored the best means to win civil equality. As had earlier conventions seeking somewhat different goals, it chose to rely on converting public opinion by "continual presentation of the first principles of political freedom, truth, and justice." This, the delegates agreed, was the best way to secure those rights which had been "wrested from a depressed people."[28] Nor did they stop with generalities, but examined the specific issue of the franchise. To it they related all other major issues of welfare and improvement. Without the ability to express themselves politically, they lacked the "vital means" for uplift and were but "nominally free."[29] Without the political power to force change, they would continue to be barred from schools and jobs, proscribed from social institutions, and denied a voice in the community until they all fell into "carelessness, intellectual inertness, and indolence."[30] The children of impotence and despair, their lives were destined to poverty, crime, and unspeakable suffering.

Although the delegates at Albany related a whole series of practical problems to their disfranchisement, they returned constantly to the theoretical arguments entitling them to the suffrage. They were men and as such deserved, "on the ground of [their] *common humanity*," the same rights which their fellow citizens enjoyed.[31] They rejected out of hand therefore one resolution which would encourage New York Negroes to increase their collective power by buying land and thereby meeting the property qualification. Eager to support land ownership, they refused to

28. *Ibid.*, January 9, 1841.
29. *Ibid.*, January 2, 1841.
30. From the Address of the Convention, *Colored American*, December 19, 1840.
31. *Ibid.*, December 19, 1840.

accept any suffrage requirement not exacted of other citizens.[32] By affirming the natural civil rights of all men and by demanding practical guarantees for those rights, the convention made its priorities clear.

This time the resolves of the convention were not left to chance. Before it adjourned, it appointed a series of committees to carry out the various activities the meeting had approved, to draw up an address, collect statistics, and develop means to achieve the franchise. And as delegates returned to their homes, they organized county committees to circulate petitions, act as committees of correspondence, and help implement the convention's work.[33]

Urged on by chairman Garnet of the central committee as well as by local committees, blacks across the state held suffrage meetings and circulated petitions. From Brooklyn, Newtown, Hudson, and Buffalo, from Long Island to the Niagara frontier, petitions were sent in: 13 signatures from Lansingburgh, 1,300 signatures from New York City, 100 signatures each from Flushing, Poughkeepsie, and Rochester, and 600 white signatures from New York and Schenectady.[34] In Troy, Garnet collected, sorted, and collated the petitions. Then, early in February 1841 he carried them to the legislature, where three sympathetic members introduced them to the Assembly. Two weeks later he was back in Albany, this time with James McCune Smith, to rehearse the arguments for Negro suffrage before a legislative committee. Systematically they argued black claims to citizenship and contested white arguments to the contrary. They pointed to their nativity in America, elaborated the degradation which disenfranchisement brought, recalled Negroes' good conduct at the polls when they were allowed to vote, asserted that a white majority was ready to accept Negro voters, and vaunted their faith in the ultimate success of their suffrage campaign.[35]

32. *Ibid.,* January 2 and 9, 1841.
33. *Ibid.,* September 12, 1840.
34. *Ibid.,* October 17, 1840. Also September 5, November 14 and 21, December 5, 12 and 26, 1840, January 9, 16, and 23, and February 6 and 13, 1841.
35. *Ibid.,* February 13 and March 13, 1841. *American and Foreign Anti-Slavery Reporter,* I (February 1841), 125.

Although Smith and Garnet were well received, their message was soon lost in a legislature preoccupied with building a bridge across the Hudson River at Albany. But, not having expected instant victory, New York Negroes continued their campaign. They held state and local conventions. They passed resolutions asserting that natural law entitled them to equal rights and, most especially, to the vote. They portrayed the social burden their disfranchisement imposed on the state, a burden of ignorance, apathy, poverty, and crime. They rehearsed the good results which accompanied black suffrage in Massachusetts.[36] And they appealed to prevailing nativist sentiment, developing the paradox of native-born Negroes being excluded from the ballot box while unqualified immigrants, schooled only in European tyranny, swarmed to the polls. "We find no fault with the laws of the land, which welcome the oppressed of other nations, (if they are white,) to the benefits of our institutions, and which furnishes them a safe asylum," the 1845 state convention in Syracuse observed, "but we complain that we, native born citizens, are denied the same rights which are so largely and freely extended to foreigners."[37]

For a while, in 1846, it seemed that this intensive campaign would bear fruit in the deliberations of a convention called that year to revise the state constitution. In January leading activists in the suffrage drive—Garnet, Smith, Ray, Wright, Van Rensselaer, Steward, and Ward among them—urged the "Voters of the State of New York" to elect delegates who were sympathetic to removing all special qualifications for black voters.[38] This time, they were more fortunate, with backing from the Liberty party and strong upstate antislavery support. The convention adopted such a revision. Yet when it was submitted to the electorate for ratification separate from other constitutional changes, it was overwhelmingly defeated. Democratic strongholds almost unani-

---

36. Address of the New York State Convention of Colored Citizens (1841), in *National Anti-Slavery Standard*, September 23, 1841. It was written by Garnet.
37. *Ibid.*, September 11, 1845.
38. *Ibid.*, January 29, 1846.

mously voted down the revision, while Whig districts were split. Only the Liberty party had unqualifiedly supported the proposal.[39] Surveying the ruinous referendum, James McCune Smith wrote to fellow abolitionist Gerrit Smith in December that "that terrible majority" weighed heavily on him for it embodied "a hate deeper than I had imagined."[40] Ironically, the stituation seemed to bear out the *National Anti-Slavery Standard's* warning against an exclusively Negro campaign for it demonstrated that the nub of the problem lay in white prejudice.

Nonetheless the dedicated few continued the struggle in succeeding years. Then, in 1855, the state assembly voted two-to-one to abolish the property qualification. Although the senate took no action on the bill, the assembly's action was enough to rekindle the franchise campaign.[41] Meeting in Troy, another convention organized the New York State Suffrage Association to press for the removal of "every legal and political disability."[42] Throughout the state local groups swung into action, lobbyists badgered legislators, and innumerable people signed and sent to Albany unnumbered petitions while statewide meetings of the Suffrage Association coordinated, encouraged, and publicized the work.[43] Finally in 1860 a new constitutional amendment to eliminate the property qualification went to the voters for ratification. Black efforts then concentrated on averting another defeat at the hands of popular prejudice.

They did not rely on friendly whites. They knew they had to convert the unfriendly. They had, as Smith put it, "to make this

39. John L. Stanley, "Majority Tyranny in Tocqueville's America: The Failure of Negro Suffrage in 1846," *Political Science Quarterly*, LXXXIV (September, 1969), 416-423.

40. James McCune Smith to Gerrit Smith, December 28 et seq., 1846, S-SU.

41. *Frederick Douglass' Paper*, May 4, 1855.

42. *Ibid.*, August 3 and September 14, 1855, quotation in the former.

43. *Frederick Douglass' Paper*, September 21, 1855. Stephen Myers to Gerrit Smith, March 22, 1856, in Benjamin Quarles, ed., "Letters from Negro Leaders to Gerrit Smith," *Journal of Negro History*, XXVII (October 1942), 447. *Frederick Douglass' Paper*, January 7, 1859. *Weekly Anglo-African*, September 10 and October 15, 1859, April 28, May 19, and June 23, 1860. *Douglass Monthly*, October, 1860.

suffrage campaign as nearly self-reliant on the part of our people, as possible."[44] "The crisis calls in the strongest language and most imperative terms upon all colored men to contribute money as they can afford, to circulate pamphlets and handbills discussing the question before the public," a suffrage convention meeting in May exhorted.[45] It was equally important, however, to avoid the mistakes which had led to the 1846 fiasco. Canvassers were cautioned against stirring up the venomous prejudice which had defeated them fourteen years earlier. They should, the Suffrage Association urged, avoid the provocative term "Negro enfranchisement" and discuss the amendment as one eliminating "property qualification" generally.[46] When Stephen Myers wanted to organize a statewide convention on the eve of the election, Smith warned against it lest it create antagonism at the critical moment. Especially was he concerned, as he confessed to Gerrit Smith, that a large suffrage convention would alienate the foreign vote just when it should be courted. Acting on this assumption, the association printed foreign language propaganda but at the same time avoided pressure on Democratic immigrant strongholds.[47]

Despite their caution and care, victory was as elusive in 1860 as it had been in 1846. "No decent man," lamented Douglass, "could assign a motive for his vote against us, without casting his eyes to the ground, or looking up with a blush of mingled shame and malignity. . . . It was an act of unmitigated pride and prejudice, intended to depress and degrade a class which, of all others in the State, need the ballot box as a means of self-elevation and popular regard."[48]

The struggle for the suffrage, frustrating enough in New York, was even more discouraging in Pennsylvania. Apparently reinvigo-

44. James McCune Smith to Gerrit Smith, June 21, 1860, S-SU.
45. *Weekly Anglo-African*, May 19, 1860.
46. *Ibid.*, May 19, 1860. Even the resolutions themselves avoid using the term "Negro enfranchisement."
47. James McCune Smith to Stephen Myers, September 21, 1860, copy, and Smith to Gerrit Smith, October 20, 1860, both in S-SU.
48. *Douglass Monthly*, December, 1860.

rated by the 1840 Albany convention, residents of the Keystone State resumed their fight against the disfranchisement which the 1838 constitutional revision had imposed. Early in 1841 Philadelphians launched a petition drive for the suffrage. Nonetheless they hesitated to commit themselves to political action as fully as did New Yorkers and shunned holding a state convention. As Philadelphians they had been barred from voting when blacks elsewhere in the state had, before 1838, enjoyed the franchise, and they were reluctant therefore to embark on too visible a project for change. In part, their stance reflected the influence of their state's apolitical abolitionism. In part, it was generated by fear of provoking violence. And in 1841, Philadelphia was clutched by racial tension which at least once broke into rioting so fierce as to discourage them even from holding a national convention in the city.[49]

To the west, however, the situation was different, and Negroes there were ready to hold a state convention. They had been voters before 1838 and welcomed the public attention which a state convention would bring to their claims for suffrage. Consequently the Harrisburg convention of August 1841 was dominated by delegates from the western counties of the state, especially from Pittsburgh where its planning had begun. Espousing goals and means similar to those of the Albany convention, they demanded "all the privileges and immunities of citizens," framed a petition campaign, and recommended grass roots organization.[50]

For the next few years county and state conventions continued to meet, and in 1848 a statewide suffrage society was organized. These groups argued, like their counterparts in New York, that natural law required civil equality as did all practical projects for race improvement. "If we admit the *fatalism* that we need to be elevated before we are fitted to possess the rights and privileges of white men," the 1848 state convention asserted, echoing New

49. *Colored American,* January 30, 1841. *Liberator,* November 5, 1841, Bell, *Negro Convention Movement,* 69.
50. State Convention of the Colored Freemen of Pennsylvania, *Proceedings...1841,* 3, 5, 8, 11-16. Quotation on 8.

Yorkers' rejection of similar premises, "we consequently acknowledge our inferiority in the scale of creation. Let us never attempt to erect the temple of freedom on such a sandy foundation. . . ."[51] But, despite this proud stance, their efforts were futile. In 1865 Harrisburg was the scene for still another equal rights convention seeking the franchise.[52] That it met at all was testimony to blacks' political impotence as well as to their perseverance.

The impact of the early state political conventions in New York and Pennsylvania was felt in the 1843 national convention. Held in political antislavery country, the Buffalo convention was largely organized and run by Garnet, who was thus responsible for its strong endorsement not only of political action but of the Liberty party as well. Not even the presence of Frederick Douglass and Charles Remond, the two strongest anti-political-action representatives whom Boston's black Garrisonians could send, was able to turn this first major national convention of the 1840s from supporting political action.[53]

Indeed, New Englanders south of Massachusetts were as concerned with suffrage as were New Yorkers and Pennsylvanians. In Connecticut the politically oriented State Temperance and Moral Reform Society undertook in 1841 a petition drive against the presumably liberal constitution of 1817, which had denied blacks access to the ballot box. Like their New York associates, they emphasized that Connecticut Negroes were native-born Americans and entitled to full civil equality. They too dwelt on the degradation to the race and the social burden to the state which disfranchisement produced. In so doing they convinced the legislature in 1846 to adopt a measure for black suffrage, subject to popular referendum. And again like their New York brothers,

51. State Convention of the Coloured Citizens of Pennsylvania, *Minutes of. . . Convened at Harrisburg, December 13th and 14th, 1848* (Philadelphia: Merrihew and Thompson, 1849. Reprint, Philadelphia: Rhistoric Publications, n.d.), 20.

52. State Equal Rights' Convention of the Colored People of Pennsylvania, *Proceedings . . . 1865*, 41-47.

53. National Convention of Colored Citizens, *Minutes . . . 1843*, 4-26. *Liberator*, August 4, 1843. Also see *ibid.*, August 25, 1843.

they were defeated, this time by a count of three-to-one, achieved, so Amos Beman contended, by the opposition of nine-tenths of the Irish vote.[54] Yet they did not give up; at conventions held in 1849, 1854, and 1855, Connecticut Negroes repeatedly demanded the franchise. The activists among them continued to agitate, to circulate public addresses, and to carry their case to the legislature. Yet they too failed to overcome the white prejudice which blocked change. When the Civil War began, Connecticut alone among the New England states still denied equal suffrage to Negroes.[55]

Only in Rhode Island did the fight for equal suffrage produce results. There, followers of Thomas Dorr, who in 1841 were in active revolt against Rhode Island's undemocratic constitution, demanded universal white manhood suffrage. When, however, the rebels denied the franchise to blacks, the latter threw their support to the conservative establishment; and, when armed violence seemed imminent, some two hundred volunteered to fight for the law and order party. Here at last Negroes had something to offer in exchange for enfranchisement. Although the conservatives lagged in fulfilling their implicit promise, the anti-Dorrite constitutional convention did finally eliminate all franchise restrictions in September 1842.[56]

Elsewhere in the North bids for the franchise were universally lost in the decades prior to the Civil War. Indeed most Northern blacks needed the Reconstruction amendments as much as did Southern freedmen. After the New Jersey constitutional convention of 1844 explicitly disfranchised them, Negroes there stayed

54. *Colored American,* September 19, 1840, Robert A. Warner, *New Haven Negroes: A Social History* (New Haven: Yale University Press, 1940), 95-96. Robert A Warner, "Amos Gerry Beman—1812-1874, A Memoir on a Forgotten Leader," *Journal of Negro History,* XXII (April 1937), 210. *North Star,* December 3, 1847.

55. *Weekly Anglo-African,* July 23, 1859. For the conventions see *Liberator,* October 12, 1849, October 27, 1854, and *Frederick Douglass' Paper,* May 4, 1855.

56. J. Stanley Lemons and Michael A. McKenna, "Re-enfranchisement of Rhode Island Negroes," *Rhode Island History,* XXX (Winter, 1971), 3-13. Irving H. Bartlett, *From Slave to Citizen, The Story of the Negro in Rhode Island* (Providence: The Urban League of Greater Providence, 1954), 39-43.

voteless until 1875.[57] In the old Northwest Territory, where federal law had forever forbidden slavery, state laws were heavily restrictive of black freedom, denying blacks virtually all civil rights. Nor was the situation different in the new western states of Iowa, Oregon, and California.[58] So Westerners, like Easterners, pressed for civil rights and political recognition.

In Ohio, state conventions beginning in 1849 and continuing through the 1850s agitated the suffrage question, while activists collected signatures on petitions and distributed hortatory addresses in efforts to gain the ballot.[59] In Michigan similar efforts by Detroit blacks were defeated in 1850 when white voters turned down a franchise referendum two-to-one.[60] While activism was not so intense in Illinois and Wisconsin, Negroes in both states made scattered attempts to gain the suffrage.[61] Everywhere, however, such efforts were futile. Throughout the 1850s, white Northerners, except in five New England states, either denied black Americans the franchise or, as in New York, obliged them to meet special qualifications.

"It is hard," observed Frederick Douglass in 1859, "to say whether we are any nearer, to-day, to Free Suffrage, than we were

57. Lee Calligaro, "The Negro's Legal Status in Pre-Civil War New Jersey," *New Jersey History*, LXXXV (Fall-Winter 1967), 174.

58. Jacque Voegeli, *Free But Not Equal: The Midwest and the Negro During the Civil War* (Chicago: University of Chicago Press, 1967), 1-2. Eugene Berwanger, *The Frontier Against Slavery: Western Anti-Negro Prejudice and the Slavery Extension Controversy* (Urbana: University of Illinois Press, 1967), *passim*.

59. Colored Men of Ohio [variant titles], *Proceedings* of Conventions for 1849, 1850, 1851, 1856, 1857, and 1858 detail the action at the convention level. The 1852 proceedings are in *Voice of the Fugitive*, October 21, 1852. For local meetings see *North Star*, March 9 and July 6, 1849; John Mercer Langston, draft fragments of addresses to the Ohio legislature, prior to 1854, John Mercer Langston Papers, microfilm, Amistad Research Center; and *Frederick Douglass' Paper*, June 16, 1854.

60. Berwanger, *Frontier Against Slavery*, 40. John Dancy, "The Negro People in Michigan," *Michigan History Magazine*, XXIV (Spring 1940), 221-240, and more importantly the *Signal of Liberty* and the *Detroit Advertiser* contain information on local meetings in Michigan; and legislative action can be followed in the Journal of the House of Representatives of Michigan. For this latter material we are indebted to David Katzman.

61. *Provincial Freeman*, December 27, 1856. Bell, *Negro Convention Movement*, 187. *Liberator*, October 23, 1857.

in 1837."[62] The few gains were minimal and were probably cancelled out by losses. Across the North thirty years of effort for the franchise had brought almost total defeat. The reasons are fairly clear. An early participant in the New York movement observed cogently that blacks in that state made up only 2% of the population, that the 98% of the population which was white overwhelmingly opposed black enfranchisement, and that Negroes had no "mode of efficiently (as a distinct people) influencing the said white majority, neither by interest, fear, nor by superior intellectual power."[63] The observations were devastatingly accurate. The situation was further worsened by the fact that in New York, where some blacks could vote, and in Pennsylvania, where until 1838 many had the franchise, and in Massachusetts, where all could vote, Negroes failed to exercise their suffrage. In New York, for example, at the time of the 1846 franchise referendum only 1,000 of a potential 3,000 black voters bothered to register. So too they gave only sporadic support to state conventions and organizations working to achieve the ballot.[64]

Yet it is difficult to credit the conclusions which the *Anglo-African Magazine* drew in 1859 that had they tried harder "the result would doubtless have been greater general progress ..., a more united front to meet past and coming exigencies, and a profounder hold upon the public attention, and a deeper respect on the part of our enemies...."[65] Certainly the apathy and negligence of others frustrated activists. But even had all Negroes been activists, statistics were against them. As the National Convention of Colored Men observed in 1864, black men had few friends.[66] Neither the antislavery societies nor the *Liberator* were

62. *Douglass Monthly,* March, 1859.

63. *Colored American,* August 8, 1840.

64. *Rights of All,* October 16, 1829. *Colored American,* July 15, 1837, and December 16, 1840. Stanley, "Majority Tyranny in Tocqueville's America," 415.

65. *Anglo-African Magazine,* I (October 1859), 309.

66. National Convention of Colored Men, *Proceedings of the National Convention ... Held in the city of Syracuse, N. Y., October 4, 5, 6, and 7, 1864 ...* (Boston: Published by J. S. Rock and Geo. L. Ruffin, 1864. Reprint, New York: Arno Press, 1969), 44.

then pressing for the black vote; and the major political parties, riddled as they were with race prejudice, did little or nothing for their enfranchisement. Lacking numbers in the North, where by the Civil War there were, according to the federal census, only 230,000 free blacks, they also lacked support from the white majority and the economic resources to develop a major educational program. As James McCune Smith pointed out in 1860, when black efforts for the New York franchise referendum were largely financed by a gift from the wealthy drug magnate Bradhurst Shieffelin, "Alas for our condition that a white man . . . can exert more influence, even in a good cause[,] on our colored men, than could any colored man."[67]

Beyond all this lay still another question, which the unfriendly New York *Sun* raised in 1845 when it observed that Negroes would get no advantage from suffrage without the property qualification without also having access to public office.[68] Most white abolitionists gave the problem as short shrift as did the *National Anti-Slavery Standard* when it responded that there was scarcely any one in New York City "so stupid as to find the measure of the value of the right of suffrage in the probability of obtaining office."[69] In arguing thusly, Garrisonians in particular were refusing to recognize that blacks needed the political power which office holding betokened. They sought not theoretical victory but access to the means which would expand their rights and opportunities and make their freedom complete. Political abolitionists glimpsed this truth, and Liberty party adherents acted on it. Not surprisingly those who sought black political power cooperated with them.

Even before the organization of the Liberty party, blacks strove to make politics serve their ends. In the middle- and late-1830s, black abolitionists joined white in questioning candidates for office

67. James McCune Smith to Gerrit Smith, September 22, 1860, S-SU.
68. Reported in *National Anti-Slavery Standard,* September 11, 1845.
69. *Ibid.,* September 11, 1845.

about issues of critical interest. In the New Bedford area, where Massachusetts' second-largest black population lived, candidates were asked how they stood on ending slavery in the District of Columbia and on abolishing the interstate slave trade, and their responses—or lack of them—were publicized.[70]

In New York the questioning focused on state laws allowing Southern visitors to retain their slaves for nine months, denying fugitive slaves trial by jury, and requiring a property qualification of black voters. Those who would pledge to change these laws won endorsement, while those who upheld them were disowned. But what was to be done when neither candidate was satisfactory? Should votes be wasted in the hardfought campaigns of the Jacksonian era? Could antislavery men justly vote for candidates politically sound on all but the slavery issue? And what if candidates straddled the issue? The dilemma was as obvious as it was acute. One group in New York City, meeting in 1838, vowed to support only candidates who stood right on repealing all the measures about which they were questioned.[71] This left them with no acceptable gubernatorial candidate. The incumbent, William Marcy, had dodged all the questions; Whig challenger, William Seward, had pledged himself in favor of jury trials for fugitives but had ducked the other questions. If they held to their purist position, New York blacks would forfeit a role in choosing a governor, while they wasted their substance supporting the only candidate who stood right on all measures, the Whig candidate for the relatively powerless post of lieutenant-governor.

Samuel Cornish snorted at such errant nonsense. Intelligent abolitionists, he argued, should support the best available candidate, choosing the lesser evil if no candidate met optimum specifications. Assuming that half a loaf was better than none, he urged support for Seward and the chance to gain legal process for alleged fugitives. To David Ruggles, already at odds with Cornish, this position was a pure and simple compromise with sin. How

70. *Liberator,* November 1, 1839. *Colored American,* November 18, 1837.

71. *Colored American,* November 3, 1838.

could abolitionists justify supporting evil—even the lesser evil—when their commitment was to the good?[72]

The Liberty party was created to insure that there were antislavery candidates and thus to eliminate this problem. Unwilling to turn their backs on political power and equally reluctant to subordinate principle to expediency, Liberty men hoped not only to give voters a meaningful choice but to elect abolitionists to those positions vested with the power to end slavery. Their political idealism provoked sharp debate. Many blacks, sharing the suspicions of moral reformers that all politics was corrupt and all politicians self-serving, doubted that the Liberty party would withstand temptation any better than the Whigs and Democrats. Many others, pragmatists who looked to power politics to achieve their goals, questioned whether a third party could be an effective vehicle.[73]

The columns of the *Colored American* were filled with this debate late in 1839. Cornish insisted that an antislavery party, rather than ending slavery, would corrupt abolitionists and divert them from their goal. Philip Bell and Charles Ray were in the opposite camp. As Ray argued, the choice was simple. One could vote for proslavery candidates and do evil; or one could refrain from voting and do nothing; or one could vote a third party antislavery ticket and do something to end slavery. The latter was the only acceptable alternative.[74]

Ray's position was that of most politically articulate New Yorkers. From his nomination, Albany Negroes backed Liberty party presidential candidate James G. Birney in the 1840 election and urged support for "the noble band of philanthropists already

72. *Ibid.*, November 17, 1838. *Mirror of Liberty*, January, 1839, 36.
73. On the whole blacks were considerably more sanguine about politics than were white abolitionists. In a closely fought vote in 1839 at the annual meeting of the American Anti-Slavery Society, blacks voted five-to-one in favor of a firm endorsement of political action. See *Liberator*, May 24, 1839.
74. *Colored American*, August 31, November 2, 9, and 16, 1839. Also *ibid.*, October 31, 1839, for a similar debate with Thomas Van Rensselaer, who supported pragmatic political activity, not restrictive abolitionist politics.

engaged in our behalf."[75] Samuel Ward, already a political abolitionist, fought hard for the new party in upstate Madison County. "To it," he recalled ecstatically, "I devoted my political activities; with it I lived my political life. . . ."[76] In 1842 Garnet was invited to travel from Troy to Boston to address the Massachusetts Liberty party convention, eager to achieve black endorsement, and the following year he was instrumental in putting the national Negro convention at Buffalo behind the new party. Even Douglass, in 1844 still a Garrisonian and presumably apolitical, ventured approval of the Liberty party, though he soon retreated when reproved by Boston headquarters.[77] Similarly New Bedford Negroes broke ranks in at least one "public meeting of the colored legal voters of the county of Suffolk" to endorse Birney in his second try for the presidency.[78] And though a few, like Salem's old organization stalwart Charles Remond consistently denounced the Liberty party,[79] black Bostonians were so split by 1848 that they could only agree to the bland statement that everybody was "under the highest obligations to remove Slavery by moral and political action."[80]

As the Liberty party sought and won black endorsement, so too they made sure that Negroes played active roles in its organization. That it should have done so reflected several special circumstances. With the American and Foreign Anti-Slavery Society as well as with antislavery missionary societies, at least in New York state, it shared a largely common leadership, black and white, and thus common attitudes. Furthermore, the party was small, and the addition of a black support bloc was strategically important. Finally, in New York, the talents of a significant professional

75. *Colored American*, May 23, 1840.

76. Ward, *Autobiography*, 75.

77. *Emancipator and Free American*, March 3, 1842. National Convention of Colored Citizens, *Minutes of. . .1843*, 15-16. Edmund Quincy to Caroline Weston, March 9, 1844, W-BPL. Garnet, for his part, rejected Boston's reproof of his Liberty party activity in firm tones; see his letter to Maria W. Chapman, November 17, 1843, in *Liberator*, December 8, 1843.

78. *Liberator*, September 20, 1844.

79. *Ibid.*, October 7, 1842, November 1, 1844, and April 18, 1845.

80. *North Star*, February 18, 1848.

middle class of Negro leaders were available to it. These they used well. Garnet, Ward, and Ray addressed both New York and other state conventions as well as national conclaves.[81] In Cortland, New York, Ward edited a Liberty party paper, the *True American.*[82] In turn, blacks appealed to Liberty party to support their goals. In 1845, for instance, its New York followers were asked to disregard party and vote for those delegates to the constitutional convention who would favor repeal of the property qualification for Negro voters.[83]

Even in New York, however, the appeal of political action was by no means universal. At the 1843 national convention in Buffalo, Stephen Myers bitterly denounced as counterproductive proposals to endorse the third party. Indeed, he said, Negroes should stand totally clear of party identification. "Lying, as we do in many of the States, at the mercy of both the great political parties, and petitioning as we do, yearly, for the restoration of our rights, we consider it consummate folly to advise our people to identify themselves with either."[84]

The results of Garnet's action to the contrary at the state convention in Rochester illuminated Myers' fears. Garnet had persuaded that meeting to condemn both Whigs and Democrats as proslavery parties. At the next state convention held in 1844 in Schenectady, the New York City delegation, led by James McCune Smith and Ulysses Vidal, attacked the resolutions. The Rochester convention had been called only on behalf of suffrage and had exceeded its charge when it presumed to judge particular political parties. More importantly, its action had antagonized Democratic Governor William Bouck, who had been prepared to back the

81. Benjamin Quarles, *Black Abolitionists* (New York: Oxford University Press, 1969), 184. *Emancipator and Free American,* March 3, 1842. Albany *Patriot,* February 24, 1847.

82. H. P. Smith, *History of Cortland County*...(Syracuse: D. Mason & Co., 1885), 131-132. On at least one occasion, at the Washtenaw (Michigan) county Liberty Convention, blacks were excluded, presumably because they did not have the franchise; *Signal of Liberty,* September 1, 1841, from the notes of David Katzman.

83. Ransom F. Wake *et al.,* to Gerrit Smith, June 13, 1845, S-SU.

84. *Liberator,* September 29, 1843.

removal of property qualifications. Through delaying tactics, Garnet managed to avoid a vote of censure,[85] but subsequent conventions refused to repeat the Rochester mistake.

National developments, too, raised doubts about the wisdom of supporting the Liberty party. Propelled by the extension of slavery which Texas' annexation represented and the Mexican War promised, political abolitionists grasped for effective means to end the war and make the land acquired by it free. The Liberty party promised little hope because its base was simply too narrow. At the same time neither major party would risk Southern support by excluding slavery from the new territories. Consequently the Free Soil party emerged in 1848 as the new alternative. Free from the stigma of radical abolition, it could attract broader support than had the Liberty party by its platform of antiextension.

Because of its very moderation, however, Free Soil confronted black leaders with a difficult decision. The national convention meeting in Cleveland in September 1848 voted support for the Free Soil party which, although it fell short of highest antislavery principles, possessed "a tendency to enhance the liberty of the colored people of the United States."[86] Douglass, who attended the convention, dissented on the floor from this endorsement. His reasons for doing so are not, however, altogether clear, since he was already well on the way to giving the new party his personal and editorial support. The preceding June he had written "that Northern men and opinions can never be respected in either of the great political organizations of this country, while slavery exists. Parties must therefore be broken up. . . ."[87] By August he was praising the Free Soil nominating convention for having "virtually adopted the leading doctrines and purposes set forth by the American Anti-Slavery Society at its formation, as the duty of the government."[88] And early in September, satisfied with the slogan "Free Soil, Free Men, Free Labor, Free Speech, and Free States,"

85. *National Anti-Slavery Standard,* October 17 and 24, 1844.
86. *North Star,* September 29, 1848.
87. *Ibid.,* June 16, 1848.
88. *Ibid.,* August 18, 1848.

Douglass placed the name of its presidential nominee on the *North Star's* masthead.[89]

Even more illustrative of the dilemma which Free Soil presented for black abolitionists was the tentative support which Liberty party stalwart Samuel Ward first gave, and then withdrew, from the new party. Chosen by Cortland County antislavery Democrats to attend the national Free Soil convention at Buffalo, he accepted in spite of the fact that his *True American* supported Gerrit Smith as the presidential candidate of a splinter group of the Liberty party. Once chosen, Ward pledged himself to oppose Martin Van Buren, were he selected as the Free Soil candidate—which he was—because as President, Van Buren had threatened to veto any bill ending slavery in the District of Columbia.[90]

The convention served to cancel out the minimal hopes which Ward had for the new party. No sooner had he arrived in Buffalo than John Hale, the Liberty party presidential candidate, whose nomination had already split that party, proclaimed his support for Van Buren. Ward was incensed, convinced that Hale had accepted the nomination only to use it in selling out the party.[91] Once the convention was over Ward hurried back home and wrote Gerrit Smith in great agitation. "Well; I have been to Buffalo. . . . Farewell to confidence in man!" Hale was but one of the traitors who had sacrificed moral principle to political advantage. The only right thing to do now was to call a state Liberty party convention and nominate Smith. Then, "God helping us, all will be well in the end."[92] Ward did not confine his dismay to private letters. In an "Address to the Four Thousand Colored Voters of the State of New York," he assured them they held the balance of power both in the state and in the nation. Thus it was urgent that they reject Van Buren and the Free Soil platform, which did "NOT include the Equal and Inalienable Rights of ALL MEN."[93]

89. Foner, *Douglass,* 2:72.
90. Cortland (New York) *Democrat,* July 26, August 2 and 9, 1848.
91. *North Star,* September 1, 1848.
92. Samuel R. Ward to Gerrit Smith, August 14, [1848], S-SU.
93. *North Star,* September 1, 1848.

Douglass balked at Ward's address. It was just so much haggling. One had to take the Free Soil candidates as the best available, despite their obvious imperfections. Yet a year of observing Free Soilers at work gave Douglass serious misgivings. By May 1849 he was complaining that the party was weak and ineffectual, that it lacked grass roots support, and that it was governed by expediency at the cost of antislavery principle.[94] The new party had promised much; it had delivered little. Martin Delany experienced a similar disillusionment. An enthusiastic Free Soil supporter in September of 1848, he despaired of Free Soilers' duplicity early in 1849. Their concern was not, he wrote then, "the extension of liberty to the black man, but . . . the protection of the liberty of the white . . . endangered by the encroachments of the slave power."[95]

For blacks, generally, the issue was not slavery's encroachment on North and West but its persistance in the South and its heritage in the North. As James McCune Smith, then a recent convert to the Liberty party, wrote in 1848, there was only "one way to attack Slavery through Political action," and that was "to make it the sole idea of that political action. . . .The *one idea* of slavery has spread its shoots and its roots and its suckers into every institution in the land," he added. "And if the one idea has wrought this, how can we remove the results except by removing the one idea in its essence and in its mode?"[96] For this end, Liberty party splinter groups continued to work.

Nonetheless the Free Soil experience had taught them the valuable lesson that they must broaden their platform to extend their appeal. Ward, for example, was arguing in 1850 that a one-plank platform spelled political impotence. Writing Gerrit Smith after a New England tour, he reported that the time was ripe to revive the Liberty party there but that its base must be extended beyond antislavery to a variety of issues popular with the major

94. *Ibid.*, September 1, 1848 and May 25, 1849.
95. *Ibid.*, January 12, 1849. For a general assessment of the relationship between the Negro and the Free Soil party see Eric Foner, "Politics and Prejudice: The Free Soil Party and the Negro, 1849-1852," *Journal of Negro History*, L (October 1965), 239-256.
96. James McCune Smith to Gerrit Smith, May 12, 1848, S-SU.

parties.[97] Yet even that technique had its dangers. Douglass, converted to Liberty party in 1851, was similarly tormented by its smallness and lack of political power. Still, he feared that taking stands on other controversial issues might both lose it some of the support it had and divert the energy needed to effect any one major change. "The abolitionist is impatient with the Liberty Party, because it will not consent to be a mere abolition party," he wrote; "and the land-reformer is impatient with it, because it will not consent to be a mere land-reform party. The free-trader expects no good from the Liberty Party, so long as it concerns itself with any other evil than tariffs; and the temperance man cannot be reconciled to it, whilst it aims at anything else than to carry Civil Government against dram-shops."[98] In Pennsylvania William Whipper expressed similar reservations. He had swung from apolitical Garrisonianism to political involvement in the late 1840s when he came to support the old Liberty party. In 1851, however, he so feared that expanding its platform had led it away from high antislavery ground that he refused to attend the party convention. In the event, both Douglass and Whipper had overreacted, for in 1851, at least, two-thirds of the platform dealt with antislavery and civil rights.[99]

For all their misgivings, blacks worked valiantly over the years to keep an antislavery party alive. They played a prominent role in party organization. They ran for office on its ticket. In 1848 Ward was a candidate for the New York State assembly; in 1850 he was nominated the vice-presidential running-mate of Gerrit Smith on a ticket which faded away before 1852.[100] Smith, for his part, in giving both moral and financial support to the *Impartial Citizen* and the *Frederick Douglass' Paper* made them unofficial organs of the Liberty party. Yet when the election of 1852 brewed, many Liberty party proponents supported the Free Soil party's presidential candidate, John Hale of New Hampshire. Despite earlier

97. Samuel R. Ward to Gerrit Smith, April 30, 1850, S-SU.
98. *Frederick Douglass' Paper*, June 26, 1851.
99. *Ibid.*, September 25, 1851.
100. *Weekly Chronotype*, June 24, 1848. Cortland (New York) *Democrat*, November 25, 1848. *Chronotype*, October 8, 1850.

criticisms, both Martin Delany and Frederick Douglass backed Hale as did many other blacks in New England and New York.[101] Indeed, Douglass' vacillation between the Liberty party in off years and Free Soil and Republican parties in presidential years suggests a pattern of irresolution between principle and pragmatism in politics. Thus, in 1853 he returned to the Liberty party, which he called "the repository of radical antislavery truth"; and the next year willingly served, along with Jarmain W. Loguen of Syracuse, on several committees at the party's state convention.[102] A year later he ran on its ticket for the office of New York's secretary of state, while George B. Vashon, lawyer and teacher at McGrawville's Central College, was its nominee for attorney-general. But when 1856 came round, Douglass threw his support to the Republican party and its presidential candidate, John Charles Frémont.[103]

Still, irresolution was not the whole story, for the logic of national events in the mid-1850s compelled party reorganization, as the Kansas-Nebraska crisis gave the death blow to the Whigs. Emerging to fill the vacuum was the Republican party which drew to it Conscience Whigs, Free Soilers, Free Democrats, and Anti-Nebraska men. Again the Liberty party rationale was challenged, as it had been in 1848, by an antiextension party which substituted hope of winning for antislavery principle. To meet this challenge the sparse remnants of New York's Liberty party, including Douglass, J. McC. Smith, Loguen, and Garnet, reorganized themselves as the Radical Political Abolitionists. Arguing that slavery was unconstitutional and that the federal government had the power to abolish it by direct action, the new group added

101. *Frederick Douglass' Paper,* August 20 and October 8, 1852. *Liberator,* August 20, 1852.

102. *Frederick Douglass' Paper,* March 4, 1853 and October 13, 1854.

103. *Anti-Slavery Bugle,* September 22, 1855. Douglass, *Anti-Slavery Movement,* 30, 35. Frederick Douglass to Gerrit Smith, August 31, 1856, S-SU. The *Bugle* misnames him John Vashon rather than George. In Ohio, in 1855, although John M. Langston ran only for town clerk, he was elected by an all-white vote. See John Mercer Langston, *From the Virginia Plantation to the National Capital or the First and Only Negro Representative in Congress from the Old Dominion* (Hartford: American Publishing Co., 1894), 144.

nothing dynamic to old formulas. After a brief existence it disappeared.[104]

Unchallenged therefore by a viable party of antislavery principle, the Republican party by 1856 attracted politically oriented Northern blacks. State conventions in Ohio and New York endorsed its ticket as did public meetings in Boston.[105] Even Douglass, somewhat guiltily, threw *Frederick Douglass' Paper* behind Frémont. It was, he wrote Gerrit Smith, "the best thing" he could do at the moment, although he assured the Liberty party leader that he had not forgotten the "doctrines and measures, inseparable from your great name and character."[106]

By 1860 whatever free black consensus there was in the North clearly supported the Republicans. The Colored Men's National Suffrage Convention of 1858 overwhelmingly backed the party and specifically rejected the Radical Abolitionists.[107] In New England, black Garrisonians who had argued in the 1840s and early 1850s that the constitution was proslavery and that only disunion would cure slavery rapidly shifted ground. In so doing, the New England convention of 1859, while not disavowing their proslavery interpretation of the Constitution, argued that it was more useful to act as though it were antislavery. Thus were they free to act within the political system and endorse the Republican party. It was not noble idealism but simple pragmatism to go, after thirty or more years of ineffective antislavery struggle, for a party which might achieve national power. So the *Weekly Anglo-African* advised New York blacks to bloc vote for the best (presumably Republican)

104. Radical Political Abolitionists, *Proceedings of the Convention . . . Held at Syracuse, N. Y., June 26th, 27th, and 28th, 1855* (New York: Central Abolition Board, 1855), 3-4. *Frederick Douglass' Paper,* July 5, 1855. *Radical Abolitionist,* December, 1855.

105. State Convention of Colored Men, *Proceedings of the State Convention . . . Held in the City of Columbus, Ohio, Jan. 16th, 17th & 18th, 1856* ([Title page missing]), 2. *Liberator,* September 5, 1856. *National Anti-Slavery Standard,* September 27, 1856.

106. Frederick Douglass to Gerrit Smith, August 31, 1856, S-SU.

107. Henry H. Garnet and J. W. Duffin to Gerrit Smith, September 10, 1858, S-SU.

candidates—not out of party loyalty but in the hope of unseating their oppressors.[108]

Ironically at this final juncture Douglass' political pragmatism deserted him. Quixotically he abandoned the Republicans to support a Liberty party even more splintered and fragmentary than it had been in the early 1850s. In urging his fellows to vote for Gerrit Smith for president in 1860, Douglass argued that principle must precede practice; that "ten thousand votes for *GERRIT SMITH* . . . would do more . . . for the ultimate abolition of slavery in this country, than two million for ABRAHAM LINCOLN. . . ."[109]

Aberrant as it was, Douglass' exhortation dramatized the failure of black political activism in the antebellum period. In a political system characterized by compromises and coalitions among divergent interests rather than by steady pursuit of ideological goals, blacks' single-minded dedication to antislavery and civil rights goals stood little chance, for they had nothing to bargain with. Furthermore their singleness of purpose bred no agreement or unity on tactics or strategy. But that greater internal cohesiveness would have made a real difference is a doubtful proposition. As a largely disfranchised minority in the North, the black community remained politically powerless, lacking even the most elemental traction necessary to initiate change. For all their struggles in the antebellum years, no blacks except those in Rhode Island had gained the simplest yet most fundamental weapon of political power, the vote. And in New York and northern and central New England, where some or all possessed the suffrage, black voters were never sufficiently numerous to be politically significant. Elsewhere black political power declined or remained totally absent. Indeed, during the years of greatest political activity the

108. *Liberator,* June 21, 1844, July 13, 1855, August 19, 1859. *Weekly Anglo-African,* July 30 and October 15, 1859.
109. *Douglass Monthly,* October, 1860.

condition of Northern Negroes became steadily worse. In the 1850s, as Congress and courts combined to curtail still further the rights of Northern blacks—be they freemen or fugitives—the future looked decidedly bleak.

10. FUGITIVES AND RESCUERS—1850: A TURNING POINT

EVER SINCE the passage of the 1793 fugitive slave law, Northern blacks, whether freed by formal emancipation or their own earlier flight, had aided Southern slaves fleeing bondage. They sheltered them, fed them, and settled them where they were, or helped them go still farther north, sometimes even to Canada. By the 1830s such efforts often were formally organized and occasionally overtly defiant as they rescued slaves retaken by privately employed slavecatchers or public officers enforcing the law. Although antislavery whites also aided fugitive slaves by providing material support and by testing the law in the courts, they were, until 1850, almost never involved in rescue attempts and did little to organize fugitive aid except through antislavery societies.

In 1850, however, the pattern changed. The fugitive slave law of that year was both more rigorous in itself and more offensive to private citizens in the North, who were compelled under threat of fine and imprisonment to aid in the capture and return of fugitives. Whites, therefore, as well as blacks, took open, organized, and vigorous action against it. They established organizations specifically designed to thwart the law, and for the first time they joined in significant numbers in violent confrontations intended to rescue individual fugitives. In these new circumstances the relationship between black and white abolitionists varied from that of the established antislavery societies. Now blacks were major shapers of the policies and methods which after 1850 many white abolitionists accepted and made their own. Thus the pattern of black resistance to both fugitive slave laws remained the same, although it intensified and became more open with the passage of the 1850 law. By contrast, the basic form of opposition by whites changed sharply in 1850, following a path new to them, but blazed by blacks during the twenty years preceding.

"LOOK OUT FOR KIDNAPPERS," a broadside warned New Yorkers on July 8, 1834. Dr. Rufus Haywood of Raleigh, North Carolina, had come North to claim and seize as fugitives John Lockley and his family, who were then residents of the city. As soon as the charge was filed, Lockley had sought a jury trial. Haywood, incensed at the legal obstacles placed in his path, immediately challenged the constitutionality of granting a fugitive due process. If Haywood's contention was upheld, the broadside pointed out, he could simply seize his alleged property on a routine certificate from the city recorder. "Will men who love LIBERTY, and believe that all *innocent men* have a right to it, tamely see such villany [*sic*] perpetrated *by law* in this city?" the broadside asked. The answer it expected was clear, for it was signed, "OPPOSITION TO TYRANTS IS OBEDIENCE TO GOD."[1]

Here, starkly portrayed, was the fear and frustration that plagued both fugitive and freeman in the North. How could they achieve the legal process and protections guaranteed other Americans? Or how could they escape the consequences when that process was denied them? One answer was provided by the vigilance committee. Probably developed first by New Yorkers, it was rapidly copied elsewhere. In these groups blacks, and sometimes whites, used a variety of devices to protect both bona fide freemen and actual fugitives who were otherwise helpless against alleged owners or their agents who threatened them with a forced return to slavery. Because the fugitive, who seldom knew anyone in the North, usually sought help from those of his own race first, the initial contact and shelter more often than not came from Negroes,

1. The broadside is included in the microfilm edition of the *Liberator*, and appears between 1833 and 1834; American Periodical Series, APS968, Reel 391.

while sympathetic whites aided with money, clothes, transportation, and the provision of legal services.[2]

In the middle 1830s the pattern of vigilance activity evolved in New York City largely through the efforts of David Ruggles. Already known for his abolitionist sentiments and his vigorous attack upon racist David Reese, Ruggles, at a meeting of the "friends of Human Rights" in November 1835, called for an investigation of kidnapping and of ways to aid its victims. From this effort emerged the New York City Vigilance Committee, with Ruggles its secretary and principal catalyst.[3] Because in New York jury trial was denied alleged fugitives and because other forms of legal protection were minimal, the action of the committee's leaders often went well beyond providing legal aid; with at least some of them advocating open physical resistance to the law. How willing some of them were to use extralegal means is suggested by Ruggles' reaction to the seizure of a George Jones, who was almost immediately sent South. "While we are subject to be thus inhumanly practiced upon, no man is safe," he exhorted the public; "we must look to our own safety and protection from kidnappers; remembering that 'self-defence is the first law of nature.' "[4]

Constantly the vigilance committee was on guard for the rights and safety of blacks.[5] Slaves accompanying their masters on visits from the South were informed that New York law prohibited their being held involuntarily for more than nine months. When, as in the case of Charity Dodge, they learned of one held beyond that time,

2. Larry Gara, *The Liberty Line: The Legend of the Underground Railroad* (Lexington: University of Kentucky, Press, 1961), *passim.*

3. *Liberator,* December 26, 1835. Dorothy B. Porter, "David M. Ruggles, an Apostle of Human Rights," *Journal of Negro History,* XXVII (January, 1943), 31-32. New York Committee of Vigilance, *The First Annual Report of the New York Committee of Vigilance . . . 1837* (New York: Piercy and Reed, 1837. Reprint, Philadelphia: Rhistoric Publications, n.d.), 4, contains a brief statement of the aims and objectives of the committee.

4. *Liberator,* August 6, 1836.

5. See, for example, New York Committee of Vigilance, *First Annual Report . . . 1837,* 13-14.

the committee sought legal redress.[6] Unwilling to wait for cases to be brought to them, they kept a constant surveillance of the comings and goings of known agents for slaveholders and of ships suspected of illegal slaving. Their actions also embraced free blacks, endangered, as were freeborn Margaret Baker and her children, by kidnapping and enslavement. Thus, during its first three years of work, so Ruggles reported, the vigilance committee averaged a case every other day.[7]

Sometimes action went well beyond upholding and publicizing the law. Ruggles regularly sheltered fugitives who came to the city, among them a young caulker from Baltimore not yet named Frederick Douglass.[8] More spectacular was the attempted rescue of William Dixon. While he was being held in the courthouse during a hearing to determine his future, a large group of blacks gathered outside. When they learned that the hearings had gone against him, they were prepared. As Dixon was led down the courthouse steps, the crowd seized him, aided his escape, and provided him with "a large dirk and a Spanish knife." Their action, however, was futile, and Dixon was soon recaptured.[9] Thereupon the vigilance committee formally sprang into action and raised money to appeal Dixon's case to the higher courts as part of their continuing struggle to achieve jury trials "for all persons hereafter claimed by man thieves as fugitive slaves in the state of New York."[10]

On the use of extralegal action in the Dixon case and elsewhere, vigilance committee opinion was badly divided and the issue soon became a bone of contention. Samuel Cornish, who was a member of its executive committee, and, incidentally, Ruggles' major critic, condemned the attempted Dixon rescue. Appalled by the ruckus which the "ignorant part of our colored citizens" had made, in front of the courthouse, Cornish sought to confine activity in such

6. *Mirror of Liberty,* July, 1838, 1-2. Dodge had been held illegally for three years as an unpaid servant. She was finally released.
7. *Mirror of Liberty,* July, 1838, 6-8.
8. Fragment, unidentified MS, p. 4, Frederick Douglass Papers, Library of Congress, microfilm edition (cited hereafter as D-LC), Reel 13.
9. *Liberator,* April 21, 1837.
10. *Colored American,* January 20, 1838.

cases to the "intelligent and efficient Vigilance Committee" and its "eminent lawyers" in the courts of law. "We have perfect confidence in the men whose business it is to conduct these matters," Cornish concluded and pleaded with future "ignorant" mobs against "going to the Courts at all, or assembling in the Park, on the occasion of fugitive trials—you can do no good, but much harm."[11]

Ruggles thought differently, and much of the difficulty over extralegal action within the vigilance committee focused on his militance. More interested in immediately effective action than in legal and organizational niceties, Ruggles incurred the doubt and displeasure of other leading New York City blacks, including, in addition to Cornish, Theodore Wright, Charles Ray, Philip Bell, and Robert Sears. Charging him with financial irregularities in his position as secretary of the vigilance committee, these men finally forced his resignation in 1839.[12] Without doubt, although he was later exonerated of charges of malfeasance,[13] his bookkeeping and financial management were chaotic. Nonetheless, the financial contretemps was only a screen for the real issue of Ruggles' flamboyant and often illegal action.

In 1836 when he had tried, albeit unsuccessfully, to rescue slaves from the Brazilian ship, *Brilliante,* owned by the mayor of Rio de Janeiro, Ruggles was jailed on charges of assisting in a slave escape and of inciting a riot.[14] The following year, 1837, his brashness brought open and head-on conflict with Cornish after he had prevailed upon the editor to publish in the *Colored American* an exposé of illegal slave trading. Ruggles charged that John Russell, a landlord to Negro seamen, had helped a trader kidnap three Gambians staying at his boarding house and ship them off to be sold in New Orleans. Cornish, assuming that Ruggles had fully checked the story, relied on his report. Once it was published, Russell sued the paper for libel, won his case, and saddled Cornish

11. *Ibid.,* April 15, 1837.
12. *National Anti-Slavery Standard,* August 20, 1840. *Mirror of Liberty,* January 1839, 34.
13. *Colored American,* September 5, 1840.
14. *Weekly Advocate,* January 14, 1837.

and the *Colored American* with a fine and court costs. Neither individually nor as secretary of the vigilance committee would Ruggles accept responsibility for the suit or aid the already hard-pressed paper in meeting its legal obligations.[15]

Ruggles' third brush with the law, in 1838, was the most personally burdensome for him. Arrested for concealing a fugitive charged with stealing $9,000 from his Arkansas master, Ruggles was taken to jail. There, so he claimed, he was deserted by a friend who refused to bail him out and left him to spend the night in a dank four-foot by eight-foot cell with four drunks. Although he refused to identify the individual publicly, it was probably Cornish or another member of the vigilance committee. When Ruggles was bailed out the next morning, his troubles in the case had only begun, for he was continued on bail for fourteen months, during which time his movements were restricted. Finally he was freed without a trial, suggesting that the case against him was scarcely conclusive.[16]

At stake in all three episodes was more than a personal difference between Ruggles and Cornish, for that clash was but part of a fundamental disagreement over what actions were appropriate in defending black rights. Ruggles, an activist by temperament, was abrasive and unconcerned about protocol. His bearing and style offended his more conservative colleagues, who preferred quieter means within legal boundaries. Consequently it was only in 1839, when Ruggles was forced out of the vigilance committee, that dissension ended. Significantly, thereafter the committee languished until 1848 when it became the nucleus for a new state organization.[17]

Elsewhere a variety of vigilance committees flourished. Pittsburgh, Detroit, Boston, and Albany all had such groups in the late

15. Porter, "David Ruggles," 39-43. Lewis and Arthur Tappan, Gerrit Smith, William Jay, James G. Birney and others finally came to the rescue of the *Colored American*. See also *Colored American*, November 3, 17, and December 1, 1838.

16. *Liberator*, October 5, 1838. *Mirror of Liberty*, January, 1839. *Liberator*, February 7, 1840.

17. *North Star*, May 18, 1849.

1830s and 1840s.[18] Although none was as dramatic as that which Ruggles led, and few publicized either their membership or their activities, most did their share of good work. Especially successful was the Philadelphia committee, organized in 1838. Although it had white members, like the New York and most other Vigilance Committees it was predominately black and black-led. During its first decade Robert Purvis guided its activity; thereafter William Still was its dominant member. His careful chronicle of its activities demonstrated that it was a major link on the underground railroad. Like the New York group, it also undertook court challenges and intervened to prevent enslavement of free blacks. Assuring William Wells Brown in 1848 that his freedom would be protected in the city, Purvis called the vigilance committee "a formidable obstacle" to any would-be kidnapper.[19] All of these groups were part of a network of vigilance committees serving, as the Detroit *Advertiser* wrote of that city's group, the "interest of the colored people."[20]

Important as they were, vigilance committees affected individual cases rather than underlying issues. Of the latter, one of the most fundamental was that Negroes in the North, fugitive or free, possessed few civil rights in the courts and, in actual practice, seldom appeared there except as the accused. A critical question therefore was how blacks could gain access to fair trials and basic justice.

State laws varied considerably. After 1820 Pennsylvania statutes required that a judge, rather than an alderman or justice of the

18. *Colored American*, December 1, 1838. Detroit *Advertiser*, April 27, 1842, from the notes of David Katzman. *Liberator*, May 24, 1844. Benjamin Quarles, *Black Abolitionists* (New York: Oxford University Press, 1969), 153.

19. Gara, *Liberty Line*, 99. Vigilant Committee of Philadelphia, "Minute Book of the Vigilant Committee of Philadelphia," (1839-1844), MS, Historical Society of Pennsylvania, *passim*. Larry Gara, "William Still and the Underground Railroad," *Pennsylvania History*, XXVIII (January 1961), 34. The quotation is a paraphrase in William Wells Brown to [?] May, August 17, 1848, in *Liberator*, September 1, 1848.

20. Detroit *Advertiser*, April 27, 1842, from the notes of David Katzman.

peace, hear cases of those claimed as fugitives under the 1793 Federal Fugitive Slave Law; after 1826, it required both that evidence offered to prove slave status meet minimum standards and that heavy fines be levied against those convicted of kidnapping free blacks. Yet the United States Supreme Court's decision in the 1842 Prigg case endangered even these limited protections, for the court found the 1826 statute an unconstitutional state interference with federal prerogative.[21]

Blacks responded to the decision instantaneously and almost always with despair. "Benezet," writing in the *Northern Star,* thought that the decision "settled it as the law of the country, that no non-slaveholding state has any right to enact laws securing a jury trial to alleged fugitives from southern slavery, nor to punish those who may choose to kidnap any inhabitant of a free state."[22] Samuel Ward was equally alarmed. "I can see no kind of legal protection for any colored man's liberties. Everything is made as easy as possible for the kidnapper. . . . Be a man, [how] ever free [,] he is liable to instant seizure, & enslavement."[23]

Yet there were those who found some benefits in the Prigg decision. If the capture and return of fugitives was purely a federal affair, then states were not only prohibited from interfering with enforcement of the 1793 law, but also from helping to enforce it. In Boston, Negroes petitioned the state legislature "to prohibit their officers and citizens from interfering to aid slaveholders in seizing and returning fugitive slaves." At the same time they decided to petition Congress "to repeal the law of 1793."[24]

21. Edward R. Turner, *The Negro in Pennsylvania, 1639-1861* (Washington: American Historical Association, 1912), 117, 233. Even before the Prigg decision, the position of Pennsylvania blacks was severely threatened. In 1832 the state legislature considered measures to restrict the immigration of blacks, and it pressed for a more vigorous enforcement of the 1793 Fugitive Slave Law by suggesting the repeal of the 1820 statute requiring a judge to hear all fugitive slave cases. In January 1832 James Forten, William Whipper, and Robert Purvis led a petition campaign against these proposals. *Liberator,* April 14, 1832. "Petition of Philadelphia Negroes to the Pennsylvania State Legislature, January, 1832," in Aptheker, *Documentary History,* 1:129-133.
22. *Northern Star and Freemen's Advocate,* March 17, 1842.
23. Samuel R. Ward to Gerrit Smith, April 18, 1842, S-SU.
24. *Liberator,* June 3, 1842.

Ruggles, who was now living in Northampton, Massachusetts, and was as militant as ever, welcomed the Prigg decision for having cleared away obstacles which impeded a direct test of the 1793 law. "I wish," he wrote Garrison impatiently, "the friends of freedom would, instead of taking issue against Justice Story, or the Supreme Court, for explaining the true bearing of the law, go against its constitutionality."[25] That these responses had merit, the action of both Pennsylvania and Rhode Island attested. Anticipating a practice common in the 1850s, both states had by 1848 adopted personal liberty laws that prohibited state officials from cooperating with federal agents to enforce the fugitive slave law.[26]

While some argued the constitutionality of the law, others negated it by direct and physical resistance. Late in June 1833, the agent of a Kentucky slaveholder had arrived in Detroit to claim a man variously known as Smith, Thornton, or Blackburn, and his wife. Speedily seized and jailed, the couple was soon visited by local Negroes, who brought with them a disguise which enabled Mrs. Smith to escape. Later a crowd gathered in front of the jail and attacked the sheriff when he brought out her husband. Engaging the sheriff and his men in armed conflict, they finally got the prisoner into a cart and drove him away.[27] Resultant black glee and white fear reduced the town to utter terror, which lasted at least a month. Blacks were charged with burning down a barn and threatening the peace of the community. Thereupon the mayor required that Negroes either "give a certificate of freedom and bond of good conduct" or leave town. Then in classic overreaction, Secretary of War Lewis Cass, who happened to be in

25. *Ibid.*, February 10, 1843.
26. Turner, *Negro in Pennsylvania*, 238. George L. Clarke to Frederick Douglass, February 18, 1848, in *North Star*, March 3, 1848, wrote triumphantly, "Rhode Island has just declared, through her highest Legislative authority, that she will no longer act the part of bull-dog for the South, to seize and hold their runaway slaves."
27. *Liberator*, July 6, 1833.

town, ordered a contingent of federal troops from nearby Fort Gratiot to guard the city. For a week thereafter the town remained a garrisoned fortress.[28]

Near Buffalo in 1835 another group of blacks rescued a fugitive family recently kidnapped from their refuge in St. Catherines, Canada. Releasing the family from the slave agent was easy enough, but it took resort to arms to circumvent the large sheriff's posse sent to intercept them on their way back to Canada. After the battle, in which William Wells Brown reputedly took some part, eight or ten of the rescuers were arrested and later fined.[29] The following year in Boston, a group of strong-minded women invaded the state supreme court and spirited away two women whose alleged slave status the court was reviewing.[30] Not only did no whites participate in this rescue, but both Garrison and the Massachusetts Anti-Slavery Society[31] censured their action.

In yet another episode, in which two fugitives from Kentucky who had sought shelter in Oberlin were tracked down and seized in their hiding place, white college students and others joined local blacks in a rescue attempt. They jeered the constable and slave agents so unmercifully that they barricaded themselves in a nearby house, which the protesters then surrounded and bombarded with threats to kill the slavecatchers unless the slaves were freed. Finally, however, all parties agreed to take the case before the local judge for a decision. The slaves were freed on a technicality, but immediately rearrested on a new affadavit. Legal maneuver continued while Jefferson and Jane Johnson languished in jail. Finally, unwilling to trust the court, they broke out and made good their escape. One unsympathetic newspaper charged that a

28. Eliza B. Mason to Catherine Armistad Mason, July 20, 1833, and a second, which contains the quotation, July 27, 1833, in John Mason Manuscripts, Burton Collection, Detroit Public Library. Lewis Cass to Marshall Chapin, July 25, 1833, in Marshall Chapin Manuscripts, Burton Collection, Detroit Public Library. From the notes of David Katzman.

29. *Liberator*, August 1, 1835, gives the figure eight to ten blacks. William E. Farrison, "William Wells Brown in Buffalo," *Journal of Negro History*, XXIX (October, 1954), 301-302, citing the 1849 edition of Brown's *Narrative*, sets the figure at forty, mostly blacks.

30. *Liberator*, December 10, 1852.

31. *Ibid.*, August 6, 1836.

"gang of Oberlin, fanatical, abolition anarchists" had stormed the jail, and "with saws, axes, &c., prepared for the purpose, liberated the negroes confined therein" and carried them off. Testimony that they acted on their own, however, is probably more accurate.[32]

In Boston in 1842 just after local blacks had founded the New England Freedom Association to aid fugitives,[33] George Latimer, formerly of Norfolk, Virginia, was seized. Immediately both black and white abolitionists held protest meetings and signed petitions urging repeal of the fugitive slave law. Black protesters, however, did not stop with this familiar response, but went on, almost at once, to draw on their 1836 experience and suggest the use of extralegal means if appeals to the courts failed to rescue Latimer. Douglass, who was lecturing in New Bedford when he heard the news, set the tone. "Now make up your minds to what your duty is to George Latimer," he exhorted his audience, "and when you have made your minds up, prepare to do it and take the consequences, and I have no fears of George Latimer going back."[34] Subsequently a mass meeting of Boston blacks late in November sanctioned the use of force. "For the safety of Liberty, and security of our happiness," read one resolution, "we will hereafter, in time of peril, use such arguments as were used by our illustrious fathers in defence of freedom, to prevent such base perversion of right and justice."[35] Violence was probably avoided only by the willingness of Latimer's owner to sell his slave to Boston abolitionists.[36]

32. *Ibid.*, March 26, 1841, and May 21, 1841.
33. *Ibid.*, April 21, 1843.
34. *Ibid.*, November 18, 1842.
35. *Ibid.*, December 23, 1842.
36. Not all were as fortunate as Latimer, the Smiths, Jefferson and Jane Johnson, or the St. Catherines family. George, a stowaway aboard the brig *Mobile* out of Savannah, was apprehended in 1846 in New York. When he appeared in court, a crowd gathered outside and twice tried without success to rescue him. Luckier than George and his would-be rescuers was another group which, the following year, seized several slaves who had been taken near Carlyle, Pennsylvania, by Maryland public officers. Although they managed to rescue the slaves and send them on their way, twelve of the rescue force were arrested, brought to trial, and found guilty of rioting. The

Dramatic as these and similar episodes were, it was the passage of the 1850 Fugitive Slave Act which pushed both black and white abolitionists into openly avowed and preconcerted action to defy the law.[37] During the spring and summer of 1850, while the bill was still pending in the Congress, blacks as well as whites met frequently to urge its defeat. From Pittsburgh and New York to Boston and Portland, they gathered. Faced with the likelihood of a law designed to make the lot of the alleged fugitive even more perilous than had that of 1793, they spoke with new determination.

New Yorkers announced that the new law simply would "have no binding force" upon them and pledged to resist it by all possible means, even "the sacrifice of life."[38] In Boston Henry Bibb proclaimed, "If there is no alternative but to go back to slavery, or die contending for liberty, then death is far preferable."[39] We shall, resolved blacks in Providence, "sacrifice our lives and our all upon the altar of protection to our wives, our children, and our fellow sufferers in common with us."[40] Admittedly not all the responses were so extreme, but their common temper was clear. They shared the determination of the Allegheny County Free Colored People, who, in petitioning Congress, emphatically opposed "all and every Act, Bill, or Provision now in existence or that may hereafter be introduced into either House of Congress of the United States, in any way or manner infringing upon our liberties as American Citizens."[41]

---

next year, in a similar action, Adam Crosswaite of Michigan was rescued from the courtroom in Detroit while being tried as a fugitive and was "conveyed . . . across the Detroit river into Canada." *Liberator,* November 6, 1846, and September 24, 1847. *North Star,* December 15, 1848.

37. Larry Gara, in *Liberty Line,* 109-111, identifies no particular pattern to black resistance, treating it as isolated instances. Stanley W. Campbell, examining the Shadrach case, in *The Slave Catchers: Enforcement of the Fugitive Slave Law, 1850-1860* (Chapel Hill: University of North Carolina Press, 1968, 1970), 151, suggests but does not explore the idea of a pattern.

38. *North Star,* April 5, 1850.

39. *Liberator,* April 12, 1850.

40. Quoted in Bartlett, *Slave to Citizen,* 45.

41. "Petition of Free Colored People of Allegheny Co. Penna. remonstrating against the law of 1793 relative to the recapture of fugitive

Petitions, remonstrances, and dire threats failed to block its passage, and in September the new fugitive slave bill became law. When New York blacks asked, in public protest, "Shall we resist Oppression? Shall we defend our Liberties? Shall we be FREEMEN or SLAVE?" they meant not whether, but how. Threatening to use force for their own safety, they also openly encouraged slaves to defend themselves "with the surest and most deadly weapons" including "bowie knives and revolvers."[42] Nor was it each man for himself for as meeting followed meeting the resolve of one old New Yorker "to strike dead the first man who dares to lay his hand upon a brother to throw him into bondage" became the commitment of many.[43] Bostonians, though their language was not so colorful, announced the same message.[44] In Buffalo, Negroes resolved to resist by all means available "every attempt to enforce any act by which an American citizen is liable to be deprived of life or liberty without due process of law, without a trial by a jury of his peers, or without the privilege of the writ of habeas corpus."[45] In Portland, Maine, they proposed a vigilance committee "to give notice of the approach of danger; to see that every person is provided with the means of defence, and that places of security are selected."[46] In Syracuse, Jarmain Loguen predicted that blacks would "have their liberties or die in their defence,"[47] and in Pittsburgh Martin Delany breathed contempt at any officer who might try to search his house for fugitives. "If he crosses the threshold of my door, and I do not lay him a lifeless corpse at my feet," Delany vowed, "I hope the grave may refuse my body a resting-place, and the righteous Heaven my spirit a home."[48]

slaves . . . [1850]" United States Senate. Petitions and Memorials on Slavery, 1820-1863. Record Group 46. National Archives.

42. *National Anti-Slavery Standard,* October 10, 1850.

43. *Ibid.,* October 10, 1850.

44. *Impartial Citizen,* October 12, 1850.

45. *Ibid.,* October 12, 1850.

46. *Liberator,* November 1, 1850.

47. Jarmain W. Loguen, *The Rev. J. W. Loguen, as a Slave and as a Freeman. A Narrative of Real Life* (Syracuse: J. G. K. Truair & Co., 1859), 391

48. Quoted in Frank A. Rollin, *Life and Public Services of Martin R. Delany* . . . (Boston: Lee and Shepard, 1868. Reprint, New York: Arno Press, 1969), 76.

On many occasions force was unnecessary and both fugitives and freemen were then willing to use legal process or nonviolent illegal means. In 1851 in Chicago, for example, an alleged slave was freed on convincing evidence that his identity had been mistaken.[49] Two years later the pressure of Boston opinion forced some Southern visitors to surrender to the court a slave they had brought with them, though ironically the woman chose to remain a slave in the household of her masters and the case was dismissed.[50] Vigilance committees were either formed or revived as a result of the new crisis. From Maine to Massachusetts to Maryland and on west to Michigan, they assisted fugitives traveling on the underground railroad. Though many of them were still exclusively black, some had a minority or majority of white members and at least one Boston group was probably exclusively white. But whatever the race, these committees acted on black precedents set in the preceding decades. Moreover by the mid-1850s, their defiance of law and government became so blatant that previously clandestine operations were openly publicized and brazenly flaunted.[51]

This new spirit was generated and sustained by a series of attempted and actual rescues which most spectacularly represented the will to resist. Widely reported in the press, capturing the imagination of antislavery enthusiasts, and reducing proslavery men to fury, they constituted a distinct challenge to federal law and the government which enforced it. The first of them occurred in Boston. There Shadrach was a waiter at the Cornhill Coffee House, hard by the *Liberator* office. In February 1851, John Caphart, agent for slaveowner John Debree of Norfolk, appeared to claim Shadrach as a fugitive from his native Virginia. Commissioner George Curtis issued a warrant for his arrest, and Deputy Marshal

49. Chicago *Journal*, June 13, [1851], reprinted in *Liberator*, July 11, 1851.

50. *Frederick Douglass' Paper*, October 28, 1853. James Pennington's experience was less satisfactory. He trusted his brother and nephews to legal process, only to have them whisked off before the counsel he had obtained for them could assist. See *Liberator*, June 2, 1854.

51. In upstate New York, for example, the Underground Railroad openly advertised for funds in the Syracuse press, listing both black and white officers and conductors.

Patrick Riley and his men were ordered to serve the warrant. On the 17th they staked out the coffee house and, in short order, took Shadrach prisoner.

By the time Shadrach faced Commissioner Curtis, who under the law had sole authority to dispose of his case, five lawyers, including the black Robert Morris, were in court to defend the prisoner. After the claimants presented their evidence, the defense lawyers won a postponement until the following day. In routine procedure, Marshal Riley then ordered the courtroom cleared and unwittingly opened the way for a rescue whose exact nature is still unclear.[52]

A large crowd of blacks had gathered outside the courtroom where the hearing was held. When the door was opened to clear the room, the crowd flowed in. There followed, at least as some reported, a scuffle with the marshal's men, though others testified that the event was characterized by singing and general good cheer. In either case, one eyewitness wrote, they came in like a cloud which "darkened the whole room," enveloped Shadrach, and swept him out the opposite door, whence he disappeared.[53] The public next heard from him in a letter he wrote from Montreal, signed Frederick Wilkins, saying that he had reached exile safely.[54]

An almost completely nonviolent rescue, the freeing of Wilkins generated a series of repercussions. First of all, those associated with his disappearance were arrested, including lawyer Morris, white abolitionist Elizur Wright, Lewis Hayden, who had come to Boston to escape the consequences of a rescue attempt in Michigan, and white lawyer Charles Davis. Subsequent testimony revealed wide variations on what had happened, but some things are clear. There is no question but that Marshal Riley had anticipated trouble. He had staked out the coffee house carefully,

52. *Liberator*, February 21, 1851.
53. *North Star*, April 10, 1851. The quotation is in John Daniels, *In Freedom's Birthplace. A Study of Boston Negroes* (New York: Johnson Reprint, 1968), 62. See also the account of Thomas W. Higginson in *Cheerful Yesterdays* (Boston: Houghton, Mifflin & Co., 1898), 135-136.
54. *North Star*, April 10, 1851. The name was incorrectly printed by the paper as Frederick Minkins.

made his arrest quickly, and immediately thereafter requested permission to hold Shadrach in custody at the navy yard (a request which the commandant refused). He was also prompt in arresting well-known antislavery activists who might be linked with the escape. It seems clear that he was intent on making an early show of law and order on behalf of the detested statute. Finally, whether as the result of conflicting testimony or of popular opposition to the law, no jury would convict those who were brought to trial. Of the two blacks, who were probably most responsible for the rescue, Hayden was released when his jury was hung on "some division as to the facts in evidence," and Morris was freed by a vote of eleven-to-one in his favor. Only Elizur Wright, involved in the Shadrach case primarily as a journalist but well-known as an abolitionist and Liberty party man, came dangerously close to conviction. The jury in one of his several trials voted eleven-to-one to find him guilty. Yet even he escaped.[55]

The excitement and impact of the Shadrach affair did not, however, lie in court proceedings or hung juries, but rather in the example it set of successfully putting the new fugitive slave law to naught. In so doing, it forced those who supported it and the entire Compromise of 1850 as the best way to preserve national harmony to demand its rigorous enforcement. With rigid determination increasing on both sides, the disputants risked polarizing the nation. Daniel Webster, speaking for the forces of law, order, and national tranquility, verbalized the Fillmore administration's total dedication to enforcing the law. "The act of taking away Shadrach from the public authorities in Boston, and sending him off," the Secretary of State told an Albany audience in 1851, "was an act of clear treason." Opposition to the law could be tolerated only if it remained orderly and within the legal process. Resort either to "force of arms or force of numbers" threatened the nation. The Shadrach case, from this point of view, was a clear and deliberate subversion of the United States government.[56]

55. *Liberator,* June 13 and, for the quotation, June 20, 1851; also November 21, 1851 and June 18, 1852.

56. *Boston Slave Riot, and Trial of Anthony Burns* . . . (Boston: Fetridge and Company, 1854), 38.

For abolitionists of both races, the pattern of the Shadrach drama established the positive value of a clear-cut and deliberate confrontation with the government over the fugitive slave law. As a result of it, white antislavery people whose aid to escapees from slavery had previously been confined almost exclusively to legal assistance and the occasional provision of shelter and transportation, now both planned and executed overtly defiant action. Just two months later, the Sims case illustrated this new situation. In April 1851, again in Boston, a police officer aided by a *"large posse of Watchmen,"* arrested Thomas Sims, a twenty-three-year-old fugitive from Georgia.[57] Once again a battery of distinguished legal aid entered the case on his behalf. Hearings were held and legal procedures set in motion. But at the same time, Thomas Higginson, a white Unitarian minister from Worcester, was plotting Sims' escape.

Tragic though the outcome was—for Sims was neither legally freed nor illegally rescued but rather returned to slavery—an element of opera bouffe surrounded the affair. The predominately white Boston vigilance committee could not agree on a plan of attack and so did nothing. Higginson, one of its members, developed various schemes, from forcing the resignation of the United States marshal in Boston to stirring up a meeting at Tremont Temple to mob the courthouse. Finally, when none of these succeeded, he concocted a plan for Sims to jump out of an upper story window onto a mattress, but meanwhile his keepers nailed the window shut.[58] Then, after judgment went against Sims, Wendell Phillips tried to bribe the captain of the vessel which was to carry Sims south, but even that failed to work.[59]

Significantly in the Sims case there was little black intervention. Doubtless there were some Negroes in the crowd which gathered around the courthouse and was once so thick that it blocked entry or exit. But there was no organized group effort—not from lack of

57. *Liberator,* April 11, 1851. Anna Mary Wells, *Dear Preceptor: The Life and Times of Thomas Wentworth Higginson* (Boston: Houghton, Mifflin, & Co., 1963), 74, gives Sims' age as seventeen.

58. Wells, *Dear Preceptor,* 74.

59. Deborah Weston to Anne Weston, April 15, 1851, W-BPL.

interest but because activists had left town in droves to avoid arrest after the Shadrach rescue.[60] Furthermore, government officials were determined there should be no more escapes and without question feared that Negroes would be the rescuers. How likely they were to be arrested is suggested by the case involving the sons of the late Reverend Samuel Snowden, who were arrested for walking back and forth in front of the courthouse during Sims' detention. They were black and, as it turned out, at least one of them was armed. But, as their lawyer argued, they lived in Cambridgeport, had often to cross the bridges late at night, and therefore carried arms for self-defense as did others in their position. Although Judge Cushing fined Isaac Snowden only $1, he placed his brother Charles under $600 bond for being *"armed offensively, to the terror of the people."* The size of the bail suggested government overreaction or judicial prejudice, for only recently one of Webster's sons had been released in an assault case on $200 bond.[61] The action seemed to justify the retreat which Lewis Hayden, still under indictment for his role in the Shadrach case, described in explaining to Higginson that black organization in the city was deplorably weak. "Practically there are no colored men in Boston," he pointed out; "the Shadrach prosecutions have scattered them all." Whatever must be done to rescue Sims had, therefore, to "be done without them."[62]

The situation was very different when Jerry McHenry was seized as a fugitive in Syracuse, New York, on October 1. On that day, the town was jammed with people attending a state Liberty party convention and the fall agricultural fair. Indeed the choice of time and place—for Syracuse was in the heartland of New York antislavery strength—suggested either ineptitude or a deliberate intent to enforce the law in the face of opposition. Furthermore McHenry had lived in Syracuse for some time and was widely known to be a fugitive. In any case, he was arrested in broad daylight and taken to the combination courthouse and jail, where a

60. Higginson, *Cheerful Yesterdays,* 140.
61. *Liberator,* April 11, 1851.
62. Quoted in Higginson, *Cheerful Yesterdays,* 140.

hearing was held in the early afternoon. When it adjourned, a group of Negroes suddenly "seized the alleged fugitive, rescued him from the custody of the officers, and rushed down Water and Genesee streets, through Market Square, and down Water street to Lock street, [and] over the Lock street bridge." There the police overtook them and recaptured McHenry.[63]

After this turn of events, the local Unitarian minister, Samuel J. May, joined Gerrit Smith, in town for the Liberty party convention, in contriving a new rescue. During the evening, a large crowd gathered around the jail and threw stones at its windows. Then about 9 p.m., ignored by the local and probably sympathetic militia, they stormed the building, and scattered the police, pushing one officer out of the window and breaking his arm. But most importantly, they rescued McHenry and carried him to Bratnall's Hotel where he was put in a carriage and sent to Canada.

Angered both by McHenry's escape and the victory over law enforcement which it represented, government officials cast a dragnet to ensnare the rescuers. Of the twenty-six finally indicted, twelve were blacks; but of those twelve, nine escaped to Canada before trial. Among those who fled were Samuel Ward, who lacked free papers, and Jarmain Loguen, well-known as a fugitive. Of the four who were finally tried, one was acquitted and two were dismissed because of a hung jury. In the end a single person was convicted: Enoch Reed, the only black man who came to trial.[64]

Similar in many ways to previous incidents, the Jerry Rescue's repercussions were somewhat unusual. The three whites who were brought to trial were charged under the 1850 Fugitive Slave Act, but Enoch Reed was tried under the 1793 statute. There was no official explanation for this arrangement, but Frederick Douglass

63. *Liberator,* October 10, 1851.
64. The Jerry Rescue and its sequel can be followed in a variety of accounts: *Ibid.,* October 10, 1851; Loguen, *A Narrative,* 417, 420, 426, 442; Samuel Ringgold Ward, *Autobiography of a Fugitive Negro* (London: J. Snow, 1855), 117-128; *Frederick Douglass' Paper,* April 8, 1852, February 4, and March 4, 1853; Samuel Joseph May, *Some Recollections of Our Antislavery Conflict* (Boston: Fields, Osgood, & Co., 1869), 373-384. Campbell, *Slave Catchers,* 156.

surmised it was because conviction under the old statute would be easier and surer since its constitutionality had long since been upheld by the Supreme Court. In choosing to indict Reed under the old law, therefore, the government implied that it was more important for it to win its case against a black.[65] It also chose to indict relatively obscure men rather than the well-known abolitionists May and Smith, who were eager to admit guilt and challenge the law on constitutional grounds. Clearly the enforcement of the new law had rapidly become of great political importance, testing, as it did, the government's power and will to carry out this most unpopular part of the 1850 compromise. It was commonly believed that Daniel Webster himself drafted the Syracuse indictments in an effort to achieve a clear-cut government victory in upholding the law and punishing transgressors. Indeed, some thought that he had planned McHenry's arrest to coincide with the Liberty party meeting in Syracuse precisely to provoke an incident and demonstrate the law's strength. And some also believed that President Fillmore considered a government victory in the trials necessary if he were to seek reelection in 1852. Not surprisingly the opinion was widespread that the trials were purely political.[66]

Further impetus was given to the federal government's need to show its ability to enforce the law by the still more dramatic armed battle which alleged slaves and their supporters had waged in Christiana, Pennsylvania, in the previous month. The bloodshed there epitomized the militant resistance blacks were prepared to make to avoid a forced return to slavery. Negroes who lived in Lancaster County, which bordered on Maryland, had long offered refuge to runaway slaves and resistance to kidnappers.[67] Hence, when the Maryland slaveholder, Edward Gorsuch, arrived in the area with his son and nephew, they were accompanied by a United States deputy marshal and his assistants to help them seize four

65. *Frederick Douglass' Paper*, February 4, 1853.
66. *Ibid.*, January 29, 1852.
67. William Uhler Hensel, *The Christiana Riot and the Treason Trials of 1851: An Historical Sketch* (Lancaster, Pa.: New Era Publishing Co., 1911), 16-18. Roderick W. Nash, "William Parker and the Christiana Riot," *Journal of Negro History*, XLVI (January 1961), 26-27.

escaped slaves for whom they had warrants. But, forewarned by a message from William Still of the Philadelphia Vigilance Committee, William Parker, leader of the local activists, had hidden the fugitives in his house. When Gorsuch and the marshal arrived at dawn and tried to serve the warrants, they were driven out of the house by Parker, who first thrust a farm fork at them and then hurled an axe. Soon the slavecatchers, who had expressed their determination to fight it out, were surrounded by local blacks whom Mrs. Parker had summoned. Caught between Parker and his associates in the house and the new defenders arriving on all sides, all of whom were armed with farm implements or guns, the marshal fled as the firing started. The claimants remained and, before it was over, Edward Gorsuch was dead and his son, Dickinson, gravely wounded.[68]

The fate of the Christiana fugitives is unclear, except that they disappeared into freedom. William Parker and his brother-in-law, whose shooting from the house probably killed Gorsuch, fled to Canada, along with at least one other person. Most of those involved in the fracas stayed where they were, for it was much harder to escape to British territory from southern Pennsylvania than from northern New York. Of their number, thirty-one blacks and five whites were arrested. Of these, some were soon released and others were indicted on charges of treason, murder, and riot. Only one, Castner Hanway, a white man, was brought to court. Tried for treason, he was acquitted.[69]

The repercussions of the Christiana rescue did not end in southeastern Pennsylvania. Almost at once Chicago blacks met to raise money for the defense of those indicted.[70] In Columbus, Ohio, the "victorious heroes" of Christiana were cheered for their

68. *Frederick Douglass' Paper,* September 25, 1851. *Liberator,* September 19, 1851. Hensel, *Christiana Riot,* 23. Nash, "William Parker and Christiana Riot," 27-30. James J. Robbins, *Report of the Trial of Castner Hanway for Treason, in the Resistance of the Execution of the Fugitive Slave Law of September, 1850*...(Philadelphia: King and Baird, 1852), 58-59.

69. Hensel, *Christiana Riot,* 43-44, 83, 89, 98.

70. *Frederick Douglass' Paper,* January 8, 1852.

"manly" and "heroic" stand, and efforts were made to secure them counsel.[71] Elsewhere the treatment of those arrested was examined. A correspondent in Bibb's *Voice of the Fugitive* noticed discriminatory court procedures, with whites released on bail while blacks were held in jail.[72] Samuel Ward commented bitterly in the *Impartial Citizen* that had the Christiana defenders been 1848 European revolutionaries rather than black Americans fighting for their freedom "no wreath of glory" would have been "too bright, no words of panegyric too warm" for them.[73] And from Rochester, Frederick Douglass concluded that the 1850 law and the government's response to the Christiana affair had "virtually made every colored man in the land an outlaw," who could be "hunted by any villain" who so wished and then tried for treason if he dared "lift his arm in his own defense."[74]

After the rescue cases of 1851 and the failure to convict the resistants in the courts, there were no major clashes over the Fugitive Slave Law until 1854. Yet in this three-year interval, blacks continued to challenge the law and to rescue fugitives in such widely separated places as Wilkes-Barre, Detroit, Sandusky, Milwaukee, and Cincinnati.[75] The key to the relative inactivity of federal officials seemed to be, as New York's Whig boss, Thurlow Weed, perceived it, a recognition of diminishing returns. "The accused knew before, and now even the Government has begun to discover that its trials of the 'Rescuers' has done more to impair the efficiency of the Fugitive Slave Law, than would have been done, if a gang of fifty 'Jerries' had marched up State Street, in broad daylight, on their unmolested road to Canada."[76]

Yet three years later the Pierce administration moved to crush opposition to the law once and for all. No fugitive case during the

71. *Ibid.*, November 13, 1851.
72. *Voice of the Fugitive*, January 15, 1852.
73. Quoted in *Liberator*, October 3, 1851.
74. *Frederick Douglass' Paper*, September 25, 1851.
75. Campbell, *Slave Catchers*, 139. Detroit *Tribune*, n.d., in *Frederick Douglass' Paper*, June 24, 1852. Campbell, *Slave Catchers*, 137-138. *Liberator*, April 7, 1854. Wilbur Siebert, *The Underground Railroad From Slavery to Freedom* (orig. publ. 1898. Gloucester, Mass.: Peter Smith, 1968), 85.
76. *Frederick Douglass' Paper*, March 4, 1853.

antebellum period was more significant than that of Anthony Burns in late May and early June of 1854. Burns, then thirty years old, had recently escaped from Virginia and was working in Boston for Coffin Pitts, a clothing dealer. Walking quietly in Court Street on the evening of May 24, he was arrested by officers from the office of the United States marshal on a warrant issued by Fugitive Slave Law Commissioner Edward G. Loring. Lodged overnight in an upper room of the federal courthouse, Burns was brought to his hearing before the commissioner the next morning. By then, the word of his arrest had spread, and three well-known Boston lawyers, including Robert Morris, were on hand to defend the fugitive.[77]

At the request of counsel, Burns' hearing was postponed until Saturday, May 27. On May 26, taking advantage of this delay, Boston abolitionists both staged a mass protest meeting in Faneuil Hall and, less publicly, devised a plan for freeing the prisoner. The latter drew upon Lewis Hayden's success in the Shadrach case and Thomas Higginson's failure in the Sims case, and the rescue was to be led by both men. They planned an armed assault on the courthouse timed to coincide with a rush of support from those attending the nearby Faneuil Hall meeting.[78] Unfortunately the speakers at Faneuil Hall were not informed of the rescue plan and so foiled the efforts of participants to move it to the courthouse square. Consequently the group which forced the courthouse door was inadequately reinforced, and after they had battled for awhile inside and killed one of the defenders, they were repulsed. There was to be no second chance for a rescue. By the following morning, the Independent Corps of Cadets, Company B of the Boston Light Dragoons, and the Boston Light Infantry had all been called up to keep the peace around the courthouse. Soon they were supplemented with other militia units—the New England Guards, the Light Guard, the Sergeants Guards of Light Dragoons, and the Lancers.

77. *Boston Slave Riot*, 5-7.
78. Higginson, *Cheerful Yesterdays*, 151.

Despite muddle and militia, Massachusetts blacks were not prepared to give up one of their number to the fugitive slave law. Although four Negroes had been arrested in the biracial attack on the courthouse and charged with riotous conduct and disturbing the peace, hundreds of Negroes from Boston, Worcester, and New Bedford, cowed neither by the arrests nor the troops, flocked the next morning to the courthouse. There, from the main steps, the mayor of Boston addressed them, warning them that the law would be enforced. When William Johnson made some "disrespectful and insulting remark" in response, he too was arrested.

Throughout that long Saturday, tension remained high. The rescue had failed on Friday. On Saturday an attempt to buy Burns' freedom, organized by Leonard Grimes, pastor of the Twelfth Baptist Church, failed when the owner changed his mind and withdrew his sale offer. The following week, the hearings, adjourned from Saturday, dragged on until Friday, when Commissioner Loring finally ordered Burns returned to Virginia. Persistently blacks sought a way to save him. A group of them followed the federal district attorney until the police arrested one of their number. Black waiters refused to serve the soldiers who tried to eat in area restaurants. Lewis Hayden entered a countersuit against the Virginia slaveholder for $10,000 damages on Burns' behalf. Throughout it all, in a quiet show of strength, several hundred Negroes kept a courthouse vigil which lasted until Burns was sent South.[79] "Through that long week of agony," a Lynn observer wrote Garrison, "the vicinity of the slave pen was thronged by colored men and women, watching from dawn till eve, and some of them the long night through, patiently awaiting . . . the fate of their poor brother in bonds; seeking in every way in their power to show their sympathy for him, and hoping and praying, to the last moment, for his deliverance from the hand of the kidnapper."[80]

79. *Boston Slave Riot, passim,* quotation on 13. For Grimes' role see Charles Emory Stevens, *Anthony Burns, a History* (Boston: John P. Jewett & Co., 1856. Reprint, New York: Negro Universities Press, 1969), 62-68, 71, 202-203.

80. *Liberator,* July 7, 1854.

The government, however, had its way. On June 2, Anthony Burns, accompanied by the United States marshal and his aides, left the courthouse. Preceding him was "a detachment of the National Lancers on the right and left of the street; a corps of United States Artillery, followed by a corps of United States Marines." He was followed by a second "corps of United States Marines; the field piece, drawn by a span of horses and manned by a detachment of six of the members of the Fourth Regiment United States artillery; [and finally another] corps of United States Marines." The streets were cleared and protected by members of Massachusetts militia units. Except for the throwing of a single bottle allegedly filled with vitriol, there was little demonstration or physical impediment as Burns marched through Boston to the waterfront, where a revenue cutter waited to take him South.[81] Boston abolitionists, both black and white, could only share the recaptured slave's bitterness and despair in helpless silence.

Their frustration was not alleviated when, a year later, Burns' freedom was purchased through the efforts Grimes had begun shortly after his arrest, for the fugitive slave law remained on the books and in force. Sporadic resistance to it continued therefore until the Civil War. In Philadelphia in 1855 Jane Johnson and her two children escaped their owner, a minor United States diplomat. As a result William Still and three other Negroes were tried and acquitted on riot charges;[82] but the white Quaker, Passmore Williamson, who was also involved, was imprisoned for provoking their escape. In Ohio, Delaware, and New York other blacks clashed with the law as they tried to aid fugitives.[83] But of the many cases in the late 1850s, only the Oberlin-Wellington rescue was of major consequence. There, in the heart of the Western

81. *Boston Slave Riot*, 85.
82. *Liberator*, August 10, 1855. *Provincial Freeman*, August 22, 1855. *Liberator*, September 7, 1855.
83. See, for example, Campbell, *Slave Catchers*, 134-135, 161-162. *Douglass Monthly*, October, 1859. *Liberator*, May 4, 1860. *Weekly Anglo-African*, May 26, 1860.

Reserve, a band of thirty or forty blacks, many of them armed, joined a group of several hundred whites to rescue John Price. As one result, Charles Langston was tried and found guilty, primarily of having refused to try to stop the rescue.[84] In his statement to the court, whose all-white proceedings he denounced, Langston reiterated his determination to defy the fugitive slave law. "No matter what the laws might be," he told judge, jury, spectators, and indirectly the United States government, "you would honor yourself for [assisting a fugitive], while your friends and your children to all generations would honor you for doing it, and every good and honest man would say you had done *right!*"[85] The many public meetings which Negroes held in Langston's support served not only to praise the man but to endorse his condemnation of the "Fugitive Slave Law, and the action of the Federal Courts."[86]

In no known rescue case was a fugitive seized from law officers without black assistance, and even after 1850 there were few or no whites involved in numerous rescues. But numbers, after 1850, were less important than their implications. Head-on confrontation with law and government was the theme of the decade's most radical abolitionists. More than that, the association of black pragmatists and white radicals defying the widely despised 1850 law heightened Northern resentment as it fed Southern fears, thus further exacerbating sectional antagonism.

More specific to black abolitionism, the conspiracy of both fugitives and freemen to thwart the law and confront its enforcers proved an effective device. If, as did happen, a few apostates sold out their fellows to the slavecatchers, they were severely punished by the community.[87] Overwhelmingly blacks acted together to

---

84. *Liberator*, June 3, 1859. Jacob R. Shipherd, Comp. *History of the Oberlin-Wellington Rescue* (orig. publ. New York: Negro Universities Press, 1969), 26-27, 31, 100, 102, 106-107, 116.

85. Langston, *Should Colored Men be Subject to the . . .Fugitive Slave Law*, 16.

86. *Douglass Monthly*, June, 1859. See also *Liberator*, June 10, 1859, for a Boston meeting praising Langston's speech to the court.

87. Examples occur in Campbell, *Slave Catchers*, 135, and *Liberator*, September 17, 1858 and April 26, 1861.

shield others and to defend themselves from the law. None of them would trust to courts which excluded them from the jury box and limited their access to the witness box. Nor could they trust a legal system which, when their liberty was at stake, denied them trial by jury and favored the claimant over the defendant. Proudly and openly they put the law to naught.

In so doing, they accomplished much. As hunted fugitives making rightful resistance, they increased white antipathy to slavery. As freemen fighting for the natural rights of life and liberty, they bound themselves together to fight their exclusion from a society and government pledged to protect those rights for others. And as political beings, although they were largely unconscious of this function, they weakened the union which had long permitted their enslavement by helping to destroy the consensus on which it rested. Their successes as well as their frustrations drove them increasingly, in the final decade before the Civil War, to a rhetoric and militance which went well beyond defiance of a single statute.

11. THE USES OF VIOLENCE—THE RHETORIC OF THE 1850s

THAT RESISTANCE to the fugitive slave law was frequently violent is but one indication of the degree to which many black abolitionists were willing to rely on force. As in other areas, here, too, their experience differed from that of their white counterparts, who seldom made a positive virtue of violence and who, if Garrisonians, were frequently committed to a pacifism so complete that they absolutely rejected using force under any circumstances. For blacks, however, the endemic civil disorder of the Jacksonian period at least partly shaped their responses. Not only slavery but urban riots had taught them that civil authority seldom shielded them from violence. Consequently they both preached and practiced the use of force in self-defense. Admittedly also, at least in the 1830s, abolitionists of whatever color were particular targets for incensed rioters. Thus Negroes, whether activists or not, often bore the double brunt of antiabolitionism and racism. Constantly threatened and frequently attacked, they turned to counterforce to protect themselves and their property.[1]

The Cincinnati riots of 1829 offer a case in point. There, white laborers, fearful of economic competition from a growing black population, tried to drive their rivals from the city. After several nights of being personally assaulted and seeing their homes demolished, Negroes fought back. When some were arrested for

1. Leonard L. Richards, *"Gentlemen of Property and Standing." Anti-Abolition Mobs in Jacksonian America* (New York: Oxford University Press, 1970), passim. David Grimsted, "Rioting in its Jacksonian Setting," *American Historical Review,* LXXVII (April 1972), 361-397.

firing into an attacking mob, the mayor ordered their release on the grounds that they were acting legitimately in self-defense. In another instance, to protect their community, Hartford blacks in 1831 attacked a white gang that had been molesting Negro women. The following year, in a situation resembling that in Cincinnati, Philadelphia blacks fought off white mobs with clubs and stones.[2] So the pattern of forceful protection of themselves and their community continued as blacks responded to direct assault with counterviolence.

Those who ventured into antislavery work multiplied the likelihood that they and their friends would be subject to mob attack. Conversely, it sometimes happened that mob violence first led Negroes to abolition. In either case, riot and violence intensified their determination to resist by physical force as well as by nonviolent protest. Thus Samuel Ward, already introduced to antislavery theory by Simeon S. Jocelyn, was wholly won to the cause when a mob attacked a meeting of blacks that he was attending in New York's Chatham Street Chapel in July 1834. First beaten and then arrested, Ward was galvanized by the experience into antislavery action rather than bitter withdrawal.

Yet the repercussions of riots presented a variety of problems. They tried the grit of older men and made them hesitant. Long a black spokesman, James Forten was troubled by the constant succession of riots in Philadelphia in the early 1830s and attributed them not only to reaction against abolitionist activity and local Negroes but to fears aroused by emancipation in the British West Indies. Still, he continued to believe that Britain had provided an example which the United States must follow.[3] Another older leader who responded to riots with sheer grit and determination rather than with the excitement of the young Ward was Samuel Cornish. Writing in his *Colored American,* he attributed mob action to deep

2. Lebanon, Ohio, *Western Star,* August 29, 1829. *Liberator,* June 4, 1831. Edward R. Turner, *Negro in Pennsylvania, 1639-1861* (Washington: American Historical Association, 1912), 160.
3. Samuel Ringgold Ward, *Autobiography of a Fugitive Negro . . .* (London: J. Snow, 1855), 45-49; *Liberator,* July, 1834, *passim.* James Forten to James McCune Smith, September 8, 1835, C-BPL.

and underlying racism. But rather than giving in to it, Cornish called upon white "men of property and standing" in the community to rise against such outrages. "No man is safe," he warned them, "neither secure in life nor property, in a country subjected to such heathen outbreakings." At the same time, he advised cohesive race support for abolition. The alternative was to become "a ruined people."[4]

While Forten and Cornish viewed violence as an unwelcome condition in which they were trapped, younger activists, especially in the 1840s and 1850s, were much readier to advocate overt force when quiet persuasion failed. This was especially true among those who had been slaves. Though he did not wish "for scenes of blood and carnage," William Wells Brown told a Lynn, Massachusetts, audience in 1848, "if a favorable opening should occur to the slave population of this country, he could hardly subdue himself to counsel non-resistance, or to act upon its principles himself."[5] Douglass told a Syracuse audience in 1854 that he "took ground against the doctrine of non-resistance." "He dropped the idea," his own newspaper reported him saying, "on seeing a dear friend assaulted and beaten in a cruel and inhuman manner."[6] And Jarmain Loguen announced to Garrison in 1854 his willingness to use force by explaining that he was a fugitive slave. "And you know," he taunted the editor, "that we have strange notions about many things."[7] So much for the *Liberator's* advice to emulate the noble and long-suffering Uncle Tom.

---

4. *Colored American,* June 2, 1838. The implicit fear in Cornish's plea was made more explicit in a resolution of the Cincinnati Union Society in 1836 against abolitionist activity which "injure[d] the interests of the coloured population of the free States by exciting the suspicion of white inhabitants; and we believe to rivet more firmly the chains of the slave." *African Repository,* XII (October 1836), 322.

5. William E. Farrison, *William Wells Brown: Author and Reformer* (Chicago: University of Chicago Press, 1969), 124.

6. *Frederick Douglass' Paper,* October 13, 1854.

7. *Liberator,* May 5, 1854. William Whipper, on the other hand, was one of the few blacks who followed the Garrisonian position. In an 1837 speech, for example, he opposed any kind of physical resistance, especially by blacks. See Carter G. Woodson, *Negro Orators and their Orations* (Washington: Associated Publishers, 1925), 104-118.

As Northern blacks were increasingly convinced that safety lay in strength, they more and more gave countenance, praise, and direct encouragement to slave revolt. Unlike white abolitionists who almost universally until the 1850s echoed Lydia Maria Child's assessment of emancipation in the British West Indies as "the right way, the safe way," Negroes cheered Nat Turner's revolt. At first their enthusiasm was heavily veiled. When word of the 1831 Virginia uprising reached Boston, city blacks proclaimed a day of "humiliation and prayer" and begged God for "the prolonged life of all strenuous advocates for the cause of the bleeding sons of Africa."[8] If their wording was ambiguous, James Forten's was less so. From Philadelphia he wrote Garrison that Turner's revolt should catalyze greater action among abolitionists for it made the alternatives clear. Eager to avoid violence, he played up the threat of revolt. It was evidence of "the evils of slavery," not the least of which was an "urgent sense of danger," which should now lead "to something more than mere hopes and wishes."[9]

Black abolitionists responded far more openly to the European revolutions of 1848, for in them they saw models for their own future. "The world is in commotion," the Cleveland national convention of 1848 apostrophized. Serfs were throwing off their yokes with "manly bearing" and "bondsmen—yea, *slaves*" in the Antilles had, "in the majesty of manhood," thrown off and crushed the remnants of that "most foul, man-debasing and heaven-daring scourge and curse of the human family."[10] The same year delegates to a Pennsylvania state convention in Harrisburg lauded Europe's progress against tyranny.[11]

Speaking in Boston's Faneuil Hall, Frederick Douglass pronounced the new rhetoric of militance. "There are many Madison Washingtons and Nathaniel Turners in the South," he chastised his largely white audience, "who would assert their rights to liberty, if

8. *Liberator,* September 17, 1831.
9. James Forten to William L. Garrison, October 20, 1831, G-BPL.
10. *North Star,* August 11, 1848.
11. Coloured Citizens of Pennsylvania, *Minutes of the State Convention . . . Harrisburg . . . 1848,* 10-11.

you would take your feet from their necks, and your sympathy and aid from their oppressors." American slaves' failure to revolt came not from cowardice but from their numerical inferiority. Comparatively so few blacks among so many whites, they were like a man fighting with his hands tied and deserved no rebuke for fighting poorly.[12] William Wells Brown in 1848 publicly compared Nat Turner to Moses and later predicted that a modern Hannibal would sometime arise in the person of a more successful Turner.[13] When, in 1859, Robert Morris praised the "noble and heroic" Nat Turner and Denmark Vesey for "conceiving the sublime idea of freedom for themselves and their race,"[14] he was dealing in the commonplace.

Nor was revolutionary enthusiasm confined to praise, for from it flowed open encouragement for slave revolt. Even before Turner, David Walker's 1830 *Appeal* had made the invitation explicit. The time, however, was not propitious for so vigorous a statement, and general response to the Turner revolt drove the *Appeal* underground. Yet its message was not lost. Even so conservative a journal as the *Colored American* saw in the annexation of Texas an opening through which to end slavery by insurrection. Cornish argued that were Texas admitted to the union, the union would dissolve. As a result, an isolated South would quickly descend into "barbarous licent[i]ousness, and mental and physical imbecility," offering slaves a golden opportunity to join with oppressed "honest white laborer[s]" to avenge themselves in "anarchy, bloodshed and rapine."[15]

Closer to Walker's *Appeal* in its direct exhortation to revolt was Garnet's "Address to the Slaves," presented to the 1843 conven-

12. *Liberator*, June 9, 1848. Madison Washington was the leader of the *Creole* mutiny in 1841.

13. William Wells Brown, *Narrative of . . . a Fugitive Slave* (Boston: The Anti-Slavery Office, 1847), Appendix, 55.

14. William Wells Brown, *The Black Man . . .* (Boston: Robert F. Wallcut, 1865), 229. Brown at the time of the Civil War saw the conflict as one which would produce another, more successful, Nat Turner. *Ibid.*, 74, 105; Farrison, *Brown*, 339.

15. *Colored American*, September 2, 1837.

tion in Buffalo. At its climax it called for insurrection. "Brethren, arise, arise! Strike for your lives and liberties. Now is the day and the hour. Let every slave throughout the land do this, and the days of slavery are numbered. You cannot be more oppressed than you have been—you cannot suffer greater cruelties than you have already. *Rather die freemen than live to be slaves.* Remember that you are FOUR MILLIONS."[16]

The address reflected the man, for Garnet's own experience was one which taught resistance. When he was only fourteen, slave-catchers descended on his family, who had escaped to New York City. Father, mother, and sister only narrowly avoided being returned to slavery. Consumed with fear and fury, Henry bought a knife and threatened to pursue the slavecatchers. By the next year, he had organized a group of young New Yorkers pledged to go South when they had finished school and start an insurrection designed to free all slaves. Garnet's experience at the Noyes Academy in New Hampshire demonstrated that this was not all adolescent fantasy. There, he defended himself and his fellow black students against an antiabolitionist mob by firing a double-barrelled shotgun at a particularly menacing attacker.[17]

Dramatic as Garnet's experience was, he was not the only one at the 1843 national convention to advocate violence. The president of the meeting, Buffalo's Samuel Davis, had set a similarly militant tone in his introductory address. Comparing black action to the Greek and Polish revolts of a few years earlier, he encouraged his auditors to unite and attack their oppressors with their own weapons. "If we are not willing to rise up and assert our rightful

16. Henry Highland Garnet, "An Address to the Slaves of the United States of America," in *A Memorial Discourse . . . Delivered in the Hall of the House of Representatives, Washington City, D.C. on Sabbath, February 12, 1865. With an Introduction by James McCune Smith* (Philadelphia: Joseph M. Wilson, 1865), 51.

17. James McCune Smith's introduction to Garnet, *Memorial Discourse,* 25-26. Alexander Crummell, "Eulogium on Henry Highland Garnet, D.D. Before the Union Literary and Historical Association; Washington, D.C., May 4, 1882," in *Africa and America* (Springfield, Mass.: Willey and Co., 1891), 300 and 280.

claims, and plead our own cause," he admonished, "we have no reason to look for success."[18]

Neither Davis nor Garnet, however, could carry the convention. The delegates spent more time on Garnet's address than on any other issue. They returned to it on several occasions. Its author made an impassioned defense of several hours, exploring the evils of slavery and the actions of Vesey, Turner, and other rebels. But when the decision on printing the address was made, it failed— almost by chance, for it came within a single vote of passage.[19] Four years later, delegates to the national convention at Troy did vote to print it. Although it had apparently been somewhat toned down by the addition of a statement about the inexpediency of "revolution with the sword," it still contained a direct plea for resistance. "No oppressed people," the revised text read, "have ever secured their liberty without resistance. What kind of resistance you had better make, you must decide by the circumstances that surround you, and according to the suggestion of expediency."[20] The message was clear and well received. Two years later, the Colored Citizens of Ohio voted to print and distribute five hundred copies of Walker's *Appeal* and Garnet's "Address," which were American Negroes' two clearest insurrectionary documents to that time.[21]

The rebellious mood was further enhanced in 1850 by the new Fugitive Slave Act. Among all abolitionists the rhetoric of nonresistance and hopes for peaceful change were subverted by pressing frustrations from declining membership in antislavery societies, free soil defeats in Congress, and the seeming futility of twenty years of antislavery effort. Although the most immediate and effective resistance to this law manifested itself in widely-

18. National Convention of Colored Citizens, *Minutes of . . .1843*, 7.
19. *Ibid.*, 13-19.
20. Garnet, "An Address to the Slaves of the United States of America," in William Loren Katz's edition of Walker's *Appeal* and Garnet's *Address* (Reprinted, New York: Arno Press, 1969), 96.
21. State Convention of the Colored Citizens of Ohio, *Minutes and Address of the . . .*, *Convened at Columbus, January 10th, 11th, 12th, & 13th, 1849* (Oberlin: From J. M. Fitch's Power Press, 1849), 18.

publicized attempted rescues, it also generated further incitement
to slave revolt. A Cazenovia, New York, biracial convention called
to protest the law not only anticipated insurrection but positively
encouraged slaves to rise. When the revolt came, the convention
declared, "the great mass of colored men of the North . . . [would]
be found by your side, with deep-stored and long accumulated
revenge in their hearts, and with death-dealing weapons in their
hands."[22] The next year, Charles Langston told an Ohio state
convention meeting in Columbus that he would not hesitate to
"call on every slave, from Maryland to Texas, to arise and assert
their *liberties,* and cut their masters' throats."[23] Thus did steps
taken to forestall threats to slavery by escape provoke among
abolitionists not only a commitment to make escape more safe but
to make slaveholding considerably less so. And as the condition of
freemen became ever more precarious, more of them extended
approval to past revolts and encouragement to future ones.

With roots in the events of the 1840s and early 1850s, the rhetoric
of revolt reached its peak with the Dred Scott decision of 1857.
For all abolitionists and free soilers, as well as for the Republican
party, the decision was a severe blow, for it seemingly cut off the
last legal possibility of halting further expansion of slavery. But the
blow to ostensibly free blacks was yet more severe, for the
Supreme Court's ruling reduced all American Negroes to a
rightlessness and impotence little different from that of slavery.
The felt perception of that rightlessness had long been central to
their experience. Response to the 1850 Fugitive Slave Bill
embraced an awareness that the distinction between slavery and
freedom was fast fading. Samuel Ward had charged that its passage
forced all blacks to fall "back upon the natural and inalienable
rights of self-defence-self-protection" because in stripping them of
the rights of habeas corpus and trial by jury, it left them only the

22. *Antislavery Bugle,* September 28, 1850, quoted in Herbert Aptheker,
A Documentary History of the Negro People in the United States (2 vols.
New York: Citadel Press, 1951, 1969), 1:301-302.
23. State Convention of the Colored Citizens of Ohio, *Minutes
of . . .1851,* 10-11.

chance of "dying freemen, or living slaves." In depriving blacks of two basic constitutional rights, it effectively divested them of all.[24] Delany agreed. If "the citizens of one State, are entitled to all the rights and privileges of an American citizen in all the States . . . ," then to deny anyone a right or privilege of American citizenship was to take citizenship from him altogether and leave him totally outside the pale of organized government.[25]

Although Ward and Delany anticipated the substance of Chief Justice Roger Taney's decision that black men had no rights which white men were bound to respect, the formal court action made of it a watershed. Not only did it publicly declare the utter rightlessness of all blacks, slave or free, it also closed to them all legal alternatives and thrust their quest for civil rights outside present or future legality. If the American Constitution denied them rights, a meeting of Philadelphia blacks concluded, it would be "at once the height of folly and the depth of pusillanimity" for them to support the government it established.[26] Yet, as Charles Langston recognized, simply withdrawing support was the weak response of a powerless group. "Ours is the poor privilege," he observed bitterly, "to protest, to remonstrate, to beg, to weep; here ends our power. . . ."[27]

There were, of course, those who desperately strove to regain some legal protection. In Massachusetts various groups petitioned the state legislature to make the issue one of states' rights and to guarantee them, as citizens of the commonwealth, the rights enshrined in the federal Constitution.[28] Taking another tack in the pages of the *Anglo-African Magazine,* James McCune Smith viewed the court's action as one of politics rather than law. Asserting that blacks born in the United States were unquestionably American

24. *Liberator,* October 11, 1850.

25. Martin R. Delany, *The Condition, Elevation, Emigration, and Destiny of the Colored People of the United States . . .* (Philadelphia: The Author, 1852), 158.

26. *Liberator,* April 10, 1857.

27. Charles H. Langston *et al.* to Salmon P. Chase, April 13, 1857, Salmon P. Chase Papers, Library of Congress (cited hereafter as C-LC).

28. See, for example, *Liberator,* February 26, July 9, August 13, 1858, and January 21, 1859.

citizens and entitled to all the rights of citizens, he advised his readers to "smile at the Dred Scott decision, and the various rulings of the minions of slaveholders, who hold for the time, the Executive power of the General Government." Their hope lay in political action, which would, in the future, undo Taney's pronouncement. Meanwhile they should "bide [their] time."[29]

Few shared Smith's optimism. Robert Morris challenged the right of young blacks to emigrate to Canada and avoid the fight at home. Slavery would, he prophesied, be overthrown not by "peaceable means" but by force, and all had a responsibility to prepare for coming battles.[30] Also opting for action outside the system, the Colored Men of Ohio resolved in their 1858 convention that Negroes were "absolved from all allegiance to a government which withdraws all protection."[31] A year later, unsure of the consequences which the Harper's Ferry raid held for him, Douglass lashed out at a government which had refused him citizenship because of his color and then sought to arrest him for treason. He had, he was sure, no government to betray.[32] In much the same mood, Robert Purvis, feeling his total deprivation of civil process, confessed that he felt nothing but *"contempt, loathing,* and *unutterable abhorrence!"* for the American government.[33]

Stripped of the rights of citizenship and implicitly of the rights of man, alienated from the government of their country, and maddened by an ever-expanding slavery which threatened them personally, more and more blacks pressed for slave insurrections. William Wells Brown encouraged such uprisings. John Rock invitingly portrayed their accomplishments elsewhere. Frederick Douglass argued their usefulness, and Charles Remond their

29. *Anglo-African Magazine,* I (May 1859), 149.

30. *Liberator,* August 13, 1858.

31. Convention of the Colored Men of Ohio, *Proceedings . . .Held in the City of Cincinnati, on the 23d, 24th, 25th and 26th days of November, 1858* (Cincinnati: Moore, Wilstach, Keys & Co., 1858), 6-7.

32. *Douglass Monthly,* November, 1859, cited in Philip Foner, ed., *The Life and Writings of Frederick Douglass,* (4 vols. New York: International Publishers, 1950-1955), 2:466.

33. *Liberator,* May 18, 1860.

inevitability. Episcopal clergyman J. Theodore Holly feared lest the escape of potential leaders defer the coming revolt;[34] and William Day, William Watkins, and John Mercer Langston joined to advocate "the right and duty of resistance by force of arms, when it was feasible."[35]

As the 1850s wore on, endorsements of insurrection were increasingly accompanied by a note of apocalypse. On the heels of the Kansas-Nebraska Act, William Wilson, Douglass' "Ethiop" correspondent, pronounced doom. "The whole land trembles with the iniquities of the accursed system of slavery usurpation. . . . Let the tocsin be sounded, and to arms every man whose skin is not whitened with the curse of God; and let our motto be, 'hands off, or death.' "[36] The Dred Scott decision increased this note. Douglass concluded that law prevailed neither in Court nor Congress nor Kansas. Everywhere God's law had been set at naught, and unless America heeded "solemn warnings" a judgment yet "more fierce or terrible" might fall upon it. "The world is full of violence and fraud," he augured, "and it would be strange if the slave, the constant victim of both fraud and violence, should escape the contagion."[37] Likewise James McCune Smith, who had not long since been willing to wait for political action, predicted in 1859 that events were making a slave insurrection unavoidable. "The glorious approach of this triumphal state here in our own land and elsewhere, no power of the tyrant, no chain of the oppressor, no skill or craft of the diplomatist, can stay," he editorialized in the *Weekly Anglo-African.* "Come it will, and come it must."[38] Even the cautious and conservative James Pennington concurred, translating the apocalypse more fully into clerical

34. *National Anti-Slavery Standard,* May 23, 1857. *Liberator,* August 7, 1857. Foner, *Douglass,* 2:438-439. *Liberator,* August 13, 1858. *Anglo-African Magazine,* I (November, 1859), 363.

35. Convention of the Colored Men of Ohio, *Proceedings . . .1858,* 17.

36. *Frederick Douglass' Paper,* June 9, 1854. On the whole question of confrontation and apocalypse, see Jane H. Pease and William H. Pease, "Confrontation and Abolition in the 1850s," *Journal of American History,* LVIII (March 1972), 923-937.

37. Quoted in Foner, *Douglass,* 2:413.

38. *Weekly Anglo-African,* July 30, 1859.

language. "Shall all these abominations be done and ratified among men on earth, and the Mighty and Holy God remain inactive upon His throne?"[39] The voice of black America answered, "No."

Militant blacks, however, showed little of Pennington's willingness to await divine intervention. Increasingly their rhetoric compared their own situation in the 1850s with that of white Americans at the time of the War for Independence. The Dred Scott decision convinced Charles Remond that the work of the Revolution was unfinished, and led him to wonder whether it would "ever be completed."[40] Bitter at America's degradation of blacks, he regretted "exceedingly" that he had "one single drop of blood in [his] veins that mingled with the blood of the men who engaged in the strife on Bunker Hill and at Lexington," for their efforts had produced a nation of "cowards" and "pander[er]s to American slavery."[41]

Blacks' revolutionary heritage was one of betrayal, for their ancestors had fought for the freedom they were now denied. But rather than renounce the Revolution, as Remond tried to do, most Boston Negroes sought to revive and fulfill it. William Nell renewed memories of the Boston Massacre when, beginning in 1858, he organized a series of Crispus Attucks celebrations, whose speakers used the example set in 1770 as a goad to militant action in the present.[42] John Rock drove the theme home in 1860. He did, it is true, refuse to idolize Attucks, whose action began the process which produced a government willing to use "every means in its power to outrage and degrade his race." Yet he found in Attucks, as in Nat

39. *Anglo-African Magazine*, I (November, 1859), 345.
40. *Liberator*, June 19, 1857.
41. *Ibid.*, July 10, 1857.
42. Robert P. Smith, "William Cooper Nell: Crusading Black Abolitionist," *Journal of Negro History*, LV (July, 1970), 192. William C. Nell to [William L. Garrison], February 22, 1859, G-BPL.

Turner and John Brown, the clear message that to be free, both slaves and free blacks must fight their own battles.[43]

More and more as revolution became a familiar theme the oppressors were defined by race. Formerly protest rhetoric had portrayed the struggle largely as one between abolitionists and the slave power or between Northern freemen and Southern slave-holders. Now it was between black and white. For a score or more years many Negroes had worked with or within the predominately white antislavery movement. Now they were impatient with its ineffectiveness and its white orientation. Douglass, the earliest and most prized slave agent, announced in the summer following the Taney decision that, after a ten-year shift, he now considered himself primarily a black rather than an antislavery leader. Remond, Nell, and William Wells Brown, all loyal Garrisonians until then, began after 1857 to reassess their roles and to support race activities which they had earlier disapproved.[44]

The more blacks turned inward, the more they defined their conflict as a racial one. Rejecting both white leadership and white organization, they came, as did the National Emigration Convention of 1854, to regard as the "common enemy every white, who proves not himself to the contrary."[45] So few whites conformed "to the contrary," and so many displayed prejudice that nearly all Negroes remembered some "deep and painful experience" which, in Samuel Ward's words, would constantly tempt them "to hate their white fellow-citizens." In 1855 he found this both reasonable and proper. "How difficult, how impossible, to deny this [injury repeatedly done Negroes], with all its telling force of historical fact! How natural is such a feeling, in such circumstances! How richly the whites deserved it!"[46]

43. *Liberator*, March 16, 1860.

44. Foner, *Douglass*, 2:436-437. *Liberator*, August 13, 1858. *Weekly Anglo-African*, July 23, 1859. *Liberator*, August 19, 1859.

45. National Emigration Convention of Colored People, *Proceedings of... Held at Cleveland, Ohio, On Thursday, Friday and Saturday, the 24th, 25th, and 26th of August 1854...*(Pittsburgh: Printed by A. A. Anderson, 1854), 20.

46. Ward, *Autobiography*, 84-85.

Speaking at the Boston Massacre celebration in 1858 John Rock answered charges made by abolitionist Theodore Parker that Negroes were inherently cowards, unwilling to fight for their freedom. Looking back, Rock noted in passing that in Russia at that very moment thirty million Caucasians were serfs and were not in revolt. More importantly, he denied that it was cowardice which kept a minority group of four million surrounded by a hostile race of twenty-seven million from rebelling. "Nothing but superior force keeps us down," he asserted. Praising those "slaves rising up by hundreds annually" and fleeing to Canada in the face of "paid men, armed with pistols, clubs and bowie-knives," hired to thwart them, and with even "the army and navy of this great Model Republic arrayed against them," Rock concluded by asking "if the charge of cowardice [did] not come with an ill-grace." Goading Parker with abolitionists' failure to end slavery, Rock added, "White men have no room to taunt us with tamely submitting. If they were black men, they would work wonders; but, as white men, they can do nothing."[47]

Despite Rock's fiery responses, charges of cowardice and apathy continued to rankle. Especially after the Harper's Ferry raid failed to stir a slave revolt, militant predictions of inevitable insurrection were strained and challenged. At its inception, there had been Negro support for John Brown's plan. In the spring of 1858, thirty-three blacks and twelve whites met in Chatham, Canada; and there, under Brown's leadership, organized a provisional government to conduct guerrilla operations in Kansas and perhaps in the slave South. But Brown's plan was unclear; he had trouble raising money, and for seventeen months little happened. In the interim, almost all the Chatham enthusiasts fell away. Martin Delany, who later claimed to have organized the Brown meeting, was immersed

47. *Liberator*, March 12, 1858. In a great show of enthusiasm the *Anglo-African Magazine*, I (January, 1859), 2-3, predicted that the Negro was the "coming man." "The European race would seem to have reached its destined development. . . . To advance still further, the tide of civilization requires . . . new blood. And whence can this be procured, unless from a race hitherto unmixed in the current of civilization?"

in his emigration project when plans for guerrilla fighting at Harper's Ferry matured. Finally, of the original thirty-three only Osborn Anderson actually accompanied Brown to western Virginia.[48]

Nor did Brown receive much more support from the black leaders in the Northern states with whom he had been in touch. Some, like Garnet, turned him down at once, not because he objected to an invasion to stir revolt but because "the time [had] not yet come for the success of such a movement." Slaves in the South were unprepared for it. They were "not sufficiently apprised of their rights and of the sympathy that exist[ed] on the part of the North for them." And blacks in the North, "in consequence of the prejudice that shuts them out from both the means and the intelligence necessary," were equally unready for the venture.[49] The Rev. John N. Gloucester, usually more conservative than Garnet, apparently collected funds for Brown but did nothing more. Douglass, who had fought Garnet's "Address to the Slaves" so vigorously fifteen years earlier, was now sympathetic to some action in the South but, in August 1859, he rejected Brown's specific plan to attack Harper's Ferry rather than to wage guerrilla activity in the Southern Appalachians as he had originally planned.[50] Had there been hope of success, Douglass wrote after the abortive raid, he would have been willing to "write, speak, publish, organize, combine, and even to conspire against Slavery"; but Brown's fantasy was simply too foolhardy to engage his support.[51] If any leading black activist supported Brown it was

48. *Weekly Anglo-African*, November 12, 1859. Fred Landon, "Canadian Negroes and the John Brown Raid," *Journal of Negro History*, VI (April 1921), 174-175. William E. Burghardt DuBois, *John Brown* (Philadelphia: George W. Jacobs, 1909), 259-266. Frank A. Rollin, *Life and Public Services of Martin R. Delany* (New York: Arno Press, 1969), 87-89. Fred Landon, "From Chatham to Harper's Ferry," *Canadian Magazine*, LIII (October 1919), 447-448.

49. *Liberator*, December 9, 1859.

50. DuBois, *John Brown*, 248-259. Foner, *Douglass*, 2:85-94.

51. Frederick Douglass to Editor, Rochester *Democrat*, October 31, 1859, quoted in *Anglo-African Magazine*, I (December 1859), 381-382; also in *Douglass Monthly*, November 1859.

Jarmain Loguen of Syracuse, who accompanied Brown to Canada in 1858 and returned in the summer of 1859 to organize blacks there into Liberty Leagues. Yet there is no evidence to indicate that Loguen was actively involved either in the planning or execution of the Harper's Ferry raid. Thus, though Douglass did flee the country in self-protection, there is no proof that leading Northern blacks gave substantial aid to the Harper's Ferry venture.

In its aftermath, John Brown drew far more support. That black, like white, abolitionists then portrayed him as a martyr to their cause may reflect changed minds, uneasy consciences, or disappointment that the rhetoric of violence and revolution had failed in the event. In any case, Negroes met across the North in Massachusetts, Rhode Island, New York, Pennsylvania, and Ohio to celebrate John Brown's raid. Like their white antislavery counterparts they apostrophized the patriarch and especially praised his five black followers. In Providence a "large and enthusiastic meeting" deplored the use of violence but called Brown a "hero, philanthropist and unflinching champion of liberty."[52] In Ohio the black state antislavery society called the participants "heaven appointed Heralds and Prophets" whose behavior in jail and on the gallows illustrated "that new lesson, the lesson of Insurrection, so thrilling and solem[n]ly taught the American people in the tragedy of Harper's Ferry."[53] Douglass, recently returned in December 1860 from his self-imposed exile, publicly endorsed "John Brown's way," for, although "all hope of general insurrection [was] vain," that single raid did "more to upset the logic and shake the security of slavery than all other efforts in that direction for twenty years."[54]

Nonetheless, Douglass' concession that widespread revolt was improbable touched on the renewed charges that slaves were

52. *Weekly Anglo-African,* November 19, 1859.
53. Ohio State Anti-Slavery Society, *Proceedings of the First Annual Meeting of . . . Held in Xenia, Ohio, January 3rd, 4th, and 5th, 1860* ([Title page missing. 1860]), 11.
54. Foner, *Douglass,* 2:535. Frederick Douglass to James Redpath, June 29, 1860, *Liberator,* July 27, 1860.

apathetic and cowardly and that Harper's Ferry had demonstrated that they would not fight for their freedom. To these assertions J. Sella Martin, young pastor of Boston's Joy Street church, responded by asking why slaves should have fought then. "They have learned this much from the treachery of white men at the North, and the cruelty of white men at the South, that they cannot trust the white man, even when he comes to deliver them."[55] The *Anglo-African Magazine* further explored the differences between white- and black-led revolts in an extended comparison of John Brown's raid with Nat Turner's revolt. "The one is the mode in which the slave seeks freedom for his fellows, and the other, the mode in which the white man seeks to set the slave free. . . .Nat Turner's terrible logic could only see the enfranchisement of one race, compassed by the extirpation of the other; and he followed his gory syllogism with rude exactitude. John Brown, believing that the freedom of the enthralled could only be effected by placing them on an equality with the enslavers, and unable, in the very effort at emancipation to tyrannize himself, is moved with compassion for tyrants as well as slaves, and seeks to extirpate this formidable cancer, without spilling one drop of christian blood." The choice was up to whites, the magazine concluded in an appeal to their vital self-interest. "So, people of the South, people of the North! men and brethren, choose ye which method of emancipation you prefer—Nat Turner's or John Brown's."[56]

The inference followed that blacks had already chosen. And Martin Delany, in the only extended exploration of slave insurrection published by an American Negro in the immediate prewar years, bore it out. His incomplete novel, *Blake,* was the story of Henrico Blacus, a free-born Cuban shanghaied into American slavery and there known as Blake. He bore his bonds until his slave wife was sold. Then he escaped to agitate for rebellion in the deep South. In his travels he met survivors of the Vesey and Turner revolts, who constituted a clear link with these earlier ventures. Yet for whatever reasons Delany failed to complete the story in this

55. *Liberator,* December 9, 1859.
56. *Anglo-African Magazine,* I (December 1859), 386.

vein but rather made Blake return to Cuba in order to plan and execute a revolt in the Caribbean. There the extant story ends abruptly.[57]

Incomplete though the novel is, its themes are clear. A massive conspiracy among slaves was both necessary and possible. The leadership for such a revolt existed. Slaves must shed the white man's religion, which preached submission and kept them in ignorance of their rights. Race solidarity was the essence of revolution; the action would be a "war upon the whites." "Whatever liberty is worth to the whites," Blake wrote his wife at one point, "it is worth to the blacks; therefore, whatever it cost the whites to obtain it, the blacks would be willing and ready to pay, if they desire it."[58] Black revolt would bring black freedom.

Clear in fiction and easy in oratory, revolution and insurrection never came in fact. Nowhere in the North was there a population density of Negroes sufficient to sustain race war—even had the inarticulate been ready to respond to its rhetoric. And the Brown raid, badly organized and occurring in an area of Virginia where the slave population was very thin, gave little real test of the likelihood of servile insurrection. What then did the rhetoric of violence mean?

Its vehemence offered no viable solutions. It was rather a gauge responding to the frustrations of rightlessness and powerlessness. Not surprisingly it never occupied the total energy of black leaders, who continued their efforts through more customary channels—or devised new race organizations—or sought fulfillment of their goals outside the United States.

57. Martin R. Delany, *Blake or the Huts of America* (Boston: Beacon Press, 1970) The novel was originally published as a serial in the *Anglo-African Magazine* in 1859 and in the *Weekly Anglo-African* in 1861-1862. Delany sought but apparently got no support for publishing it in book form from Garrison. See his letter to the latter, February 19, 1859, G-BPL. It is not certain whether Delany ever finished the novel or whether the final chapters are lost.

58. Delany, *Blake*, 290, 192.

12. SEPARATISM AND EMIGRATION—THE NATIONALISM OF THE 1850s

THE CONDITIONS and events which produced determined resistance to the fugitive slave law and appeals for revolt shaped also a new will to build separate race institutions. The discussion which surrounded these proposals drew on experience gained in establishing churches, mutual aid societies, and schools as well as in organizing race conventions and civil rights campaigns. At the end of the 1840s and throughout the 1850s, however, new urgency marked the quest for distinctly black solutions to Afro-American problems. Increasingly excluded from economic opportunity, denied suffrage and other civil rights, and rendered ever more unsafe in person and property, free Negroes collectively and individually sought different approaches to dignity and security either within the United States or outside its boundaries.

For Frederick Douglass, a new pattern of organization marked the way for blacks to stay in America and improve their position. Urging "the wisdom and the necessity of combination," he proposed to his readers in the summer of 1849, a National League of Colored People "to grapple with the various systems of injustice" perpetrated against them and to aid them to "regain [their] plundered rights." He used as a foil an article from the New York *Hyperion* reprinted in the same issue of the *North Star*, which developed an elaborate theory of nationalism and cultural unity. Since Afro-Americans, the article contended, were linked not by their African roots but by their common life experience in the Western Hemisphere, they shared, from Canada to South America, "a common social destiny." To control it, they must achieve cultural nationhood. The *Hyperion,* however, stopped short of advocating "an independent political confederacy" and sought only "equal civil and political rights" in already established governments.[1]

William Whipper doubted the viability of such dreams as things then stood. He opposed separatist action until blacks developed strong internal social bonds. "While we have no national existence 'as a people,' we can have no national institutions," Whipper contended in a letter to Douglass. Only "a distinct civil and religious code" could rally and unite any people, and these Afro-Americans lacked. Believing religion to be the basis of all cultural and civil values, Whipper insisted that until they completely rejected white American religion and established their own independent faith, blacks could not hope to build national organization. "If our people ever become united in the prosecution of objects for the promotion of their common welfare," he concluded, "it will be when they have erected the altar of a new religion over the grade of Sectarianism."[2] In propounding the priority of cultural cohesion, Whipper had moved far from his earlier opposition to separate race action and had evolved a bold demand for an independent society derived from the Afro-American experience. Nonetheless his proposal demanded a choice between immediate action and long-range effectiveness.

Despite Whipper's criticism, Douglass' plan for a national union failed less from lacking a strong cultural base than from being premature. The fugitive slave law crisis the next year conclusively demonstrated that fact. In Canada blacks soon envisaged a race organization embracing at least North America and the Caribbean. The 1851 North American Convention in Toronto urged "a great

1. *North Star,* August 10, 1849.
2. *Ibid.,* November 23, 1849. Douglass agreed at least in part with Whipper's analysis, suggesting that blacks had sufficiently rid themselves of the white man's religion to begin to lay their own autonomous cultural base. *Ibid.,* December 14, 1849.

league of the colored people of the North and South American continents, and of the West Indies."[3] Though the Toronto meeting generated nothing formal, a meeting in Amherstburgh two years later tried to create a Canadian Council for the Africo-American League.[4] And, in the United States, Douglass pressed his earlier idea at the Rochester national convention of 1853. After considerable debate and no little acrimony, he won his essential point when the delegates adopted James McCune Smith's similar plan for a national council supplemented by auxiliary state councils.[5]

Local response to these developments was favorable. Returning home from the Rochester meeting, Boston delegates reported its work to an enthusiastic audience. Within the month Chicagoans approved the plan for a national council. By the end of the year meetings in Albany, New York, and Providence had chosen representatives to the new council. And in New York State, small cities and towns like Geneva, Elmira, and Syracuse formed local auxiliaries.[6]

Yet the initial enthusiasm rapidly evaporated. From the very start council meetings were hamstrung by attendance too small to make a quorum, and wrangling about procedure and representation took a heavy toll. In New York, where support for the council was strongest, the state council, jealous of its prerogatives, worried lest it sacrifice its autonomy to the national council or be underrepresented there.[7] Bitter personal differences split the Massachusetts council. At its January 1854 meetings separatists

3. *Voice of the Fugitive*, September 24, 1851. A North America and West India League was less sweeping in scope, but at least got to the constitution-writing stage. *Ibid.*, February 26, 1852.

4. General Convention for the Improvement of the Colored Inhabitants of Canada, *Minutes and Proceedings of the ... Held by Adjournments in Amherstburgh, C.A. June 16th and 17th, 1853* (Windsor: Bibb & Holly, 1853), 8, 21-23.

5. *Frederick Douglass' Paper*, July 15, 1853.

6. *Liberator*, July 29, 1853. *Frederick Douglass' Paper*, January 13, 1854. Also *ibid.*, August 19, November 21, December 30 and 16, 1853, and March 17 and 31, 1854.

7. Howard H. Bell, *A Survey of the Negro Convention Movement, 1830-1861* (New York: Arno Press, 1969), 166-180. *Frederick Douglass' Paper*, December 2, 1853, and February 3, 1854.

traded epithets with assimilationists. H. O. Remington, of New Bedford, charged that Remond was "wholly unworthy of the confidence of the Colored People," and likened him to John C. Calhoun.[8] William Nell, incensed at the attack on his assimilationist colleague, threatened to quit the council altogether and later reported that the proceedings were "disgraceful to an assembly of freemen."[9]

In the West, local interests also impeded national harmony. At the national council meeting in Cleveland in July 1854, the Ohio delegation could make or break a quorum. Unhesitatingly they used their strategic advantage to attack decisions made by the New York State council and by the earlier Rochester session of the national council. Their ultimate objective, it seemed, was to sabotage the national council system and to replace it with one in which Ohio leaders would have a greater voice. So effective was their stranglehold, one observer reported, that the meeting's ending was its greatest triumph, for "in order to effect a creditable adjournment" Amos Beman had to seize a passing instant to terminate the proceedings "when there happened to be just at that time a quorum."[10]

Shamelessly victimized by the parochialism of its members, the national council, which met in Philadelphia in 1855 for the last time, verified the assessment that Johnson Woodlin had made two years earlier. A national council, the Philadelphian had written Douglass, would not serve the needs of the race, for blacks had to be "*instructed* in matters pertaining to a radical change; and this *instruction* no 'national council' or convention can confer." Although sympathetic to the idea of such a council, Woodlin, like Whipper, was convinced that some theoretical consensus had to precede it. Whipper had sought cultural cohesion; Woodlin's goal was self-government. "The social relations of our race must be *governed,* and the principles of that *government* is [*sic*] within us,

8. *Frederick Douglass' Paper,* January 13, 1854.

9. *Liberator,* January 27, 1854.

10. *Frederick Douglass' Paper,* September 1, 1854. Also *ibid.,* July 28, 1854.

and only needs an outward manifestation in the form of a *national political existence.*"[11]

By mid-1855 the national council idea was dead, killed by parochial interests, personal bickering, and insufficient theoretical underpinnings. In its place stood its triumphant rival: the nationalism of emigration. But, like preceding movements seeking resettlement outside the United States, it also generated considerable opposition and controversy, not least of all because it rekindled the old suspicions engendered by the hated American Colonization Society.[12]

In the first National Convention of the Free People of Color, held in Philadelphia in 1830, the delegates, responding to the Cincinnati riots of the previous year, had devoted much of their energy to marshalling aid for Canadian emigration. But their enthusiasm contradicted prevailing black opposition to resettlement outside the United States. Ever since they had first condemned the American Colonization Society in 1817, blacks have overwhelmingly rejected flight and resettlement elsewhere as a solution to discrimination and inequality. Even though several other conventions evinced an interest in Canadian settlement in the early 1830s, resistance to emigration of any kind was the norm for most Northern Negroes from 1817 until 1850. The passage of the new fugitive slave law, however, radically changed all that. With their freedom immediately menaced by the hazards of the new fugitive slave law, several national leaders chose temporary or permanent exile. Garnet, who had been lecturing in England, prolonged his stay for two years and then went to Jamaica, where he remained until 1855.[13] Loguen and Ward both fled to Canada to escape possible arrest and punishment for their parts in the Jerry rescue case; and though Loguen shortly returned, Ward never

11. *Ibid.,* May 6, 1853.
12. For a general survey of this activity see Bell, *Negro Convention Movement,* 124-161.
13. [Leeds Anti-Slavery Society] , *Fugitive Slaves: Douglass, Pennington, Wells Brown, Garnett, Bibb and Others* (Leeds Anti-Slavery Series, No. 34. London: n.p., n.d. [ca. 1853]).

did.[14] Among the rank and file the exodus was much more pronounced. Hundreds of unknown fugitives and freemen fled across the northern border. Only weeks after the passage of the hated law, the Governor-General reported to his home government that Canada was "likely to be flooded with blackies."[15] Within six months, Henry Bibb had established the *Voice of the Fugitive* in Windsor to encourage black settlement under the British flag.[16] When the North American Convention met in Toronto in 1851, it urged northward emigration.[17] As fast as refugees arrived, groups and individuals organized and proffered assistance, like that extended by the Refugee Home Society, which was established by Canadian Negroes and Michigan abolitionists to provide cheap land, self-government, and adequate schooling to the newcomers.[18] By the end of the decade perhaps as many as 20,000 American-born blacks were living in Canada.

The new willingness to emigrate was not solely the product of fear. It also betokened an emerging identification with a distinctive black culture. Although many race activities and institutions of the earlier period—the societies, churches, conventions, schools, and press, as well as the appeals to race pride and African history—were components of this phenomenon, their original goal had been the assimilation of Negroes into the mainstream of American life. Now, in the 1850s, they were eyed as a base for a black identity which would be realized in more complete separatism.

A new nationalism began to emerge by the late 1840s. Rooted in long-felt imperatives for distinctive race action, it expanded

14. Jarmain W. Loguen to George Whipple, February 14, 1851, Copy, AMA-ARC. Jarmain W. Loguen to [J. R. Johnson?], December 18, 1851, in *Frederick Douglass' Paper*, January 8, 1852. Samuel R. Ward to George Whipple, October 13, [1851], AMA-ARC. Samuel Ringgold Ward, *Autobiography of a Fugitive Negro* . . .(London: J. Snow, 1855), 102-120.

15. James Bruce, Eighth Earl of Elgin, to Henry George, Third Earl Grey, October 6, 1850, in *The Elgin-Grey Papers, 1846-1852,* edited by Sir Arthur Doughty (Ottawa: J. O. Patenaude, I.S.O., Printer to the King, 1937), 720.

16. *Voice of the Fugitive*, January 1, 1851.

17. *Ibid.*, August 13, 1851.

18. *Ibid.*, June 1 and August 13, 1851.

until, in some cases, it embraced complete and total separation from the United States. In the 1849 Convention of the Colored Citizens of Ohio, the delegates split over supporting plans for a Negro nation. The majority report of the committee on colonization proposed creating an Afro-American republic once slavery had been ended. "We are willing, it being optional," the report read, "to draw out from the American government, and form a separate and independent one, enacting our own laws and regulations, trusting for success only in the God of Liberty and the Controller of human destiny."[19] The report touched off a rancorous debate and was finally rejected, but not before it had driven a wedge into the traditional anticolonization position. John Langston, one of the authors of the convention's report, continued to explore the possibility of a separate black existence in "the newly acquired territories" of the West where, he said hopefully, "we may peaceably settle & enjoy our own Political regulations as do the inhabitants of other Territories."[20]

When Indiana blacks met in 1851, they readily concluded that they could always emigrate to Canada, Jamaica, Mexico, or Central America; but they insisted they would never go to Liberia.[21] At the same time, however, Lewis Putnam of New York City tried to break that old pattern. He organized an United African Republic Emigration Society, sought funds from the state legislature, and even won some support from Governor Washington Hunt.[22] But this new venture could not overcome twenty years of anticolonization feeling. Across the state local meetings voted their disapproval. A group in New York City, at which George Downing and Cornish lashed out against Putnam, asserted that the Emigration Company was no better than the old colonization society and dubbed it "our

19. State Convention of the Colored Citizens of Ohio, *Minutes and Address...1849,* 11. The anticolonizationist minority report, which was adopted by the convention, is on 13-14.
20. Charles H. Langston and John M. Langston to Salmon P. Chase, September 12, 1850, C-LC.
21. *Voice of the Fugitive,* August 27, 1851. *Frederick Douglass' Paper,* October 2, 1851.
22. *African Repository,* XXVII (November, 1851), 324.

enemy and vilifier."[23] Three months later, in January 1852, a similar group condemned Governor Hunt for requesting legislative appropriations to assist emigration. Upstate, Albanians, equally incensed with the request, denied the governor's premises that Negroes in the state were destined to an inferior status; and in February a "Committee of Thirteen" denounced Putnam's project in a direct address to the legislature. In April still another New York meeting protested the Putnam-Hunt proposals and applauded when Pennington, Reason, Smith, and Cornish set out various arguments against the plan.[24]

Elsewhere the response to emigration was much the same. A tentative plan for colonization, launched by H. Ford Douglass of Columbus, P. H. Clark of Cincinnati, and both Ohio Langstons at the 1852 Ohio convention, left their associates largely unimpressed. The delegates voted 36-9 to reject their proposal that a special convention meet to consider voluntary emigration within North America, or outside it if necessary.[25] Not long after a Free Colored People's Convention in Maryland decided that "in the face of constantly increasing emigration and growing prejudices" they had little choice but to go to Liberia.[26] But their conclusion was quickly challenged by a meeting of Baltimoreans, who likened the convention to the reviled American Colonization Society and denied that it spoke for more than ten per cent of their number.[27]

Clearly, therefore, emigration sentiment in the early 1850s failed to engender race unity or to win widespread black support. Many leaders continued to see in it a white plot to exile free blacks

---

23. *Frederick Douglass' Paper*, November 13, 1851.
24. *Ibid.*, February 5 and 26, 1852. *Liberator*, May 14, 1852.
25. Convention of Colored Freemen of Ohio, *Proceedings . . .[1852]*, 5, 9.
26. The word should be "immigration." It clearly refers to the pressures against blacks created by increasingly large numbers of European immigrants. *Frederick Douglass' Paper*, August 6, 1852, Convention of the Free Colored People of the State of Maryland, *Proceedings of the . . . Held in Baltimore, July 26, 27, and 28, 1852*, in *Journal of Negro History*, I (July 1916), 323-338; and *Frederick Douglass' Paper*, August 13, 1852.
27. *Liberator*, August 20, 1852.

and further entrench slaveholding. Their attitude was little moderated by new arguments from James G. Birney, respected abolitionist and Liberty party leader and long an outspoken opponent of the American Colonization Society. He, succumbing to despair that white prejudice was unconquerable, recommended in an 1852 pamphlet that free Negroes emigrate to Liberia.[28] Both Samuel Ward and George Downing rejected his argument and denounced his counsel.[29] Incensed when the white-dominated executive committee proposed that the American and Foreign Anti-Slavery Society assist those who wished to settle in Africa, Downing, joined by James McCune Smith, charged it with selling out. "There is a manhood in the colored race here in the United States, and you cannot see it," Smith taunted the whites. "You want to go to Africa to see gorgeous temples and governorships. You are so blind that you cannot see the grand throbbings of humanity in the heart of every black man. I say the resolution [for emigration assistance] ought to be struck out, and no aid ought to be given to a man to leave his country."[30]

Race meetings throughout the North in the early fifties repeated the same determination. Bostonians thought that in America there was "no particular fault . . . save in respect to some of its customs, institutions and laws." It was their "duty and determination to rectify [them] with speed" rather than to emigrate.[31] A New Bedford meeting rejected Horace Mann's assertions that blacks' intellectual and emotional qualities were best suited to life in a warm climate, and they denounced the covert endorsement of colonization the assertions implied.[32] Elsewhere—in Philadelphia, Syracuse, Paterson, and Rochester—

28. James G. Birney, *Examination of the Decision of the Supreme Court of the United States, in the Case of Strader, Gorman and Armstrong vs. Christopher Graham, Delivered at its December Term, 1850: Concluding with an Address to the Free Colored People* (Cincinnati: Truman and Spofford, 1852), 43.

29. *Frederick Douglass' Paper*, March 11 and 25, 1852.

30. *Ibid.*, May 27, 1852.

31. *Liberator*, April 4, 1851.

32. *Frederick Douglass' Paper*, October 22, 1852. *Ibid.*, February 27, 1852, for an earlier New Bedford anticolonization meeting.

blacks identified emigration with the American Colonization Society and scorned it as a way to "coerce" them into leaving the United States.[33]

Lecturing to English and Scottish audiences, James Pennington epitomized most black response. *"The colored population of the United States have no destiny separate from that of the nation of which they form an integral part*," he said. Moreover, he added in a letter back to Douglass, not even in Africa could Negroes escape the white man. "The Saxon is there! The real, landstealing, unscrupulous, overreaching Saxon is even in Africa, and is pushing his way into the interior!"[34]

Regardless of the opposition, emigration could not be written off. The earlier colonization thrust had been broken in part by the prospects for improvement at home, which the new antislavery movement of the 1830s had promised. But its failure to achieve significant change by the 1850s and the tenseness which gripped black Americans in that decade forced them to reassess all alternatives. Just as, twenty years earlier, the hopelessness produced by race riots and harsh enforcement of discriminatory laws in Ohio had driven Negroes to support resettlement in Canada, so now a greater hopelessness impelled them to reconsider colonization in the Caribbean and Africa.

Leader of the new emigrationist enthusiasm was Pittsburgh's Martin R. Delany, physician, erstwhile editor of the short-lived *Mystery,* and author of *The Condition, Elevation, Migration, and Destiny of the Colored People.* A late convert, Delany had opposed emigration at the North American Convention in Toronto in 1851 and the next year had declined to endorse the idea on at least two separate occasions. Shortly thereafter, however, his conversion

33. *Ibid.,* April 29, 1852, and *Liberator,* October 7, 1853. *Frederick Douglass' Paper,* April 1, 1853. *Voice of the Fugitive,* April 22, 1852. *Frederick Douglass' Paper,* July 15, 1853.

34. William C. Nell, *The Colored Patriots of the American Revolution . . .*(Boston: Robert F. Wallcut, 1855), 356. *Frederick Douglass' Paper,* April 22, 1852.

began.[35] He increasingly believed that black freemen were becoming as rightless as slaves. "I am not in favor of caste, nor a separation of the brotherhood of mankind, and would as willing[ly] live among white men as black," he wrote Garrison in 1852, "if," he added significantly, "I had an *equal possession and enjoyment* of privileges" now withheld by the "blind selfishness" and "deep prejudice" of whites. "I must admit," he concluded, "that I have no hopes in this country—no confidence in the American people—with a *few* excellent exceptions. . . ."[36]

Further elaborating his argument in the *Condition and Elevation*, published the same year, he wrote:

The bondman is disfranchised, and for the most part so are we. He is denied all civil, religious, and social privileges, except such as he gets by mere sufferance, and so are we. They have no part nor lot in the government of the country, neither have we. They are ruled and governed without representation, existing as mere nonentities among the citizens, and excrescences on the body politic—a mere dreg in the community, and so are we. Where then is our political superiority to the enslaved?[37]

In America, clearly, there was none. The only alternative for black men was to leave the United States, which excluded them from the benefits of society and government and whose politics offered them no vehicle for change.

35. *Voice of the Fugitive,* September 24, 1851. *Frederick Douglass' Paper,* April 29, June 10, 1852. *Weekly Anglo-African,* October 1, 1859. In his essay, " 'The Father of Black Nationalism': Another Contender," *Civil War History,* XVII (December 1971), 310-319, Floyd J. Miller contends that Delany came to emigration through the direct influence of Pittsburgh's Lewis Woodson. It seems a tenuous connection at best since, as Miller's article suggests, Woodson's emigrationism is hard to demonstrate decisively, and Delany failed to embrace emigration until late in his career, although he had been a close friend of Woodson for years.

36. *Liberator,* May 21, 1852.

37. Martin R. Delany, *The Condition, Elevation, Emigration, and Destiny of the Colored People of the United States...*(Philadelphia: The Author, 1852), 14-15.

The only other question, then, was where to go. Delany rejected Liberia because of its unhealthful climate and its domination by American whites. Canada had better climate, but it was also subject to American influence. At first, therefore, Delany proposed settlement somewhere in Central or South America, where the climate was excellent, the land rich, and racial discrimination totally absent.[38] But in proposing an exploration of Africa's east coast—across the continent from Liberia—he left the door open for African settlement as well. There, economic wealth lay buried in mineral deposits and could be exploited by an east-west transcontinental railroad. Developing its economic potential, Afro-Americans could find both national identity and free community. "We must MAKE an ISSUE, CREATE an EVENT, and ESTABLISH a NATIONAL POSITION for OURSELVES," Delany apostrophized. Only by undertaking "some fearless, bold, and adventurous deeds of daring—contending against every odds—regardless of every consequence" could American Negroes "expect to be respected as men and women."[39]

Since emigration and settlement had to be a race adventure, Delany neither expected nor wanted the help of white abolitionists. He charged them with having disrupted discussions of emigration in the early convention movement and with having pushed aside black efforts in their attempts to "make full amends for the injuries . . . inflicted on an unoffending people." Negroes who had welcomed the white antislavery movement, he said, had, "instead of realising what we had hoped for," found themselves "occupying the very same position in relation to our Anti-Slavery friends, as we do in relation to the pro-slavery part of the community—a mere secondary, underling position, in all our relations to them."[40]

Race progress, Delany insisted, militated against consultation with or reliance upon whites. Whatever the project, blacks must counsel among themselves and act for themselves. When Douglass

38. *Ibid.,* 169-174, 178-182.
39. *Ibid.,* 209-215.
40. *Ibid.,* 24, 27.

sought Harriet Beecher Stowe's aid and advice for a manual labor school, Delany objected. The issue was not, he said, accepting funds from whites but allowing them to influence decisions in race matters.[41] Thus he felt free to seek contributions from English and French donors to help finance his projected African explorations. In 1858, he solicited Henry Ward Beecher's aid in convincing the American Missionary Association to give him monetary assistance. Two years later he gladly accepted assistance from the white African Aid Society in England. But he consistently denied donors the right to control the expenditure of the funds contributed or to dictate policy.[42]

Having completed his conversion to emigration by mid-1853 and having decided to work within an exclusively black framework, Delany called a national convention to launch an emigrationist program. No sooner had he announced his plans than opposition to them developed. He had publicized his project almost immediately after the 1853 Rochester national convention had rejected the idea of settlement outside the United States. To many, the timing indicated his intention to undercut the national council and its program for race unity. Douglass, for whom the Rochester meeting meant real progress, immediately challenged Delany, particularly condemning his exclusion of all but supporters from the proposed emigration convention as "narrow and illiberal."[43] Public meetings throughout the North took up Douglass' complaint; in New Bedford, Boston, Chicago, Elmira, and Columbus blacks chose the nationalism of the Douglass council system over Delany's emigration plan and condemned the latter's unrepresentative attempt to overthrow it.[44]

41. *Frederick Douglass' Paper,* April 1, 1853.
42. Delany, *Condition and Elevation,* 209-215. Martin R. Delany to Henry Ward Beecher, June 17, 1858, AMA-ARC. Delany to George Whipple, 1858, AMA-ARC. Martin R. Delany, *Official Report of the Niger Valley Exploring Party* (New York: T. Hamilton, 1861), 124.
43. *Frederick Douglass' Paper,* August 26, 1853.
44. *Ibid.,* September 30, 1853. *Liberator,* February 24, 1854. *Frederick Douglass' Paper,* November 18, 1853, March 17, 1854, and October 28, 1853.

The hue and cry his opponents raised did not, however, deter Delany. In August 1854 the National Emigration Convention met in Cleveland, and delegates chosen for their assured support eagerly endorsed his proposals. Their geographic distribution not only testified to Delany's control of the movement, but also reflected a pattern of support primarily from the Ohio River valley and cities on the Great Lakes. Although officers of the convention represented a variety of states, the one hundred forty-one elected delegates were concentrated in three: Eighty-one came from Delany's own Allegheny County in western Pennsylvania, twenty-five came from Ohio and seventeen from Michigan. The remainder came in ones and twos from other states as scattered as Louisiana, New York, and Rhode Island.[45]

The skewed distribution of the delegates suggests a concentration of emigrationist interest in those Western areas where black population was most dense and where civil rights activity had been both strong and futile. It also demonstrates the commanding position of Delany, whose friends and neighbors were so ubiquitous on the convention floor that George Vashon asked whether it was only a "Convention of Pittsburghers" and wondered why it had not been held at home to save transportation costs.[46] Such cavils worried neither Delany nor the delegates. In their official report of their deliberations they flatly claimed that they had "transacted business equal to the duration of a season, and of vastly more importance than any other similar body of colored people ever before assembled in the United States."[47]

Despite its hubris, the Cleveland convention had fashioned a new emigration program. Although, like all other race conventions, it stressed the importance of civil rights, equality, economic advancement, freedom, and political power, it also contended that blacks must seek them outside a hostile United States, suggesting

45. National Emigration Convention of Colored People, *Proceedings...Cleveland... 1854,* 16-18.
46. *Frederick Douglass' Paper,* November 17, 1854.
47. National Emigration Convention of Colored People, *Proceedings... 1854,* 15.

that the best places to go were Central and South America and the Caribbean.[48] The central flaw in American life, which made emigration necessary, the official address, later published as *The Political Destiny of the Colored Race on the American Continent*, argued, was "not a question of the rich against the poor, nor the common people against the higher classes, but a question of white against black—every white person, by legal right, being held superior to a black or colored person." "For more than two thousand years, the determined aim of the whites has been to crush the colored races wherever found," the *Political Destiny*, which was mostly Delany's handiwork, asserted.[49] In the process American blacks had experienced an oppression similar to that of Latin American Indians, with whom they could now join in establishing a new nation south of Mexico.[50] The goal of emigration was not to escape but rather to gain control over their own lives. Emigrationists must form compact settlements where Negroes would be "the *ruling element* of the body politic."[51] Suffrage in the United States, even were it granted, would provide no substitute, the address was quick to add, for it would be a "*privilege*" not a "*right*," and would not provide any access to power.[52] "The white race," the emigration convention concluded, "will only respect those who oppose their usurpation, and acknowledge as equals those who will not submit to their rule."[53]

To implement its dynamic program, the convention created a National Board of Commissioners to investigate the condition of blacks everywhere and to publicize its findings. A separate Foreign Commission was directed to explore possible areas for settle-

48. *Ibid.*, 24-27, 33-70. The latter pages constitute the official address.
49. Martin R. Delany, *Political Destiny of the Colored Race on the American Continent* (Address to the Colored Inhabitants of the United States, which was the official address of the Cleveland Emigration Convention), printed as an appendix in Rollin, *Delany*, quotations at 355, 336.
50. *Ibid.*, 346-347.
51. *Ibid.*, 333.
52. *Ibid.*, 329.
53. National Emigration Convention of Colored People, *Proceedings . . .1854*, 42.

ment.[54] But these projected activities, even though many were never carried out, only provided additional impetus for the unconverted to attack the whole idea. As soon as the convention adjourned, public gatherings and newspaper articles pounced upon its work. Many, who likened Delany's plan to that of the American Colonization Society, thought it would skim off enterprising free blacks who should stay at home to continue the struggle against slavery. Colonization, under any auspices, they asserted, would only prolong slavery in America.[55]

Most of the charges were familiar. But the one that emigrationists were neglecting the slaves deserved careful pondering, for the convention did seem to have turned its back on them by creating a sharp distinction between bondsmen and free. Like all other free black efforts to extend their freedom in the North, opposition to the fugitive slave law excepted, the emigration project promised little to slaves. The Cleveland convention recognized that fact and freely admitted its distance from them. "Let none be found to shield themselves behind the plea of our brother bondsmen in ignorance; that we know not *what* to do, nor *where* to go. We are no longer slaves, as were our fathers, but freemen; fully qualified to meet our oppressors in every relation which belongs to the elevation of man, the establishment, sustenance and perpetuity of a nation."[56] Furthermore, the contention of emigrationists that slavery would cease when blacks had created a separate nation because then whites would no longer dare enslave them did not convince many. It all sounded neatly automatic; but, as John Gaines of Cincinnati asked about Haiti, so others might ask of any new black nation: "What benefit is this to us? Has it abated one jot of prejudice? Has it removed one unholy law?" With a genuine

54. *Ibid.*, particularly Articles 6, 11, 13, and 14 of the Constitution of the National Board.
55. See, for example, *Frederick Douglass' Paper,* October 20, 1854, February 16, March 2, 1855, January 18, 1856, and *Provincial Freeman,* March 21, 1857, for protest meetings in Ohio, California, Illinois, New York, and Iowa.
56. National Emigration Convention of Colored People, *Proceedings . . . 1854,* 56.

awareness of realpolitik, he concluded that "a Negro Republic, on the coast of Africa, the Caribbee Islands, or South America, will never induce the haughty Saxon to respect us at home, unless it be a power physically as strong as Russia, and morally [as strong] as England or France."[57] Meanwhile, Frederick Douglass asserted, the emigration furor was only diverting attention from slavery and indefinitely postponing emancipation.[58]

But what, the emigrationists asked, were the likely alternatives? As a young Pittsburgher protested, the old ways had not worked. Twenty years before, his father's generation had exclaimed, "Here (in the United States) we were born—here will we live, by the help of the Almighty—and here we will die, and let our bones lie with our fathers." To cling to their wisdom would be to enshrine an anachronism. One might as well, he concluded, go back still further to the "creed of our grandfathers, in import like the following: Here (on Massa's plantation) we were born—here will we live, if Massa don't sell us—and here we will die, and let our bones lie with the rest of Massa's niggers."[59]

As proposals for mass emigration gained currency, so too did proposals for selective emigration. Delany stood out as the major spokesman for the former. For the latter Garnet was the leading proponent. Central to the ideas of the selective emigrationists was that of sending out Afro-Americans to develop Africa's economic potential. That vast continent, Garnet hoped, would become the frontier and safety valve for blacks which the American West was for whites. An early anticolonizationist, Garnet never gave up his belief that Negroes could win freedom, gain status, and achieve full citizenship in the United States.[60] But late in the 1840s he

57. *Frederick Douglass' Paper*, January 27, 1854.
58. Frederick Douglass to Benjamin Coates, April 17, 1856, in Foner, *Douglass*, 2:388.
59. *Frederick Douglass' Paper*, January 4, 1856.
60. Henry Highland Garnet, *The Past and Present Condition and the Destiny of the Colored Race* . . . (Troy: J. C. Kneeland and Co., 1848), *passim*.

modified his earlier opposition to all colonization and fashioned an approach to emigration which would extend the opportunities of talented young blacks without contravening civil rights activity in the United States. Long an advocate of migration westward, Garnet wrote Douglass in January 1849 that the frontier, free of Eastern aristocracy and decadence, offered Negroes a chance to make their mark. Then he added that non-American areas might also perform the same function.[61] Indeed, even Liberia might serve as a base from which Afro-Americans could aid Africa in "a commercial and a political" way.[62]

Although Garnet by now countenanced the work of the American Colonization Society—for he "would rather see a man free in Liberia, than a slave in the United States"[63]—he did not endorse the Society's preference for massive emigration. As he understood it, his own ideas were much more precise. Drawing upon his experience with the American free produce movement, Garnet thought that a carefully nurtured economic development in Africa would effectively end the slave trade. Growing and selling free labor cotton from Africa would not only make fortunes for young black entrepreneurs but supply the European market so well that Americans would be forced by economic self-interest to end slavery. These hopes were buttressed by his 1850 lecture tour for the English free produce movement which exposed him to the African Aid Society, established a decade earlier by Thomas Folwell Buxton to further Anglo-African economic growth and to christianize and westernize Africans. Already a free labor enthusiast and a clergyman as well, Garnet was readily influenced by Buxton's plan and made much of it his own.[64]

61. *North Star*, January 26, 1849.

62. Henry H. Garnet to Samuel R. Ward, February 10, 1849, in *North Star*, March 2, 1849.

63. Henry H. Garnet to Frederick Douglass, January 21, 1848[9], in *North Star*, January 26, 1849.

64. Richard K. McMaster, "Dr. Martin Delany, the Rev. Henry Highland Garnet, and the African Civilization Society, 1856-1861," a paper delivered to the Association for the Study of Negro Life and History, Baltimore, 1966, mimeographed copy, 5. *African Repository*, March 15, 1840. *American and*

The forces of religion and economic advancement, coupled with constant interest in the history and culture of Africa as a source of race pride, drew Garnet irresistibly to the new emigration. He was further convinced by his sojourn in Jamaica, from 1852 to 1855, where he carefully observed the free labor cultivation of semi-tropical crops.[65] In a variety of ways, therefore, he was won to the potential of selective emigration. Consequently in 1858, when the African Civilization Society was organized, Garnet was one of its principal supporters.

The new society differed from Delany's movement in several ways. It was a biracial group with relatively few black members. It eschewed mass emigration in favor of carefully planned economic development and missionary activity in Africa. For Garnet it represented not the only solution for black Americans, but one of several options. "Let those who wished to stay, stay here—and those who had enterprise and wished to go, go and found a nation, if possible, of which the colored Americans could be proud," the New York *Tribune* reported him saying in the summer of 1858.[66] There must be no coercion, and only those who would help Africa as well as themselves should go. Most American Negroes, Garnet thought, would stay where they were and achieve full freedom and equality, while an enterprising and talented few would migrate to Africa to farm, trade, and preach. As a result of it all, Africa would once again be great.

The African Civilization Society offered Garnet much of the machinery needed to pursue his goals. By exercising vigilance and care, the settlers it sponsored could end the slave trade and curtail slavery. By enterprise and the use of American techniques, they could insure Africa's economic growth. By pursuing rigorously the society's program of white-financed but black-implemented

Foreign Anti-Slavery Reporter, I (January, 1841), 110-111. Howard R. Temperley, "The British and Foreign Anti-Slavery Society, 1839-1868," (Ph.D. Yale University, 1960), 243.

65. During his stay in Jamaica, he encouraged emigration there. See his open letter in *Frederick Douglass' Paper*, September 2, 1853.

66. New York *Daily Tribune*, August 11, 1858.

evangelization, they could make of Africa a Christian community. "Thus the preaching of Christ, and the introduction of Christian civilization and lawful commerce," wrote the society's directors, "will elevate the nations of Africa, and also afford a sphere for the development of Christian zeal and commercial activity among the educated men of color in the United States, thus aiding the work of elevation HERE, which is so imperatively necessary."[67]

The Achilles heel of the African Civilization Society was its dependence on whites, who provided the bulk of its funding. Most active among them was Benjamin Coates of Philadelphia, a Quaker philanthropist and businessman long associated with the American Colonization Society. Accordingly many blacks thought the new society was only a mask for the hated older one.[68] Therefore whatever it gained in support among clerics drawn by its missionary dimension,[69] it quickly lost in the denunciations of those who feared another white conspiracy to drive independent freemen into exile. Finally, those who opposed emigration of any kind rejected not only Garnet's, but Delany's program as well. George Downing, Charles Reason, Charles Remond, and, most persistently, Frederick Douglass among the leaders all fought the African Civilization Society;[70] they were supported by the rank and file in numerous meetings, particularly in New England.[71]

67. Henry H. Garnet and the Board of Directors to Dear Sir, 1859, an open letter from the African Civilization Society, AMA-ARC. The African Civilization Society is treated by Garnet in his speech at Cooper Union, March 1860, in *Weekly Anglo-African,* March 17, 1860; in McMaster, "Delany, Garnet and the African Civilization Society"; and in Howard Bell, ed., "Introduction," *Search for a Place, Black Separatism and Africa 1860* (Ann Arbor: University of Michigan Press, 1969), 14-16.

68. Garnet took great pains to deny any connection between the two societies. See *Weekly Anglo-African,* September 17, 1859. For Coates' role, see Benjamin Coates to Frederick Douglass, September 1, 1858, *Frederick Douglass' Paper,* September 17, 1858; and Coates to Alexander Crummell, April 14, 1862, Society Collection, Historical Society of Pennsylvania.

69. For a list of early supporters see William Herries to Douglass, June 27, 1859, in *Frederick Douglass' Paper,* July 8, 1859.

70. George T. Downing to William L. Garrison, April 5, 1860, G-BPL. *Liberator,* May 27, 1859. *Douglass Monthly,* February 1859. George T. Downing and Charles L. Reason to Gerrit Smith, March 25, 1860, S-SU.

71. Opposition meetings are reported widely in *Liberator, Weekly Anglo-African,* and *Douglass Monthly* during 1859-1860.

Nowhere was opposition more vicious or damaging, however, than at a meeting held in New York City's Zion Church on April 12, 1860. Speaking for the Society were Garnet and J. Sella Martin of Boston. Opposing them were George Downing and Charles Reason. From the beginning, the meeting went poorly for the emigrationists. In clashes over procedure, the election of officers, and other tangential issues, they were handily defeated. When the debate on substance began, Reason and Downing read anticolonizationist letters from abolitionists of every known stripe which explicitly attacked the Civilization Society and which, the opposition implied, implicitly linked it to the Colonization Society. Some called Garnet's organization a nefarious plot of the Republican party to rid the United States of Negroes. Vigorously protesting and ignoring the fifteen-minute limit for each speaker, Garnet tried to answer each point in turn. Before long decorum gave way to bitter ad hominem exchanges, each side charging the other with lying and slavishness. Eventually words were replaced by fists, and church officials threatened to turn out the lights if the meeting did not adjourn. It was, the *Weekly Anglo-African* reported, like a "lot of toads caught in a July shower"; or, as the *Liberator* noted, a veritable "representation of 'Donnybrook Fair.' " "Thus ended," the *Anglo-African* concluded laconically, "one of the most unsatisfactory and unhappy demonstrations ever made in this city, and fairly illustrated the truthfulness of the suggestion of one of our dailies, that there is much work here for a civilization society."[72]

Unwilling to let that fiasco stand, Martin and Garnet called a second meeting for April 16 and made sure that they controlled it. At the beginning of the meeting, held in the Metropolitan Assembly Rooms, Garnet spoke; then, according to the *Anglo-African* report, he threw the floor open to statements from the opposition. The controls had worked all too well, and there was none to counter him. So he spoke again for about an hour and then answered questions to everybody's satisfaction. Before the meeting

72. *Weekly Anglo-African*, April 21, 1860. *Liberator*, May 4, 1860.

adjourned, it adopted a resolution endorsing the African Civilization Society and its work. That there was no opposition at the second meeting George Downing explained with more than a touch of pique. Why should any opponents come forth? "What assurance had they of fairness in a meeting which they had reasons for believing was a packed meeting of rowdies, who would disregard all law, all decency, and every decent precedent?"[73]

Such meetings did nothing to further the work of the African Civilization Society or to meet the attacks made on it. Even so avid an early supporter as J. Sella Martin was turned off by them; and, although he still endorsed the goals of the society, he withdrew his active support. He explained his action on the grounds that England's Manchester cotton supply association was developing adequate African resources.[74] Yet it was probably the persistent rumors that the Civilization Society was a tool of the American Colonization Society and the constant bickering it produced which made him change his mind. Within the year even Garnet's enthusiasm cooled, and he turned his attention to Haitian, rather than African, emigration.

While the battle over the African Civilization Society raged, Delany was exploring the Niger River. What made him shift attention from eastern to western Africa is not clear, but it had occurred by August 1858 when a General Convention for the Promotion of the Interests of the Colored People of Canada and the United States met in Chatham, Canada, to implement the emigration program set forth four years earlier at Cleveland. They agreed to send out an exploring expedition under Delany's leadership in order to ascertain whether the Niger River valley was suited to permanent settlement by Afro-American emigrants.[75]

73. *Weekly Anglo-African*, April 28, 1860. Quotation, *ibid.*, May 26, 1860.

74. *Ibid.*, May 5, 1860.

75. *Liberator*, September 24, 1858. Chatham *Planet*, August 26, 1858. Delany, *Official Report*, 39, 43.

Of the large expedition originally planned only two men actually went—and they went separately.[76] Robert Campbell, a naturalist from Philadelphia, accepted aid from the African Civilization Society and set out at once on his own. Delany hastened to raise funds for himself, fearful that Campbell might take over the expedition completely. Finally he too was on his way and by July 1859 he was in Monrovia. There, in a public address, he reaffirmed his basic contention that blacks could not live in America with dignity. More than that, he announced that their hope lay in Africa rather than in the Western Hemisphere.

Yet hardly had he rehearsed the details of his emigration theory than he began to change his mind about it. Temporarily debilitated by a bout with fever and suffering from poor health, he stopped feuding with Campbell and joined his party. Together they explored Yoruba country and concluded treaties with the chiefs in Abbeokuta which allowed American Negroes to settle there. The treaty terms, reflecting the change in Delany's outlook, rested not on mass migration but on the select settlement of persons with specific skills and crafts needed to develop the area economically. Thus Delany had moved very close to the position of the African Civilization Society. By May 1860, after he had left Africa, he was ready to give it public, if limited, support.

In his official report of the expedition, written in the spring of 1860, Delany elaborated his new position. He had pledged to the Yoruba leaders that "no heterogeneous nor promiscuous 'masses' or companies, but select and intelligent people of high moral as well as religious character" would be "induced to go out."[77] And already Delany, who was then traveling in England, was planning the first such group with William King, white leader of the Canadian Elgin community. The Scottish Presbyterian minister was in Britain at the time, raising funds and generally assisting Elgin settlers who planned to settle in Africa. He already had the support

76. The African venture can be followed in *Weekly Anglo-African*, October 1, 1859, and February 11, April 21, and June 30, 1860. Also Bell, ed., "Introduction," *Search for a Place*, 1-22.
77. Delany, *Official Report*, 77.

of the African Aid Society and shortly agreed with Delany that the latter would lead the Elgin group out to Yoruba country.[78]

These plans as well as his official report brought Delany even closer to the African Civilization Society and its English counterpart, the African Aid Society. He stressed the benefits of cultivating free labor cotton to sell to Great Britain; of introducing Christianity to Africa and thereby curtailing the slave trade; and of fostering commerce and manufacture for the economic benefit of Africans and Afro-American entrepreneurs alike. Then, when he returned to the United States, Delany officially joined forces with the Civilization group. Immediately he was endorsed as leader for the Elgin emigrants. And when the society reorganized in November 1861 to allow blacks a larger voice, Delany became one of its vice-presidents.[79]

The organizational rapprochement, however, accomplished little in furthering African emigration. Both the Delany and the Garnet strands had lost momentum by 1861; more importantly, the Civil War had refocused attention on working in America to end slavery and gain civil equality. But even in wartime, interest in Caribbean and Central American settlement did survive. Partly it was logistics which made emigration within the Western Hemisphere seem more feasible. Partly it was the support it enjoyed from prominent whites. Several years earlier, in 1858, Congressman Frank P. Blair had presented a plan for Central American emigration to the House of Representatives,[80] and many black emigrationists supported it.

78. William King, "Autobiography," MS, King Papers, Public Archives of Canada, 416-419.

79. Delany, *Official Report,* 111-119. African Civilization Society, *Constitution of the . . . ; Together with the Testimony of Forty Distinguished Citizens of New York and Brooklyn, to the Importance of the Objects Contemplated by its Friends . . .* (New Haven: Thomas J. Stafford, Printer, 1861), 7-8. Alfred I. Churchill to William King, March 9, 1861, King Papers, Public Archives of Canada. Churchill to London *Daily News,* March 16, 1861, in Chatham *Planet,* April 11, 1861. African Civilization Society, *Constitution,* 1-6.

80. Frank P. Blair, *Speech of Hon. Frank P. Blair, Jr., of Missouri on the Acquisition of Territory in Central and South America, to be Colonized with Free Blacks, and Held as a Dependency by the United States. Delivered in the House of Representatives, on the 14th Day of January,*

James M. Whitfield of Buffalo, who had favored emigration for twenty years, was apparently encouraged by Blair to investigate settlement possibilities in Central America, which he did in 1859. James Theodore Holly, long an advocate of Haitian emigration, sought to incorporate Blair's thinking in his own. In a long letter to the congressman, Holly, who in 1854 had been charged with investigating Haiti for the Cleveland Emigration Convention, detailed his conclusions. Because Haiti had had a legitimate revolution and possessed its own government, albeit a monarchy, it was the best place to create a "negro nationality" capable of guaranteeing American blacks both political rights and social acceptance. In turn, a settlement there of skilled workers and professionals from the United States would bring the island a flourishing middle class capable of elevating settlers and natives alike.[81]

Increasingly Haiti was the focus for emigrationist sentiment. When Delany's treaty for land in the Niger Valley was wiped out by warfare among the Yorubas, the Caribbean island seemed for many emigrationists the most likely spot. William J. Watkins,

---

1858 . . . (Washington: Buell and Blanchard, 1858). Blair's idea was not new. Thoughout the 1840s and early 1850s blacks had discussed the pros and cons of emigration to the British West Indies, made free by emancipation in the 1830s. References to such projects appear in the *North Star, Voice of the Fugitive,* and particularly for the early period in the *Colored American.* For a specific Canadian illustration see Toronto *Globe,* December 10, 1859.

81. James T. Holly to Frank P. Blair, January 30, 1858, from Frank P. Blair, "An Address Delivered Before the Mercantile Library Association of Boston, Massachusetts, January 26, 1859," reprinted in "Letters to Anti-Slavery Workers and Agencies, by Negro Writers," *Journal of Negro History,* X (October, 1925), 758-768. Howard H. Bell, "Negro Nationalism: A Factor in Emigration Projects, 1858-1861," *Journal of Negro History,* XLVII (January, 1962), 45-48. Joan R. Sherman, "James Monroe Whitfield, Poet and Emigrationist: A Voice of Protest and Dissent," *Journal of Negro History,* LVII (January 1972), 173-175. James Theodore Holly, *A Vindication of the Capacity of the Negro Race for Self-Government, and Civilized Progress, as Demonstrated by Historical Events of the Haytian Revolution; and Subsequent Acts of that People Since their National Independence* (orig. ed. 1857. In Howard H. Bell, ed. *Black Separatism and the Caribbean 1860,* by James Theodore Holly and J. Dennis Harris. Ann Arbor: University of Michigan Press, 1970), 24-25, 64-66, quotation on 64. *Anglo-African Magazine,* I (September 1859), 300, and I (October 1859), 327-329.

briefly an assistant to Douglass, threw his support to Holly's plans and, it was reported, nearly converted Douglass. William Wells Brown, J. D. Harris, an Ohio emigrationist, and Garnet all voiced their approval. Actual emigration began in 1861 when Holly led a band of fifty Philadelphians to the Caribbean country. How many others joined him is uncertain, but the settlement did not thrive. Although Holly himself stayed on and eventually became the island's Episcopal bishop, most of his fellows found the island physically disastrous and economically ruinous. Few of them were farmers and Haiti had little employment for the skilled workers Holly had convinced to accompany him.[82]

In both the Caribbean and Africa, the dream of creating a new black nationality failed. Weakened by the distress of settlers in Haiti, African warfare, dissension among rival leaders, sparse and tepid support, and organizational and logistical difficulties, it fell final victim to President Lincoln's attempt to link emancipation with compulsory colonization in a disastrous experimental settlement in Central America.

In a moment of utter despair in 1862 the Colored Men of Philadelphia addressed a plea to Lincoln. Appalled by his Chiriqui colonization scheme, they laid their fears and sense of injustice before him. "Many of us in Pennsylvania, have our own houses, and other property, amounting, in the aggregate, to millions of dollars. Shall we sacrifice this, leave our homes, foresake our birthplace, and flee to a strange land, to appease the anger and prejudice of the traitors now in arms against the Government . . . ?"[83]

82. Bell, ed., "Introduction," *Black Separatism,* 4-6. William E. Farrison, *William Wells Brown, Author and Reformer* (Chicago: University of Chicago Press, 1969), 334-336. *Douglass Monthly,* January, 1861. Robert A. Warner, *New Haven Negroes, A Social History* (New Haven: Yale University Press, 1940), 109. Bell, ed. "Introduction," *Black Separatism,* 7-8.

83. "An Appeal from the Colored Men of Philadelphia to the President of the United States" (1862), in Herbert Aptheker, *A Documentary History of the Negro People in the United States* (2 vols. New York: Citadel Press,

Then, propelled by the pressures of war and foreign policy, conscious of the failure of colonization, and driven by antislavery hounding, the President reversed his course. On New Year's Day in 1863 it seemed for a moment that black America had at last begun to win.

1951, 1969), 1:474. For anticolonizationist sentiment during the Civil War see James M. McPherson, "Abolitionist and Negro Opposition to Colonization During the Civil War," *Phylon*, XXVI (1965), 391-399.

PART V

Some Assessments

THE DEGREE to which any movement succeeds or fails depends on its strategy and tactics, its leaders and participants, and the time and context in which it exists. No one or two factors alone can account for its course.

13. WHO WOULD BE FREE

FOR OVER thirty years free blacks in the North worked to end slavery and to gain equal rights and opportunities for themselves. Like their white antislavery colleagues, they employed various means to achieve their goals. Some early Garrisonians followed the *Liberator* editor throughout the following decades while others, dismayed at his opposition to church and state, in 1840 followed white moderates into new antislavery societies and the Liberty party. Some like Charles Remond and William Wells Brown continued to work primarily in white organizations throughout the 1850s, but most gave their major efforts in the 1840s and 1850s to distinctive race activity. Moreover, like many white abolitionists, most blacks readily changed affiliation and techniques of action as occasion demanded. Thus, though their ultimate goals remained relatively constant, their activity at any given time was shaped by pragmatic considerations not only of present needs and possibilities but of what had and had not worked in the past. To attempt to type individuals or groups, except at a particular moment, is to impose a stasis and structure which, with rare exceptions, existed in neither white nor black abolitionism. Whether one was a Garrisonian or not in 1840 was essentially irrelevant in the 1850s when the issues had changed from the nature and possibilities of reform to the wisdom and likelihood of revolt and emigration.

Indeed, the immediacy of their concern for civil rights as well as their pragmatic involvement with slavery made the need for visible results a more crushing burden for black than for white abolitionists. As they struggled against constant and overwhelming odds, they measured victory by a slight gain here, a perceptible lessening of discrimination there. In organizing their efforts, they forged a sense of community and established institutions conducive to their welfare. Yet success demanded more than a coherent collective experience. Blacks also had to sway white Americans, who controlled political and economic power, and who had numerical superiority.

Much of their effort went to education. On their own or with the aid of white philanthropy and government subsidy, they established a number of primary and secondary schools. Although they achieved some significant changes, these efforts produced no overall pattern of educational equity. Except for Ohio, no Western state provided public funds for black schools; elsewhere the facilities provided at public expense ranged from quite good to totally inadequate. In higher education their efforts to establish advanced academic or vocational institutions were almost uniformly defeated.

Even so, many Northern Negro children did receive an education of sorts. Though schooling was largely in segregated institutions, some areas with both a small black population and a concentration of white antislavery sentiment allowed all children to attend the common schools. Moreover, some attempts to integrate schools succeeded. The petitions and boycotts of Boston blacks forced change in a state where widespread abolitionist concern finally made government officials receptive to desegregation. In Rochester black pressure and white awareness that segregated schools were disproportionately expensive produced integration in city schools. Elsewhere, as in most Massachusetts towns outside of Boston, integration occurred largely by a process of chance or accident. Nonetheless, in 1860 it was still true that the prevailing pattern in the East was segregation and in the West, an absence even of separate schools.

Agitation to end other forms of legal discrimination also met with modest success. Massachusetts repealed its antimiscegenation law, though primarily in response to pressure from antislavery whites. More in response to black pressure, Jim Crow railroad facilities, never provided for in Massachusetts law, were gradually abandoned in the state in the 1840s. In New York City at least one test case against segregated streetcars was won in the 1850s, though de facto segregation continued. Of more sweeping impact, Ohio partially repealed its Black Code in 1849, though that was less a response to Negro protest than to political juggling among white Whigs, Democrats, and Free Soilers.[1] In Rhode Island blacks won the franchise by throwing their badly needed support to the conservative faction during the Dorr War. Yet the transitory nature of the power gained by the vote was demonstrated in the 1850s when they were unable to force an end to segregated schooling in the state.

Wherever black abolitionists made these modest achievements they affected only the free Northern population—yet a major part of their goal was to end Southern slavery. Geographically remote from it and with no grasp on Southern consciences or government, they had to rely on indirect pressure. Their constant and dramatic resistance to the fugitive slave law, especially after 1850, comprised such action and was, in fact, the most effective part of the movement for civil rights and freedom. Although successful resistance sometimes took the form of legal appeal and court challenge, its most stirring forms were illegal and defiant slave rescues frequently aided by the underground railroad and by occasional violence. These rescues made mockery of the national commitment to defend slave property, which the 1850 Fugitive Slave Law enshrined. Consequently, even though most fugitives apprehended were in fact returned to their owners, the security that the compromise of 1850 promised the South was gravely eroded, especially as Northern white opinion increasingly encouraged defiance.

Here, as in other areas, achievement was not unalloyed, for it may well be that the individual freedom promised by successful escape lured potential insurrectionary leaders from the South. Alexander Crummell was sure that Garnet, for one, would have led an uprising had he not fled slavery as a young boy.[2] Less specific

1. See Allan Peskins' comment in his edition of the *Autobiography of John Malvin*, reprinted under the title *North Into Freedom. The Autobiography of John Malvin, Free Negro, 1795-1880* (Cleveland: Press of Case Western Reserve University, 1966), 66, note 7.

2. Alexander Crummell, *Africa and America: Addresses and Discourses* (Springfield, Mass.: Willey and Co., 1891), 298.

allusions as well as the militance of other fugitives suggest that Garnet was not alone in this potential.

Yet despite the limitations under which they constantly worked and the qualifications with which all their accomplishments seem laden, the very real successes which black abolitionists had are not to be gainsaid. Pressing always against slavery and for meaningful freedom, they wrenchèd modest improvements from a reluctant society during the antebellum years. In doing so they also created a variety of organizations and institutions. A fair number of blacks found needed coherence and direction in the general antislavery movement. Others looked to the black press, which led a persistent if sporadic existence throughout the antebellum period. Increasingly the activists organized race conventions and established exclusive associations, local, state, and national, to achieve freedom and equality.

The ways proposed to achieve these goals sparked constant internal controversy, perhaps because the goals were so broad and all-encompassing. Fierce debate was not, to be sure, confined to black abolition. The white antislavery movement was constantly torn by controversy as well. Yet the purpose of the white movement was, compared with the black, narrowly defined. White abolitionists would eliminate slavery and free the bondsmen.[3] For blacks, however, the issue was more complex. What whites saw as a single and unified goal, blacks perceived as a diverse and multiple spectrum. Although ending slavery was a central concern, achieving freedom did not stop there. Every child sent to school, every youth learning a trade, every adult getting a job, or voting, or serving on a jury, every right extended or opportunity fulfilled was part of the long continuum toward complete freedom. Black abolitionists consequently chose to act in a variety of spheres and in many ways, both in the North and the South. White antislavery activity,

3. White antislavery, particularly in its Garrisonian wing, embraced multi-reformism and might therefore be considered a very broad movement indeed. While this very engagement in various causes effectively created tensions and cleavages, it is also true that, if one considers the ending of slavery as the central issue, white abolition was, compared with black, much more singularly focused on a precise goal.

on the contrary, was directed more precisely to the distant South, where accomplishment was still more elusive than in Northern civil rights efforts.

The diversity and pragmatism that gave the black movement so much of its strength also saddled it with ever-nagging questions of priorities. At one point Samuel Cornish advised blacks to work primarily for civil rights and leave the antislavery fight to the abolition societies. But embedded in his advice was the danger that individuals and groups would, as he later put it, "Take care of Number One" and neglect broader race aims.[4] Charles Remond shared these misgivings, and attributed the slow progress in desegregating Boston's schools in the 1850s to black unwillingness to participate in general antislavery work.[5] Frederick Douglass was still sharper in his criticism. Addressing an 1848 convention, he bluntly asserted that free Negroes in the North "cared very little about the fettered bondman, and less about their own elevation and improvement."[6] Furthermore, most black leaders believed that action close to home had a better chance of visible and immediate results than simply opposing an institution they could not directly confront.

That this choice did not set them so far apart from the general antislavery movement the frustration of white abolitionists in the 1850s attests. After more than twenty years of constant effort they had had virtually no direct effect upon the peculiar institution at the South. Their papers were unread, their lectures were unheard, their moral suasion was unfelt. Slavery seemed as firmly entrenched in 1860 as it had been in 1830. Yet there was more to it than that. Partisan victories and visible changes in social institutions were not the only measures of success. Judged by the extent to which the antislavery crusade reshaped the national mood and remolded available alternatives in the 1850s, the assessment is very different.

4. *Colored American*, January 27, 1838.
5. *Liberator*, December 14, 1849.
6. *North Star*, September 9, 1848.

Much of that reshaping and remolding was done by blacks, not so much by their work as antislavery agents and lecturers, though that was important, but by their widespread resistance to the fugitive slave law. In either case, those who contributed most to the general antislavery impulse were avowedly and openly fugitives because their testimony and action convinced Northern whites that slaves sought and could handle freedom. Those who were born free or who had never even lived in the South, though they too participated in abolition societies and slave rescue attempts, were most active and effective in the Northern struggle for civil rights, focusing on that part of the spectrum of liberty which they had not yet realized. Where individuals found themselves on the continuum of freedom and how they understood its meaning was, in short, the most important single fact shaping the black crusade in the antebellum North.[7]

Not only did Northern blacks have to choose where to concentrate their energies, they had also to consider how best to expend them. That they who would be free must strike the blow was common enough as adage, but the question remained whether they should strike alone or in concert with sympathetic whites.

7. Limited biographical information on a number of those active in antislavery and other civil rights activities makes a statistically significant analysis of black leaders hazardous. Of some seventy-five men and women on whose roles this book has touched and about whom information beyond their antislavery and civil rights activity is available, at least eighteen had been slaves and forty-four had fairly definitely not been so, with no reasonable information for the rest. Of those we know to have been slaves, three were freed from slavery in Northern states by emancipation and two had lived in de facto freedom from childhood when they escaped the upper South with their parents. Some of those whose freedom from birth we have no reason to question may well have been slaves and have found it strategic or prestigious not to have admitted that status. Theodore Hershberg, in a paper delivered at the Conference on Comparative Systems of Slavery, University of Rochester, March 9-11, 1972, suggests that in Philadelphia being freeborn and mulatto were the statistically predominant factors in membership and leadership in abolitionists, civil rights, and improvement societies, but also that these societies had a higher proportion of ex-slaves as members (11.5%) and officers than did literary and sport societies. Unhappily the Philadelphia Social History Project, whose computerized analysis of federal and city censuses and society memberships has generated Hershberg's information and analysis, is unique and there is no comparable information for other cities to test whether his findings would hold true elsewhere.

Would action through exclusive race organizations be more or less effective than working with predominately white groups? Those who chose the separate path—and their numbers increased over the years—contended that Negroes had special needs that they alone could meet. By working on their own they intended to demonstrate their capacity and thus change white attitudes. Thirty years of labor, however, gave the lie to that hypothesis, for whites continued to disfranchise, segregate, and otherwise deny civil rights to them.

Those thirty years also proved that apathy among blacks remained a constant problem. Newspapers, books, pamphlets, conventions, local gatherings, and private exhortation notwithstanding, race leaders were tormented by the small numbers who responded to their pleas for action of whatever sort.[8] Frequently their impatience boiled over in public and drove them to probe the reasons for apathy. "The cause of suspension" of the *Colored American*, Charles Ray charged in 1840, explaining its poor circulation, "is, primarily, 'the mental enslavement of the entire free colored population. . . .' "[9] Charles Remond blamed the persistence of apathy on a faulty sense of family obligation. Parents should be driven by concern for their children's future to work in the antislavery cause.[10] George Downing thought that indifference was bred by the ignorance of blacks "as to their [own] interest."[11] Whatever the causes, leaders lamented their paucity of followers. Garnet, Ward, Watkins, and Douglass[12] had all recognized the frustration which J. Sella Martin summed up in 1861. "We are not even alive to the promises of this war," he

8. The multiple effects of this apathy were set forth in the complaint of the Executive Board of the Ohio State Anti-Slavery Society, which noted in 1860 that local and county auxiliaries were dormant, that funds were scarce, that agents and lecturers were a mixed lot of the diligent and the apathetic, that fund-raising produced minimal returns, and that even the Executive Board found it hard to muster a quorum for its meetings. Ohio State Anti-Slavery Society, *Proceedings of the First Annual Meeting . . . 1860*, 5-8.

9. *Liberator*, January 3, 1840.

10. *Ibid.*, October 23, 1840.

11. George T. Downing to William L. Garrison, October 3, 1859, G-BPL.

12. See, for example, *North Star*, April 13, 1849. *Impartial Citizen*, May 31, 1851. *Liberator*, December 5, 1851. Foner, *Douglass*, 2:435.

fumed, "and it does seem that in peace or war we constantly alternate between the two points of social and political paralysis— from the apathy of indifference, to the apathy of despair."[13]

Haunted by the syndrome of paralysis, various spokesmen tangled with the problems of being leaders without followers. James McCune Smith was acutely aware of the chasm which separated the two. Bluntly asserting that there were no race leaders because there were no followers, he blamed the fact on a preference for white leadership. Just as Negroes patronized white businessmen and professionals rather than black, so they looked to white spokesmen on political and social issues. Feeling the futility of his own efforts, Smith sympathized with others who sought to serve the race.

> If we have no "leaders" among the colored people, by what term are we to distinguish the colored men who assemble in conventions, write addresses, pass first rate resolutions, &c., &c., for the elevation of "our people"? These men, who are, or have been—for some have passed away—men of public spirit, earnest for the general good and zealous for the advancement of the down-trodden, men willing to spend and be spent; but, alas! they have never had the masses to support them, nor even to give an approving cheer of God's-speed to their well meant efforts: so far from being leaders of the people, they are "like unto children sitting in the markets, and calling unto their fellows and saying, 'We have piped unto you, and ye have not danced; we have mourned unto you, and ye have not lamented.' "[14]

Why were these men unheard? Part of the answer may lie simply in who they were. Overwhelmingly they were free men. Considerably fewer than one-third of them, probably, had experienced slavery, although some of the most dynamic had

13. *Douglass Monthly,* June, 1861.
14. *Frederick Douglass' Paper,* September 21, 1855.

indeed been slaves. Predominantly they were urban, a characteristic they shared with most Northern blacks. Yet their provenance did not reflect directly the density of black population concentration.[15] Philadelphia, which in 1860 had, with its surrounding area, the largest urban black population in the North, contributed relatively few leaders after the early days of protest activity, and those first spokesmen were often men of considerable wealth and substance. James Forten was a prosperous sailmaker; Robert Purvis, the son of a Charleston, South Carolina merchant, was independently wealthy; William Whipper and Stephen Smith ran a flourishing lumber yard in nearby Columbia; and Abram Shadd was a substantial landowner in neighboring Chester county. The subsequent failure of the city to generate leaders in proportion to its population may well have lain in the declining economic position of its black community.[16]

New York, with scarcely more than half the black population of Philadelphia, generated at least twice as many leaders—a proportion which also holds when the respective parameters are extended to include all of Pennsylvania and New York State. In New York, early leadership was drawn heavily from the professions—which continued to furnish new spokesmen throughout the antebellum period. Perhaps because of the clerical tone of early abolitionism in New York City, ministers there were more visible as activists than they commonly were elsewhere.[17] In the early years Peter Williams, Theodore Wright, and Samuel Cornish stood out; they were later joined by Henry Garnet, Alexander Crummell, Charles Ray, Samuel Ward, and Jarmain Loguen. From other professions came Thomas Jinnings, dentist; James McCune Smith, physician and

15. For black population see Wilbur Zelinsky, "The Population Geography of the Free Negro in *Ante-Bellum* America," *Population Studies,* III (1949-1950), 398.

16. Theodore Hershberg, "Free Blacks in Antebellum Philadelphia: A Study of Ex-Slaves, Freeborn, and Socioeconomic Decline," *Journal of Social History,* V (Winter, 1971-1972), 183-209.

17. The clerical pattern tended also to be true in Connecticut, whose leaders were closely allied with the New York syndrome. Of twenty-one activist clerics, twelve operated in New York State and Connecticut, including James Pennington and both Bemans from the latter.

druggist; George Vashon, lawyer; and teachers William Allen and Charles Reason. Furthermore the concentration of the black press in the state gave scope to those who served as its editors and publishers—among them Cornish, Ward, Douglass, Van Rensselaer, Garnet, Ray, Myers, and Bell. In addition to professional outlets, New York offered scope for political activity with its black middle class access to the ballot and a Liberty party more flourishing and enduring than elsewhere. In sum, a heavy supply of professionals and a variety of outlets for black abolitionism encouraged in New York a high proportion of visible leaders.

In Boston, the other major Eastern center of black activism, the Negro population in 1860 was less than one-fifth that of New York City. Yet there, more than in New York or Philadelphia, a large proportion of individuals participated visibly in antislavery work. The dominance of Garrison and his *Liberator,* the relocation there after 1843 of the American Anti-Slavery Society central office, and strong abolitionist sentiment in the state all contributed to this phenomenon. Massachusetts Negroes lived and worked in a peculiarly sympathetic environment. Furthermore they had almost full civil rights, including the suffrage and access to public education funds. These external circumstances shaped a peculiar pattern of leadership. Very few were ministers—doubtless a reflection of Garrisonian anticlericalism—although in the early days Samuel Snowden was prominent and later Leonard Grimes and J. Sella Martin were important spokesmen. Other professions were also represented: lawyer Robert Morris; dentist and lawyer John Rock; and clerk-copyist William Nell. Many leaders in the Boston area, however, were small businessmen engaging in personal service, especially barbering, or in selling secondhand clothing and furniture and were, in consequence, close to their constituencies in education and everyday contact. Charles Remond and John Barbadoes were both barbers; David Walker was a clothes dealer; John T. Hilton, a used furniture dealer; and Lewis Hayden, a general trader.

In the West, patterns were not so clear. In Ohio, while the black population was most concentrated in Cincinnati, leadership was widely dispersed in Cincinnati, Cleveland, Columbus, and Oberlin.

On occasion Pittsburgh too acted as part of the Ohio syndrome. Farther west there were centers of activity in Chicago and Detroit. In the West leaders were also frequently professionals though it may be significant that some of them had started their lives as barbers or purveyors of personal service. In Pittsburgh Martin Delany was a physician and Lewis Woodson, a clergyman. In Oberlin was lawyer John M. Langston, and in Columbus, his brother Charles, a teacher. Peter Clark taught school in Cincinnati, William Monroe preached in Detroit, William Day edited a newspaper in Cleveland, and on the West Coast, Jeremiah Sanderson both preached and taught in Sacramento. Outstanding among businessmen activists were John B. Vashon, barber and bathhouse operator, in Pittsburgh; and William Lambert, a tailor and clothes-cleaner in Detroit.

By contrast, most Negroes in the North did unskilled, menial, or domestic work, usually for whites, and were thus widely separated, socially and economically, from their would-be leaders. The latter were the elite of the black community and constituted an early version of a black bourgeoisie. Because of their differences in economic security, education, and relative independence from white control, they frequently failed to understand the moods, needs, and life-style of their would-be followers. Critical of devices which the rank and file used to survive in hostile surroundings with limited resources and unpredictable futures, the leaders often seemed paternalistic and overbearing. Ex-slave Frederick Douglass, addressing a Cincinnati audience in 1854, spoke of "the faults of the colored race—of their clannishness—of their desire to live together in one street, and of their fondness for getting too many in one house, also of their improvidence, [for] they desired to harvest their corn as soon as they had planted it, to receive a reward for their labor before it was done."[18] Freeborn Samuel Cornish, associating lower-class behavior patterns with "slavish origin," editorialized on the nature of Negro shortcomings. "We are harsh, coarse and uncouth in our manners; we are deficient in

18. *Frederick Douglass' Paper*, May 5, 1854.

refinement and good taste; we are crude and boorish in our social intercourse; we are low and vulgar in our religious ideas and our religious actions; we convert a religious meeting into a very Babel, men and women sometimes acting in any other manner than genteelly, and our preachers encourage it. . . ."[19]

Martin Delany, sharing with Douglass and Cornish both a life experience of having risen from extreme poverty to relatively prosperous respectability and an intellectual commitment that the race must do likewise, chastised the masses for taking domestic jobs and doing menial work. So concerned was he with upward social and economic mobility that he overlooked the simple need to survive and admonished Negroes to refuse all work which promised no chance to rise. Seldom did those on the bottom rungs reply, but a J. D. Patterson did speak their sentiments. A waiter, Patterson was appalled at hearing Delany say "he would rather receive a telegraphic dispatch that his wife and two children had fallen victims to a loathesome disease, then [sic] to hear that they had become servants of any man—[and] he thought that he must speak." How dared leaders who were "not in places of survants [sic] . . . cast slurs upon those, who were in such places from necessity?" What told most was that Delany, when he replied to Patterson, assumed that since he was so articulate, he must be a clergyman or theological student.[20]

Despite such insensitivity, there was also a current of awareness among the leaders about the gap which separated them from the masses. Replying to an article by James McCune Smith in *Frederick Douglass' Paper*, Brooklyn's William Wilson resented Smith's uses of obscure literary references. "Belonging, as I do, to the toiling masses, I have no back office with cushioned chairs, nor idle time for readings of that sort."[21] Garnet, also of the articulate elite, took both Smith and the Rev. John Gloucester to task for their unconcern and snobbery. They not only reveled in conspicuous consumption, but held themselves apart from the persons and

19. *Impartial Citizen*, June 28, 1851.
20. *North Star*, September 29, 1848.
21. *Frederick Douglass' Paper*, January 26, 1855.

economic needs of other Negroes. Gloucester, who owned considerable real estate in New York City, refused to employ black carpenters to build the houses which he then refused to rent to black tenants. Likewise Smith lived in a large mansion on Sixth Avenue built by white labor and wore clothes made by white tailors and hatters and would go to a white barber, Garnet charged, could he find one who would shave him.[22]

If Wilson's and Garnet's castigations seem peevish as well as perceptive, they reflect still another attitude which deprived leaders of followers. They were frequently suspicious of each other's motives and spent much time and energy in fruitless bickering. Chief among their concerns was that others were using the cause to advance themselves. Mere circumstances gave substance to the charges, for even the elite could ill-afford the lost business or salary which devoting so much time, money, and energy to antislavery or civil rights campaigning involved. Many therefore willingly took fees, sought profit from their writings, or gave other evidence of making money from their activism. Moreover, the prestige and recognition which taking prominent roles as race leaders involved were of great importance because blacks were excluded by white prejudice from most other avenues for the exercise of power. Overbearing and grasping as they may have been at times, their behavior was doubtless as much a result of frustration as of arrogance or greed.

Nonetheless leaders' "number-oneish-ness" constituted an ever-festering sore on the body militant. In 1840 the *Colored American* leveled charges of venality against David Ruggles' conduct on the New York Vigilance Committee.[23] When Jarmain Loguen took fees for registering the deeds of recipients of Gerrit Smith's land grants, Samuel Ward charged him with making a profit on philanthropy.[24] When Ward and Garnet failed to appear at

22. *Weekly Afro-African,* January 19, 1861. Jarmain Loguen was a notable exception to this pattern. Not only did he work with the poor and with prisoners in his Syracuse-Auburn mission field, but he seems to have preferred it. See his letter to George Whipple, March 21, 1851, AMA-ARC.

23. *Colored American,* September 12, 1840.

24. *Voice of the Fugitive,* July 29, 1852. Loguen denied the charge in a letter to editor Henry Bibb, August 13, 1852, *ibid.,* September 9, 1852.

Buffalo's celebration of West Indian Emancipation in 1849, their disappointed hosts charged that they had been lured by lucre to break the engagement and speak elsewhere. In 1852 Robert Purvis charged that Douglass' motive in breaking with Garrison had been to seize power and primacy in the antislavery movement.[25] Five years later Purvis elaborated the charge that lack of principle and "basest selfishness" motivated all Negroes who attacked Garrisonianism. "They value anti-slavery not for what it is in itself, or for what it is doing for the slave," he concluded, "but for what it does or fails to do for themselves personally."[26] And from the emigrationist camp came similar aspersions in 1854 charging integrationist leaders with devising schemes to benefit themselves rather than the race.[27]

Often these charges led to bitter and prolonged personal feuding well removed from the original issue. Cornish charged Ruggles with being "reckless of principle," and Ruggles branded him a "land speculator" in turn.[28] Douglass and Garnet, who fell out in the middle 1840s over issues like supporting slave insurrections and initiating a black press, had descended to personal insult by 1850. Douglass was, Garnet charged, inordinately "ambitious of fame."[29] Douglass thereupon questioned Garnet's honesty and Christian character, and noted his innate viciousness.[30] In Canada, in the 1850s, Henry Bibb and Samuel Ward both cried foul while reporting the other's dishonesty and inefficiency in aiding fugitives; and Bibb's *Voice of the Fugitive* and Ward's *Provincial Freeman* publicized the charges. Similarly the *Liberator* and *Frederick Douglass' Paper* were used to air the piques of Garrisonians Nell, Purvis, Remond, and Brown on the one hand and Douglass on the other. Finally, at the end of the 1850s, there was the bruising exchange over selling out, packing meetings, and the like which

25. *North Star,* August 24, 1849. *Frederick Douglass' Paper,* May 20, 1852.
26. *Liberator,* May 22, 1857.
27. *Provincial Freeman,* August 5, 1854.
28. *Colored American,* July 27, 1839.
29. *North Star,* June 22, 1849.
30. *Ibid.,* August 17, 1849.

marked the African Civilization Society controversy.[31]

Ironically, although those who feuded agreed with those who criticized them for disrupting the movement, they persisted. When in 1840-1841 the issue of separate race conventions prompted dispute, "Sidney" lamented that the people were "perishing by oppression" while their leaders were "one opposing the other, upon a *word*; . . . metaphycising upon *things,* when they should be using the resistless energy of principle, to vindicate their wronged and deeply injured brethren."[32] Sometime later Pliny Sexton, distressed by the verbal vituperativeness of the Garnet-Douglass brawl, concluded that "if talented and influential colored men, must fill their papers with such kind of Anti-Slavery, . . . considerate and conscientious persons will not think the cause of humanity and the brotherhood of the race will be much promoted by their support."[33] In 1850, when Douglass and Ward clashed over Ward's addressing a segregated audience, Delany tried to stem the exchange. It is "painful in the extreme, and mortifying," he wrote Douglass, "to see talent, usefulness, ability, and acknowledged greatness among our leading men, unconscious though they may be of their attitude in the eyes of the public, brought to no higher aim than driving each other into obscurity!"[34]

Yet three years later, when he charged Douglass with editorial malfeasance, Delany proved unable to take his own advice. Their exchanges brought from Johnson Woodlin of Philadelphia the wry observation that "when 'leaders' disagree, division will result as a natural consequence among the masses; and this appears to be the legitimate fruit of all our efforts.—The fact is, the masses have lost confidence in the 'leaders.' "[35] This time Douglass saw the danger.

31. See, for example, *Frederick Douglass' Paper, Liberator, Voice of the Fugitive, Weekly Anglo-African,* and *Provincial Freeman* during the 1850s. See also Frederick Douglass to Gerrit Smith, January 14, 1853, S-SU; and Robert Purvis to William L. Garrison, September 12, 1853, G-BPL.
32. *Colored American,* March 13, 1841.
33. Pliny Sexton to Henry H. Garnet, September 29, 1849, in *North Star* October 12, 1849.
34. *Ibid.,* July 11, 1850.
35. *Frederick Douglass' Paper,* May 6, 1853.

"The fact is, brother Delany," he wrote his opponent, "we are a disunited and scattered people, and very much of the responsibility of this disunion must fall upon such colored men as yourself and the writer of this."[36] Yet the disunion continued and brought still other knowing laments. As the Providence correspondent to the *Weekly Anglo-African* wrote of the emigration disagreements late in 1859, "It puzzles me to conceive how it is that our people cannot look a question in the face without such wrangling and bitterness."[37]

This personal wrangling and bitterness also distracted attention from fundamental disagreements over the nature and substance of race action which underlay much of the feuding. The questions were not confined solely to means, for, although the goals of freedom and equality were universal, their context, especially in the 1850s, became cloudy. Yet the actual debates over emigration and considerations of resistance got at the underlying problems only obliquely. Foremost among them was whether assimilation, which integration within the United States embodied, or separation, common to emigration and other forms of nationalism, would best produce freedom and equality.[38] Corollary to it was the question whether activists should work within the prevailing political and social system, which in the 1850s had probably come to include resistance to the fugitive slave law and the Dred Scott decision, or attack it from the outside. It is true that on the level of practical action and specific issues the substance of these questions was debated from 1830 to 1860. Yet it was only on rare occasions that they were consciously considered as theoretical possibilities. Therefore inchoate and unspoken, but nonetheless

36. *Ibid.*
37. *Weekly Anglo-African,* October 22, 1859.
38. The problem is common to both races in a multiracial society according to Harmannus Hoetink, *The Two Variants in Caribbean Race Relations: A Contribution to the Sociology of Segmented Societies.* Hoetink contends that each group seeks for "homogenization" either through the total assimilation of intermarriage or through elimination of the races by physical or symbolic removal. See George M. Frederickson, *The Black Image in the White Mind: The Debate on Afro-American Character and Destiny, 1817-1914* (New York: Harper and Row, 1971), 131.

differing, philosophical assumptions prolonged the acrimony which almost always focused on specifics and ignored the long-range implications. Whether either the dichotomies of assimilation or separatism and of working within or against the national structure could have been resolved it is impossible to say. Their consideration might possibly have clarified the meaning of the choices available though indeed it might also have narrowed those choices. Surely the failure to consider them encouraged a day-to-day pragmatism which further splintered the community. "The result is," James McCune Smith wrote Douglass in 1854, "that each man feels his particular wrong, but no hundred men together feel precisely the same oppression; and, while each would do fair work to remove his own, he feels differently in regard to his neighbor's oppression."[39]

Whether assessed by its goals or its organizational efficiency, black abolitionism was a failure. Yet to dwell upon its leaders' quarrels and their remoteness from their community, or to concentrate on irresolution, parochialism, indifference, and apathy is largely to miss the meaning of free black activism in the antebellum North. The question of failure centers most meaningfully around the interrelated conditions of rightlessness and powerlessness. Only here does one find a coherent explanation of why a struggle for freedom, equality, personal dignity, and group identity was futile in a society whose dominant group avowedly espoused the values these goals embraced.

There were, of course, internal impediments to power, for its effective use implies a group sufficiently unified over purpose and means to be able to marshal its full resources and exert its full strength. On all counts, black abolitionism fell short. Black pride and separatism competed with assimilationism and "Americanization"; feuding and dissension vitiated collective and individual endeavor. But had all this been otherwise, economic self-interest,

39. *Frederick Douglass' Paper,* May 12, 1854.

political and social stability, and racism made the overwhelming majority of white men unalterably opposed to the goals for which black men struggled. And whites not only constituted the vast majority of the population, especially in the North, but controlled the nation's economy and politics.

In one word, then, black America was powerless. In petitioning President Lincoln in 1862 against his Chiriqui colonization project, a group of Philadelphians shatteringly revealed their condition: "Beyond this, our humble appeal, we are almost powerless in our own great cause."[40] Fully entitled to vote only in New England— Connecticut excluded—and enfranchised in New York and Ohio[41] only under special conditions, they lacked the most basic tool of political power. Poor and probably, as in Philadelphia and New York, getting poorer, blacks lacked economic might to make their interests felt.[42] If it is true that revolution is sired by rising expectations, they lacked even the potential to revolt, for in the 1850s the clear perception was that things were getting worse.

No matter what means they chose, they necessarily relied, to some extent, on whites. Even at its most militant, black abolition utilized white resources and either consciously or unconsciously was shaped by its white benefactors. Even if they did not attach restrictions, donors made choices among potential recipients and thus strengthened one faction or approach as against another. Even more pronouncedly, black abolitionists depended on white willingness to accede to their demands. How could they acquire political power, if those who possessed it refused to share it? The defeat of enfranchisement measures in New York, Connecticut, and various Midwestern states clearly illustrated the dilemma. Blacks could perhaps persuade white legislators who sought the rewards that might come from an indebted voting bloc, but they could not offer even that potential benefit to prejudiced voters whose support they

40. "An Appeal of the Colored Men of Philadelphia to the President of the United States," in Herbert Aptheker, ed., *Documentary History of the Negro People in the United States* (2 vols. New York: Citadel Press, 1951, 1969), 1:475.
41. In Ohio only those who were more than 50% Caucasian could vote.
42. See Hershberg, "Free Blacks in Antebellum Philadelphia," 185-187.

needed. And if even abolitionists held to their racial prejudices, how could Negroes expect to convert slavery's supporters? How then were the rightless to acquire rights? How were the powerless to acquire power?

Occasionally blacks found power and used it effectively—to gain the suffrage in Rhode Island, to desegregate schools in a few communities, and, most importantly, to nullify the fugitive slave law as a political device. But even in these exceptional cases their power was defined by the actions of others to which they reacted. They were unsuccessful in effecting legislation for full civil rights or universal emancipation. They were unable to foment slave rebellion, and they failed to win significant numbers of white men to their side. By 1861 Northern blacks had gained little, except in race pride and organization, beyond what they had in 1830. In some cases, they had lost ground.

By 1852 Martin Delany had lost hope for black improvement within the United States. If, as he contended, "A child born under oppression, has all the elements of servility in its constitution" and cannot hope to achieve "freedom and independence of feeling,"[43] emigration and separatism were the sole solution. Yet most articulate blacks, even in the troubled 1850s, shared the angry hopes of William Watkins that, if they could but gain civil and political rights in the United States, they would enjoy the power, wealth, and social advantages of white America. "We are told we cannot rise! Take the millstone from off our necks. . . . *Give us our rights.*"

But Watkins' very plea contained the obstacle. The power to effect change was the white man's to give, not the black man's to take. "Give us our rights, we ask no more." If white America refused, what then?[44]

43. Martin R. Delany, *The Condition, Elevation, Emigration and Destiny of the Colored People of the United States* . . . (Philadelphia: The Author, 1852), 208.

44. William J. Watkins, *Our Rights as Men* . . . (Boston: Benjamin Roberts, [1853]), 10.

Bibliography

SOURCES FOR the study of the history of American blacks in the early nineteenth century are relatively meagre. Despite this paucity, however, there exists a good core both of primary and of secondary material, much of it reasonably accessible as a result of several recent reprint series in black studies.

Principal among the sources for our study were the proceedings of various conventions and societies, national, state, and local. Of those available most were separately printed, although some can be found only in newspaper reports, and a few are available only in manuscript form. Also of considerable importance for our work were the various black newspapers which flourished during the antebellum period. Although the coverage of the press was very uneven, qualitatively and quantitatively, it gave us indispensable insights into the thought and action of the articulate black community and its leadership. We supplemented the black press with the general antislavery press. We also made considerable use of the books, tracts, essays, and narratives of fugitive slaves and free blacks, as well as of other similar material. Finally manuscript correspondence threw useful light for us on the history of the antebellum black community. While no substantial collections exist devoted to any individual or individuals—the Douglass Papers at the Library of Congress being largely of a later period—it was possible to draw together a small but useful body of manuscript material by carefully searching major antislavery and related collections.

Within the past few years there has been a considerable outpouring of writing in black history. Yet on the particular subject of our book relatively little has been done. Invaluable as the older work was for us—and in some cases indispensable—it nevertheless was generally uncritical and incomplete; more recent work has only begun to scratch the surface of potential black historiography.

The bibliography which follows is designed to list sources cited in the notes and text, to cite other particularly useful works, and to provide a finding guide for relatively rare and elusive items. It is not intended to be exhaustive, but to point out the most important works. Occasionally, therefore, we have added an annotation to an entry if we thought that the annotation would prove helpful. Finally we call particular attention (as we have done in the footnotes) to several of the major reprint series in black history, among them especially the Arno Press (New York), Johnson Publishing Company (Chicago), Mnemosyne Publishing Co. (Miami), Negro Universities Press (a division of Greenwood Publishing Co., Westport, Connecticut), and Rhistoric Publications (Philadelphia), now merged to form SR Scholarly Resources (Wilmington, Delaware). In order to facilitate the use of this bibliography we have tried, where reprints are not readily available, to note at least one library where the less accessible items may be found.

I. Proceedings, Minutes, and Constitutions of conventions and societies.

    A. National.

        Bell, Howard H., ed. *Minutes of the Proceedings of the National Negro Conventions, 1830-1864* (New York: Arno Press, 1969). Photographic reproductions of the convention proceedings for 1830-1835, 1843, 1847, 1848, 1853, 1855, and 1864. This is the most important single source of primary material available for a study of antebellum black conventions.

        In addition to the convention proceedings in Bell, the following national proceedings are also very important.

        Minutes and Proceedings of the General Convention, for the Improvement of the Colored Inhabitants of Canada, Held by Adjournments in Amherstburgh, C. W. June 16th and 17th, 1853 (Windsor, C. W.: Bibb & Holly, 1853). Howard University.

        Proceedings of the National Emigration Convention of Colored People; Held at Cleveland, Ohio, On Thursday, Friday and Saturday, the 24th, 25th, and 26th of August, 1854 (Pittsburgh: Printed by A. A. Anderson, 1854). Cornell University.

B. State (arranged alphabetically by state).

Proceedings of the First State Convention of the Colored Citizens of the State of California. Held at Sacramento Nov. 20th, 21st, and 22d in the Colored Methodist Church (Sacramento: Democratic State Journal Print, 1855). Cornell University.

Proceedings of the Connecticut State Convention of Colored Men Held at New Haven on the September 12th and 13th, 1849 (New Haven: William H. Stanley, Printer, 1849). Howard University.

Proceedings of the Convention of Free Colored People of the State of Maryland. Held in Baltimore, July 26, 27, and 28, 1852, reprinted in *Journal of Negro History,* I (July 1916), 323-338.

Minutes of the State Convention, of the Colored Citizens of the State of Michigan...26th and 27th of October 1843 . . . (Detroit: William Harsha, 1843). University of Michigan.

Proceedings of the State Convention of Colored Men of the State of New Jersey, Held in the City of Trenton, N. J., July 13th and 14th, 1865 ...(Bridgeton, New Jersey: J. B. Ferguson, Printer, 1865). Rutgers University.

Minutes of the State Convention of Colored Citizens Held at Albany, on the 18th, 19th, and 20th of August, 1840, for the Purpose of Considering their Political Condition (New York: Piercy and Reed, 1840).

Minutes and Address of the State Convention of the Colored Citizens of Ohio, Convened at Columbus, January 10th, 11th, 12th, & 13th, 1849 (Oberlin: From J. M. Fitch's Power Press, 1849). Harvard University. Oberlin College.

Minutes of the State Convention, of the Colored Citizens of Ohio, Convened at Columbus, January 9th, 10th, 11th, and 12th, 1850 (Columbus: Gale & Cleveland, 1850). Harvard University.

Address to the Constitutional Convention of Ohio, from the State Convention of Colored Men, Held in the City of Columbus, January 15th, 16th, 17th, and 18th, 1851 ([Columbus]: E. Glover, Printer, [1851]). Oberlin College.

Minutes of the State Convention, of the Colored Citizens of Ohio, Convened at Columbus, Jan. 15th, 16th, 17th, and 18th, 1851 ([Columbus]: E. Glover, Printer, 1851). Harvard University.

Proceedings of the Convention, of the Colored Freemen of Ohio. Held in Cincinnati, January 14, 15, 16, 17 and 19 [sic] [1852] (Cincinnati: Printed by Dumas & Lawyer, 1852). Harvard University.

Official Proceedings of the Ohio State Convention of Colored Freemen. Held in Columbus, January 19th-21st, 1853 (*Aliened American-Extra.* Cleveland: Printed by W. H. Day, Aliened American Office, 1853). Harvard University.

Proceedings of the State Convention of Colored Men, Held in the City of Columbus, Ohio, Jan. 16th, 17th & 18th, 1856 (Title page missing). Harvard University.

Proceedings of the State Convention of the Colored Men of the State of Ohio, Held in the City of Columbus, January 21st, 22d & 23d, 1857 (Columbus: John Geary & Son, 1857). Harvard University.

Proceedings of a Convention of the Colored Men of Ohio, Held in the City of Cincinnati, on the 23d, 24th, 25th and 26th days of November, 1858 (Cincinnati: Moore, Wilstach, Keys & Co., Printers, 1858). Western Reserve Historical Society, Harvard University.

Proceedings of the First Annual Meeting of the Ohio State Anti-Slavery Society, Held in Xenia, Ohio, January 3rd, 4th, and 5th, 1860 (Title page missing). Harvard University.

Proceedings of the State Convention of the Colored Freemen of Pennsylvania, Held in Pittsburgh, on the 23d, 24th and 25th of August, 1841, for the purpose of considering their Condition and the Means of Its Improvement (Pittsburgh: Matthew M. Grant, 1841). Oberlin College.

Minutes of the State Convention of the Coloured Citizens of Pennsylvania Convened at Harrisburg, December 13th and 14th, 1848 (Philadelphia: Merrihew and Thompson, 1849). Reprint, Rhistoric Publications.

Proceedings of the State Equal Rights' Convention, of the Colored People of Pennsylvania, Held in the City of Harrisburg, February 8th, 9th, and 10th, 1865 . . . (Philadelphia: McC. Crummill, Printer, Printed For and By the Order of the Convention, 1865). Reprint, Rhistoric Publications.

C. Other.(Arranged alphabetically by title of organization).

African Civilization Society. *Constitution of the African Civilization Society . . .* (New Haven: Thomas J. Stafford, Printer, 1861). University of Michigan, Western Reserve Historical Society, Historical Society of Pennsylvania, Harvard University.

Agricultural and Mechanic Association [of Pennsylvania and New Jersey]. Constitution and Shareholder List. MS. Leon Gardner Collection. Historical Society of Pennsylvania.

American Anti-Slavery Society. *Annual Reports* (Title varies), 1834-1861 (none issued 1840-1854). A complete listing may be consulted in Dwight L. Dumond, *A Bibliography of Antislavery in America* (Ann Arbor: University of Michigan Press, 1961), 8-9. Variously available University of Michigan, Howard University, Oberlin College, and Cornell University.

The Minutes and Proceedings of the First Annual Meeting of the American Moral Reform Society, Held in Philadelphia . . . the 14th to the 19th of August, 1837 (Philadelphia: Merrihew and Gunn, 1837). Reprint, Rhistoric Publications.

Glasgow Emancipation Society. Minute Books. MS. Mitchell Library, Glasgow, Scotland.

The First Annual Report of the New York Committee of Vigilance, for the Year 1837, Together with Important Facts Relative to their Proceedings (New York: Piercy and Reed, 1837). Reprint, Rhistoric Publications.

Proceedings of the Convention of Radical Political Abolitionists Held at Syracuse, New York June 26th, 27th, and 28th, 1855 (New York: Central Abolition Board, 1855). Harvard University, Cornell University.

Social, Civil and Statistical Association of Colored People of Philadelphia. Minute Book, 1860-1867. MS. Historical Society of Pennsylvania.

Vigilant Committee of Philadelphia. "Minute Book of the Vigilant Committee of Philadelphia," 1839-1844, MS. Historical Society of Pennsylvania.

II. Newspapers and Periodicals.

A. Black Press.

Despite the interest among antebellum blacks in a race press, there were very few newspapers which had an extended existence or have survived. Many existed for only a few issues and today there remain only scattered copies or no trace whatever. Only those papers which had a significant impact in the antebellum period are listed here. Others are noted in the text and footnotes.

Freedom's Journal (New York) 1827-1829
Rights of All (New York) 1829
Colored American (New York) 1837-1841
Northern Star and Freemen's Advocate (Albany) 1842-1843
North Star (later *Frederick Douglass' Paper*, then *Douglass Monthly*) (Rochester) 1847-1863
Impartial Citizen (Syracuse, Boston) 1849-1850
Voice of the Fugitive (Windsor) 1850-1852
Provincial Freeman (Windsor, Toronto, Chatham) 1853-1856
Weekly Anglo-African (New York) 1859-1863
Anglo-African Magazine (New York) 1859-1860

B. Other newspapers and periodicals particularly useful for their inclusion of material about black America.

African Repository (Washington) 1825-1865
Liberator (Boston) 1831-1865
National Anti-Slavery Standard (New York) 1840-1865
American and Foreign Anti-Slavery Reporter (New York) 1840-1846

III. Printed primary materials.

A. Collections.

Aptheker, Herbert. *A Documentary History of the Negro People in the United States* (2 vols. New York: Citadel Press, 1951, 1969).

Bell, Howard H., ed. *Black Separatism and the Caribbean in 1860* (Ann Arbor: University of Michigan Press, [1970?]).

Bell, Howard H., ed. *Search for a Place. Black Separatism and Africa, 1860* (Ann Arbor: University of Michigan Press, 1969).

Katz, William Loren, ed. David Walker. *Walker's Appeal in Four Articles.* Henry Highland Garnet, *An Address to the Slaves of the United States of America* (New York: Arno Press, 1969).

Porter, Dorothy B., ed. *Negro Protest Pamphlets: A Compendium* (New York: Arno Press, 1969).

Woodson, Carter G., ed. *Negro Orators and their Orations* (Washington: Associated Publishers, 1925).

B. Individual titles.

Allen, William G. *The American Prejudice Against Color. An Authentic Narrative, Showing How Easily the Nation Got into an Uproar* (London: W. & F. G. Cash, 1853). Duke University, Boston Public Library.

[Armistead, Wilson]. *Calumny Refuted, by Facts from Liberia; With Extracts from the Inaugural Address of the Coloured President Roberts; an Eloquent Speech of Hilary Teage, a Coloured Senator; and Extracts from a Discourse by H. H. Garnett, a Fugitive Slave, on the Past and Present Condition, and Destiny of the Coloured Race* (New York: W. Harned, 1848). Howard University.

Bibb, Henry. *The Narrative of the Life and Adventures of Henry Bibb, An American Slave, Written by Himself, With an Introduction by Lucius Matlack* (New York: Published by the Author, 1849). Reprint, Rhistoric, Negro Universities Press, Mnemosyne.

Birney, James G. *Examination of the Decision of the Supreme Court of the United States, in the Case of*

Strader, Gorman and Armstrong vs. Christopher Graham, Delivered at its December Term, 1850; Concluding With an Address to the Free Colored People, Advising them to Remove to Liberia (Cincinnati: Truman & Spofford, 1852). Harvard University, New York State Library.

Boston Slave Riot, and Trial of Anthony Burns . . . (Boston: Fetridge and Company, 1854). New York State Library.

Brown, Henry "Box." *Narrative of Henry Box Brown* . . . (Boston: Brown and Stearns, 1849). Reprint, Rhistoric.

Brown, Paola. *Address Intended to be Delivered in the City Hall, Hamilton, February 7, 1851, on the Subject of Slavery* (Hamilton: Printed for the Author, 1851). Metropolitan Toronto Library.

Brown, William Wells. *The American Fugitive in Europe* . . . (Boston: John P. Jewett, 1855). University of Maine.

Brown, William Wells. *The Black Man, His Antecedents, His Genius, and His Achievements* (orig. ed. 1863. Boston: Robert F. Wallcut, 1865). Reprint, Mnemosyne.

Brown, William Wells, *Narrative of William W. Brown, a Fugitive Slave* . . . (Boston: The Anti-Slavery Office, 1847). Reprint, Johnson.

Campbell, Robert. *An Account of a Journey among the Egbas and Yorubas of Central Africa in 1859-60* (np, nd), in Bell, *Search for a Place.*

Chapman, Maria Weston. *"How Can I Help to Abolish Slavery?" or, Counsels to the Newly Converted* (Anti-Slavery Tract Number 14. New York: American Anti-Slavery Society, [1855]). New York State Library, Cornell University, Harvard University.

Colored People of Providence. *Will the General Assembly Put Down Caste Schools?* ([Providence]: n.p., December 1857). Providence Public Library.

Condition of the American Colored Population, and of the Colony at Liberia (Boston: Pierce & Parker, 1833). Oberlin College.

Cornish, Samuel E. and Theodore S. Wright. *The Colonization Scheme Considered, in Its Rejection by the Colored People—in Its Tendency to Uphold Caste—in Its Unfitness for Christianizing and Civilizing the Aborigines of Africa, and for Putting a Stop to the African Slave Trade* . . . (Newark: Printed by Aaron Guest, 1840). Howard University, Library of Congress, New York State Library.

Crummell, Alexander. *Africa and America: Addresses and Discourses* (Springfield, Mass.: Willey and Co., 1891). Library of Congress.

Delany, Martin R. *Blake or the Huts of America* (orig. publ. 1859. Boston: Beacon Press, 1970).

Delany, Martin R. *The Condition, Elevation, Emigration, and Destiny of the Colored People of the United States Politically Considered* (Philadelphia: The Author, 1852). Reprint, Arno.

Delany, Martin R. *Official Report of the Niger Valley Exploring Party* (New York: T. Hamilton, 1861), in Bell, *Search for a Place.*

Delany, Martin R. *Political Destiny of the Colored Race on the American Continent,* printed as an appendix to Frank A. Rollin, *Life and Public Services of Martin R. Delany* . . .(Boston: Lee and Shepard, 1883). Reprint, Arno.

Douglass, Frederick. *The Anti-Slavery Movement. A Lecture* . . . *Before the Rochester Ladies' Anti-Slavery Society* (Rochester: Lee, Mann & Co., 1855). Harvard University, Howard University.

Douglass, Frederick. *Narrative of the Life of Frederick Douglass* . . . (Boston: Anti-Slavery Office, 1845. New York: Dolphin Books, 1963).

Drew, Benjamin. *A North-side View of Slavery. The Refugee: or, the Narrative of Fugitive Slaves in Canada. Related by Themselves, With an Account of the History and Condition of the Colored Population of Upper Canada* (Boston: John P. Jewett Company, 1856). Reprint, Addison-Wesley.

Easton, Hosea. *A Treatise on the Intellectual Character, and Civil and Political Conditions of the Colored People of the U. States, and the Prejudice Exercised Towards Them* . . . (Boston: I. Knapp, 1837), in Porter, *Negro Protest Pamphlets.*

Foner, Philip, ed. "John Browne Russwurm, A Document," *Journal of Negro History,* LIV (October, 1969), 393-397. The text of Russwurm's Bowdoin College commencement address, 1826, "The Condition and Prospects of Hayti."

Forten, James, Jr. *An Address Delivered before the Ladies' Anti-Slavery Society of Philadelphia* . . . *14th of April, 1836* (Philadelphia: Merrihew and Gunn, 1836). Harvard University.

Garnet, Henry H. *A Memorial Discourse. . . Delivered in the Hall of Representatives, Washington City, D. C. on Sabbath, February 12, 1865* . . . (Philadelphia: Joseph M. Wilson, 1865). Howard University.

Garnet, Henry Highland. *An Address to the Slaves of the United States of America* (orig. publ. 1848). Reprint, Katz, ed., Arno.

Garnet, Henry Highland. *The Past and the Present Condition, and the Destiny of the Colored Race* . . . (Troy: J. C. Kneeland and Co., 1848). Reprint, Mnemosyne.

Garrison, William Lloyd. *Thoughts on African Colonization* (orig. publ. 1832. New York: Arno Press, 1969).

Hall, Nathaniel. *The Iniquity: A Sermon Preached . . . Dec. 11, 1859* (Boston: John Wilson & Son, 1859). New York State Library.

Hamilton, William. *Address to the Fourth Annual Convention of the Free People of Color of the United States . . .* (New York: S. W. Benedict, 1834). Reprint, Porter, *Negro Protest Pamphlets.*

Holly, James Theodore. *A Vindication of the Capacity of the Negro Race for Self-Government, and Civilized Progress, as Demonstrated by Historical Events of the Haytian Revolution; and the Subsequent Acts of that People Since Their National Independence* ([n.p.: n.p., 1857]), in Bell, *Black Separatism*).

Langston, Charles H. *Should Colored Men Be Subject to the Pains and Penalties of the Fugitive Slave Law? Speech . . . before the U. S. District Court Delivered When About to Be Sentenced for Rescuing a Man from Slavery* (Cleveland: Ohio Anti-Slavery Society, 1859). Amistad Research Center.

Langston, John Mercer. *From the Virginia Plantation to the National Capitol or the First and Only Negro Representative in Congress from the Old Dominion* (Hartford: American Publishing Co., 1894). Reprint, Arno.

Leeds Anti-Slavery Society. *Fugitive Slaves: Douglass, Pennington, Wells Brown, Garnett, Bibb and Others* (London: [Leeds Anti-Slavery Series] , n.d.). Howard University.

Loguen, Jarmain W. *The Rev. J. W. Loguen as a Slave and as a Freeman. A Narrative of Real Life* (Syracuse: J. G. K. Truair & Co., 1859). Howard University.

Nell, William Cooper. *The Colored Patriots of the American Revolution with Sketches of Several Distinguished Colored Persons; To Which is Added a Brief Survey of the Conditions and Prospects of Colored Americans* (Boston: Robert F. Wallcutt, 1855). Reprint, Arno.

Paul, Nathaniel. *An Address, Delivered on the Celebration of the Abolition of Slavery in the State of New York, July 5, 1827 . . .* (Albany: Printed by John van Steenbergh, 1827). Reprint, Porter, *Negro Protest Pamphlets.*

Pennington, James W. C. *The Fugitive Blacksmith; or, Events in the History of James W. C. Pennington, Pastor of a Presbyterian Church in New York, Formerly a Slave in the State of Maryland* (3rd ed. London: Charles Gilpin, 1850). Reprint, Negro Universities Press.

Pennington, James W. C. *A Text Book of the Origin and History, &c. &c. of the Colored People* (Hartford: L. Skinner, Printer, 1841). Reprint, Negro Universities Press.

Robbins, James J. *Report of the Trial of Castner Hanway for Treason, in the Resistance of the Execution of the Fugitive Slave Law* . . . (Philadelphia: King and Baird, 1852). Reprint, Negro Universities Press.

Ruggles, David. *The Extinguisher Extinguished! or, David M. Reese, M. D. "Used Up."* . . . (New York: David Ruggles, 1834). Reprint, Rhistoric.

Walker, David. *Walker's Appeal in Four Articles* (Boston: David Walker, 1830). Reprint, Katz, ed., Arno.

Ward, Samuel Ringgold. *Autobiography of a Fugitive Negro. His Anti-Slavery Labours in the United States, Canada and England* (London: J. Snow, 1855). New York State Library, Howard University, Cornell University.

Watkins, William J. *Our Rights as Men. An Address Delivered in Boston, Before the Legislative Committee on the Militia, February 24, 1853 . . . in Behalf of Sixty-Five Colored Petitioners, Praying for a Charter to Form an Independent Military Company* (Boston: Benjamin Roberts, [1853]). Reprint, Porter, *Negro Protest Pamphlets.*

IV. Collections of letters and related material.

A. Manuscript. Both the Frederick Douglass Papers in the Library of Congress (D-LC) and the John Mercer Langston Papers at the Amistad Research Center, the two major collections of papers of antebellum black leaders, contain almost no antebellum material. In a number of the various antislavery collections, however, very useful caches of material are available.

American Missionary Association Papers,
    Amistad Research Center (AMA-ARC)
Antislavery Collection, Boston Public Library
    Chapman Papers (Ch-BPL)
    Child Papers (C-BPL)
    Garrison Papers (G-BPL)
    May Papers (M-BPL)
    Phelps Papers (P-BPL)
    Weston Papers (W-BPL)
Salmon P. Chase Papers, Library of Congress (C-LC)
Foster Papers, American Antiquarian Society (F-AAS)
Sydney H. Gay Papers, Columbia University (G-CU)
Gerrit Smith Miller Papers, Syracuse University (S-SU)
Edmund Quincy Papers, Massachusetts Historical Society (Q-MHS)
Elizur Wright Papers, Library of Congress (W-LC)

B. Printed Collections.
Barnes, Gilbert H. and Dwight L. Dumond, eds. *Letters of Theodore Dwight Weld, Angelina Grimké Weld, and Sarah Grimké, 1822-1844* (New York: D. Appleton-Century Co., 1934).
Doughty, Arthur G., ed. *The Elgin-Grey Papers, 1846-1852* (4 vols. Ottawa: J. O. Patenaude, 1937).
Dumond, Dwight, ed. *Letters of James Gillespie Birney, 1831-1857* (2 vols. New York: D. Appleton-Century Co., 1938).
Foner, Philip, ed. *The Life and Writings of Frederick Douglass* (4 vols. New York: International Publishers, 1950-1955).
Harris, Sheldon H., ed. *Paul Cuffe: Black America and the African Return* (New York: Simon and Schuster, 1972).
"Letters to Antislavery Workers and Agencies," *Journal of Negro History*, X (July and October 1925), 345-567, 648-774; XI (January 1926), 62-214.
Porter, Dorothy B., ed. "Early Manuscript Letters Written by Negroes," *Journal of Negro History*, XXIV (April 1939), 199-210.
Quarles, Benjamin, ed. "Letters from Negro Leaders to Gerrit Smith," *Journal of Negro History*, XXVII (October 1942), 432-453.
Woodson, Carter G., ed. *The Mind of the Negro as Reflected in Letters Written During the Crisis, 1800-1860* (Washington: Association for the Study of Negro Life and History, 1926).

V. Secondary material.

A. Unpublished.
Drake, Richard B. "The American Missionary Association and the Southern Negro, 1861-1888" (Third draft, Ph.D. Emory University, 1957. On deposit, Berea College Library).
McMaster, Richard K. "Dr. Martin Delany, the Rev. Henry Highland Garnet, and the African Civilization Society, 1856-1861" (Paper presented to the Association for the Study of Negro Life and History, Baltimore, 1966. Copy in authors' possession).
Rice, C. Duncan. "The Scottish Factor in the Fight Against American Slavery, 1830-1870" (Ph.D. University of Edinburgh, 1969).
Temperley, Howard R. "The British and Foreign Anti-Slavery Society, 1839-1868" (Ph.D. Yale University, 1960).

312   *Bibliography*

Wyatt-Brown, Bertram. "Partners in Piety: Lewis and Arthur
    Tappan, Evangelical Abolitionists, 1828-1841" (Ph.D.
    Johns Hopkins University, 1963).

B. Published.
Andrews, Charles C. *The History of the New-York African
    Free-Schools, From Their Establishment in 1787, to the
    Present Time* . . . (New York: Printed by Mahlon Day,
    1830). Reprint, Negro Universities Press.
Bardolph, Richard. "Social Origins of Distinguished Negroes,
    1770-1865," *Journal of Negro History*, XL (July 1955),
    211-249.
Barnes, Gilbert H. *The Antislavery Impulse, 1830-1844* (orig.
    publ. 1933. Gloucester: Peter Smith, 1967).
Bartlett, Irving H. *From Slave to Citizen: The Story of the
    Negro in Rhode Island* (Providence: The Urban League of
    Greater Providence, 1954).
Bell, Howard H. "The American Moral Reform Society,
    1836-1841," *Journal of Negro Education*, XXVII (Winter
    1958), 34-40.
Bell, Howard H. "Expressions of Negro Militancy in the
    North, 1840-1860," *Journal of Negro History*, XLV
    (January 1960), 11-20.
Bell, Howard H. "Free Negroes of the North, 1830-1835: A
    Study in National Cooperation," *Journal of Negro Educa-
    tion*, XXVI (Fall 1957), 447-455.
Bell, Howard H. "National Negro Conventions of the Middle
    1840s: Moral Suasion vs. Political Action," *Journal of
    Negro History*, XLII (October 1957), 247-260.
Bell, Howard H. "The National Negro Convention, 1848,"
    Ohio Historical Quarterly, LXVII (October 1958),
    357-368.
Bell, Howard H. "The Negro Convention Movement,
    1830-1860: New Perspectives," *Negro History Bulletin*,
    XIV (February 1951), 105.
Bell, Howard H. "The Negro Emigration Movement,
    1849-1854: A Phase of Negro Nationalism," *Phylon*, XX
    (Summer 1959), 132-142.
Bell, Howard H. "Negro Nationalism: A Factor in Emigration
    Projects, 1858-1861," *Journal of Negro History*, XLVII
    (January 1962), 42-53.
Bell, Howard H. *A Survey of the Negro Convention
    Movement, 1830-1861* (New York: Arno Press, 1969).
Berwanger, Eugene. *The Frontier Against Slavery: Western
    Anti-Negro Prejudice and the Slavery Extension Contro-
    versy* (Urbana: University of Illinois Press, 1967).

Boyd, W. D. "James Redpath and American Negro Colonization in Haiti, 1860-1862," *Americas: A Quarterly Review of Inter-American Cultural History*, XII (October 1955), 169-182.

Brewer, William M. "Henry H. Garnet," *Journal of Negro History*, XIII (January 1928), 36-52.

Brewer, William M. "John B. Russwurm," *Journal of Negro History*, XIII (October 1928), 413-422.

Calligaro, Lee. "The Negro's Legal Status in Pre-Civil War New Jersey," *New Jersey History*, LXXXV (Fall-Winter 1967), 167-180.

Campbell, Stanley W. *The Slave Catchers: Enforcement of the Fugitive Slave Law, 1850-1860* (Chapel Hill: University of North Carolina Press, 1968, 1970).

Cooper, Frederick. "Elevating the Race: The Social Thought of Black Leaders, 1827-50," *American Quarterly*, XXIV (December 1972), 604-625.

Dancy, John C. "The Negro People in Michigan," *Michigan History Magazine*, XXIV (Spring 1940), 221-240.

Daniels, John. *In Freedom's Birthplace: A Study of Boston Negroes* (orig. publ. 1914. New York: Johnson Reprint, 1968).

Du Bois, W. E. Burghardt. *John Brown* (Philadelphia: George W. Jacobs, 1909).

Dykes, Eva B. *The Negro in English Romantic Thought; or a Study of Sympathy for the Oppressed* (Washington: Associated Publishers, 1942).

Farrison, William E. *William Wells Brown: Author and Reformer* (Chicago: University of Chicago Press, 1969).

Farrison, William E. "William Wells Brown in Buffalo," *Journal of Negro History*, XXIX (October 1954), 298-314.

Farrison, William E. "William Wells Brown, Social Reformer," *Journal of Negro Education*, XVIII (Winter 1949), 29-39.

Filler, Louis. *The Crusade Against Slavery, 1830-1860* (New York: Harper and Brothers, 1960).

Fisher, James A. "The Struggle for Negro Testimony in California, 1851-1863," *Southern California Quarterly*, LI (December 1969), 313-324.

Foner, Eric. "Politics and Prejudice: The Free Soil Party and the Negro, 1849-1852," *Journal of Negro History*, L (October 1965), 239-256.

Fox, Dixon Ryan. "The Negro Vote in Old New York," *Political Science Quarterly*, XXXII (June 1917), 252-275.

Frederickson, George M. *The Black Image in the White Mind: The Debate on Afro-American Character and Destiny,*

1817-1914 (New York: Harper & Row, 1971).

Gara, Larry. *The Liberty Line: The Legend of the Underground Railroad* (Lexington: University of Kentucky Press, 1961).

Gara, Larry. "The Professional Fugitive in the Abolition Movement," *Wisconsin Magazine of History,* XLVIII (Spring 1965), 196-204.

Gara, Larry. "William Still and the Underground Railroad," *Pennsylvania History,* XXVIII (January 1961), 33-42.

Garrison, Wendell P. and Francis J. Garrison. *William Lloyd Garrison, 1805-1879: The Story of his Life as Told by his Children* (4 vols. New York: The Century Co., 1885-1889).

George, Carol V. R. *Segregated Sabbaths: Richard Allen and the Emergence of Independent Black Churches 1760-1840* (New York: Oxford University Press, 1973).

Grimsted, David. "Rioting in its Jacksonian Setting," *American Historical Review,* LXXVII (April 1972), 361-397.

Gross, Bella. "Freedom's Journal and the Rights of All," *Journal of Negro History,* XVII (July 1932), 241-286.

Hensel, William Uhler. *The Christiana Riot and the Treason Trials of 1851: An Historical Sketch* (orig. publ. 1911. New York: Negro Universities Press, 1969).

Hershberg, Theodore. "Free Blacks in Antebellum Philadelphia: A Study of Ex-Slaves, Freeborn, and Socioeconomic Decline," *Journal of Social History,* V (Winter 1971-1972), 183-209.

Hickok, Charles T. *The Negro in Ohio, 1802-1870* (Cleveland: Press of the Williams Publishing and Electric Company, 1896). Case Western Reserve University.

Higginson, Thomas W. *Cheerful Yesterdays* (Boston: Houghton Mifflin Co., 1898).

Hirsch, Leo H., Jr. "New York and the Negro, from 1783 to 1865," *Journal of Negro History,* XVI (October 1931), 382-473.

Jacobs, Donald M. "David Walker: Boston Race Leader, 1825-1830," *Essex Institute Historical Collections,* CVII (January 1971), 94-107.

Jacobs, Donald M. "William Lloyd Garrison's *Liberator* and Boston's Blacks, 1830-1865," *New England Quarterly,* XLIV (June 1971), 259-277.

Johnson, Franklin. *The Development of State Legislation Concerning the Free Negro* (New York: Arbor Press, 1918).

Katzman, David M. *Before the Ghetto: Black Detroit in The Nineteenth Century* (Urbana: University of Illinois Press, 1973).

Kraditor, Aileen S. *Means and Ends in American Abolitionism. Garrison and His Critics on Strategy and Tactics, 1834-1850* (New York: Pantheon Books, 1967, 1969).

Landon, Fred. "Canadian Negroes and the John Brown Raid," *Journal of Negro History,* VI (April 1921), 174-182.

Landon, Fred. "From Chatham to Harper's Ferry," *The Canadian Magazine,* LIII (October 1919), 441-448.

Lapp, Rudolph M. "Jeremiah Sanderson: Early California Negro," *Journal of Negro History,* LIII (October 1968), 321-333.

Lapp, Rudolph, M. "The Negro in Gold Rush California," *Journal of Negro History,* XLIX (April 1964), 81-98.

Lemons, J. Stanley and Michael A. McKenna. "Re-enfranchisement of Rhode Island Negroes." *Rhode Island History,* XXX (Winter 1971), 3-13.

Lerner, Gerda. "The Grimke' Sisters and the Struggle Against Race Prejudice," *Journal of Negro History,* XLVIII (October 1963), 277-291.

Litwack, Leon F. "The Abolitionist Dilemma; The Antislavery Movement and the Northern Negro," *New England Quarterly,* XXXIV (March 1961), 50-73.

Litwack, Leon F. "The Emancipation of the Negro Abolitionist," in Martin Duberman, ed., *The Antislavery Vanguard: New Essays on the Abolitionists* (Princeton: Princeton University Press, 1965),137-155.

Litwack, Leon F. *North of Slavery: The Negro in the Free States, 1790-1860* (Chicago: University of Chicago Press, 1961).

Mabee, Carleton. "A Negro Boycott to Integrate Boston Schools," *New England Quarterly,* XLI (September 1968), 341-361.

McManus, Edgar J. *A History of Negro Slavery in New York* (Syracuse: Syracuse University Press, 1966).

McPherson, James M. "Abolitionist and Negro Opposition to Colonization During the Civil War," *Phylon,* XXVI (Winter 1965), 391-399.

McPherson, James M. *The Struggle for Equality, Abolitionists and the Negro in the Civil War and Reconstruction* (Princeton: Princeton University Press, 1964).

Malvin, John. *Autobiography of John Malvin, A Narrative, Containing an Authentic Account of His Fifty Years' Struggle in the State of Ohio in Behalf of the American Slave, and the Equal Rights of All Men Before the Law Without Reference to Race or Color...* (orig. publ. 1879. Cleveland: Press of Western Reserve University for Cleveland State University, 1966).

May, Samuel Joseph. *Some Recollections of Our Anti-Slavery Conflict* (Boston: Fields, Osgood & Co., 1869).

Mehlinger, Louis R. "The Attitude of the Free Negro Toward African Colonization," *Journal of Negro History*, I (July 1916), 276-301.

Miller, Floyd J. " 'The Father of Black Nationalism': Another Contender," *Civil War History*, XVII (December 1971), 310-319.

Nash, Roderick, W. "William Parker and the Christiana Riot," *Journal of Negro History*, XLVI (January 1961), 24-31.

Nichols, Charles H. *Many Thousand Gone: The Ex-Slaves' Account of Their Bondage and Freedom* (Bloomington: Indiana University Press, 1963, 1969).

Olbrich, Emil. *The Development of Sentiment on Negro Suffrage to 1860* (Bulletin of the University of Wisconsin, 477. History Series, Vol. 3, No. 1. Madison: University of Wisconsin, 1912).

Pease, Jane H. and William H. Pease. "Black Power—The Debate in 1840," *Phylon*, XXIX (Spring 1968), 19-26.

Pease, Jane H. and William H. Pease. "Ends, Means, and Attitudes: Black-White Conflict in the Antislavery Movement," *Civil War History*, XVIII (June 1972), 117-128.

Pease, William H. and Jane H. Pease. "Antislavery Ambivalence: Immediatism, Expediency, Race," *American Quarterly*, XVII (Winter 1965), 682-695.

Pease, William H. and Jane H. Pease. *Black Utopia: Negro Communal Experiments in America* (orig. publ. 1963. Madison: State Historical Society of Wisconsin, 1972).

Pease, William H. and Jane H. Pease. "Boston Garrisonians and the Problem of Frederick Douglass," *Canadian Journal of History*, II (September 1967), 29-48.

Penn, Irving G. *The Afro-American Press and Its Editors* (orig. publ. 1891. New York: Arno Press, 1969).

Perlman, Daniel. "Organizations of the Free Negro in New York City, 1800-1860," *Journal of Negro History*, LVI (July 1971), 181-197.

Porter, Dorothy. "David Ruggles, An Apostle of Human Rights," *Journal of Negro History*, XXVIII (January 1943), 23-50.

Porter, Dorothy B. "Sarah Parker Remond, Abolitionist and Physician," *Journal of Negro History*, XX (July 1935), 287-293.

Quarles, Benjamin. *Black Abolitionists* (New York: Oxford University Press, 1969).

Quarles, Benjamin. "The Breach Between Douglass and Garrison," *Journal of Negro History*, XXIII (April 1938), 144-154.

Quarles, Benjamin. *Frederick Douglass* (orig. publ. 1948. New York: Atheneum, 1968).

Rammelkamp, Julian. "The Providence Negro Community, 1820-1842," *Rhode Island History,* VII (January 1948), 20-33.

Richards, Leonard L. *"Gentlemen of Property and Standing:" Anti-Abolition Mobs in Jacksonian America* (New York: Oxford University Press, 1970).

Rollin, Frank A. [Frances Rollin Whipper] *Life and Public Services of Martin R. Delany* . . . (orig. publ. 1868. New York: Arno Press, 1969).

Ruchames, Louis. "Race, Marriage and Abolition in Massachusetts," *Journal of Negro History,* XL (July 1955), 250-273.

Ruchin, Judith P. "The Abolition of Colored Schools in Rochester, New York: 1832-1856," *New York History,* LI (July 1970), 376-393.

Sheeler, J. Reuben. "The Struggle of the Negro in Ohio for Freedom," *Journal of Negro History,* XXXI (April 1946), 208-226.

Shepperson, George. "Frederick Douglass and Scotland," *Journal of Negro History,* XXXVIII (July 1953), 307-321.

Sherman, Joan R. "James Monroe Whitfield, Poet and Emigrationist: A Voice of Protest and Despair," *Journal of Negro History*, LVII (April 1972), 169-176.

Shipherd, Jacob R., comp. *History of the Oberlin-Wellington Rescue* (orig. publ. 1859. New York: Negro Universities Press, 1969).

Siebert, Wilbur H. *The Underground Railroad from Slavery to Freedom* (orig. publ. 1898. Gloucester: Peter Smith, 1968).

Smith, Robert P. "William Cooper Nell: Crusading Black Abolitionist," *Journal of Negro History,* LV (July 1970), 182-199.

Stanley, John L. "Majority Tyranny in Tocqueville's America: The Failure of Negro Suffrage in 1846," *Political Science Quarterly,* LXXXIV (September 1969), 412-435.

Stanton, William. *The Leopard's Spots. Scientific Attitudes Toward Race in America, 1815-1859* (Chicago: University of Chicago Press, 1960).

Staudenraus, Philip J. *The African Colonization Movement, 1816-1865* (New York: Columbia University Press, 1961).

Stevens, Charles Emery. *Anthony Burns, A History* (orig. publ. 1856. New York: Negro Universities Press, 1969).

Tappan, Lewis. *The Life of Arthur Tappan* (New York: Hurd and Houghton, 1870).

Thomas, John L. *The Liberator. William Lloyd Garrison, A Biography* (Boston: Little, Brown and Co., 1963).

Thornbrough, Emma Lou. *The Negro in Indiana: A Study of a Minority* (Indianapolis: Indiana Historical Bureau, 1957).

Turner, Edward R. *The Negro in Pennsylvania, 1639-1861* (Washington: American Historical Association, 1912).

Voegeli, Jacque. *Free But Not Equal: The Midwest and the Negro During the Civil War* (Chicago: University of Chicago Press, 1967).

Wade, Richard D. "The Negro in Cincinnati, 1800-1830," *Journal of Negro History,* XXXIX (January 1954), 43-57.

Warner, Robert A. "Amos Gerry Beman—1812-1874, A Memoir on a Forgotten Leader," *Journal of Negro History,* XXII (April 1937), 200-221.

Warner, Robert A. *New Haven Negroes: A Social History* (New Haven: Yale University Press, 1940).

Wells, Anna Mary. *Dear Preceptor: The Life and Times of Thomas Wentworth Higginson* (Boston: Houghton, Mifflin, 1963).

Wesley, Charles H. "The Negro in the Organization of Abolition," *Phylon,* II (Third Quarter 1941), 223-235.

Wesley, Charles H. "Negro Suffrage in the Period of Constitution-Making, 1787-1865," *Journal of Negro History,* XXXII (April 1947), 143-168.

Wesley, Charles H. "The Negroes of New York in the Emancipation Movement," *Journal of Negro History,* XXIV (January 1939), 65-103.

Wesley, Charles H. *Richard Allen, Apostle of Freedom* (Washington: Associated Publishers, 1935).

Work, Monroe N. "The Life of Charles B. Ray," *Journal of Negro History,* IV (October 1919), 361-371.

Wyatt-Brown, Bertram. *Lewis Tappan and the Evangelical War Against Slavery* (Cleveland: The Press of Case Western Reserve University, 1969).

Zelinsky, Wilbur. "The Population Geography of the Free Negro in *Ante-Bellum* America," *Population Studies,* III (1949-1950), 386-401.

Zilversmit, Arthur. *The First Emancipation: The Abolition of Slavery in the North* (Chicago: University of Chicago Press, 1967).

VI.In addition to the material in this bibliography, there is a considerable literature which no one interested in the subject can afford to ignore. Though it was not published until we had essentially completed our own work, the best starting guide to the literature of all aspects of black history in America is James M. McPherson *et al.: Blacks in America. Bibliographical Essays* (Garden City: Doubleday & Co., 1971).

Bibliographic Addendum

WHEN AUGUST MEIER proposed that the University of Illinois Press issue a new paperback edition of *They Who Would Be Free,* we, of course, reread the original and contemplated how and whether we should revise it. Concluding that we should not tinker with the text, we nonetheless decided that, because so much black history has been published since 1974, we should bring our original bibliography up to date. The purpose of this brief essay, however, is not a comprehensive survey of all the works that might clarify the goals, nature, and means of Northern blacks' efforts to expand their own freedom and to end slavery. Rather it is to present a selection of historical and other works, particularly those using previously unexploited sources and innovative research methods or those offering new interpretations of how African-Americans in the pre-Civil War North struggled to extend their own civil rights and to end slavery in the South.

Among new editions of primary sources the best known, although still largely incomplete, is John Blassingame's edition of the Frederick Douglass papers, which Yale University Press began publishing in 1979. Of considerably wider scope is the University of North Carolina Press' extensively annotated *Black Abolitionist Papers,* edited by Peter Ripley. Of the five projected volumes, the first two, dealing with activity in the British Isles and Canada, were published in 1985 and 1986. The volumes dealing exclusively with the United States are currently in process. *Maria Stewart, America's First Black Woman Political Writer: Essays and Speeches,* edited by Marilyn Richardson (Bloomington: Indiana University Press, 1989), gives new attention to the first black female antislavery lecturer. Howard H. Bell's *Minutes and Proceedings of the National Negro Conventions, 1830-1864* (New York: Arno, 1969) has now been supplemented by Philip S. Foner and George E. Walker, eds., *Proceedings of the Black State Conventions* (Philadelphia: Temple University

Press, 1979-80), which, in addition to the primary texts, also contains useful biographical and bibliographical information. To guide students to the black press, Donald M. Jacobs, Heath Paley, Susan Parker, and Dana Silverman have edited *Antebellum Black Newspapers: Indices to New York "Freedom's Journal" (1827-1829), "The Rights of All" (1829), "The Weekly Advocate" (1837), and "The Colored American" (1837-1841)* (Westport: Greenwood Press, 1976). And Penelope L. Bullock's *The Afro-American Periodical Press, 1838-1909* (Baton Rouge: Louisiana State University Press, 1981), though it deals more extensively with the post-Civil War period, does contain some data on earlier papers.

The lives of black leaders have captured the imagination of a number of writers. William L. Andrews, in *To Tell a Free Story: The First Century of Afro-American Autobiography, 1760-1865* (Urbana: University of Illinois Press, 1986), approaches the subject from the vantage point of literary analysis rather than from a historian's perspective. *North into Freedom: The Autobiography of John Malvin,* edited by Allen Peskin (Kent, Ohio: Kent State University Press, 1989), adds to the store of autobiographies. Richard J. M. Blackett's *Beating against the Barriers: Biographical Essays in Nineteenth-Century Afro-American History* (Baton Rouge: Louisiana State University Press, 1986) discusses half a dozen antebellum black leaders, including James W. C. Pennington, Robert Campbell, and J. Sella Martin. Among other biographical studies are Blackett's "William G. Allen: The Forgotten Professor," *Civil War History,* XXVI (1980), 39-52; Wilson J. Moses, *Alexander Crummell: A Study of Civilization and Discontent* (New York: Oxford University Press, 1989); Stanley J. Robboy and Anita W. Robboy, "Lewis Hayden: From Fugitive Slave to Statesman," *New England Quarterly,* XLVI (1973), 591-613; William F. Cheek, *John Mercer Langston and the Fight for Black Freedom, 1829-1865* (Urbana: University of Illinois Press, 1989); George A. Levesque, "Boston's Black Brahmin: Dr. John S. Rock," *Civil War History,* XXVI (1980), 326-346; and Richard P. McCormick, "William Whipper: Moral Reformer," *Pennsylvania History,* XLIII (1976), 23-48. Of biographies of more visible and controversial figures,

Joel Schor's *Henry Highland Garnet: A Voice of Black Radicalism in the Nineteenth Century* (Westport: Greenwood Press, 1977), expressly defends "black radicalism as a positive force with the Negro community," as does his "The Rivalry between Frederick Douglass and Henry Highland Garnet," *Journal of Negro History,* LXIV (1979), 30-38. For another and controversial account of Garnet's life see Sterling Stuckey, "A Last Stern Struggle: Henry Highland Garnet and Liberation Thought," in Leon F. Litwack and August Meier, eds., *Black Leaders of the Nineteenth Century* (Urbana: University of Illinois Press, 1988), 129-148. As might be expected, the life of Frederick Douglass continues to intrigue and challenge scholars. Dickson J. Preston examines Douglass' formative years as a Maryland slave in *Young Frederick Douglass: The Maryland Years* (Baltimore: Johns Hopkins University Press, 1980); David W. Blight looks at Douglass' views about the Civil War in *Frederick Douglass' Civil War: Keeping Faith in Jubilee* (Baton Rouge: Louisiana State University Press, 1989); Leslie F. Goldstein discusses Douglass' willingness to use force, physical and moral, in the war against slavery in "Violence as an Instrument for Social Change: The Views of Frederick Douglass," *Journal of Negro History,* LXI (1976), 61-72; Waldo E. Martin ventures a more extensive treatment in *The Mind of Frederick Douglass* (Chapel Hill: University of North Carolina Press, 1984); and Peter F. Walker presents a complex social-psychological-historical discussion of Douglass in part 3 of his *Moral Choices: Memory, Desire, and Imagination in Nineteenth-Century American Abolition* (Baton Rouge: Louisiana State University Press, 1978).

Other studies focusing on specific kinds of activity suggest the large range of black activism. For education, Harry C. Silcox provides a contextual background in "Delay and Public Neglect: Negro Public Education in Antebellum Philadelphia, 1800-1860," *Pennsylvania Magazine of History and Biography,* XCVII (1973), 444-464; Lawrence Grossman deals with "George T. Downing and Desegregation of Rhode Island Public Schools, 1855-1865," *Rhode Island History,* XXXVI (1977), 99-105. In matters religious, Carol V. R. George looks at "Widening the Circle: The Black Church and the Abolitionist Crusade, 1830-1860," in Lewis Perry and Michael Fellman, eds., *Antislavery Reconsidered: New Perspectives on the Abolitionists* (Baton Rouge: Louisiana State University Press, 1979), 75-95. Dealing with a single denominational group, George A. Levesque, in "Inherent Reformers—Inherited Orthodoxy: Black Baptists in Boston, 1800-1873," *Journal of Negro History*, LX (1975), 491-519, analyzes the role of one black church in the welding of a black community and the internal struggles that beset that process. Other writers emphasize still other issues: Emma J. Lapansky, "Since They Got Those Separate Churches: Afro-Americans and Racism in Jacksonian Philadelphia," *American Quarterly*, XXXII (1980), 54-78; David E. Swift, *Black Prophets of Justice: Activist Clergy before the Civil War* (Baton Rouge: Louisiana State University Press, 1989).

A number of studies deal, in a variety of different ways, with the general subject of black community. Although he deals with the South as well as the North, Ira Berlin, in "The Structure of the Free Negro Caste in the Antebellum United States," *Journal of Social History*, IX (1976), 297-318, provides a solid basis for studying similarities as well as differences between blacks in the North, the Upper South, and the Lower South, paying particular attention to such issues as urbanization, discrimination, occupational status, and community autonomy. Focusing more specifically on individual cities, James O. Horton and Lois E. Horton dissect the antebellum Boston black community in *Black Bostonians: Family Life and Community Struggle in the Antebellum North* (New York: Holmes and Meier, 1979); Julie Winch looks at a particular Philadelphia group in her *Philadelphia's Black Elite: Activism, Accommodation, and the Struggle for Autonomy, 1787-1848* (Philadelphia: Temple University Press, 1988); and the early pages of David M. Katzman's *Before the Ghetto: Black Detroit in the Nineteenth Century* (Urbana: University of Illinois Press, 1973) discuss the city's blacks before and during the Civil War. Leonard P. Curry's *The Free Black in Urban America, 1800-1850* (Chicago: University of Chicago Press, 1981) deals with occupations, property ownership, mortality, and religious and racial unrest in American cities, including Albany, Cincinnati, Boston, and Philadelphia. The most complete and complex study of black life in an antebellum city is Gary B. Nash's *Forging Freedom: The Formation of Philadelphia's Black Community, 1720-1840* (Cambridge: Harvard University Press, 1988). Emma J. Lapansky charts a distinctive community of Philadelphia women in "Feminism, Freedom, and Community: Charlotte Forten and Women Activists in Nineteenth Century Philadelphia," *Pennsylvania Magazine of History and Biography,* CXIII (1989), 3-19.

In the area of intellectual history broadly considered, Leonard I. Sweet examines blacks' perceptions of themselves and their attempts to find points of contact with and to identify areas of difference from a dominant white American culture. *Black Images of America, 1784-1870* (New York: W. W. Norton, 1976) principally focuses on the burden of black history in the context of the American Dream. Robert C. Dick focuses on the intellectual history of Northern blacks in his *Black Protest: Issues and Tactics* (Westport: Greenwood Press, 1974). And, in an intriguing challenge to the received wisdom about blacks' economic status and activity, Juliet E. K. Walker posits that there was a dynamic, if limited, entrepreneurialism among antebellum blacks in "Racism, Slavery, and Free Enterprise: Black Entrepreneurship in the United States before the Civil War," *Business History Review,* LX (1986), 343-382.

A major theme that runs through much contemporary black history is the search for self-identity and self-determination as well as a conscious and sometimes aggressive black nationalism. Vincent P. Franklin approaches the subject briefly in his chapter "Let Your Motto Be Resistence," in *Black Self-determination: A Cultural History of the Faith of the Fathers* (Westport: L. Hill, 1984). Understanding antislavery and other political activity is enhanced by Jamie Sokolow, "Jerry McHenry and the Growth of Northern Antislavery Sentiment during the 1850s," *Journal of American Studies,* XVI (1982), 427-445; Earl F. Mulderink, " 'The Whole Town Is Ringing with It': Slave Kidnapping Charges against Nathan Johnson of New Bedford, Massachusetts, 1839," *New England Quarterly,* LXI (1988), 341-357; and Richard J. M. Blackett, *Build-*

ing an Antislavery Wall: Black Americans in the Atlantic Abolitionist Movement, 1830-1860 (Baton Rouge: Louisiana State University Press, 1983). How unsuccessful were the attempts of blacks to break into antebellum politics is demonstrated by Phyllis F. Field in *The Politics of Race in New York: The Struggle for Black Suffrage in the Civil War Era* (Ithaca: Cornell University Press, 1982).

The dynamics of black nationalism were clearly evident in debates and activities centering on colonization and emigration. A useful general survey of the issues and evolution of emigration activity is Ellen Ginzburg Migliorino, "Blacks Debate Emigration before the Civil War," *Storia Nordamerica,* III (1986), 93-115. Richard J. M. Blackett has devoted much time to exploring aspects of emigrationist history. For example, see his "Anglo-American Opposition to Liberian Colonization, 1831-1833," *Historian,* XLI (1979), 276-294; "In Search of International Support for African Colonization: Martin R. Delany's Visit to England, 1860," *Canadian Journal of History,* X (1975), 307-324; and "Martin R. Delany and Robert Campbell: Black Americans in Search of an African Colony," *Journal of Negro History,* LXII (1977), 1-25. The Pan-African dimension of black nationalism has been treated in Cyril E. Griffith's *The African Dream: Martin R. Delany and the Emergence of Pan-African Thought* (University Park: Pennsylvania State University Press, 1975). Robert L. Harris has addressed the subject in "H. Ford Douglas: Afro-American Antislavery Emigrationist," *Journal of Negro History,* LXII (1977), 217-234. One of the finest works dealing with the evolution of black nationalism and the search for a sense of community among antebellum blacks is Floyd J. Miller's *The Search for a Black Nationality: Black Emigration and Colonization, 1787-1863* (Urbana: University of Illinois Press, 1975).

In addition to the published studies noted above, there are specialized and detailed dissertations dealing with the complex history of antebellum Northern free blacks. Among them are Kwana Mbiassi Kinshasa's "Free Blacks' Quest for a National Identity: Debates in the African American Press on Assimilation and Emigration, 1827-1861," (New York University, 1983), and Janice S.

Lewis' "The Fortens of Philadelphia: An Afro-American Family and Nineteenth-Century Reform" (Georgetown University, 1978).

In sum, the past fifteen years have seen a broad variety of approaches to understanding blacks' search for freedom in the antebellum North, and the literature continues to grow.

Index

BOOKS IN THE SERIES BLACKS IN THE NEW WORLD

Making Their Own Way: Southern Blacks' Migration
to Pittsburgh, 1916-30
Peter Gottlieb

My Bondage and My Freedom
Frederick Douglass, edited by William L. Andrews

Black Leaders of the Nineteenth Century
Edited by Leon Litwack and August Meier

Charles Richard Drew: The Man and the Myth
Charles E. Wynes

John Mercer Langston and the Fight for Black Freedom, 1829-65
William and Aimee Lee Cheek

The Old Village and the Great House: An Archaeological and
Historical Examination of Drax Hall Plantation,
St. Ann's Bay, Jamaica
Douglas V. Armstrong

Black Property Owners in the South, 1790-1915
Loren Schweninger

The Sociogenesis of a Race Riot: Springfield, Illinois, in 1908
Roberta Senechal

Coal, Class, and Color: Blacks in Southern West Virginia,
1915-32
Joe William Trotter, Jr.

No Crooked Death: Coatesville, Pennsylvania, and the Lynching
of Zachariah Walker
Dennis B. Downey and Raymond M. Hyser

Reprint Editions

King: A Biography, Second Edition
David Levering Lewis

The Death and Life of Malcolm X, Second Edition
Peter Goldman

Race Relations in the Urban South, 1865-1890
Howard N. Rabinowitz, with a Foreword by C. Vann Woodward

Race Riot at East St. Louis, July 2, 1917
Elliott Rudwick

W. E. B. Du Bois: Voice of the Black Protest Movement
Elliott Rudwick

The Negro's Civil War: How American Negroes Felt and Acted
during the War for the Union
James M. McPherson

Lincoln and Black Freedom: A Study in Presidential Leadership
LaWanda Cox

Slavery and Freedom in the Age of the American Revolution
Edited by Ira Berlin and Ronald Hoffman

Diary of a Sit-In, Second Edition
Merrill Proudfoot, with an introduction by Michael S. Mayer

They Who Would Be Free: Blacks' Search for Freedom, 1830-61
Jane H. Pease and William H. Pease